Brazil and the struggle for rubber

STUDIES IN ENVIRONMENT AND HISTORY

Brazil and the struggle for rubber

*A study in
environmental history*

WARREN DEAN

*Department of History
New York University*

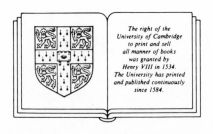

The right of the
University of Cambridge
to print and sell
all manner of books
was granted by
Henry VIII in 1534.
The University has printed
and published continuously
since 1584.

CAMBRIDGE UNIVERSITY PRESS

*Cambridge
New York   New Rochelle
Melbourne   Sydney*

Published by the Press Syndicate of the University of Cambridge
The Pitt Building, Trumpington Street, Cambridge CB2 1RP
32 East 57th Street, New York, NY 10022, USA
10 Stamford Road, Oakleigh, Melbourne 3166, Australia

First published 1987

Printed in the United States of America

Library of Congress Cataloging-in-Publication Data
Dean, Warren.
Brazil and the struggle for rubber.
(Studies in environment and history)
Bibliography: p.
1. Hevea – Brazil – History.   2. Rubber industry and
trade – Brazil – History.   3. Hevea – Diseases and pests –
Brazil – History.   4. Hevea – History.   5. Rubber industry
and trade – History.   6. Hevea – Diseases and pests –
History.   I. Title.   II. Series.
SB291.H4D43   1987   338.1′738952′0981   87-5130

British Library Cataloguing in Publication Data
Dean, Warren
Brazil and the struggle for rubber : a
study in environmental history
– (Studies in environment and history)
1. Rubber industry and trade – Brazil
– History
I. Title
338.1′738952′0981   HD9161.B62

ISBN 0-521-33477-2

For Elizabeth

Contents

Explanatory notes

Currency The Brazilian currency was called the milreis until November 1942, thereafter the cruzeiro, until February 1986, when it was changed to the cruzado. Extreme inflation in the post-World War II period makes evaluation difficult, therefore the equivalent in current U.S. dollars is provided where relevant.

Rubber yields Yields have been converted throughout the text, for purposes of comparison, into dry rubber equivalent, on the basis of a standard tapping technique: Every other day (150 times a year), on a single half spiral panel. They have also been converted to a standard 300 trees per hectare. Although groves are normally planted more densely, 300 is usual by the age tapping can be commenced.

Abbreviations used in text and footnotes

The author apologizes for this appallingly extensive list that represents, nevertheless, only the essential abbreviations. Several that were used only once in the text have been omitted, but all those referring to Brazilian institutions or programs are here displayed in the original Portuguese as well as the English translation.

ABSSFMS	*Agricultural Bulletin of the Straits Settlements and Federated Malay States*
Agr. Amer.	*Agriculture in the Americas*
ANPRC	Association of Natural Rubber Producing Countries
BASA	Banco da Amazônia, S.A.
BBATT	*Bulletin of the Board of Agriculture of Trinidad and Tobago*
BCA	Banco de Crédito da Amazônia (later BASA)
BDLS	*Bulletin Department van den Landbouw in Suriname*
Belém-MRR	U.S. Consulate, Belém, Monthly Rubber Report, Brazil
BMI-K	*Bulletin of Miscellaneous Information-Kew*
BMTIC	*Boletim do Ministério de Trabalho, Indústria e Comércio*
CEPEC	Centro de Pesquisas de Cacau, Itabuna, Bahia (Center for Cacao Research)
CNB	Conselho Nacional de Borracha (National Rubber Council)
CNPSD	Centro Nacional de Pesquisa em Seringueira e Dendê, Manaus (National Center for Research in Rubber and Oil Palm)
COPERBO	Companhia Pernambucana de Borracha Sintética (Pernambucan Synthetic Rubber Company)
CPATU	Centro de Pesquisas Agropecuárias do Trópico Húmido, Belém, Pará (Center for Agricultural Research of the Humid Tropics)
CPI-49/67	Brazil, *Diário do Congresso Nacional*, Secção I, Projeto de Resolução No. 114, de 1970 (1 May 1970), Suplemento,

	"Aprova as conclusões da Comissão Parlementar de Inquêrito destinada a verificar as razões do desestímulo à produção da borracha (Da CPI criada pela Resolução No. 49/67)."
EMBRAPA	Empresa Brasileira de Pesquisa Agropecuária (Brazilian Enterprise for Agricultural Research)
EMBRATER	Empresa Brasileira de Assistência Técnica Rural (Brazilian Enterprise for Rural Technical Assistance)
ERT	Estabelecimento Rural do Tapajós (Rural Establishment of the Tapajós, i.e., Belterra)
ETA	Escritório Técnico Agrícola, Rio de Janeiro (Agricultural Technical Office, of USAID)
FABOR	Fábrica de Borracha, Duque de Caxias, Rio de Janeiro (Rubber Factory, a synthetic plant)
FTRC-A	Firestone Tire and Rubber Company Archives, Akron, Ohio
GEPLASE	Grupo Executivo do Plano de Seringueira (Executive Group of the Rubber Plan)
HFMA-D	Henry Ford Museum and Archives, Dearborn, Michigan
IAC	Instituto Agronômico de Campinas (Agronomic Institute of Campinas)
IAL	Instituto Agronômico do Leste, Una, Bahia (Agronomic Institute of the East)
IAN	Instituto Agronômico do Norte, Belém (Agronomic Institute of the North)
INCRA	Instituto Nacional de Colonização e Reforma Agrária (National Institute of Colonization and Land Reform)
INIC	Instituto Nacional de Imigração e Colonização (National Institute of Immigration and Colonization)
IOLRC-RFC	India Office London Records Centre, Revenue Forests Home Correspondence
IPEAL	Instituto de Pesquisas e Experimentação Agropecuárias do Leste (Institute for Agricultural Research and Experimentation of the East, successor to IAL)
IPEAN	Instituto de Pesquisas e Experimentação Agropecuárias do Norte (Institute for Agricultural Research and Experimentation of the North, successor to IAN)
IRCA	Institut de Recherches sur le Caoutchouc de l'Afrique (Rubber Research Institute of Africa)
IRRDB	International Rubber Research and Development Board
JBABG	*Journal of the Board of Agriculture of British Guiana*
MRPRA	Malaysian Rubber Producers Research Association, Brickendonbury, Hertfordshire

PAB	*Pesquisa Agropecuária Brasileira*
PHW-P	Philip H. Williams Papers, Mudd Library, Princeton University, Princeton, New Jersey
PNB	Plano Nacional de Borracha (National Rubber Plan)
PRO	Public Records Office, London
PROBOR	Programa de Incentivo à Produção de Borracha Natural (Natural Rubber Production Incentive Program, of SUD-HEVEA, 1972–)
PROHEVEA	Projeto de Heveicultura na Amazônia (Amazon Rubber Cultivation Project)
PROMASE	Programa Especial de Controle do Mal-das-Folhas da Seringueira (Special Program of Hevea Leaf Blight Control)
RBG-K	Royal Botanic Gardens, Kew, England
RDC	Rubber Development Corporation
REBAP	Reunião de Estudos da Borracha para Aumento da Produção (Rubber Study Meeting for the Increase of Production)
RG 54-BPI	U.S. National Archives, Record Group 54, Bureau of Plant Industry, Field Crops Research Branch, Brazil
RG 166-FAR	U.S. National Archives, Record Group 166, Foreign Agricultural Relations Reports, Brazil
RG 234-RFC	U.S. National Archives, Record Group 234, Reconstruction Finance Corporation, Brazil
RRIM	Rubber Research Institute of Malaysia
SES	Serviço de Expansão da Seringueira (Rubber Expansion Service, in São Paulo)
SNS-1	Seminário Nacional da Seringueira, 1, Cuiabá, *Anais*
SNS-2	Seminário Nacional da Seringueira, 2, Rio Branco, *Anais*
SNS-3	Seminário Nacional da Seringueira, 3, Manaus, *Anais*
SPVEA	Superintendência do Plano de Valorização da Amazônia (Superintendency for the Amazon Valorization Plan)
SUDAM	Superintendência da Amazônia (Superintendency of the Amazon, successor to SPVEA)
SUDHEVEA	Superintendência da Borracha (Superintendency of Rubber)
TORMB	Taxa de Organização e Regulamentação do Mercado da Borracha (Tax for the Organization and Regulation of the Rubber Market)
USDA	United States Department of Agriculture

xiii

Acknowledgments

The author wishes to acknowledge funding provided by the John Simon Guggenheim Memorial Foundation, the Social Science Research Council, the Fulbright Commission-Brasília, and the Department of History and Faculty of Arts and Sciences of New York University.

Many persons provided information, criticism, encouragement, and assistance. The author especially wishes to thank Barry Machado, K. H. Chee, Paul Holliday, Brian Avery-Jones, Paulo de Tarso Alvim, Paulo de Souza Gonçalves, Richard Graham, Carl Prince, Irwin Unger, Thomas Glick, G. T. Prance, Norman Gall, Oscar Pardiñas Borreani, P. W. Allen, Reinhard Lieberei, and the editors of the Cambridge Studies in Environment and History series, Donald Worster and Alfred Crosby, and Frank Smith of Cambridge University Press. Versions of the thesis of this book were presented to the faculty and students of the Universidade Estadual de São Paulo-Assis, the Center for Latin American Studies, Sophia University-Tokyo, and the Program in Agricultural Resource Development, Cornell University. Their useful criticisms were much appreciated. Of course, none of these persons bear any responsibility for failings that may persist in this text.

Among many who gave generously of their services, the author wishes especially to thank archivists and librarians Richard Crawford, David R. Crippen, Shirley Evans, S. M. D. Fitzgerald, Paula Jescavage, and Lothian Lynas, and draftsman Thomas Dean. The hospitality and many kindnesses of friends were also much appreciated, especially those offered by Clélia, Gabriel, Camila and Flávia Bolaffi; Anna Verônica Mautner; Nancy, Anthony, Eugênia, and Sandro Naro; Fumio Nakagawa; and Ruy Alencar. Finally, the author wishes to express his gratitude to Elizabeth McArdle, without whose support and encouragement this research may never have been carried out.

Introduction

The domestication of plants is one of humankind's most consequential achievements. Plant cultivation was the technique that multiplied human numbers, launched civilization, and for better or worse established human dominion over nature. Domestication, in prehistoric times a gradual and partly accidental process of selection and hybridization, gradually expanded and stabilized food and raw material supplies of the human population. The exchange of seeds and plant materials, along with relevant techniques, was certainly one of the most important forms of cultural diffusion. Thus, for example, was maize passed from the Tamaulipas region of Mexico in which it was hybridized to places as remote as Massachusetts and Paraguay, at least a millennium before the Europeans arrived in the New World.

The voyages of Columbus marked the beginning of a deliberate and wholesale transfer of domesticates, of great importance for the steady growth of human numbers, for the expansion of world commerce, and for the spread of European imperialism. Thus, for example, did sugar cane, brought from the Mediterranean and the Atlantic islands to Brazil and the Caribbean, provide a growing supply of carbohydrate to the inhabitants of the north temperate zone, while engendering a ghastly trade in kidnapped African labor and the phenomenon of industrialized yet politically retrograde plantation colonies.[1]

At the same time that Europeans were expanding their agriculture through the selection of new cultivars and of more propitious locations for their cultivation, they were also interfering ever more aggressively with relations among plants and their parasites and pests. These changes, although inadvertant and unnoticed, were nevertheless also historical events, inextricable from the social and political changes that succeeded the introduction of the new cultivars. The transfer, for example, of the potato to northern Europe from its central Andean hearth was followed, at an interval of less than two centuries, by the transfer – or "invasion," as such events are denominated by aggrieved human onlookers – of *Phytophthora infestans*, the potato blight, with catastrophic consequences for European populations from the Shannon to the Volga.[2]

1

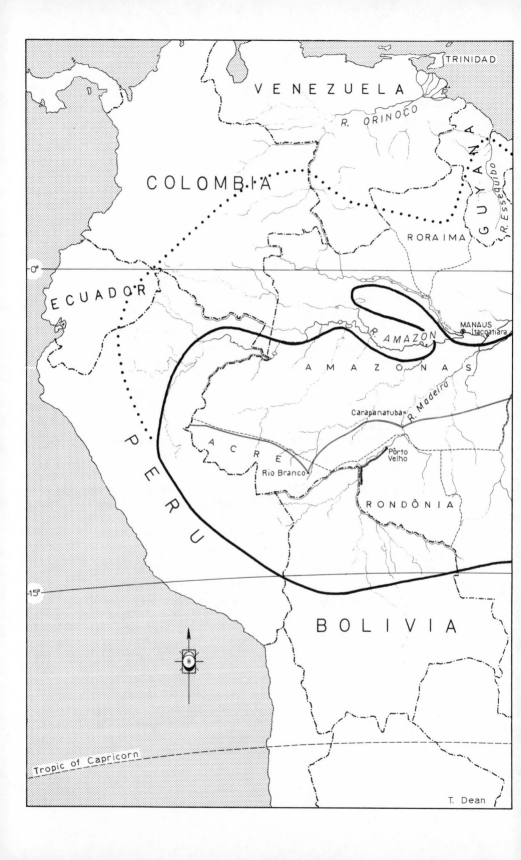

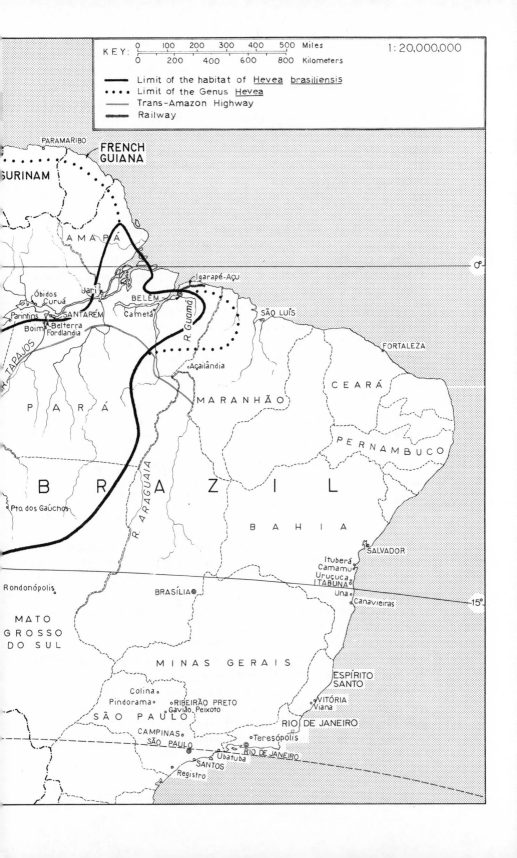

Introduction

By the nineteenth century, the transfer of exotic plants and the search for wild plants that might be domesticated were activities that were becoming rationalized and organized and put at the service of industrial capitalism. Collectors were sent from Europe to the farthest reaches of the earth in search of unknown species that might serve as raw material, remedy, or ornament. This enterprise, even though it was the expression of scientific and state bureaucracies, nevertheless partook of romance: It was a quest for the rare, the precious, and the danger-scented.

Of all the great feats of that era of botanical discovery, none was more imposing than that of the domestication of rubber. New World inhabitants had shown rubber, which they obtained from several tropical plant species, to early explorers, including Columbus. Since it was an unstable product, it remained for more than three centuries a mere curiosity. Then, in 1839, it was found that through treatment with sulphur and heat, rubber's elastic properties could be made more permanent. Its applications multiplied and the exploitation of many wild rubber-bearing plants, including some that were soon discovered in Asia and Africa, was much intensified.

It happened that the wild tree that yielded the purest and most elastic rubber, and also most abundantly, was native to the Amazon basin. Known as *Para rubber* in commerce, it soon became the object of an immense and unwieldy trading system that stretched from Belém, at the river's mouth, 3,000 kilometers into the interior of the world's largest and densest tropical forest. The rubber trade became a mainstay of the Brazilian economy, providing at its height almost 40 percent of its export revenues, nearly equaling coffee in importance.

It was not long before the idea was conceived of domesticating rubber. The project involved many complex problems: The botanical identification of the wild plants from which rubber was obtained, the collection of information about their growing conditions and the manner in which they were tapped in the wild, the organization of expeditions to collect plant materials and acclimatize them in advantageous locations, and, finally, the undertaking of experimental programs to determine optimal techniques of cultivation and exploitation. All these questions were resolved, and plantation-grown rubber entered the world market at the beginning of the twentieth century.

But Brazil was not the site of the successful commercialization of rubber. Rubber cultivation was, instead, transferred to Southeast Asia. Malaya, Ceylon, Sumatra, Java, and Cochin China became immense fields of investment, binding those colonies more straitly to their imperial metropoles. Soon abundant and cheap, rubber was put to thousands of uses. Its reduced cost was an important factor in the emergence of a mass market for automobiles; from two-thirds to three-quarters of the demand for rubber soon came from the makers of tires and tubes for motor vehicles.

Meanwhile, Brazil, the original and major supplier of wild rubber, suffered disaster. Its economic growth diminished and its vast Amazon region relapsed into stagnation and despair. Few modern events demonstrate as well the interrelatedness of human affairs. Ever since, Brazil has struggled impatiently at a task that has continued to elude it: to install in its own territory the rational cultivation of the plant of which it was so long ago despoiled.

These events, though dimmed by time, were not without consequences for the present and for the foreseeable future. Despite the invention of synthetic elastomers, natural rubber, still indispensable for certain industrial purposes, has continued to maintain nearly a third of the world market. The colonial planters and governors long ago departed their tropical domains, but they left behind a resource of immense value that the newly independent states have ceaselessly tried to improve. And other tropical countries, notably India and China as well as Brazil, anxious to supply their expanding industries with raw materials domestically produced, yet poorly endowed with the crude oil that is necessary to manufacture synthetic elastomers, have intensified their development of rubber plantations. In Africa the Ivory Coast, like Liberia before it, has tried to develop rubber as a major export crop.

This study attempts to view the history of rubber cultivation in a global context, while concentrating upon the Brazilian struggle. It sets out to answer the questions that Brazilians have repeatedly put to themselves. Only a little empathy is required to realize that the first question must necessarily be: How was the Brazilian rubber monopoly lost? The answer, pursued in Chapters 1 and 2, is important to an understanding of the ecological relationship that provides the thesis of this study, and it shatters a myth that has survived into the present, distorting comprehension and deflecting effective action.

The next, inevitable question is: Why did the Brazilians not take up rubber cultivation themselves in response to the Southeast Asian threat? The answer, as will be demonstrated, is that they did, but not successfully. Numerous explanations have been offered to account for this failure. When a system such as an agricultural regime fails, many interrelating weaknesses may be seen to have some influence on the outcome. The essential problem, however, is usually identifiable as that which remains even when the others are rectified. Rubber cultivation in Brazil suffered in different places and times from shortages of labor, capital, and technique. But even when these difficulties were overcome, rubber trees were too low-yielding to justify their costs. Essentially, as rubber specialists are well aware, the problem is ecological. There is a certain plant fungus that attacks the rubber tree within its native range. Up to now, adequate and economical defenses against the fungus have not been devised. The revelation of these historical realities are to be found in Chapters 3 and 4.

The next question that literate and distracted Brazilians have pondered has been: How could it be that the United States, which poured capital and technique into rubber planting in Brazil for more than twenty years, failed to achieve success (and, by implication, if the rich and powerful Americans failed, how could they, the Brazilians, succeed on their own)? The story of the Ford Amazon plantations and wartime efforts to develop rubber supplies in the Amazon is therefore detailed in Chapters 5 and 6. These chapters offer abundant confirmation of the thesis put forward in Chapter 4, but perhaps none for the thesis that the United States was inherently better equipped to develop the Amazon.

Finally, the Brazilians in recent years asked how it could be, with all the technical competence that their country was developing in agricultural research, and with all the success that it was experiencing in the cultivation of other newly introduced crops – even in the Amazon, supposedly hostile to any form of commercial agriculture – that rubber persisted in refusing to grow! This paradox was so much more painful since Brazil was industrializing and had urgent, even desperate need for rubber as a raw material in its own factories. Chapters 7, 8, and 9 deal with the evolution of Brazilian rubber research and development in the postwar period up to the present. It is a costly, anguished, and conflict-ridden tale that has, let the reader be forewarned, no happy ending.

This account of the Brazilian struggle to cultivate rubber has a purpose beyond its relevance to the economic history of a single country or a single commodity. It is hoped that this study has implications for the historical understanding of agricultural regimes in general. In particular, historical accounts of tropical plantation agriculture seem customarily to be written as though the subject of study were an industrial rather than a biological process, and as though the ecological conditions of production were unimportant to historical outcomes. More broadly still, this account is designed to be a contribution to the field of environmental history, which the author sees as a kind of cultural history that analyzes the capacity of our species, under differing circumstances, to understand and manage its relationships with its natural environment. It is hoped that to some degree, this study represents a contribution to those understandings and relationships themselves.

1

Prometheus in reverse, 1855–1876

The native peoples of Brazil believed that their domesticated plants had been won for them at the cost of martyrdom. Thus maize had sprouted from the corpse of Abati, a warrior who had allowed himself to be vanquished in battle at the command of Nhandeiara, the great spirit. Thus manioc had grown from the corpse of a child who had been born to a virgin princess. Myths like these are universal; agriculture was so great a benefaction that it must have been in the beginning wrested from the gods by a heroic or supernatural benefactor. So magical a prize must have been paid for in blood.[1]

The domestication of rubber did not take place in a remote and fabled past. That achievement was modern – too recent, one would suppose, for myth to crystalize upon it. But myth fulfills a need too deep. Although the documents lie near at hand, abundant and unfaded, a marvelous version of events prevails. The myth is modern, nonetheless, and prideful moderns admit no debts to Nhandeiara. Our heroes make no sacrifice. They retire, comfortably pensioned, to their clubs, where they polish their own legends, cast in our tribal vanity and our faith in pluck and luck. This history, the history of Brazilian rubber, must begin with the myth, because it lives on and has captured the world's imagination, and because it is powerful and malign. This is the myth of Henry Wickham, the English hero, bestower of rubber seeds. This is the myth of Henry Wickham, the English rogue, thief of rubber seeds.

The transfer of rubber out of the Brazilian Amazon and its domestication in Southeast Asia was truly a remarkable event; alas, it was not so much an adventure as it was a complex bureaucratic project, some fifty years in the execution. It was in the 1850s that the Royal Botanic Gardens, in the London suburb of Kew, first turned its attention to the wild trees that were the sources of rubber, and it was not until the end of the 1890s that the first few pounds of plantation-grown rubber were offered for sale. In the interval, programs of investigation and experiment, many of them inevitably in wrong directions, had to be carried out.

The first problem to be solved was the identification of the rubber-yielding plants that were arriving at the London and Hamburg docks. Rubber is a

Plate 1

HEVEA BRASILIENSIS Muell. arg.

The first botanical drawing of *Hevea brasiliensis*, from James Collins's report, 1872. (Courtesy The New York Public Library Special Collections)

hydrocarbon, a polymer of isoprene, elastic because of its organization in long, crinkled chains. New World Indians had learned to extract rubber from at least eight of the many tropical species in which it occurs as an ingredient in a milky fluid called *latex*, which courses through special tubes found in the inner bark, probably as a defense against insect predators. The quest for rubber therefore had to begin with observation of indigenous peoples. In this there was nothing novel. Botanists who wandered through the South American wilderness depended on its inhabitants for instructions in the uses of strange species; these were then tested in the laboratories of Paris, London, and Berlin. This methodology, which paradoxically rendered homage to cultures the Europeans thought otherwise primitive, was chosen out of necessity: Confronted with thousands of unfamiliar plants, they could hardly discover the potential of all of them. In a sense, the method limited the range of discovery, since indigenes were unable to puzzle out the uses of more than a fraction of the plant life that surrounded them. Tragically, since researchers were accompanied by the advancing frontier, native cultures were often destroyed before scientific transcription could begin.

The earliest reports of rubber came from Central America, where balls and other objects were made of it. This rubber was obtained from the latex of trees of the genus *Castilla*. Gathered in the wild, Castilla rubber, or Caucho, was a modest article of international trade by the middle of the eighteenth century.

At Belém, near the mouth of the Amazon, another sort of rubber came to the attention of Portuguese colonial authorities. This type was called *Seringa*, or syringe, rubber from its earliest application. By the 1750s, army boots, knapsacks, and other articles were sometimes sent from Lisbon to Belém to be waterproofed. But the first published notice in Portugal of goods made of this sort of rubber dates only from 1799. Just a year later, New England merchants began to place orders in Belém for shoes made of Seringa rubber. By 1839, that city was carrying on a brisk trade: 450,000 pairs were exported. The American travelers William Edwards and William L. Herndon both thought the manufacture of these shoes a curiosity worth including in their reports.[2]

Meanwhile, however, their compatriot Charles Goodyear greatly expanded the potential applications of rubber through his discovery that rubber could be chemically stabilized by mixing it with sulphur in the presence of heat, a process that came to be known as vulcanization. Rubber was soon the preferred material for the confection of gaskets for steam engines, so that this obscurely gotten raw material accompanied iron and steel wherever factory machinery, mining pumps, and railroads were installed. Rubber was also essential in machine belting and tubing, and in buffers between railway carriages. In 1830, Britain imported 211 kilograms of raw rubber; by 1857, it imported 10,000 kilograms; and by 1874, as rubber was coming to be applied to telegraph wiring, imports jumped to 58,710 kilograms.

9

Prometheus in reverse, 1855–1876

In 1736, Charles Marie de La Condamine sent samples of Castilla rubber from Ecuador, where it was called *Caoutchouc* or *Hévé*. When, a decade later, he found Seringa rubber on his voyage down the Amazon, he confused it with Castilla. In 1775, another French naturalist, Fusée Aublet, published an accurate description of a rubber tree native to the Guianas that he named *Hevea guianensis*, still apparently unaware of the unrelatedness of the Castilla-Hévé and Seringa rubber trees. In 1785, Jean-Baptiste Lamarck received the first dried specimen of Seringa to reach Europe. Lamarck suspected it to be a species different from that identified by Aublet, but could not be sure since it was without flowers. These were at last secured in 1807 by F. G. Sieber. He sent his specimen to Carl Ludwig Willdenow, director of the Berlin Botanical Gardens, who, in 1811, applied to it the epithet *brasiliensis*.[3]

The first dried specimens of this plant to reach the Royal Botanic Gardens at Kew were brought back by a collector in 1830, but these were also flowerless. Complete specimens arrived only in 1854, upon the return of Richard Spruce from his extensive South American travels. These were examined by George Bentham, who identified them with Willdenow's specimens and drew up a list containing seven species. Finally, in 1865, Jean Mueller von Argau published a monograph in *Linnaea* in which the alternate generic name *Siphonia* was suppressed and *Hevea brasiliensis* was applied to the species that had been brought from Belém by Sieber and that appeared to be the true Seringa rubber of commerce. At last the rubber tree had received a stable scientific designation and future collectors would know more or less what they were looking for.

This *Hevea brasiliensis* is a tree of the tropical forest, rising to the forest canopy, thirty to fifty meters high. It was at first more commonly exploited along watercourses, where it was easily encountered since its seeds can float. But the largest specimens are usually located on higher ground, on soils moderately well drained. The tree was not to be found in pure stands; instead, there might be no more than two or three tappable specimens to a hectare. As the demand for rubber grew and the search for Hevea widened, it was discovered that *H. brasiliensis*, except for a few small incursions, grew only on the right bank of the Amazon, within a broad semicircle centered west of Manaus, as far south as Mato Grosso, Acre, northern Bolivia, and eastern Peru, up to an altitude of about 800 meters, within that portion of the basin that experienced at least 1,800 millimeters of well-distributed rainfall annually.

Richard Spruce was the first to describe accurately the techniques of rubber gathering. In 1855, in *Hooker's Journal of Botany*, he explained how the gatherer made numerous random cuts in the bark of the tree with a little hatchet and allowed the latex to flow from the wounds down the trunk into a clay gutter, whence it was collected in a gourd. The rubber was then coagulated by laboriously dripping the liquid over a slowly turned spit suspended over a damped fire. He remarked on higher prices for the material, a sign of increasing demand. Despite this interest, naturalists Henry Bates and Alfred Russel Wallace, both of whom collected in the Amazon in the 1850s, and Louis Agassiz, who collected there in the 1860s, devoted slight attention to it in their reports and seem not to have sent back further specimens.[4]

The Amazon, in the European imagination a trackless waste, had a long history of settlement. Portuguese control of the greater portion of the basin was established by 1750, and strengthened by the decision of the Portuguese king to transfer his court to Rio de Janeiro when, in 1807, Portugal was invaded by a Napoleonic army. The departure of the king in 1820 led directly to Brazil's independence two years later. The new government, a constitutional monarchy, had at first only a weak hold on its far-flung northern territories, which were divided into two provinces: Pará in the east and Amazonas in the west, with provincial capitals at Belém and Manaus, respectively. Brazil opened the Amazon to foreign commerce in the 1850s, permitting the operation of a British-owned steamboat company. Scientific exploration of the period was carried out under license of the government, which, although with good reason nervous concerning the intentions of foreigners, was determined to undo the secrecy of the colonial past and to apply liberal principles of trade and diplomacy. Although the region exported agricultural goods, the mainstay of the economy of the upper river had traditionally been gathered products of various kinds. By the 1850s, the rising demand for rubber was rapidly shifting regional resources: Spruce noted that 25,000 persons had taken up rubber gathering, mostly around Belém.

Most ironically, it was a Brazilian who was the first to bring to the attention of Europeans the possibility of planting Hevea. In 1861, and again in 1863, João Martins da Silva Coutinho, long engaged in exploring the rubber-bearing areas of the Amazon, recommended rubber cultivation to the provincial government of Pará. His suggestions were not followed, but rubber seeds were soon sent, possibly by Silva Coutinho himself, to Rio de Janeiro, where they were planted on the grounds of the National Museum. These trees were in flower by 1872. Meanwhile, the Brazilian government sent Silva Coutinho to Paris to take part in the Universal Exposition of 1867. Made chairman of the jury that evaluated the rubber samples sent to the exposition from various countries, he demonstrated that Brazilian Hevea was in all ways superior, and he estimated the costs of plantation production. His report was published the following year and was taken note of in London by James Collins.[5]

Collins, then the curator of the museum of the Pharmaceutical Society, had been reading the reports of Amazon travelers and corresponding with them. He had also been frequenting the London docks for several years, inspecting shipments of rubber in order to learn more about the product and the several species from which it was derived. He published, in 1868, an article in *Hooker's Journal*, in which he told what he knew of these commodities. The next year, in the *Journal of the Royal Society of Arts*, he provided more detail and expressed his desire to obtain further information from the journal's readers.[6]

Collins's articles engaged the attention of Clements R. Markham, a remarkable figure in nineteenth-century British imperialism. An enthusiastic supporter of geographical exploration, later to become the head of the Royal Geographical Society, Markham was at the time an India Office functionary. Collins's second article paid due respect to Markham's great adventure of the previous decade, the successful transfer of the cinchona plant from its native Peru to India, an exploit in which he personally involved himself. The cultivation of cinchona for quinine was an event of immense historical importance, since it facilitated European colonialism in the tropics. It is to Markham's credit that he conceived his enterprise as a means of improving the condition of the mass of the Indian population, and not merely that of the armies of occupation, a conception later to be thwarted by the Anglo-Dutch quinine cartel.[7]

Markham decided "that it was necessary to do for the india-rubber or caoutchouc-yielding trees what had already been done with such happy results for the cinchona trees." He expected that the cultivated product could be brought to market more cheaply than that gathered in the wild, and expressed the fear, already voiced by Silva Coutinho, that the stock of wild trees might be insufficient to meet growing demand and that the methods of tapping were wasteful and destructive. These considerations had also impelled his search for cinchona plants.

Markham did not give any consideration to the cultivation of rubber in situ. In the case of cinchona that strategy would not have been practical. The native habitat of cinchona was remote from transport and cinchona was to be consumed in Britain's tropical Asian colonies. Rubber, on the other hand, was to be consumed in England, and the Amazon was a good deal more convenient to Liverpool and Southampton than was the Irrawaddy. Markham, nevertheless, did not address the question directly. Rather he seemed to obscure it. His purpose may well have been to achieve a monopoly under imperial control. The India Office was on the lookout for potential export crops. Markham, however, did not suggest that rubber planted in India might be sold for export, but that it be utilized by India's railroads and telegraph.

What seems likely is that Markham, as an employee of the India Office, found it expedient to seek the office's funding, but that his personal motive was merely to repeat his exploit of ten years before, for the glory of it. It is interesting that he later complained that the viceroy of India took no interest in this venture. It should also be noted that although Hancock, the most important of the English rubber manufacturers, accompanied Collins's inquiries and Markham's schemes, he appears not to have taken any direct interest in them, certainly not to the extent of wondering whether his raw material might be more cheaply transported from plantations in the Amazon rather than Bengal.[8]

Markham stated that the idea to transfer rubber occurred to him in 1870, at which time he may have begun prodding the India Office to make some sort of commitment. Finally, in late 1871, Collins was appointed by the office to provide a report on the utility of the various species of rubber-bearing trees. Collins's report favored Hevea, along with Castilla and *Ficus elastica*, an Indian species, and recommended the acquisition of their seeds. This opinion was sent to several experts in the field, not all of whom concurred. A naturalist queried by the governor of the Straits Settlements thought Hevea would never be more than a "botanical curiosity," but Dietrich Brandis, inspector general of the Forest Department of the government of India, sent an endorsement that Collins appended to his published report. Although Brandis recommended planting on the southern Indian and Burmese coasts, he thought that Ceylon, where rain was less seasonal, might be better.[9]

Markham next caused the India Office to send Collins's report to the Foreign Office, with a request that copies be forwarded to the consul at Belém along with an instruction to obtain Hevea seeds. This request, dated 10 May 1873, also made mention of "a Mr. Wickham, at Santarem, who may do the job." On 7 May, another letter was sent, to Joseph D. Hooker, director of Kew Gardens, with more copies of the report, asking for his advice. Hooker replied that Kew Gardens stood ready to sow the perishable seeds and transfer them to the Orient. It appears that Markham had already informally contacted Hooker, since Hooker was the source of the information about Wickham. Henry A. Wickham had sent Hooker a letter from Santarém in March 1872, offering to collect botanical specimens. Hooker had not troubled to reply, but Wickham had nonetheless sent Kew a small packet of tubers and palm seeds that had arrived a few weeks before the India Office query. Hooker, probably at Markham's urging, had already written to Wickham on 5 May.[10]

Before any reply could be received from Brazil, however, rubber seeds suddenly appeared in the London market. James Collins, in his extensive correspondence, had not omitted to request seeds as well as information. On 2 June 1873, he informed Markham that a Mr. Charles Farris, who had been residing at Cametá, a town about 100 kilometers south of Belém, had returned to London, ill with a fever but bearing with him a collection of rubber seeds "quite fresh and in a fit state for planting." Markham notified Hooker immediately and authorized Collins to buy the seeds from Farris for £2/10 per thousand. Markham initialed a memorandum at the India Office warning that the French and U.S. consuls had already made bids. The Farris seeds, 2,000 of them, were received at Kew two days later, and immediately sown. Unfortunately they were not as fresh as Farris had claimed and only twelve germinated. On 22 September, half of these plants were taken to India by the new superintendent of the Calcutta Botanic Gardens.[11]

An attempt was made to propagate them by cuttings, but the climate of Calcutta was unfavorable, and only three were left a year later. It is not clear what happened to these remaining plants, or to the six retained at Kew, but they appear not to have survived. The only good that came of this episode was the decision to send further shipments to a warmer locale. For Collins there was no material gain at all. A record of his contribution exists only because he was never paid for it. He was obliged to send a second bill, along with a lengthy memoir, in 1878. Unfortunately, Collins padded his account somewhat, and Markham, when questioned by India Office accountants, claimed to remember nothing at all about the case. Undersecretary Louis Mallet then rejected the bill, accusing Collins of "a gross attempt to impose on the Secretary of State" and complained that he had "already succeeded in obtaining £80 from this office for an utterly worthless report on Gutta Percha." Collins, at the time probably without employment, deserved better the self-assessment he inserted in his memoir: "I would like to take this opportunity to place on official record, that if any honor be due for being the first person through whose instrumentality live plants of the Para India Rubber tree have been introduced into India, that honor is undoubtedly due to me."[12]

While the Collins seeds were anxiously tended at Kew, Joseph Hooker received a response from Santarém. Wickham, with a conspiratorial air that was to be his stock-in-trade, assured the director that he was "glad to accept your offer to put me into communication with the partie [*sic*] you refer to in your letter," a clear reference to the consul at Belém. Wickham was about to enter into the adventure of his life, but at that moment it represented for him simply a chance to escape another agonizing failure. It is not clear at what point Hooker and Markham became aware that Wickham had much experience of the tropics and had already written a travel account. Henry Alexander Wickham was in 1873 a young man of 27, son of a solicitor who had died when Wickham was only four. He had shown some talent for art and studied it for a while. When only 20 he voyaged to Central America, where he remained for three years, dealing in bird plumage. He returned to England, then set out again, this time to the Orinoco, where he engaged briefly in rubber gathering. Beset by ill fortune and fever, he decided to find his way home via the Rio Negro and the Amazon. On this return trip he called at Santarém, where he found a few Americans and Englishmen to befriend him, and at Pará, where the consul arranged his passage home.[13]

In London Wickham married Violet Cave, daughter of W. H. J. Carter, a Regent Street book dealer, who published Wickham's report and apparently subsidized his wanderings for many years after. Wickham persuaded his bride to accompany him to Santarém, of which he had pleasant memories. He also persuaded his mother, brother, sister, and brother-in-law, and several laborers to join them. This was an ample household that he thought to install in a life of gracious plantation ease. Enthusiastically he wrote Hooker that his house was on "a spur just off from the forest covered table highlands S. of Santarem which occupy the triangle formed by the junction of the Tapajós with the

Amazon. The waters of both rivers, islands and estuaries are taken into the view from my new home.'' At Santarém Wickham struggled for three years to raise sugar, tobacco, and manioc. When his English laborers quit him, he hired Indians, and finally he worked the fields himself. He came to depend more and more on the neighborliness of the community of U.S. Confederate emigrés, whose circumstances were little better than his, but whose practicality was much greater. His mother and then his sister died. Violet helped him move his residence twice during these three years, to ever more modest quarters.[14]

Although Wickham's situation was disastrous, his book was helping to establish his reputation as a rubber expert. Other travelers had merely observed rubber gathering, but he had engaged in it. Furthermore, he had included in his book sketches of the leaves, seed, and seed pod of what he took to be *Hevea brasiliensis*, proof enough for Markham that he could, in fact, identify the tree. Although it would not have been realized in London at the time, Wickham's Indian assistants must have been tapping another species of Hevea, since *H. brasiliensis* does not occur on the Orinoco. A sketch he drew of the tapping, moreover, shows the removal of the entire bark of the trunk, a procedure never reported on the Amazon and immediately lethal to the tree. His drawings of the leaves and seeds, if they did indeed represent *H. brasiliensis*, must have been of specimens found along the Amazon on his journey home, or after his return to Santarém. Wickham, a convenient instrument of Hooker's and Markham's purposes, was evidently less knowledgeable than they supposed.

The letter sent by the Foreign Office to the consul at Pará was received by Thomas Shipton Green, manager of the important commission house of Singlehurst and Brocklehirst, a Liverpool firm. Green had just taken over the office, his predecessor having departed Belém suddenly after interfering in local political quarrels. The letter had thus gone unread for some time, but Green assured the Foreign Office on 29 September that he had been in touch with Wickham, whom he had asked for an estimate of costs. Not until mid-December did he forward Wickham's counter-proposal. Wickham asserted that Hevea seed was highly perishable, since it was oily and quickly turned rancid. Therefore he thought it most practical to establish a nursery at his farm – by then Wickham had moved across the river to Curuá and had shifted his attention to coffee – and forward the resulting seedlings to Kew. Green evidently thought this excessive effort, because he appended his own offer to ''obtain any quantity that may be necessary at small expense.''[15]

At the India Office the Wickham proposal seems to have lain dormant for nearly six months. Probably Markham's attention had been diverted to another project and no one else had thought to reply. By July 1874, Markham reported to Hooker that the office was willing to pay Wickham £10 for a thousand seeds. Wickham responded in October that it was not worth his while to collect such a small amount. By November the Office at last decided, on Hooker's recommendation, to turn down the nursery proposal, but only in December was a memo initialled to increase to 10,000 the number of seeds the office would buy from Wickham. Oddly, but very significantly, Markham instructed Hooker to tell Wickham that the office would buy any amount he might supply![16]

In the meantime, Markham had interviewed in London, probably through the offices of Consul Green, a Bolivian named Ricardo Chávez. He had been engaged in the rubber trade as a *patrão*, that is, a merchant intermediary who provided advances to tappers of the wild trees, sold them supplies, and bought their rubber. He had moved down the Madeira River with 200 Moxos Indians and established himself at a place called Carapanatuba. Markham obtained authorization from the India Office to purchase any seeds that Chávez might ship. Chávez, upon his return to the Amazon, called upon Green and said that he would provide up to 220 kilograms of seed, which Green agreed to forward. On 6 May, Green reported to the India Office that these seeds, packed in four barrels, were en route.[17]

The barrels arrived in London on 6 July 1875. Unfortunately Markham was not at the India Office. The clerk who received the barrels did not know what to do with them, but decided ten days later to send a few of the seeds to Kew. Hooker sent back a requisition, but in the meantime, on the advice of the Secretary of the Revenue Forest Department, the Store Department had consigned the barrels to India – one to Madras and three to Calcutta. By the time the seeds arrived, they were no longer viable. Later accounts have mentioned this shipment rather vaguely, some presuming them to have been sent by Wickham. Clearly the principals involved preferred not to dwell on their errors, especially one as costly as this. The India Office, so incensed at Collins's bill for £10, was obliged to pay Chávez's bill of £114 and another for freight to India. Worse, another growing season was lost.[18]

Wickham had received in April 1875 a letter from Hooker, transmitting the news that he would be paid for as many seeds as he cared to send. Wickham replied that it was almost too late to find seed from that season, which had begun in January, but he would collect what he could. He did dispatch some seeds, which reached the India Office 9 September and were duly paid for. Like Chávez's seeds, there is no record at Kew of their arrival. On 29 January 1876, Wickham informed Hooker that the fall of seeds was just beginning and he was about to start collecting. He would send them as soon as he thought it safe, since he was worried about "European frosts.''[19]

On 6 March 1876, Wickham wrote Hooker from a place called Seringal, on the Tapajós River, that he was collecting seeds and packing them carefully. The source of these seeds has been a matter of extreme curiosity, for reasons that will later become clear. There are four witnesses of the event, none of whom is very enlightening. David B. Riker, one of the Confederate emigrés at Santarém, recalled seventy years afterward that Wickham, in whose house Riker had stayed as a boy, got the seeds at Boim, on the west bank of the Tapajós. This was confirmed by Júlio David Serique, whose father was a patrão at Boim at the time. Wickham himself produced several vague and somewhat contradictory versions, but one he wrote in 1902 stated that the seeds had been collected at exactly 3 degrees south latitude, confirming these other accounts. He also made much of another point, which he repeated invariably: The seeds had been found on highlands, not at the water's edge. And Wickham's wife kept a diary that contains an entry indicating that the seeds, or some of them, were gathered on the course of two or more canoe trips, lasting several days.[20]

The manner of collection is also a question of later consequence. Violet Wickham mentioned an Indian boy who accompanied her husband as a helper. Wickham is vague on the point, but his best-known account, that of 1908, stated that he had gotten some Indians together to assist him. According to his wife, he also bought seeds, "all that were brought to him." Wickham's recollection and his wife's diary suggest haste, the gathering of seeds all at once, yet his letters to Hooker suggest that the collecting was long drawn out, and so did Riker, who reported that it had gone on for a year. The seeds, according to Wickham, were from trees that were being tapped. Even so, the gathering must have required intensive effort, since Hevea seeds are quickly consumed on the ground by small animals. If, however, the seeds were gathered all at once, with several helpers and sellers, then, as Edward V. Lane pointed out, it is not likely that Wickham could really vouch for their provenance, whether highland or lowland, nor indeed if they were all *Hevea brasiliensis*. On the other hand, if the collection was long drawn out, then the seeds were certainly not fresh.

According to Wickham's account of 1908, haste was necessary because he had suddenly been presented with a "providential" opportunity to transport the seeds. A British ship, the *Amazonas*, on its inaugural voyage between Liverpool and Manaus, had touched at Santarém. Wickham related that the ship's cargo had been unloaded at Manaus by two crafty supercargoes who sold it and disappeared. The ship's captain, a Mr. Murray, therefore had nothing to bring back to England. Wickham had no funds, but, he recalled, "boldly chartering the ship in behalf of the government of India," he sent word to its captain to come to Santarém.[21]

The *Amazonas* arrived on the appointed day and Wickham loaded the rubber seeds, carefully layered in wild banana leaves and packed in split-cane baskets. Then, instead of waving the captain farewell, he climbed aboard with his wife and belongings. He intended not merely to dispatch the seeds, but to accompany them! Wickham's dream of a tropical planter's easy life had shattered, but he was free and clear, and in his possession was a treasure that would pay his passage and even stake his next adventure.

But first, and this is the most dramatic moment of the account he published in 1908, the ship had to pass customs at Belém. Wickham feared that if the Brazilian authorities there were to guess what was in the baskets, they might hold up the ship for instructions from Rio de Janeiro, or they might even "interdict" the cargo altogether. Upon the ship's arrival at the port, therefore, Wickham enlisted the assistance of Consul Green. Together they went to the chief of customs, whom Wickham identified mysteriously as the "Baron do S——." To him they declared the ship to be laden with "exceedingly delicate botanical specimens specially designated for delivery to Her Britannic Majesty's own royal gardens of Kew." Wickham told him that he had ordered the captain to keep up steam, hoping that he would gain the Baron's permission to proceed. The latter graciously acceded to the pair's request and the *Amazonas*, bearing the most fateful cargo ever to descend that river, steamed forth into history.[22]

Wickham told his story long after the other principals had died; there is nothing in the correspondence of Kew, the India Office, or the consulate to confirm or refute his version. Yet the circumstances, as they may be reconstructed, reveal a number of inconsistencies. To begin with, the ship: There was indeed an SS *Amazonas*, built in 1874 for the Liverpool and Amazon Royal Mail Steam Ship Company, in which E. S. Inman owned an interest. The company lasted only four years, during which time it may have been subsidized by the British government. Ironically, it did receive a subsidy from the government of the state of Amazonas, which was trying to draw traffic from Belém to Manaus. The first voyage of this line was not in 1876, however, but in 1875, and already in 1874, Alexandre Brito de Amorim, a Portuguese merchant resident in Manaus and another of the Liverpool company's organizers, was leasing steamships that sailed directly to Manaus.[23]

Furthermore, it was not necessary for Wickham to wait for one of the infrequent steamers bound direct for England. Santarém was the third largest town on the Amazon. By the mid-1870s, it was visited every ten days by the river steamboats of the English company, and almost daily by an assortment of steamboats owned by importers and local shippers. There was even in Santarém a steam launch built there by a Swiss resident who hired it out. All these craft were capable of making the run to Belém in a few days. Already in 1869, three-quarters of the town's 6,000 tons of produce were shipped in steam vessels. From Belém, English steamers departed nearly every week. The arrival of the *Amazonas*, then, was in no way a providential event.[24]

It seems very unlikely that Wickham chartered the *Amazonas* from its captain, who Inman company records indicate was named J. L. Beesley. The India Office, which kept careful accounts of the cost of the Wickham seeds, does not include an invoice from the shipping line for any amount. The steamer, according to Wickham, made its scheduled call at le Havre on the way to Liverpool, forcing him to debark there and go on alone to Kew to arrange for the reception of the seeds by night train from Liverpool. It therefore appears that he had not diverted the captain from his normal run. Nor is it clear why the theft of the outbound cargo, if that occurred, would have stranded the captain without any hope of a return cargo. The line's connections with Amorim and the import house represented by Consul Green would have resolved any temporary financial embarrassment. In any case, Beesley surely did not own his cargoes; he merely accepted them on consignment. Finally, the botanist Thomas Petch, in his study of rubber in Ceylon, stated, "There is no mention of rubber seeds on the ship's manifest: 141 cases of rubber were shipped at Manaus." Petch provides no source, but his work is accurate in other details. What seems most likely, then, is that Wickham managed to persuade the captain to accept himself, his wife, and their baggage on credit, and that he later reimbursed the line with money the India Office paid for his seeds.[25]

As for the historic encounter at the customs house, it may have occurred. Not with a baron, however, since the only baron with the initial *S* who made his home in the Amazon at the time was the Baron of Santarém, a venerable gentleman who had been one of Wickham's neighbors. The port director at Belém at the time was a simple commoner named Ulrich. Green did not report on the interview, but it would have been part of his duties, and he was later to assist Robert Cross.[26] Further, the wording of the request suggests someone who knew Brazilian tariff law well. Wickham's account leaves up to the reader's imagination whether the removal of the rubber seeds was legal. The appeal to the customs chief, however, was clearly based on article 643 of the Brazilian customs regulations, which stated: "Products destined for Cabinets of Natural History, collected and arranged in the Empire by professors for this purpose expressly commissioned by foreign Governments or Academies, or duly accredited by the respective Diplomatic or Consular Agents, national or foreign, will be dispatched without opening the volumes in which they are encased, a sworn statement by the naturalist sufficing, and duties will be charged according to the value which he gives them, in accordance with a list in duplicate which he must present."[27]

This regulation appears to refer to dried or stuffed specimens, and not, perhaps, to live or viable ones. Possibly, however, "volumes" might refer to portable greenhouses, cages, or even seedbeds. Of course, the specimens in question had no particular scientific purpose, only a commercial one. Though they were destined for royal botanic gardens in England and Ceylon, those gardens were merely to germinate the seed and raise the resulting plants to maturity, to obtain stock to sell to commercial nurseries and planters. The regulation under which the seeds were removed was, it may be argued, inapplicable, and the declaration of Wickham and Green, if any such was made, was false.

It is not the case, however, that the export of rubber seeds was prohibited.

19

There was no such law. Evidently not: the British consul had already unsecretively forwarded two earlier shipments, one from Wickham himself.

The India Office and the Foreign Office might be criticized, even so, for failing to notify the Brazilian government of their intentions. The historian René Bouvier claimed that, although both governments had self-interested reasons to deny it, the British consul-general at Rio de Janeiro had indeed officially requested seeds but had been refused. Only then did Britain act on its own. No such documentation was found in the archives of either foreign ministry; in any case, this assertion, considering contrary evidence, appears fanciful. With the publication of Collins's book under the auspices of the India Office, numerous accounts in the London press spread the notice of the office's intention to obtain Para rubber. Markham's lectures on rubber at the Royal Society of Arts were public and were reported in the newspapers. Only if the Brazilian ambassador in London had been unable to read English could he have missed them. Markham and his companions had indeed suffered delays and humiliations at the hands of some Peruvian authorities when they were collecting cinchona plants, but Markham appears to have given no thought to the possibility of similar embarrassments in Brazil. Perhaps he was observing greater circumspection, but even the internal correspondence of the India Office and Kew shows no hint of caution. They went ahead, not against the desires of the Brazilian government, but for all the world as though the Brazilian government did not exist and the only authorities in that quarter of the world were British consuls.[28]

It has also been claimed that, contrary to Wickham's version, the Brazilian authorities were aware of what he was doing. O. Labroy and V. Cayla, who in 1913 wrote a semiofficial study of rubber in the Amazon, said that he had succeeded "thanks to the good offices of the Brazilian government, which had these seeds collected by Indians in the rubber groves of the uplands." These authors were most likely engaged in face-saving. No one else has repeated this assertion, or provided proof, yet it does seem odd that Wickham could have collected rubber seeds for a period of a year or more without authorities, at the local level at least, becoming aware of it. There were, after all, a police chief and judge in Santarém, and they were not ineffectual. Herbert H. Smith, an American who spent several years in the region, and who may have been acquainted with Wickham, recounts a somewhat similar event that took place at about the same time. A young girl, an orphan of one of the American families of Santarém, was taken aboard a United States naval vessel by its captain, with the intention of returning her to relatives. Brazilian authorities quickly discovered what had occurred, however, and forced the vessel to anchor at Belém and undergo formalities. Brazilian law forbade the removal of a minor from the country without official sanction, no matter what the circumstances.[29]

Local authorities may well have been aware of Wickham's purposes, then, but they did not hinder him. Even in the absence of a specific law, they might have taken some action, as Wickham feared. Yet they did not. It may only be hindsight that perceives an omission. In 1876, the trade in rubber was still modest, there were other species that were also being tapped, and the idea that there might be on the other side of the world a place where the Para rubber tree could be cultivated would have been much beyond the imagining of most Brazilian civil servants. It certainly seems not to have been perceived clearly by Wickham himself, then or even much later, since he did not himself try rubber planting during his later wanderings in Southeast Asia, at least until 1907, during a residence in New Guinea.

It is possible to cast doubt upon many aspects of Wickham's account. But it is almost impossible to dispel the myth that he himself cultivated so assiduously. Shortly before his death, Wickham added another detail: The seeds, he told a reporter, had been loaded aboard the *Amazonas* by stealth, under the nose of a gunboat "which would have blown us out of the water had her commander suspected what we were doing." When this last, most marvelous version was published, Wickham was in his eighties, a man whose entire fame, indeed whose only success in life, had derived from this one episode. He refined his tale for twenty years, for fellow club members, for potential silent partners, for delegates to international rubber congresses. The garrulous old man with the handsome sunburned leonine head and drooping mustachio was the very image of a planter-hero. And so, thought one or another of the rubber manufacturers, why not award him a pension? Done. But did not the symbol of British daring and enterprise, the father of the rubber industry, deserve more, some honor in recognition of his great achievement? Thus, forty-four years after the inspired deed, did Henry Wickham gain a knighthood.[30]

Essential to Wickham's tale was the element of duplicity. Had he not experienced danger, there would have been no triumph; had his exploit not appeared to have constituted a theft, paradoxically there could be no honor. For the retired servants of the Empire who gathered at the Royal Colonial Institute, where Wickham customarily held forth in later years, much of the charm of his narrative lay, no doubt, in a victory slyly won over the natives. Wickham helped his confreres preserve their sense of superiority and the value of their civilizing mission.

In Brazil, on the other hand, Wickham's name was in later years reviled, and the British government reproached that it had rewarded villainy. According to Roberto Santos, a historian of the Amazon, it was an "exploit hardly defensible in the light of international law." He asserts that no one has the right "to appropriate the goods of others when there is a sure owner or a defined jurisdiction" even in the absence of a specific law. It appears, however, since Wickham obtained his seeds in groves that were being tapped, that the relevant owners had given permission and that they or their workers may have received some kind of payment. Santos appears to possess some higher vision of property, of nature constituting a national patrimony, a principle applied in Brazilian law no earlier than 1934.[31]

Wickham's act perhaps needs to be viewed from a more elevated perspective than the temporary reinforcement it provided British imperialism or the frustration it caused bourgeois ambitions in Brazil. As long as Brazilian rubber was gathered in the wild, the harvest could not rise above 40,000 tons a year, no matter how exaggerated the price. This quantity was insignificant in light of growing industrial applications. In a broader sense, therefore, what was taken from Brazil and what was gained by the British was trifling compared to the global economic benefits of the spread of rubber cultivation, including those to the Brazilians themselves, for whom the cost of rubber goods was soon reduced by three-quarters and whose own rubber manufacturing industry was later based on imported cultivated rubber. Of course, the distribution of these benefits was simultaneously rearranged: Great numbers of Asian peasants were transported to rubber plantations, where they were transformed into ill-paid coolies, while great numbers of Brazilian backlanders were relieved of debt peonage and relapsed into subsistence activities or migrated out of the Amazon. For these masses, all that had changed was the location, not the dimensions of their misery.

No matter how great the loss to Brazil of the monopoly in rubber, the losses might have been enormously greater if the principle expounded by Roberto Santos were to be generalized. The transfer of seeds, even across national borders, even for the sake of crass profit, even in behalf of imperialism, may be counted as a foremost means of the aggrandizement of the human species. Had the Portuguese colonialists not introduced Mediterranean cultivars to Brazil, its array of food and fiber plants would be short indeed. The continuing import of plant materials, cited with approval by Santos himself in regard to sugar, tobacco, and coconut varieties, has enabled Brazil to improve the productivity of its agriculture. Much of this exchange was carried out in cooperation with British botanic gardens and commercial nurseries, who were as willing to sell seeds to Brazil as to carry them off. In particular, the transfer of Liberian coffee to Brazil was at least in part the work of Kew, and foreigners appear to have collaborated in the introduction of eucalyptus, mango, numerous ornamentals, and even the principal Asian rubber tree, *Ficus elastica*. All this was occurring at about the same time as Wickham's deed, and about the same time that Kew was also acquiring from Brazil, via more prosaic channels, manioc, Brazil nuts, ipecac, and pineapples.[32]

Finally, Brazil profited extensively from feats quite similar to Wickham's and Markham's. In 1797, the captain-general of Pará, Francisco Inocêncio de Souza Coutinho, in league with French counterrevolutionaries resident in Cayenne, smuggled seeds of pepper, nutmeg, cloves, and cinnamon from that colony to the new Botanical Garden at Belém. Then in 1811, a Portuguese expeditionary force invaded Cayenne, in reprisal for Napoleon's invasion of Portugal. Its commander took full advantage of the occasion to dispatch numerous plants, including spices, lavender, jackfruit, sweetsop, avocados, breadfruit, and a new variety of sugarcane, which came to be known as *Cayena*. That Brazilian scientists might deal generously with former enemies, on the other hand, can be demonstrated by the remittances of seeds of various native species to Cayenne sometime between 1816 and 1823 by Leandro do Sacramento, director of the Botanical Garden of Rio de Janeiro.[33]

Brazil even tried, a few years after Markham, to duplicate his introduction of cinchona. In 1868, the Brazilian minister to Bolivia, F. Lopes Netto, obtained seeds of cinchona that he forwarded to the Ministry of Agriculture. These were planted out, apparently unsuccessfully, on land belonging to Escragnolle Taunay in Teresópolis, Rio de Janeiro province, in the presence of the imperial princess and her consort. Astoundingly, in the same Brazilian journal that recalled this event, may be found a reference to Henry Wickham, excoriated for having "singlehandedly prejudiced Brazil as much or more than an army of a hundred thousand men."[34]

Although some Brazilians still harbor animosity for Wickham, they cherish a Prometheus of their own. In 1727, the governor of Belém sent Francisco de Melo Palheta on a diplomatic mission to Cayenne. There he is said to have charmed the French governor's wife, Madame d'Orvilliers, into providing him seeds of coffee, *Coffea arabica*, that had been newly brought to the colony and were forbidden to foreigners. Palheta's brilliant exploit was the beginning of a plantation industry that was the mainstay of the Brazilian economy for a century and a half.[35] If it is necessary to view the transfer of plant species as theft, then perhaps Palheta may be looked upon as evening the score.

2

Awaiting developments, 1876–1906

Henry Wickham's rubber seeds arrived at Kew on 15 June 1876. The chief gardener, R. Irwin Lynch, was put in charge. According to Wickham, he had to make room for the seeds by emptying trays full of orchids. Indeed, the germinating beds took up more than twenty-five square meters. Within four days a few sprouts were beginning to appear; within ten there were more than a hundred. By 7 July, however, only 2,700, or 3.6 percent, had germinated. Wickham, perhaps embarrassed by this very low rate, preferred later to recall that 7,000 survived and avoided mentioning how large a number he had delivered. The records at Kew are not entirely consistent, but refer nearly always to 70,000 seeds. Hooker directed a letter to Markham on 24 June introducing him to Wickham, "who has been collecting seeds for you. He has brought 74,000 which have all been planted." Wickham was issued payment of £740 based upon this letter. The poor performance of his seeds constitutes further evidence that he had gathered them helter-skelter, in order to present a quantity massive enough to cover his passage back to England.[1]

In addition to the rubber seeds, Wickham delivered a number of Amazonian plants that he thought might have some value. He addressed a note to Hooker, making mention of them, and suggesting their possible uses. It was his intention to display himself as something of an amateur botanist, in order to obtain a further commission from Kew to accompany the seedlings all the way to Ceylon. Wickham claimed that he had "made some experiments in planting" rubber, and alleged that his experience would be useful. In fact Wickham had already suggested such a commission in a letter from Santarém in April 1875. He made similar representations to Markham, who wrote Hooker twice in mid-July on his behalf: "Mr. Wickham seems to have taken very great pains with the seeds," a reproachful hint that their successful collector was owed something more.[2]

But Hooker had no interest in Wickham's services. Coolly the director noted on the margins of Wickham's letter the Latin names of his specimens, as if to underscore his ignorance of botany and Kew's already perfect familiarity with them. To Markham, Hooker expressed his doubt that Wickham

Henry Wickham's rendering of "our first temporary home" near Santarém, his wife in foreground. (Courtesy The New York Public Library Special Collections)

possessed any horticultural ability. Markham told Wickham to "await developments" and wrote a memorandum at the India Office, recommending that Wickham be sent to India to choose sites for the eventual planting of the trees. This was finally disapproved in late September. A few days before, Wickham, discouraged at the lack of a reply, had already set out with his wife for Queensland, to try once again to realize his dream of becoming a successful planter. This time he took with him a portable greenhouse full of coffee seedlings, a gift from Kew's gardener. Wickham bore no grudge against Hooker, but wrote him occasionally, sending seeds and asking for recommendations. Unaware that the director had opposed appointing him to an Indian position, he remained ever grateful, imagining that the permission to return with an unlimited number of seeds had originated with Hooker.[3]

Markham was unable to obtain a post for Wickham because his own position at the India Office was shaky. While the rubber transfer was reaching its culmination, Markham's bureaucratic career was reaching a crisis, and he was soon to resign. Even though he had been instrumental in obtaining cinchona for the British empire and was on the way to repeating the feat with rubber, he was looked upon as a dilettante by the irascible Louis Mallet, Secretary of State for India, a holdover from earlier days when prompt, daily appearance at the office was not yet the chief virtue of the civil servant. Markham did indeed have too many interests, but he had carried out the planning and coordination of the rubber project. Had it not been for him, the lumbering behemoth that was the India Office would never have focused its attention sufficiently to issue proper orders to Kew and pay invoices on time. It was, for

25

example, on an occasion when Markham was absent that the India Office refused to purchase Charles Ledger's variety of cinchona, the best ever discovered. Ledger easily sold it to the Dutch, who planted it in Java.[4]

Luckily, Markham was still on hand to perform one more critical service. It had already been decided that the most suitable place for the acclimatization of the rubber trees was Ceylon. There the energetic H. K. Thwaites, director of the botanic gardens at Peradeniya, was prepared to receive the new plant as he had cinchona years before. On 9 August 1876, a shipment of 1,919 of Wickham's seedlings, packed in portable greenhouses, was entrusted to a gardener newly hired by Peradeniya. The shipment arrived at Colombo on 13 September, 90 percent of the seedlings having survived. Then it was discovered that no provision had been made for payment of the freight charges. The shipping company refused to release the plants! Thwaites desperately telegraphed Kew for instructions. Markham spent nearly a week carrying the freight documents from desk to desk, all the way to Louis Mallet himself. He raged, in a letter to Thiselton-Dyer, then Hooker's assistant, at the "fatuous processes" needed to gain approval even for small payments and the "senseless routine" that had accumulated under Mallet and Lord Salisbury. "This [letter] is not official," he ironically wrote Thiselton-Dyer, "otherwise you would not get it for a month." Another shipment of 100 plants, sent on 11 August to Singapore, as a hedge against the possible loss of the Ceylon cargo, did not fare as well. It was unaccompanied, and on arrival it was also held on the dock for nonpayment of freight. All, or nearly all, of the plants died. Markham learned of this disaster only in late December.[5]

Markham's planning involved one other, much less successful operation. In February 1876, worried at the delays in arrangements with Wickham and fearing that the seeds would indeed prove too perishable to survive a transatlantic crossing, he had recommended that Robert Cross be sent to Belém. Cross had taken part in the search for cinchona, and had already completed a voyage, commissioned by Markham, to Central America to gather Castilla seeds. This time Cross was to collect Hevea seedlings and bring them to Kew in portable greenhouses. This operation was at last sanctioned on 13 April. Cross prepared slowly for his journey, studying the herbarium specimens at Kew, and did not embark for Belém until 19 June. Oddly, this was four days after Wickham's return and it is entirely possible that he passed Wickham's baskets of seeds somewhere on the railroad between London and Liverpool. Apparently neither Markham nor Hooker thought to head him off; perhaps they thought that he had already departed.[6]

In Belém, Cross set to work with dispatch, quickly gathering a collection of seedlings in the neighborhood of the city, replanting, tending, and carefully packing 1,080 for shipment. Consul Green was in contact with him and reported that he had "rendered him every assistance possible." Cross embarked on the *Paraense*, of the Liverpool Red Cross Line, which normally called at the port of Fortaleza on the return voyage. Cross knew that place was the source of an inferior sort of commercial rubber, called Maniçoba in Brazil, Ceara in England, and *Manihot glaziovii* by botanists. There were as yet no Ceara plants at Kew. Cross rode a few miles inland on the newly built railway to the dry country in which the Ceara tree flourished, and he managed to obtain sixty of them. The *Paraense* returned him to England on 22 November.[7]

At Kew the Hevea plants were found to be in poor condition. It was decided to keep 400, which were the most promising of the lot, and to give the rest to a commercial nurseryman, William Bull. He reported the following spring that only fourteen of the Hevea plants had survived. There is no record at Kew to show that Bull returned them, nor is it known what else may have happened to them. The Kew report stated that only 3 percent of the plants retained there survived, implying a stock of only twelve plants.[8]

After the two initial shipments of seeds to Ceylon and Singapore, another lot of 100 was dispatched to Ceylon and smaller lots were sent to other British tropical colonies. Of the remaining seedlings, nearly 700 were donated to botanical collectors in the British Isles and elsewhere. By the end of 1876, more than 2,900 plants had been distributed. Then again, between mid-June and late September 1877, there was a series of small shipments, totalling 225 plants. Since these shipments totaled several hundred more than the combined total of the Wickham and Cross shipments, it appears that there had been some propagation through cuttings.[9]

Evidently, the Wickham selection provided the overwhelming genetic stock for the spread of cultivation in the British colonies. Yet the Collins plants have been a subject of considerable speculation. The early planters observed an extraordinary variability in their trees that might have been the result of intrusion of Cross's material, which had come from a population quite different from Wickham's. If the shipment sent to Singapore on 11 June 1877 consisted of Cross's seeds, then they may have constituted a disproportionate share of the Malayan genetic material. This hypothesis was frequently advanced by Malaya's most energetic rubber propagator, Henry N. Ridley.[10]

The second shipment to Singapore acquires very great importance if it is accepted that the shipment of 1876, undoubtedly Wickham's selection, had perished on the Singapore docks. The Kew Report of 1876 stated that by the time they were retrieved from customs, they were "nearly all dead," which still implied that some had survived. H. Murton, the director of the Singapore botanical garden, did write Kew on 6 September that "the plants sent last year" were flourishing. But the shipment had included other species, and Murton may have been thinking of the shipment in general, rather than the Hevea seedlings in particular. Ridley claimed invariably that the Hevea in the first shipment was entirely lost, without, however, citing evidence. There is indeed a letter in the India Office archive that supports his assertion: On 30

September 1876, William Adamson, chairman of the Raffles Library and Museum at Singapore, wrote to the colonial secretary that Murton had informed him that by the time he had been notified of the arrival of the first shipment of seedlings, "they were all dead."[11]

Yet there has been no certainty that any of the plants sent in the second shipment, in June 1877, were Cross's. Indeed, in 1914, David Prain, then director of Kew, in a retrospective article questioned "whether a single plant brought back by Cross ever became fit to send" anywhere in Asia. He reported being unable to find "any entry in our archives which could be so interpreted." Nevertheless, an earlier director, Thiselton-Dyer, had written in 1898 that Cross's surviving plants had been propagated from cuttings and that about 100 of them had been sent, not to Malaya, but to Ceylon. This apparently refers to the third, final shipment, that of 15 September 1877. Thomas Petch, in his history of rubber cultivation in Ceylon, published in 1914, surmised that the Kew director had adopted this statement from a report sent from Ceylon. But Thiselton-Dyer had been present at the time of the transfer and would not have needed prompting. The problem seems to be solved by a letter Thiselton-Dyer sent Louis Mallet, dated 8 September 1877: Kew still had in its possession ten cases of Hevea, Castilla, and Ceara rubber. "The whole of these have been derived from the proceeds of Mr. Cross's mission." These cases, he told Mallet, ought not to be delayed for shipment any longer, and were to be sent to Ceylon ten days hence. A few months later he reported that they had been sent, on 15 September.[12]

In Ceylon a new experimental garden had been laid out for the Brazilian seedlings at Heneratgoda, thought more suitable than highland Peradeniya. Early reports showed that the plants were vigorous and well suited to the climate. Nevertheless, by 1880 only 320 of the original stock of more than two thousand remained. In the meantime, Heneratgoda had sent out more than 600 supposedly propagated seedlings to India and Burma. Thomas Petch deduced that these early exports were not propagated at all, but part of the first shipment. The Ceylon gardens were apparently quite unsuccessful at propagation, and so were obliged to await the maturation of the trees to be able to supply further planting material.[13]

The Ceylon gardeners, meanwhile, were struggling with several uncertainties concerning the tree. Not the least of these was its competitiveness with other species. Despite Collins's 1872 report, the great variety and easy availability of Asiatic species caused many planters to experiment with them, especially *Ficus elastica*. Robert Cross was hired by the India Office in 1881 to scout likely sites for planting his selections, and once again he devoted more attention to Castilla and Ceara rubber. Indeed, the faster maturation of Castilla and Ceara trees caused planters to favor those species at first. Only after a few tapping seasons did they convince themselves that Hevea was superior.[14]

It was also thought that Hevea had to be planted in swamps. The usual source for this view was Cross's 1877 report to the India Office, in which he recommended planting on "flat, low-lying moist tracts, lands subject to inundation, shallow lagoons, water holes. . . ." This was the general opinion of Europeans who had made quick forays into rubber groves around Belém, where the trees were indeed often rooted below the flood line. In fact, as numerous trials showed, seedlings planted in standing water invariably died or were stunted. Ridley was later to show that trees planted in soggy ground failed to develop an adequate root system. Indeed Wickham's report to the India Office had contradicted Cross. He noted that the best specimens were to be found not along the river banks but on higher ground. Wickham's report, however, had been published without clear indication of its authorship and without Wickham's illustrations. It was only a few pages long and much less circumstantial than Cross's; therefore, it was rarely cited or reprinted. Furthermore, the Wickham report contained a hedge: It recommended rich alluvial lands and assured the reader that it would not "prove a serious drawback if they should be planted on lands which become annually flooded to the depth of a foot or so for a few weeks in the year."[15]

The Hevea in Ceylon began to bear seeds in 1882, and each year thereafter bore larger quantities. Most of the seed harvest, until 1893, was reserved for further government plantings in Ceylon, India, and Burma, but there seems at first to have been little demand from local planters. In August 1887, the director at Peradeniya dispatched 2,000 seeds to Kew, saying "no one here wants it." Meanwhile, the trees planted in Malaya, the result of the second shipment of 1877, had been preserved and were also bearing seeds. A stand of about 1,000 trees had been planted in the botanical gardens at Singapore, and there were several hundred more in Perak.[16]

The first experiments in tapping began in 1881 at Heneratgoda; the resulting samples were sent to England and found to be satisfactory. Henry Trimen, the director at Peradeniya, was extremely cautious in his program of tapping, and only in 1894 did he decide that it would be feasible to tap each year. His successor, John Willis, was equally cautious, and continued to believe that Hevea ought to be planted on land subject to flooding and that they should be planted close together for self-shading. Some Ceylon planters were outdistancing the government gardeners, making experimental plantings of their own and becoming convinced of the tree's commercial promise. The botanical gardens were therefore becoming a modest source of seed for the plantations. In 1893, 91,000 seeds were sold at five rupees per thousand. It was reported in the 1890s that planters were finding it so profitable to harvest rubber seeds, that they were not tapping the trees. According to Thomas Petch, dispatches of seeds to other tropical colonies, including non-British colonies, retarded the growth of Ceylon plantations. By 1898 the island exported 434 kilograms of seed.[17]

In 1888, Henry Ridley passed through Ceylon on his way to his new post at Singapore. He observed the techniques employed there and was granted a supply of 11,500 seeds. In Malaya, Ridley was a whirlwind, and much of his energy for the next twenty-four years was directed toward the encouragement of rubber planting. He was employed full-time to run the botanical gardens, maintain a herbarium and library, and edit a journal. He accomplished all this while collecting some 50,000 specimens, training local collectors, and providing varied agricultural extension services. Nevertheless, he found time to engage in further rubber planting, experiment with tapping and coagulating methods, investigate plant diseases, and stuff rubber seeds in the pockets of anyone who appeared to be a potential rubber planter. He did all this, according to his account, with no help from the colonial government, which disdained agriculture and was only interested in tin. During all this time he carried on a running feud with the Peradeniya gardens and with anyone else who claimed a share of the credit for promoting rubber. He was even more long-lived than Wickham, surviving to the age of 101, and in retirement he similarly polished his reputation. It rankled him that he had done so much to earn it, while Wickham, whom he once met and upbraided for the "ridiculous nonsense" that had been written about him, "for merely travelling home with a lot of seeds had received a knighthood."[18]

By the end of the decade of the 1890s, the combined, even though uncoordinated, efforts of Ridley and his collaborators, botanists at Peradeniya, and numerous planters and tappers had resolved most of the uncertainties surrounding *Hevea brasiliensis*. Planting in swampy ground was proved to be a mistake. Initial spacing of about 350 trees per hectare was shown to permit the most rapid growth. It appeared possible to begin to tap within seven years, suggesting that plantation operations might be expected to yield a profit. Tapping methods were much improved over those employed in the Amazon. To take the place of the small hatchet, knives were designed that excised thin slices of the bark. Repeated excision of the same portion of bark was found to increase, rather than reduce, the flow of latex. It was discovered that the tree could be tapped on alternate days the year through, and that annual yields of about a kilogram per tree were possible, with yields tending to increase as the tree matured. It was found that coagulation of the latex with acetic acid was an adequate substitute for the arduous process of smoking. Samples of coagulated rubber were sent to England and gradually achieved evaluations approaching that of the best grades of Brazilian wild smoked rubber.[19]

In Malaya the first successful commercial planter was not an Englishman, but an emigré Chinese, Tan Chay Yan, who planted a grove in 1896. In 1897, Heneratgoda's plan to increase its rubber groves to 1,200 hectares was canceled on account of the protests of planters, who wanted the seed sold to them. The year following was the first that commercial seed was available in Ceylon. Even so, Heneratgoda was able to sell its own seeds at twenty-seven rupees a thousand. In 1898, Malaya registered its first commercial sale of rubber, 145 kilograms, for £61. The season 1897–8 was in fact the turning point: A drop in the price of coffee accompanied by a sharp increase in the price of rubber convinced planters in Ceylon and Malaya to shift their resources. In 1905, these early plantings yielded no more than 230 tons, but seedlings were being planted at a constantly increasing rate. In the same year there were already more than 20,000 hectares laid out in Malaya, and in another year that area doubled.[20]

Only Ceylon and Malaya, of all the tropical colonies to which Kew had sent seeds, reached the point of commercial exploitation. In India and Burma, originally intended as the final recipients of the rubber materials, the plants did not develop satisfactorily. If Petch is correct in supposing that they were sent Wickham's seedlings, they may have already been too mature to resist the shock of transfer. Turned over to the forest conservator, they were planted on sites too dry or too wet and suffered from neglect and interruption.

It should be noted that Kew did not regard its newly cultivated Hevea seedlings as its monopoly: One of its 1876 shipments had been consigned to the botanic garden at Buitenzorg (now Bogor), in the Netherlands East Indies. Later there were shipments to German eastern African colonies, to Portuguese Mozambique, and more shipments to Java. This was normal practice for Kew and the other British botanical gardens, which seemed to lack a policy of exclusiveness in regard to their output. For botanists, the advantages of exchanging plant materials freely was immensely greater than maintaining exclusivity. Furthermore, in contrast to Wickham's bemused public, the botanists of Kew and other research centers were too aware of the ease with which seeds could pass man-made borders ever to consider a policy of monopoly.[21]

The growing demand for seeds within and beyond the British tropical colonies led to improvements in packing. The extremely low germination rate of Wickham's selection had engendered an exaggerated concern for the viability of seeds. In fact, quite satisfactory results could be obtained over moderate distances with no special care at all, as long as the seeds were fresh. The 11,500 seeds that Ridley brought, or had sent, from Ceylon in 1888 were simply stuffed in gunny sacks, but a large percentage survived the 2,800 kilometer journey. The seeds sent from Ceylon to Kew in 1887, packed in soil and coconut fiber, kept for three weeks and 95 percent of them germinated. By about 1900, however, the most generally employed packing medium was charcoal, much lighter in weight than soil. It was slightly moistened and packed in cracker tins. Ridley reported very high survival rates with this technique, even for periods of two or three months. A shipment of charcoal-packed seeds received at Buitenzorg in 1913 had been delayed six months, yet 50 percent germinated.[22]

By 1900, there were a number of commercial seed distributors in competition with the botanical gardens. The importance of the commercial distributors cannot be overlooked. For example, J. P. Williams, a firm located in Heneratgoda, guaranteed 75 percent germination of its seeds and claimed to have customers in Java, Sumatra, and Hawaii, where it had sent 250,000 seeds at the request of the United States Department of Agriculture. By 1906, firms such as Williams were supplying the market adequately and the director of the Ceylon botanical gardens decided to sell off groves that had been maintained for the purpose of supplying seeds.[23]

The high price of rubber seeds, and their lack of availability in the last years of the 1890s caused commercial seed dealers to consider collecting more of them in Brazil. A Scottish merchant named A. Scott Blacklaw sent two tins of Hevea seeds from Belém via England in 1881 and advertised in a Colombo newspaper that he was ready to ship any amount requested. In a letter to the same newspaper, however, he professed himself unsure whether seeds so long in transit would keep. It is not known what happened to the trial seeds or if anyone took him up on his offer. Much later, in 1897, Thomas Christy, a London merchant, advertised in Colombo that he was introducing "thousands" of seedlings from Brazil. A Ceylon planter who complained to Christy that seeds he had received from him had not germinated was told by the merchant that some of the seeds in the same lot had been sent to British Guiana, where 83 percent had germinated. Furthermore, he claimed that he had shipped Hevea seeds "to all parts of the world with perfect success."[24]

It does not appear that the British botanical gardens made any further attempts to transfer *Hevea* plant material out of Brazil. Ridley's statement in 1891 that "seed has been successfully sent from South America via England, though usually with much loss," suggests more than one introduction, but in 1898 he commented: "This plant seems never to have been successfully introduced again." He maintained that assertion in later years, although he has himself been suspected of having organized an attempt to introduce more seed.[25]

Meanwhile, however, seed dealers and planters in the tropical colonies of the other imperialist powers were becoming anxious to gain a steady supply of seed, and naturally turned to what appeared to be an inexhaustable source: the Amazon habitat of Hevea. Eugène Poisson, sent to Belém by the French Ministry of Public Instruction in 1898, found many Germans, Americans, Englishmen, and other Frenchmen there, all clamoring for seeds. Apparently there were Dutch and Belgians as well, since an estate in Java is said to have received seeds directly from Brazil in 1896 and 1898, and there were some 2,000 hectares of Hevea in the Belgian Congo by 1904, reportedly also grown from seeds brought directly from Brazil. Still other plantations were set out in Mozambique and German colonies in western Africa, apparently with seeds sent directly from Brazil. J. Orton Kerby, the U.S. consul at Belém, claimed that he had exported seeds on a small scale, apparently to Florida, and he advocated large-scale planting in the Phillipines. Poisson managed to return to Paris with 100,000 seeds, an amount considerably larger than Wickham's, and he claimed that 70 percent of them germinated. Part of this selection was dispatched to Cochin China and Cambodia, where French planters introduced rubber in 1897 or 1898.[26]

Both Poisson and Kerby warned their readers that, although many Brazilians offered to sell seeds, quite often they were seeds that had been boiled. Boiling the seeds would indeed ruin them, more surely than simply soaking them in water, since a characteristic of seed dissemination in the genus is the ability of seeds to float downstream and retain their viability. It might be imagined that the Brazilian vendors, in employing this practice, were acting on some patriotic, albeit crafty, impulse. More likely they were simply increasing their immediate profits, since seeds were sold by weight, and the boiled seeds were much heavier.[27]

Under these circumstances Brazilian seeds were evidently at a disadvantage in the international seed market, and the picaresque seed trade in Belém must have died off rather quickly. In 1884, the interior state of Amazonas had imposed a prohibitive export duty on rubber seeds of 1,000 milreis per kilogram, and in 1918, it passed a law prohibiting their export entirely. This law was repealed in 1921. More important than legal sanctions or chicanery, however, was the improductivity of all the latterly introduced materials. They overwhelmingly had been collected in the neighborhood of Belém, a region of low-yielding trees. Quite a few of the earliest plantations in Africa and Southeast Asia proved to be failures for other reasons, but in every case the local rubber estates had to be rebuilt, when they were, with seeds of the Wickham selection, sent from Ceylon or Malaya. This choice was made, also, because seeds collected on the uncluttered floors of the plantations were much cheaper than those gathered in the wild.[28]

The Netherlands East Indies possessed in the Buitenzorg garden a far more impressive research facility than Malaya had, but its director was no Henry Ridley. For a number of years he pressed on with studies of *Ficus elastica* and species of gutta-percha native to the islands. Only two trees had survived of the eighteen Kew had sent to Buitenzorg in 1876. Unfortunately, they proved to be quite low yielders. Small quantities of seeds were obtained from Ceylon and Malaya in the 1880s and 1890s, but not much attention was paid to the resulting trees until the plantations of Malaya had already proved commercially successful. Some of Poisson's seeds were purchased for the Buitenzorg garden, through a commercial seed dealer, but they also resulted in low-yielding trees. By then, however, the Dutch colonial government was determined to catch up with the British. Remembering that the acquisition of a superior variety had made that possible in the case of cinchona, the Dutch government ordered P. J. S. Cramer, a botanist at the Buitenzorg garden, to travel to the Amazon to make further collections.[29]

Cramer visited rubber plantations in Malaya and Ceylon and was appointed head of the Surinam department of agriculture. Late in 1912 he made a three-month tour of the Amazon. Influenced, no doubt, by Ernst Ule's report of 1906, which stated that the best Hevea was to be found neither near Belém nor on the Tapajós, where Wickham had collected, but on the headwaters of the Amazon's southern tributaries, Cramer continued upriver. Unfortunately for the future of Indonesian rubber cultivation, he arrived at the season of low waters and could not ascend. And so he had to content himself with some seeds from trees planted at Manaus that reportedly had been grown from seeds from the Acre territory. By 1914, Cramer was back at Buitenzorg, with 250 Hevea seedlings in his nursery. But these, too, proved to be poor yielders. Dutch breeding programs accordingly proceeded with no more stock than that which could be bought in the markets of Colombo and Penang.[30]

Surprisingly, Cramer's expedition appears to have been the last effort for many years by colonial authorities to enlarge the genetic pool of their most important plantation crop, even though it was generally believed that Wickham's selection was of inferior and perhaps even hybrid origin. Thus, the vast estates of Southeast Asia were based upon the offspring of a trifling number of plants. Henry Wickham, evidently, had indeed merited recognition: For all the amateurism and desperation of his exertions, he had succeeded where dozens, perhaps hundreds, of better-equipped adventurers and even professional botanists had failed. Within thirty years a few basketsful of seeds had been transformed into an agricultural resource of immense consequences in world trade and industry. This achievement had suffered considerably from inertia, inattention, and cross-purposes, but there had been many obstacles to overcome. As it happened, the principal sites of rubber cultivation were to be located thousands of miles from those originally envisioned.

The transfer of rubber took place just as new technologies were coming to be applied on a world scale. The steamship and the undersea cable evidently played crucial roles. The standardization of organization through Kew, which nominated personnel for the colonial gardens and which served to interchange information as well as planting materials, was another critical factor, even though operatives within this rather imperfect system had disregarded useful information and overvalued other sources that proved incorrect. Once the project was successful, however, the Kew-centered experimental organization seems to have lost its energies. Ridley was about to return to England. He had performed admirably, but he had not left behind an organization able to frame the next set of questions. The task of selection, breeding, and phytopathology were to be taken up by Dutch researchers at Buitenzorg and other centers.[31]

Shipments of plantation-grown rubber reached 1,000 tons by 1907. By then it had become a feverish speculation, and the area planted to rubber expanded enormously. Between 1907 and 1910, it multiplied ten times in Malaya, to 400,000 hectares; by the latter date there were almost 100,000 hectares planted in Sumatra and Java. It is likely that there was more *Hevea brasiliensis* growing on Far Eastern plantations than growing wild in the Brazilian Amazon! By 1913, 47,618 tons of plantation rubber were sold in the world market, more than all the rubber gathered in Brazil.

Paradoxically, the shift to rubber by eastern planters was to a certain extent the result of improved competitiveness on the part of Brazilian coffee planters. Only the Brazilians were able to achieve a profit in the face of falling coffee prices in the late 1890s. Ceylon planters, therefore, had to cast about for an alternate crop, and many chose Hevea.

In turn, the Amazon economy was ravaged by competition from Ceylon and Malaya. Wages fell along with prices, to a quarter of their level during the boom. Despairing traders, exporters, bankers, and brokers joined their tappers in an exodus from the region. Manaus and Belém, the glittering equatorial capitals of the gathering trade, battened down for an ice age of bankruptcies and stagnation. Rearguard directors of the gathering trade ransacked their vast hinterland for another wild product that might reanimate their fleets of steamboats and languishing backwoods gatherers, but could find none as highly prized.

For lack of a new resource, they would have to begin to cultivate some tropical plant for which they were particularly fitted. To some it seemed logical that that product should be *Hevea brasiliensis*. Why not? They were nearer industrial markets than the Southeast Asian growers, they had greater experience, and theirs was the original and obviously the most suitable habitat of the tree.

3

Production and folklore, 1876–1910

While the Southeast Asian colonies of the British and Dutch were rapidly developing their rubber estates, what was occurring in Brazil? Were the Brazilians aware of the competition that was gathering on the far side of the earth? What prospects did they entertain of imitating the British and Dutch in their endeavors?

It must be noted that the Brazilian economy had historically displayed a sort of vocation for extractive activities. Indeed the very name of the country was derived from a dyestuff obtained from the wood of a forest tree. During most of the eighteenth century its principal exports were alluvial gold and diamonds. Despite the regimentation of labor in the coastal sugar plantations, in each generation some of the slaves and freedmen broke free and mingled with the indigenous population along the fringes of the elite-controlled plantation colony. There they engaged in farming manioc and took up hunting and gathering as a means not only of subsistence, but also of commercial engagement with the formally organized and controlled colony. In the port cities merchants and landowners mounted expeditions to range the interior for products to sell on the coast. Their most valued prey was human – tribal peoples – to sell as slaves, and they never failed to reconnoiter for gems and precious metals. As time went on, however, their stock in trade became more prosaic: medicinals, dyestuffs, pelts, nuts, herbs, live animals, and plants – the *drogas do sertão*, or *drugs of the backlands*. Other important productive activities, such as cattle raising, reverted in Brazil to methods that were closer in technique to hunting and gathering than cultivation. Wild rubber collecting in Brazil, therefore, was far from being an aberrant form of enterprise.

The techniques of rubber gathering are easy to explain but hard to imagine. *Hevea brasiliensis* is a species typical of the climax stage of the Amazon rain forest. Like nearly all such species, it was found not in groves or clusters, but scattered widely in the forest, commonly only two or three trees to a hectare. The hopeful tapper had first to locate the trees and then clear trails to connect them. This task might take six or seven months, during which time little or no tapping could be done. Normally, the tapper cleared two or three trails of

Henry Wickham, second from right, receiving prize of U.S. Rubber Manufacturer's Association from David Figart, on right. London, 1926. (Courtesy David Figart)

60 to 150 trees each, the most that one person would be capable of tending. Tapping methods were slightly improved: Instead of allowing the latex to flow down the trunk from numerous small hatchet wounds, small cups were suspended under each of the incisions. Since the latex vessels are located in the inner bark, close to the cambium, it was difficult to avoid cutting into the cambium layer. Most tappers took no care to moderate their incisions. Trees that had been tapped over a period of years therefore developed knarled and almost impenetrable trunks.

Tapping was carried out on each trail on alternate days to allow the trees to recover. On each trail the tapper made two rounds. During the first, in the early morning when latex flow was heaviest, the incisions were made. Then during a second tour the latex was collected from the cups. In the afternoon the tapper squatted before a fire fueled by palm nuts over which a stick was suspended. The tapper constantly turned the stick while slowly dripping the liquid latex over it, and gradually a large ball of solid rubber was formed. The gathering season lasted only during the six months of the year of relatively lower rainfall because the trails became marshy and the tin cups filled

37

with water in the rainy season. Depending on the varying characteristics of trees, weather, soils, and tappers, these techniques provided yields of 200 to 800 kilograms per year per tapper, with the average below 500 kilograms.

These gathering practices were the result of accumulated empirical knowledge, some of which had to be relearned in Ceylon and Malaya, yet this knowledge was also extremely primitive and easily improved upon in plantations. The tapping procedure was often carried out in such a way as to exhaust the tree quickly or to damage its bark so severely that it could no longer be tapped. Although the finished product, if carefully "smoked," achieved price quotations as high as the best plantation coagulated rubber, it often was full of impurities, moisture, and adulterates that were introduced to elevate the price to the dealer. The tapper must have felt that he deserved some kind of bonus. The excruciating conditions of isolation, deprivation, and danger he was subjected to limited his career to a few brief seasons, during which the contraction of malaria, Chagas disease, and leishmaniasis were virtual certainties. No wonder that, when rubber gathering was described to the Brazilian poet Rubem Braga, wounded by his country's backwardness he protested, "This isn't production, it's folklore!"[1]

Hevea brasiliensis was not the only kind of rubber gathered in the wild in Brazil. It was also obtained from other species of Hevea, notably *H. guianensis* and *H. benthamiana*, locally called Seringa Itaúba and Seringa Chicote. Neither of these was as productive as *H. brasilienis*, however. Castilla rubber trees, native to a very large region that stretched from Central America to the western and northern reaches of the Brazilian Amazon, came to be tapped mainly by Peruvians moving eastward as they exhausted those on their side of the border. This was an extremely itinerant form of gathering, since the technique they employed normally killed the tree. The distinction between Castilla and Hevea output was not altogether clearly maintained in the reporting of exports, but those data suggest that Castilla gathering increased at a faster rate than Hevea gathering as the price of rubber rose sharply from the mid-1890s, reaching, it appears, 16 percent of Brazil's rubber exports by 1906. Thus despite continuously increasing inputs of capital and labor into the gathering regime, at least until 1911, there appeared to be a practical ceiling on Hevea output of about 32,000 tons.

There were still other kinds of rubber gathered commercially in Brazil, apparently more responsive to rising prices than Hevea. There was Maniçoba, or Ceara rubber, brought to England by Robert Cross. There was Murupita (of the genus *Sapium*), tall trees that yielded good quality rubber, but in small quantities. Mangabeira (*Hancornia speciosa*), another tree that grew along the coast as far as Bahia, yielded a lower-quality rubber. Massaranduba, known as Balata in the British market, derived from several species of the genus *Manilkara*, found in the Guiana highlands. It supplied a substitute for gutta-percha, of low elasticity, but highly valued for machine belting.[2]

The gathering of rubber, then, was a typical and widespread response in Brazil to economic opportunity. Like ipecac, yerba maté, sarsaparilla, Brazil nuts, guaraná, and many other lesser products, its cultivation had not been attempted, in spite of the prospect of an enlarging and bouyant market. Yet it was not impossible that rubber might be planted. Cacao, another of Brazil's principal gathered commodities, a plant that was native to the Amazon, came to be cultivated within Brazil well before the period that rubber was becoming a vast industry in Southeast Asia. Why did cultivation not occur in the case of rubber?

It might be supposed that, in the absence of competition, the mix of economic factors in the Amazon was such that gathering was the cheapest way of obtaining rubber. There was no lack of wild trees at hand. Despite the fears voiced by some, there was no possibility at the time that the tree could be made extinct in its native habitat. Even at the height of the rubber boom, no more than half the groves already marked were in production, and hundreds of thousands of square kilometers of virgin forest still remained unsurveyed. Planted trees, on the other hand, could not be tapped for some uncertain number of years, usually supposed to be fifteen or more. In a region so absolutely lacking in capital, this was a formidable obstacle to planting by large proprietors, who would have to pay others for tending the trees to maturation.

Labor was nearly as scarce as capital. African slavery had been in frank decline in the Amazon region since the rebellions of the 1830s; it was almost unknown in the gathering sector of the regional economy. Outright abolition occurred in the province of Amazonas in 1884 and in the rest of Brazil in 1888. The forced labor of pacified, sedentary Indians, those called *tapuios*, was to some degree available, through a sort of corvée system overseen by local officials, but it was, in fact, quite difficult to commandeer the labor of Indians to accomplish any task not to their liking. As for Indians who preserved their tribal way of life, they were sometimes drawn into gathering, but it was more common, along the rubber frontier, for them to suffer massacre and displacement. The rest of the population, mestizo, was regarded by contemporary observers, foreign and Brazilian, as "lazy," which was to say that they were not inclined toward steady agricultural work at the wages that employers deigned to pay.[3]

The tapping of wild rubber trees, on the other hand, was not undertaken for wages, or at least the tappers, called *seringueiros,* did not regard their compensation as such. The gathering of rubber in the early years had been carried out by independent workers who voyaged singly or in groups to uninhabited and unclaimed sites near the town of Belém, returned with the rubber in their own canoes, and received payment from dealers in such goods. As the more imposing and ruthless among the gatherers established rights of ownership to the groves, however, they took on the position of intermediaries. They received trade goods on credit from the dealers, and in turn they furnished these goods to the tappers. The tappers, accepting these advances, were also granted the "right" to tap in the groves of the intermediary, whom they now recognized as their *patrão*, or *patron*, on condition that they deliver all their rubber to him and buy all their supplies from him. This system was highly exploitative of the tappers, since the profit to the patron was achieved through the sale of trade goods, the prices of which were manipulated so that the tapper's balance at year end was often negative. Nevertheless, this system did not involve the enforcement of steady labor. Not only was the tapping season limited to six months a year, the manner and intensity of the tapper's work efforts were his own affair.

This system of labor and capital employment became more intricate as the rubber business expanded in volume, but it did not develop into cultivation. The rubber dealer, known as the *aviador*, or *forwarder*, was himself merely an intermediary who sold to the exporter, who was the direct source of overseas, mostly British, capital. More ample funds became available to the aviadores, but they used the money to launch fleets of steam vessels, not to plant rubber. The riverboats enabled them to range ever further up the headwaters of the Amazon's southern tributaries. There the trees were still untapped, thicker in girth, less scattered, and reputed to yield a finer and more copious rubber. Wandering seringueiros had reached the territory of Acre in the 1870s. The aviadores could supply them, at least during the annual high water of the rivers. This implied an even larger input of capital, however, for the stores of the patrons would have to be stocked for a year at a time. Furthermore, the local population was, in those remote locations, quite inadequate to supply the necessary labor power. The aviadores had to send out recruiters, who brought back men from the coastal towns of the northeast, from São Luis as far south as Salvador.[4]

Capital requirements for gathering were thus not inconsiderable and as the trade developed, capital inputs were certainly increasing faster than rubber output. Estimates for the installation and operation of the rubber posts suggests that each seringueiro represented an investment of about 5,400 milreis (£337) circa 1910, which implies a total investment, for the upriver sector of the rubber trade, of more than 700 million milreis (£43 million). By 1910, in comparison, British capital invested in Malayan plantations amounted to £ 50 million, or about £210 per worker.[5]

The labor requirements of this gathering system were, in the long run, more onerous than those of the plantations. In 1910, extraction of rubber employed some 150,000 laborers in tapping and transport, compared to 240,000 Malayan tappers, but the potential output of the latter, once the plantations were mature, was at least three times that of the Brazilians. The extractive system, furthermore, suffered a higher labor turnover. Elevated mortality was a principal cause of labor shortages, which impelled continued recruitment of northeasterners, perhaps 14,000 a year by the decade 1900 to 1910.[6]

Those who observed the living conditions of the gathering system reported invariably that they were miserable and dangerous. According to one knowledgeable explorer of the region, Colonel George Church, these conditions "imposed greater loss of health, life and material than an active military campaign, and the human suffering is appalling." The exploitation to which the seringueiros were subjected was so extreme that, in the words of Brazil's greatest journalist of the day, Euclides da Cunha, it constituted "the most criminal labor organization that could be imagined by the most revolting egoism." Still, this form of organization was believed to be, even by some of the same observers, the only one in which the seringueiros would enlist.[7]

This labor regime does appear to have been based principally on the workers' expectations of higher incomes rather than upon force, chicanery, or debt slavery. Had the gatherers' compensation been higher in subsistence activities, the Amazon would not have suffered constant shortages of foodstuffs. Although the northeastern migrants were no doubt lured into the rubber trade through fraudulent representations, they also seem to have been able to use their own savings or cash advances from the patrons in order to return home on leave, readily returning again to the rubber wilderness, even to the same groves. The advances that the patron provided the seringueiros may have been regarded by them not as a burden forcibly imposed but as a bonus. The patron had good reason to minimize this cost of doing business; the seringueiro, who was quite capable of heading downstream in the middle of the night, was not objectively under any great obligation to repay. That he usually did repay, as the patron usually repaid the aviador, suggests that some mutual advantage was seen to inhere in the relationship.[8]

A potential solution to the problem of an ineffective and exploitative labor regime may have been emerging within the gathering system itself. By 1910, a more sedentary form of Hevea exploitation was beginning to appear in the older groves, along the more settled routes. There, where rubber yields were lower, the seringueiros devoted part of their efforts to planting and tending their own farm plots, lessening their dependence on the stores of the patron. In these plots they were able to engage to some extent in raising crops for cash, even export crops like cacao, and they planted rubber seeds as well.[9]

The idea of shifting from rubber gathering to rubber planting was available in Brazil well before Henry Wickham made off with his 74,000 seeds, and even before João Martins da Silva Coutinho's report of 1861. The earliest recommendation to plant seems to have come from Gustavo Schuch de Capanema, in a talk delivered in 1856 to the Palestra Scientifica, a learned society in Rio de Janeiro. Capanema had been a member of the Brazilian commission to the Universal Exposition of 1855 and had been impressed by Dutch efforts to cultivate cinchona. (Thus can the two quests be seen intertwining once again!) This recommendation was included in the full commission report, published in 1858 by Antônio Gonçalves Dias, its chairman. Interestingly, the principal advantage he alleged was not economic, but social: to "civilize" the seringueiros through sedentary farming. The 1869 report of Franz Keller-Leuzinger, a German engineer commissioned to survey the Amazon, recommended planting to the Brazilian government. The English version, published in 1874, blamed the "indolence of the mestizos" and the "shortsightedness of the government" for the lack of such an initiative before then. Robert Cross also felt "perplexed and surprised," as he waded miserably through the tidal swamps around Belém, "that the natives have not yet seen the advantages that would be derived from forming plantations."[10]

In 1882, M. A. Pimenta Bueno, later governor of Amazonas, wrote an article in a Rio de Janeiro newspaper that correctly noted that the British effort to procure rubber dated from 1867. He also acknowledged, albeit inaccurately, possibly for the first time in print in Brazil, the transfer of seeds by the English. Although he thought that their experiment would fail, he still recommended planting, and positive actions to improve the living conditions of the seringueiros. A year later André Rebouças, an entrepreneur and statesman who proposed numerous agricultural and conservationist reforms, suggested acclimatizing rubber outside the region of its natural habitat, in the province of Maranhão. No further public attention seems to have been given to the possibility of planting rubber trees in Brazil for nearly twenty years.[11]

In the interval, the Brazilian Empire fell, along with slavery, and a Republic was installed in its place. The Amazon region gained some advantages thereby. The new constitution was less centralized: The provinces, now denominated states, gained the right to levy export duties and to contract debts abroad and were given ownership of public lands within their boundaries. Nevertheless, the federal government, dominated by the powerful southeastern coffee states, transferred the Amazon's import revenues to Rio de Janeiro and intervened in the affairs of the northern states at will. When, in 1901, a dispute with Bolivia led to the transfer of the Acre region to Brazil, the federal government designated it a territory so as to retain its revenues. With the Republic came the beginnings of economic growth and industrial development and the first achievements in science and technology, but these advances were limited to the southeastern region. Coffee profits and revenues, unlike those from rubber, were spent in the region where they were earned. Belém and Manaus had little to show for their wealth save their opera houses and the fanciful mansions of their politicians and merchants.

In 1900, João Barbosa Rodrigues, director of the Botanical Garden of Rio de Janeiro, urged planting in the Amazon as a way of reversing the harm that the gathering trade had wreaked on the region. A native of the Amazon region, and formerly head of the Belém botanical garden, he was appalled at the social costs of rubber extraction. Where once there had been extensive plantations of coffee, tobacco, indigo, and cotton, he saw a wandering, barbarized people, drunken and destitute. Large areas of the valley were already unproductive, the trees ruined by careless tapping. He believed, however, that the British attempt to plant rubber in Ceylon was fated to failure. It was only in the Amazon, he thought, in the tree's native habitat, that it could be cultivated, a measure that he urged, as a material base upon which to rebuild the civilization that he saw in ruins.[12]

The promotional literature of the time ignored the situation of the seringueiros and viewed the stock of wild trees as inexhaustible. It was claimed that if plantations were really called for, the Amazon was the only place where Hevea could be made to grow. A commemorative volume produced in 1904 by the evidently self-interested Amazon Steam Navigation Company claimed that experimental plantings in other parts of the world "have so far not been very encouraging, notwithstanding that the trees have been treated with all the care that experience could suggest," no doubt because only the Amazonian climate was appropriate. Another album, dated 1908, dedicated lavishly by the government of Pará to itself, alleged that the decline already experienced in rubber prices was not the result of competition, but of speculation. Para rubber, it insisted, was invincibly superior to planted rubber. The Amazon state government therefore expressed confidence that, as demand burgeoned, the Amazon would attract more and more foreign capital that would lower the costs of gathering, thereby stimulating the native supply. Hevea could be planted in the Amazon at any future time that Amazonians might be pleased to do so, and the rubber thus produced would always be cheaper and of higher quality than Asian rubber.[13]

Such arguments had a basis in reality, since there had in fact been numerous failures in rubber cultivation. A good deal of money had been lost by planters in Central America, the Caribbean, Ceylon, and Southeast Asia on rubber-bearing species other than *H. brasiliensis*, and it was still not too late to imagine that this experiment would also prove a failure. Those who scoffed at the Ceylon plantations had only to point to the spectacular collapse of coffee on that island a few years before. Scoffers also made light of the yields reported from Ceylon in the early years, without considering that these were the result of uncertain tapping techniques practiced on trees that had not yet reached maturity. Nor had the question of the relative quality of plantation rubber been settled. The first lots of Asian rubber samples had sold for prices lower than the best grades of Brazilian rubber; for this reason it was conjectured that Wickham had brought back the seeds of some species other than *H. brasiliensis*. This price differential was not overcome until 1904, and it was not until 1910 that Asian rubber was accepted for automobile tires.[14]

The complacency of contemporary writings on the future of rubber nevertheless owed less to logic than to self-interest. The funds already invested in gathering were entirely at risk, everyone engaged in the trade was deeply in debt, and still more investments would have to be lured to the Amazon if the trade was to remain competitive. Bravado was therefore characteristic of publications Brazilians published abroad in foreign languages. Among themselves they exchanged less optimistic sentiments.

In 1906, Asian exports of Hevea rubber surged from 145 to 500 tons. This was still a trifle compared to Brazil's export of 29,000 tons, but it was becoming clear to a few members of Brazil's directing elite that gathered rubber might soon be facing intense competition. The Southeast Asian plantations were for the first time mentioned in the Brazilian Chamber of Deputies. There it was proposed that the exporting of rubber be made a government monopoly, a measure that might have lowered slightly the price of Para rubber and that would have pleased the aviadores, who believed their difficulties were caused by speculation and felt exploited by the mostly foreign export houses. But clearly the proposal did not affect the central problem of relative costs of production. Estimates were beginning to appear that showed that Malayan costs were half those of the Amazon.

The Chamber of Deputies appointed a committee led by the very able Miguel Calmon du Pin e Almeida, who had already undertaken a tour of inspection of the eastern plantations to investigate rumors of their potential output. In November he reported to the chamber. He recounted the odyssey of the rubber seeds under the sponsorship of the India Office, a story evidently still unfamiliar to some of his colleagues, and he described the rapid advances made by eastern plantations. He estimated, conservatively as it turned out, that within ten years they would be exporting 25,000 tons. He criticized Barbosa Rodrigues severely for asserting that the Hevea tree would grow only in the Amazon. He attacked the extreme exploitiveness of the patron system and recommended that it be substituted by rational cultivation. His committee submitted a bill that would have granted free land and a fifty-year export tax exemption to planters of rubber and would have funded an agricultural experiment station. These measures and other similar ones were debated desultorily in the Congress for the next six years.[15]

Calmon's report was immediately influential beyond the walls of the Chamber of Deputies. A newspaper campaign in Rio de Janeiro took as its motto, "Against the *mal de Ceylon*, large-scale planting." Calmon was quoted by Guilherme Catramby, in a publication issued the following year under the aegis of the governor of the state of Amazonas. Catramby reviewed the objections to planting rubber: (1) The wild rubber groves were inexhaustible indeed, but each ton cost five lives; (2) rising demand might exercise an upward pressure on the price of rubber, but Brazilian rubber would become more costly as the seringueiros were obliged to range further and further up the rivers while oriental rubber costs could easily be further reduced. He provided instructions for planting and tapping, derived from Ceylon manuals, and he made estimates of local costs and yields. He tempted potential planters with the reminder that planted groves of trees would be subject to extremely rapid increases in value as they approached maturity, making them an excellent speculation. Catramby soon afterward organized a company of his own to plant rubber in the state of Rio de Janeiro.[16]

The same lines of argument were taken up by Jacques Huber, director of the Goeldi Museum in Belém. He had planted a few rubber trees in the Belém botanical gardens some ten years before, when, he remarked, one risked being laughed at for such a waste of time. He had begun to tap them experimentally, attempting to imitate the employment of the Malayan knife. His results were poor, but he supposed the soil his trees were planted in was too sandy. He recommended planting and pointed out the great advantages Brazil enjoyed in limitless sources of seeds and cheap land, and noted the significance of the discovery of Asian planters that the tree could be tapped in six years, not in fifteen or thirty, as had been imagined. He thought the tree could be interplanted with other crops, as was being done with coffee in southern Brazil.[17]

In fact there already were numerous planted Hevea rubber trees in the Amazon. Wickham stated in his report to the India Office that he had "occasionally known them planted," in their native habitat. The Brazilian commission to the Philadelphia Exposition of 1876 also claimed that "regular cultivation" was "already undertaken." The earliest planting of which there is printed notice was that carried out by the heirs of Joaquim Antonio da Silva, a Portuguese merchant enriched in Belém but retired and deceased in Portugal. His will had required them to plant a rubber grove. This apparently was carried out in 1865. Some 20,000 trees were set along the Guamá River, just south of Belém. Unfortunately they were on land so low that all but a thousand were carried off by river floods. A. C. Tavares Bastos's treatise on Amazon trade, written in 1866, referred to this planting. A grove of nearly 200,000 that was still standing in the municipality of Maués in the early 1920s was said also to have been planted in 1865. In 1884, the Rikers, one of the Confederate families who had befriended Wickham, planted 20,000 trees on their lands at Santarém, and this may not have been their first attempt. They were later to sell this grove to an English company. There were quite a few other commercial-sized plantations laid out before the crisis struck. A report of 1899 mentions groves of Hevea in seven municipalities in Pará state. Two small groves near Manaus, planted in 1900 and 1904, and two others near Óbidos, planted in 1908, were often visited by travelers. And a survey of the state of Amazonas in 1913 found planted groves in seven municipalities besides the capital.[18]

There were many more thousands of rubber trees scattered in small clusters at hundreds of settled places along the rivers. The trees were valued by Amazon dwellers not only for their latex but also because their seeds were edible. Indeed this quality has been suggested as the original reason that Hevea came to be of interest to humans, thus the practice of planting its seeds may well be prehistoric. Seringueiros sometimes planted seeds along their trails or at their campsites, and planted trees were often found in groves of declining yield, where seringueiros were gradually shifting to agriculture. There they sometimes interplanted Hevea and cacao in their manioc plots. Unfortunately, these trees and those planted experimentally in groves invariably proved to be low-yielding.[19]

Late in 1909, the state of Pará, under the leadership of a new governor, passed a law that provided considerable incentive to potential planters. The government offered a reduction of 50 percent in export taxes, reduced rail charges, guarantees of 5 percent profit on half the issued capital, and ninety-nine-year rent-free leases on state-owned land, up to 20,000 hectares. In return the state required the planting of 20,000 trees a year. Earlier state laws in 1886 and 1896 that had granted prizes to cultivators of various crops, including rubber, seem to have been fraudulently administered and were, in fact, a means of rewarding political loyalty. The law of 1909 stimulated requests for grants to assist the planting of six million trees, but it is doubtful that more than 340,000 were planted under its provisions before the collapse of state revenues two years later.[20]

A conference held in Manaus early in 1910 brought together some seventy leaders in the rubber trade who recognized the "urgent and unpostponable necessity" to plant rubber. Measures were proposed to the federal government similar to the Pará state law. The sponsors also sent Jacques Huber to trace the same path that Miguel Calmon had taken in 1906. He left for Ceylon and Malaya, hoping to find that Wickham's seeds had been some sort of hybrid or inferior variety of Hevea. Indeed at a rubber conference he attended in London on his way east he expressed that doubt in the presence of Wickham, who happened to be in attendance. In Ceylon and Malaya, Huber was disappointed to find quite flourishing specimens of *H. brasiliensis*, and he returned late in 1911 with alarming estimates of rubber investments.[21]

His warnings were hardly necessary. From 1911 onward, the price of rubber plummeted as more and more of the plantation-grown product came on the market. Brazilian rubber had risen on a speculative wave to fifteen milreis a kilogram in April 1910; by June 1911 it had fallen to six milreis. In the Amazon, rubber traders urgently demanded that the federal government inject funds into the gathering business. They sought help from the Bank of Brazil to support the price of rubber, and a federal guarantee for funding to float a regional bank. When neither of these schemes was realized, they persuaded Congress to approve a vast and comprehensive plan to improve the competitiveness of rubber gathering, through investments in transport, public health, labor recruitment, and rubber processing. The plan, called the Economic Defense of Rubber, included prizes for persons attempting "rational cultivation" and funding for agricultural experiment stations, but overwhelmingly the benefits were designed to save the gathering sector. The headquarters of the defense scheme was located in Rio de Janeiro, absurdly remote from the scene of the problem, and a self-serving staff managed to spend several millions of milreis in needless activities in the first year of operations. Congress thereupon repented of its generosity and in effect abolished the scheme by omitting it from the budget of 1913.[22]

The stunning indifference of the federal government to the fate of the Amazon economy seems almost suicidal, considering that the region, with only one-twenty-fifth of the country's population, had provided one-sixth of federal revenues. Over the period 1890 to 1912, the federal government had collected, in the states of Amazonas and Pará, 656 million milreis more than it had spent. This was in addition to the revenues of the territory of Acre, which accrued entirely to the federal government. On the other hand, outlays that the federal government had put into the Amazon, such as the extremely expensive Madeira-Mamoré railway (built as a treaty obligation to provide Bolivia an outlet to the ocean via the Amazon), were not particularly effective in promoting regional growth. In spite of its own shortcomings, Congress was piqued at the improvidence the northern states had displayed in handling their own revenues. They habitually overspent income, borrowing haphazardly on expectations of constantly rising income, yet they invariably left their bills unpaid. They had set export taxes, constitutionally reserved to the states, at rates approximating a stultifying 20 percent, and had wasted most of these revenues, amounting to 241 million milreis between 1890 and 1912, on the beautification of the state capitals and on payoffs to local politicians.[23]

Once the crisis was upon the region, private credit collapsed quickly along with that of the government. The aviadores and patrons were all heavily in debt, with little collateral to satisfy the exporter-creditors. Losses in 1913 were said to have amounted to more than £4 million. The regional elite struggled to persuade foreign investors to renew their inputs into rubber gathering. Foreign funds were sought for the proposed regional bank, for additional local purchasing offices of rubber manufacturers, and for more takeovers of wild rubber groves by so-called plantation companies. They continued to extol their "inexhaustible natural supplies," their "experience of centuries" in the trade, and the "unrivaled quality" of fine hard Para rubber. The state governments were called upon to grant "great territorial expanses" to foreign companies.[24]

Indeed, even though European and U.S. investors were presumably better informed about the relative viability of Southeast Asian plantations versus the rubber gathering trade, they seem to have greatly increased their stake in the Amazon during the decade 1903 to 1913, at least as far as can be measured by the Brazilian government's authorizations of foreign corporate investments; these rose ten times, to £6 million, two-thirds of it British. The Pará law of 1909 and the speculative price rise of 1910 encouraged a number of North American and European firms to buy up wild rubber groves and the federal law of 1912 attracted still more companies to register under the terms of its concessions to colonizing companies. The foreign companies that attempted to manage wild groves proved unprofitable, as did the only one that appears to have made an effort at planting, the Moju plantation of a subsidiary of the United States Rubber Company. These investments were abandoned when the price of rubber crashed.[25]

In spite of the absolute lack of new capital after 1913, small plantations of Hevea continued to be set out. Several of them survived and were noted by le Cointe in 1922 and by the joint Brazilian-American delegation in 1923. They included Seringal Mirim, near Manaus, planted in 1915, Maicá, a grove the Rikers planted after selling out their earlier one to British investors, and another near Santarém at Altar do Chão, all being tapped in 1922 and 1923. In 1912, J. Virgolino de Alencar, a patron engaged in gathering on the upper Yaco river in the Acre territory, planted 175,000 trees on 700 hectares. Alencar had more than nine years' experience in the trade and his report demonstrates considerable familiarity with the problems and prospects of planting. Among other remarkable observations, he informed the National Agricultural Society in Rio de Janeiro that he selected his seeds: He did not tap trees whose productivity he found to be very high, but saved them for reproduction since he had observed that seeds from untapped trees were more likely to germinate and showed greater vigor. He strongly recommended that others in the trade follow his example.[26]

In Bahia, Hevea was planted under the sponsorship of the state government. Miguel Calmon, the same who had presented the prescient congressional committee report of 1906, hired, when he became Bahia's secretary of agriculture, Leo Zehntner to direct the state agricultural school at São Bento das Lages. Calmon had met Zehntner in the Netherlands East Indies where he was director of an agricultural school. It was Calmon's idea that Bahia enjoyed natural conditions propitious to Hevea, and he was bent on repeating the commercial success of cacao, which had also been transferred to and domesticated in his state. Zehntner arrived in Bahia from the east with numerous seedlings, including 200 of Hevea, and these were successfully planted. In 1909 or 1910, Wilhelm Behrmann, an agent in Bahia for a German shipping line, imported 150,000 seedlings from Ceylon. Only 4,100 of these survived. They were planted in two groves in the municipalities of Una and Canavieira. There were also Hevea trees in Rio de Janeiro state, planted in the municipality of São Francisco de Paula in the 1890s. In Gavião Peixoto, in the state of São Paulo, a grove of Hevea was planted in 1915 with seeds sent from Mato Grosso by General Cândido Rondon.[27]

It is evident that until 1911 there was sufficient labor and capital to carry on rubber planting. Since these were scarce resources and planting would have been a more economical use of them, it appears paradoxical that the productive system did not shift massively toward cultivation. Even after the crash of 1911, however, when capital inputs had evaporated and northeastern laborers were leaving by the thousands, there were some local landowners who went on planting rubber. It clearly is not the case that Brazilians did not or would not plant Hevea. By the early 1920s, there were as many as two million planted rubber trees in Brazil. By that date, there were many persons acquainted with Southeast Asian plantation practices, judging from copies of imported contemporary manuals that are to be found in Brazilian libraries. Even more interesting, some seem to have been evolving their own techniques, allowing forest to regrow, so as to imitate wild conditions. But the planted trees rarely reached maturity, were rarely tended, and even more rarely were they tapped. There have been various explanations to account for this curious lapse, all the more curious in a country that was the very prototype of the tropical plantation regime.

It has been suggested that the Amazonian bourgeoisie was unable to resume direction of an agricultural regime because its economic role had become constricted. The foreign-owned exporting houses limited their ability to accumulate capital, while the patron-seringueiro labor regime made it impossible for them to take control of the productive process. Foreign investors were unable to intrude into this process because they were used to managing wage laborers and were unable to fathom the seringueiros' eccentricities. The intermediary role to which the local bourgeoisie was relegated, furthermore, accustomed them to speculative pursuits; the lure of striking it rich had become more attractive to them than the prospect of moderate profits over the long run. Their inclination, upon the fall of rubber prices, was not to revert to agriculture but to cast about for some other extractive trade to monopolize.[28]

This analysis propounds the model of a bourgeoisie that Amazonian novelist Marcio de Souza has called "stupid and incompetent," remaining in power not through control of the means of production, which means barely existed, but through control of the state, through whose instrumentality all vexing attempts at entrepreneurship could be taxed or harried out of existence. This characterization of the bourgeoisie has as its obverse one of a peasant mass as symmetrically self-indulgent and undynamic. Although the gathering system imposed upon them death rates and exploitation so severe as to render their reproduction impossible, they are alleged to have preferred that itinerant existence to planting, out of a befuddled pride and an identical preference for get-rich-quick schemes over steady remuneration.[29]

This characterization of the Amazonian bourgeoisie offers a certain surface validity, since the situation in which they found themselves seems to have lacked the absolute rigidity attributed to it; it is easy to imagine them taking upon themselves the measures needed to transform it. Like their counterparts in Cuba, they could have imported labor to perform agricultural work, if their compatriots did not suit their needs. The several thousand Peruvians, Venezuelans, Barbadians, and Trinidadians already attracted to the Amazon showed that they would not have had to go far afield. If the bourgeoisie found the capital to effect this purpose in short supply, it seems to have been due more to their inefficient use of it than to their inability to skim enough profit from the trade. Few plantation elites, if any, controlled the export business; therefore the Amazonian elite was no worse off in that regard. The ghastly state of the seringueiros attests to their ability to extract as much from their labor force as if they were themselves engaged in planting. Under similar conditions, the coffee-planting bourgeoisie of São Paulo imported nearly two million immigrants at modest expense, and the cacao-growing bourgeoisie of Bahia hired northeasterners, apparently the very same migrants who allegedly could not be persuaded to accept a wage labor regime in the Amazon.

On the other hand, it may be incorrect to suppose that the Amazon bourgeoisie was unusually incompetent. It should be noticed that their capital assets, at the moment the crisis struck, were quite inapplicable to any sort of agricultural pursuit. They consisted of a fleet of steamboats and a mountain of accounts receivable from an army of discouraged, fever-ridden tappers. It should also be noticed that despite the shortage of capital, some agricultural activity was undertaken. By the 1920s, the Amazon was again producing cotton, cacao, tobacco, and corn for the internal market. Of course the region had no monopoly on these products; therefore profits were modest and the Italian *prime donne* did not return to its opera houses. Even so, by the late 1930s, members of the Amazon bourgeoisie engaged in the gathering trade had established two of the first rubber tire factories in Brazil, an achievement that is difficult to reconcile with the presumption of incompetence.

Social structures evidently do contain rigidities that hinder change, and evidently social classes often act out of false perceptions and contrary to their own best interests. The nature of the world economy has been such as to replace such groups. One need only listen to James Collins's indignation at a temporary interruption in the supply of Brazilian Massaranduba rubber in 1869: "Such has been, and will be, the case, where the native populations have to be depended on. No amount of persuasion will induce many of them into making an effort beyond their own inclinations." In Africa, he went on, equating the Brazilian government with tribal chiefdoms, "the trading stations are, in most cases at least, dependent on the caprices of the natives."[30]

In Malaya, no sympathy was shown the caprices of the natives. When Hevea rubber first arrived, the local society, both upper class and lower, for the most part refused to interest itself in planting. Some of the local tribespeople had engaged in gathering gutta-percha, but tapping trees for wages did not appeal to them. No matter, the British swamped the countryside with tens and then hundreds of thousands of Tamil laborers from southern India. Many of the plantation owners, furthermore, were immigrant Chinese who had arisen from among those brought in to work the tin mines. The Malayans were relegated to civil service positions and consoled with the thought that the immigrants would have to learn their language if they were to obtain any sort of government services. This bitter experience was repeated in nearly every plantation society, because it was nearly always the case that plantations demanded the import of labor and entrepreneurship in the absence of tractable and opportunistic native populations.[31]

Clearly the British had an easier job of demolishing and reconstructing a comfortable indigenous society where they were able to grasp political power. But Brazil was in essential ways similar to Malaya. Its sovereignty was a ductile and malleable quality, and investment in itself was an effective inducement to collaboration. Certainly it could be used to fortify potential entrepreneurs among the local elite and to hem in the intransigent. One of the ways in which a foreign presence could be inserted was outlined by vice-consul Temple, reporting from Manaus in 1900. Acknowledging that the local working class was "independent, not to say unruly," he suggested that as a first step "that class of men which has done so much in opening up other tropical countries, men of resource and adaptability who prefer a rough life" might be encouraged to set up in business there. Once these had "opened the way," he thought, "there will be more opportunity for companies to work with success." Such men were already present in the region. Henri Coudreau calculated that some 600 Frenchmen, plus Moroccan Jews, Spaniards, and Portuguese were operating on the rivers as merchants, steamboat owners, and cacao planters, speaking Indian languages as well as Portuguese. These men were indeed devising paths along which the patron regime might have been transformed into one adapted to plantation management. In one way or another an empire that extracted labor out of several hundred wildly disparate native societies could surely have had its way with one more.[32]

Another line of analysis that might be taken in order to explain the failure of experimental plantings to grow into true cultivation is that of relative costs. This is impossible to undertake adequately, since many factors would have undergone changes had the plantations come into successful production. Certainly Brazil had an advantage in its proximity to industrial consumers. Land was very cheap; in fact public land was granted free under the 1909 law to those who announced an intention to plant rubber on it. Although export taxes were twenty times higher than in Malaya, the state governments were evidently inclined to arrange total exemptions for planted rubber. The cost of labor was apparently higher in Brazil, and productivity was lower. Yet cheaper transport, better health conditions, and more abundant foodstuffs would have brought Amazonian labor costs close to Malayan levels. When the wild rubber boom collapsed, wage levels fell to those of the coffee-growing region of southeastern Brazil, a level evidently quite competitive with Southeast Asian coffee estates. Most important, had the yields of Brazilian plantation rubber proved superior, as some expected, Amazonian labor productivity would certainly have been brought lower than that of Southeast Asia.[33]

Yields, however, were the most problematic aspect of trees planted in the Amazon, and in the short run the main reason for the lack of interest in carrying on with the plantations that had been undertaken in so many places. Despite expectations of high returns, wherever measurements were taken they showed a meager flow of latex. It was reported that many of the trees had been planted in soils that were too sandy, or were planted much closer together than was the practice in Southeast Asia. It is likely that to some degree, poor initial yields were the result of a lack of diligence in cultivating the trees to maturity and to a failure to apply Eastern methods of tapping. This is not surprising since there were no government agricultural agents in the Amazon, and the only assistance available was the occasional manual imported from London or Paris.[34]

Nevertheless, the results were discouraging. For thirty years Brazilians had been reassuring each other that the Amazon was the *pátria* of rubber, that it would undoubtedly yield better there than anywhere else. Deputy Luciano Pereira had disputed this supposition, it is true, and raised a contrary proposition with more significance than he realized: "Let my worthy colleague not put forward the argument that here in Brazil the *seringueira* should produce better than abroad, since it is in its country of origin, because I will remind him that very often certain products do better transplanted than in their own habitat. I need only mention to him the case of coffee, which in the purple soil of São Paulo found its ideal, yielding there better than in Arabia, where it originated."[35]

Indeed, there in the Amazon, the native habitat of *Hevea brasiliensis*, some sort of problem, not yet identified, was discouraging the first rubber planters and causing their potential imitators to turn to other crops. That very problem was being identified in the nearby Dutch colony of Surinam.

52

4

The reason why, 1904–1923

Although intimations of an ecological limitation upon the practical commercial planting of Hevea were appearing in Brazil, it was Brazil's colonial neighbors who first experienced the problem in epidemic form, diagnosed it, and drew the inevitable conclusions. Twelve of the seedlings grown from the Wickham selection had been sent by Kew to the botanical garden at Trinidad. Only two of these survived, and they had been rather indifferently regarded by the garden's directors, who preferred Castilla rubber and tried as well to cultivate the rubber-bearing African *Funtumia* vines. Nevertheless, by the late 1890s, reports from Malaya of successful tapping encouraged a few local planters to set out Hevea on a small scale. They bought the botanical garden's small crop of Hevea seeds, which they planted for the most part to shade cacao. There was some further planting a few years later, the result of what a Trinidadian government report described as "the fit of enthusiasm which encircled the tropics about 1905–6." In 1909, J. B. Carruthers, a botanist with experience in Asia, became assistant director of the Trinidad garden. He pointed out that Hevea yielded much more copiously than Castilla, and persuaded the garden to order some two million seeds from Ceylon. The local planters were already ordering their seed directly, from Brazil as well as Ceylon, enduring in these shipments very low rates of germination.[1]

Meanwhile, botanists employed by the government of British Guiana, most notably G. S. Jenman, occupied themselves with exploration for new rubber-bearing plants. These expeditions were inspired, apparently, by the hope that some local species of *Hevea* would prove superior to *H. brasiliensis*. *Sapium*, another genus of latex-bearing plants, seemed promising to Jenman and his associates, who were no doubt also influenced by the hope of repeating the commercial success of the nonelastic but durable Balata, known in Brazil as Massaranduba. In 1895, the first Hevea seeds were introduced by Sir Everard im Thurn, apparently from Ceylon by way of Kew, to be planted in a settlement scheme he was promoting. The department of agriculture of British Guiana, anxious to reduce the colony's excessive dependence on income from sugar exports, imported more seeds between 1896 and 1899 from Trinidad.

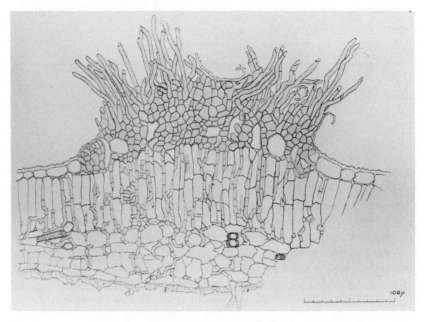

Gerold Stahel's rendering of the conidial form of *Microcyclus ulei*, 1917. (Courtesy Library of the New York Botanical Garden)

A few planters received seeds from abroad as well, so that by 1900, Hevea was to be found at nine different locations. From 1906 onward, shipments were received from Singapore that germinated quite successfully. By 1911, more than 170,000 seedlings had been sold to planters, and the earliest trees planted by the agriculture department were beginning to provide seeds.[2]

Some of the seeds imported by the planters of British Guiana were from Surinam. That colony had introduced Hevea by way of a London merchant in 1897, and nine trees had resulted. Another 480 had been grown from seeds brought directly from Brazil in 1901. Further importations of seeds from Ceylon were carried out privately in 1905 and 1907. By 1910, several estate owners who were casting about for a substitute for cacao, then being ravaged by a fungus endemic in the Amazon, had interplanted Hevea in banana groves.[3]

In both colonies Hevea was set out initially along the coast, but it was discovered that it grew slowly there and was susceptible to wind damage. Beginning in 1902, Hevea was planted at various points in the interior of British Guina, in order to test for suitable soils. In 1907, an experimental station was organized in that colony especially to acclimatize rubber. Along the Essequibo river, plantings were carried out in places where native species of Hevea were found. It was decided that the trees would thrive on well-drained soils as well as on river margins. The department of agriculture congratulated itself that Guiana enjoyed a climate so similar to the Amazon basin, including annual rainfall of 2,100 to 3,700 millimeters.[4]

By 1911, there were almost 400 hectares of Hevea in British Guiana; five years later, the planted area had expanded to almost 2,000 hectares, of which the oldest surviving trees dated from 1903. In Surinam by 1916, there were 1,000 hectares in Hevea. In Trinidad, where experiments with rubber were restrained by greater success in planting cacao, sugar, and coconuts, there were probably fewer than 500 hectares in Hevea by 1917, including 69 hectares at the well-managed Non Pareil estate. Experimental tapping had been carried out at the Trinidad botanical garden in 1898. It is not clear when the first commercial shipments of Hevea rubber occurred, since export lists did not at first discriminate one kind of rubber from another, but it may be that some was sent from Trinidad beginning in 1907, and from British Guiana in 1909. The Non Pareil estate began tapping in 1914, achieving 330 kilograms per hectare. By 1916, combined exports of Hevea rubber from British Guiana, Trinidad, and Surinam amounted to a little over 20 tons, more than half of it from Surinam.[5]

Meanwhile, botanists at several experimental stations were beginning to encounter worrisome phenomena. In 1907, Jacques Huber mentioned that he had observed several species of leaf-attacking fungi on the Hevea rubber trees at the Belém botanical garden. He did not think them much of a problem for potential rubber planters, however. In Paramaribo, where some 30,000 seeds were laid out early in 1908, some sort of leaf fungus spread like wildfire among the seedlings, defoliating nearly all of them. They quickly produced new foliage, but the explosive virulence of the disease caused concern. Deliberate attempts to infect other plants cultivated in the nursery were unsuccessful, so that it was supposed that this fungus was a parasite limited to Hevea. A. E. van Hall de Jonge, who reported this phenomenon, supposed that older trees were not susceptible since nearby mature trees were unharmed, and she speculated that some special circumstances might have been responsible for the attack.[6]

The identity of this disease was not determined, but in 1911 another fungus was found in nurseries and on several upriver plantations, even on plantations in virgin forest. Jan Kuyper bestowed a name on this fungus, *Fusicladium macrosporum*. Kuyper thought the fungus capable of damage only to nursery seedlings, but he also mentioned that it had been found to be lethal to another species of Hevea, *H. guianensis*, growing in the wild. Two years later, in British Guiana, C. K. Bancroft found a fungus that produced small round holes on the leaves of cultivated Hevea. He reported that in the wild it attacked *H. benthamiana*, as well as *H. guianensis*. He sent specimens to Kew, where it was named *Passalora heveae* by G. Massee. Still another novel fungus was collected in Belém, on trees growing in the experimental station, by the French mycologist Victor Cayla. This he sent to Paris, where E. Griffon and A. Maublanc determined that Cayla had encountered the same species as that collected in the upper reaches of the Amazon thirteen years before by Ernst Ule. Its description had been published in 1904 by Paul Hennings, who had named it *Dothidella ulei*.[7]

Cayla, upon comparing this information with Kuyper's article, concluded that *F. macrosporum* was a form of *D. ulei*. The next year, Thomas Petch, writing from Ceylon, suggested that Bancroft's material was also *D. ulei*. François Vincens, who had been working at the Goeldi Museum in Belém, reached the same conclusion independently and noted that *D. ulei* attacked several species of *Hevea*. Evidently the fungus occurred over the entire range of the genus. If it was a parasite specializing in *Hevea*, capable of attacking both young and mature trees, Petch realized, then phytopathologists might not easily be rid of it. Nevertheless, none of the researchers who had seen it live thought the fungus particularly dangerous. Cayla reported that the trees damaged at Belém were only a few hundreds among thousands, and that they probably suffered low resistance from being planted in sandy soil, in a depression in which water collected. Nevertheless, Jacques Huber, when he visited Ceylon in 1911, had told Petch that the fungus did indeed cause serious damage, even defoliating the trees. These remarks were in striking contrast with those he printed in his 1907 handbook for prospective planters.[8]

Hennings and Griffon and Maublanc described the fungus as one that produced a mold, or *mycelium* – a dense network of filamented microscopic tubes, called *hyphae*, spreading outward from each infecting spore. The hyphae penetrate the epidermis of the leaf and multiply between the cell spaces in the leaf interior. They develop quickly in newly sprouted leaflets, blackening and tearing them and causing them to fall. On somewhat older leaves the mycelia form lesions that are greyish green to olive in color, a centimeter or two in diameter, on the underside of the shiny pale green leaf, and the bunched tips of the hyphae, erect and somewhat curled, feel velvety to the touch. On the upper side of the leaf the lesion appears as a colorless patch at first, then becomes olive grey or blackish. Often these patches rot away, giving the leaf the appearance of having been blasted with shot.

Hennings had classified Ule's material as two distinct species, but Kuyper showed that they were merely different forms of the same fungus. Single- or two-celled asexual spores, called *conidia*, are produced at the external tips of the hyphae. These conidial spores are by far the most common infecting agent; borne by air currents, they spread the disease from leaf to leaf and from tree to tree. On leaves that survive the initial attack, other conidial spores are produced in tiny sacs, called *pycnidia*. These, much less numerous than conidia, appear as tiny spherical black spots on the upper side of the leaf, sometimes in a ring around the shot holes left from the hyphal invasion. Pycnidia apparently release their conidia, or *pycnospores*, at lower nighttime temperatures, thus extending the duration of conidial dispersal. Griffon and Maublanc discovered, among Cayla's material, the final, sexual stage of the fungus. This is produced in cavities, called *ascostromata*, that develop in the mycelium, resulting in clusters of *ascospores*, each of them enclosed in a resistant shell, and each containing eight double-celled haploid spores called *asci*. This sexual stage, which facilitates genetic recombination, also preserves fungal materials during periods unfavorable for reproduction and dispersal.[9]

In 1915, Gerold Stahel took up investigation of the fungus at the agricultural station in Paramaribo. He sought to designate it *Melanopsammopsis ulei*, convinced as he was that both Henning and Kuyper had erred in their classification. Nevertheless, the fungus continued to be known as *Dothidella ulei* until 1962, when it was placed by Muller and von Arx in the genus *Microcyclus*, a classification that gained general acceptance. Stahel was more influential in his choice of a name for the disease caused by the fungus; he called it South American Leaf Disease (or Blight), arguing that it was potentially the most serious leaf disease encountered in the native habitat of Hevea. By this name it has indeed become known in the several languages of the region.[10]

Stahel remarked drily in his report that he had plenty of material upon which to base his observations: The blight, which had seemed at first not to be a matter of great concern, had spread all over Surinam. Since 1915, he reported, whole groves had been destroyed, and he provided the example of a two-year-old plantation of 20,000 trees that had been reduced to 3,000. C. K. Bancroft, who visited Surinam the following year, was told that the fungus was present in every estate, affecting trees of all ages. Tapping had been suspended, because latex flow had declined. So widespread and virulent was the disease that he thought it would be the end of Hevea cultivation if a solution could not be found. By 1916, the fungus was also epidemic in British Guiana; only the experimental station of the department of agriculture was free of it. It had been reported even in the northwesternmost district of the colony, eighty kilometers distant from the nearest wild specimens of Hevea.

In the same year, J. B. Rorer found the blight occurring on several plantations in Trinidad. He presumed that it had been present on the island for several years. In 1917, he reported the disease still more widespread. The appearance of blight in Trinidad was remarkable, since no species of *Hevea* was native there. Either the inoculum was capable of reaching the colony on its own, or it had been spread by human agency and had reproduced entirely upon the small available pool of cultivated trees.[11]

The disease was seen to require constant high humidity. In British Guiana and Surinam, nevertheless, it spread faster during the season of lower rainfall. This circumstance, Stahel hypothesized, was the result of the drying up of the conidia during sunny intervals between rain showers and of the washing of the inoculum from the leaves by the rain. During the dry season, on the other hand, the fungal spores, which needed ten hours to penetrate the leaf cuticle, were able to develop overnight on normally dew-laden foliage. *Hevea brasiliensis* is a tree that *winters*, losing its leaves for a period of four to six weeks during the season of lower rainfall. Its refoliation, in the case of some populations, is repeated later in the year, without passing through a second loss of foliage. The deciduous character of Hevea had been emphasized by those who favored planting the tree in Southeast Asia. They supposed that it would protect the tree against endemic leaf fungi, under the assumption that the fungal inoculum would not be able to survive the wintering period. Thomas Petch, however, upon hearing of the reports from the Guianas, pointed out that some leaf-attacking fungi were specially adapted to deciduous behavior, having developed means of surviving the prolonged absence of host leaf tissue.[12]

Jacques Huber realized that Hevea did not occur in dense stands, because in such a situation the fungal inoculum would build up and overcome the tree's limited resistance. The scattered distribution of Hevea therefore represented the densest mass possible, under natural conditions, of the host in the presence of its highly specialized parasite. Once the tree was deliberately planted in large numbers, however, the fungus was given the opportunity to reproduce enormously and overwhelm resistance. The inherent danger of cultivation was enhanced by typical plantation practice. The trees on a given plantation were usually of varying provenance and genotype; therefore, they passed through the phase of leaf flush at varying times. Thus the fungus was presented the opportunity of attacking the highly vulnerable young leaves for a period, not of a few days, but of several weeks. Hevea is capable of replacing an unsuccessful leaf flush, but under plantation conditions, successive flushes on the same tree might be killed until the branches began to die back, ultimately resulting in the death of the tree. Even when the tree was not killed, however, the effect of leaf blight was depressive. Tree growth was slowed and latex yields were lowered.[13]

Confronted with a highly virulent and infectious leaf fungus, the plant specialists at Paramaribo and Onderneeming were unable to suggest suitable countermeasures to their planter clients. As Cayla lamented, leaf diseases, "when they attack trees, are the only ones against which men are disarmed." Nursery seedlings could be protected with sprayings of fungicide, and the customary "Bordeaux mixture" of copper sulfate and lime water was found to be effective. But mature Hevea grow to 25 or 30 meters in height. There were no spraying apparatuses available that could protect the leaf flushes in the canopies of such trees. Stahel recommended sending workers up in the branches to cut off and remove affected branches, a procedure Petch condemned. He estimated that it would take a worker an entire day to prune a single tree, and that it would have to be done simultaneously on every plantation in a given area to have any chance of success. In any case, the danger would remain of reinfection from Hevea in the wild. Bancroft mused on the effect of cutting down all the native specimens in a given area, though he was aware of the impracticality of such a project.[14]

South American Leaf Blight quickly damped enthusiasm for Hevea cultivation. In British Guiana, demand for seedlings evaporated. Repeated destruction of foliage lessened latex yields of the surviving trees, and as yields declined planters lost interest in tapping. In Surinam, Hevea rubber output declined from 10,800 kilograms in 1916 to 1,718 kilograms in 1918. Nevertheless, the continued slump in the price of rubber after 1918 was partially responsible for the near elimination of rubber from the export lists of the Guianas by 1923. The formation of a British rubber cartel the following year led to some renewal of tapping in groves that had nearly been abandoned. In Trinidad, output may have reached 74,272 kilograms in 1927, a yield of 248 kilograms per hectare, but then quickly fell away as the cartel collapsed. Many of the trees not removed before 1923 were then cut down. Where rubber had been interplanted with coffee or cacao, it was eradicated, and the coffee and cacao were left standing. In British Guiana, the total area planted in rubber declined from 2,065 to 670 hectares between 1917 and 1924 and stood at 318 hectares by 1931.[15]

During the early years of the acclimatization of Hevea in Ceylon, Malaya, and Sumatra, it was often argued that the tree would never be successful because it was an exotic. For this reason the experimental programs of more than one botanical station were directed toward proving the potentialities of plants native to Southeast Asia, such as *Ficus elastica* and various species of gutta-percha. This was precisely the same point of view, of course, as that of Brazilians who complacently assumed that Hevea would grow better in the Amazon than anywhere else, no matter what degree of artful care was bestowed upon it. As the French botanist Paul le Cointe asserted in 1922, long after such a remark could be considered realistic, "In the Amazon the Hevea is *chez lui*, thus equipped to resist enemies in the environment in which it has always won. No serious malady has ever been observed in the wild groves, even those most anciently exploited, such as those of the delta or the lower Madeira."[16]

C. K. Bancroft was much closer to the mark in pointing out that "the risk of disease affecting a cultivation in the tropics is increased if the species is a native of the country in which it is being cultivated." This was so, he thought, because, among other reasons, the inoculum was always present. A similar thought occurred a few years later to William A. Orton of the United States Department of Agriculture, in addressing the problem of establishing rubber plantations in the Amazon: "It is interesting to note that the principal tropical crops entering international commerce have been introduced from other parts of the world into the region where they are now grown." It was still not entirely clear to the principal researchers engaged in plant breeding and disease control, but success in the cultivation of tropical crops on a commercial scale usually depended on transfer out of their native habitat. Exotic plant species were more viable, because they had been removed from the pests and parasites that had coevolved with them. Crop plants of the tropics, in contrast to those of temperate regions, were especially favored by transfer because their native habitats contained predators and parasites that were more specialized and a climate that facilitated their rapid reproduction and adaptation. Much later the concept of *escape* was to be applied to this phenomenon and it was to be adopted as a conscious strategy.[17]

In the case of Hevea, it was even more advantageous that it escape from its native habitat, because it was a tree of the forest climax. *Climax* is a concept referring to the most highly evolved and complex phase of ecosystem development. Typically, cultivated plants are not climax but pioneer species, at home in disturbed environments. Specializing in rapid invasion of areas fortuitously available, such as river floodplains or forest windfall clearings, pioneer species multiply and grow rapidly, quickly produce abundant seeds, and are usually to be found in large numbers in any location. Although they require more sunlight and richer soils, they are relatively easy to cultivate, because they usually resist extremes of temperature and water supply and have developed defenses against pests and parasites that might otherwise overcome them through their rapid rates of reproduction. The concepts of *climax* and *pioneer*, it should be noted, somewhat overlap those of *temperate* and *tropical*, since temperate species tend toward pioneerism: The temperate zone offers a harsher climate, so that even its climax species present adaptations typical of pioneer habitats. Thus temperate zone agriculture is, from this point of view, more stable than that of the tropics.

Another unconscious stratagem, commonly employed by the original primitive farmers in their selection of crop plants, was hybridization. Cultivars such as wheat and maize are the result of genetic transformations that not only provided a more abundant harvest for their domesticators, but also rendered them less recognizable to the pests and predators that had evolved with their progenitors.

The Hevea rubber tree, in comparison with hybridized, temperate zone pioneer cultivars, was a very risky venture. Like other species of the climax, it is slow growing, requiring seven years to put on sufficient girth to withstand tapping. A lethal attack on such a plant by a virulent parasite cannot be stoically written off as one might a crop of rice that can be brought in within three months. And since the tree's principal defense against such parasites is to hide, isolated in the forest, it cannot be said to collaborate with the efforts of plant breeders.

This theoretical discussion of the difficulties that Hevea was experiencing in the Guianas offers, it must be emphasized, no great predictive value. It is not possible to predict the effect of transferring a given plant to a new habitat.

Although Hevea was supremely successful in Southeast Asia, and its Burmese counterpart, *Ficus elastica*, has been planted as an ornamental on miles and miles of streets in every Brazilian coastal city, the Castilla rubber tree appears to have encountered some kind of damaging fungus in Malaya, and that is one of the reasons why it was abandoned. Thus it may happen that in the new habitat some pest or parasite may be only too ready to attack the immigrant cultivar. The interrelationships of any ecological system, it must be admitted, are much too complex to offer the hope of a deterministic explanation.[18]

Nevertheless, it is evident that the India Office, by removing Hevea from its dangerous parasites, had immensely simplified the problem of cultivating this difficult species. Curiously, however, not until much later was this accomplishment realized to be the principal benefit of that brilliant exploit. Ironically, Markham, Hooker, and Wickham, obsessed as they were with advancing the interests of the British Empire, justifying the budget of Kew Gardens, or merely securing passage out of the jungle, were unable to comprehend the real nature and ultimate consequences of their enterprise.

It was, nevertheless, obvious enough to Stahel, who in 1919 warned of the possibility that the fungus that caused South American Leaf Blight might some day follow the planted Hevea trees to their new home. W. N. C. Belgrave, a botanist sent from Singapore to British Guiana in 1921 to investigate the new leaf disease, also realized that *Microcyclus ulei* represented a potential danger to the Asian plantations. He therefore recommended a quarantine on plant materials sent from the Amazon to Southeast Asia. Belgrave's brief research note initiated a long history of anxious watchfulness that still preoccupies Southeast Asian rubber growers.[19]

Much earlier on, Kew botanists had worried that Hevea might encounter endemic pests or parasites in Southeast Asia that would endanger its acclimatization. These fears were largely unfounded; none of the Asian plant-attacking fungi was prepared to parasitize this unfamiliar tree. As late as 1911 there were almost no diseases to report. Huber was "very impressed," during his tour of Asian plantations, by the "magnificent aspect of the foliage of the cultivated Heveas." He searched for signs of infection among leaves fallen to the ground (an action suggesting his concerns about the Belém plantings), but even there "it is not possible to discover a single spot of parasitic fungi." Another, much later observer remarked on the stillness of the groves, only the occasional bursting of a seed case in the midday heat interrupting their utter silence – a clear sign that even then, birds and insects native to Asia had not yet found the trees an agreeable habitat.[20]

In time, among simple endemic parasites like fungi a certain number may come to adapt themselves to exotic plant tissue. By the time of Petch's survey of 1921, a few fungal parasites or saprophytes native to the region had learned to invade Hevea. Several root diseases had appeared, but it was learned that they could be avoided by burning off existing vegetation, uprooting stumps, and digging isolating ditches. A disease of the tapping panel was found to be the result of too-intensive tapping. Two leaf fungi, *Oidium heveae* and *Glomerella cingulata*, the latter a cosmopolitan species encountered in the Amazon as well, began to attack Hevea, but neither was at all as virulent as Microcyclus. Endemic fungi, as was to be expected, had not come to attack Hevea preferentially, but only opportunistically. Thus, as late as the 1940s, a survey of Asian rubber planting was able to report that "the rubber plantations in the Netherlands East Indies have never been seriously endangered by any disease," while in Malaya no more than 0.5 percent of planting costs went for disease control. This advantage was to prove of decisive importance as Hevea breeding programs were initiated. It was possible to concentrate entirely on the problem of increasing latex output, without confronting the necessity of improving simultaneously the tree's disease resistance.[21]

Bancroft's and Stahel's reports, limited as they were in their understanding of the nature of the fungus and the host-parasite relationship, and of the potential for control of the disease, remained the most advanced information available for at least forty years. They suggested that there might be local environments in which the fungus might not be easily established and they recommended selection of surviving stock for the breeding of resistant trees. But as planters abandoned their Hevea, plant researchers abandoned further efforts to seek solutions to the deadly disease. Instead they advised planters to shift to coffee or cattle. In British Guiana the local economy reverted to gathering Balata rubber.

In Brazil, where Hevea had been planted in patches large and small along the main river courses as far as Acre, there was no report concerning the prevalence of Microcyclus, except for Huber's worried remark to Petch in the botanical garden at Peradeniya. The rubber survey carried out in the Amazon basin in 1923 by the U.S. Department of Agriculture reported the presence of fungal disease in many places, but not the sort of devastation suffered by the plantations of British Guiana and Surinam. It happens that very small stands of planted Hevea, up to a few dozen or even more, may not incur epidemic infections of the blight. Others of the relatively small stands may well have been infected, but the blight may have gone unnoticed, because many of the small plantings carried out enthusiastically after the state and federal laws of 1909 and 1912 were soon after abandoned. Still other stands may have remained in more or less continual cultivation without suffering attacks because of specific local conditions. Bancroft believed that the windiness of the Demerara coast, for example, reduced the ability of spores to settle on leaves.

But most of the Hevea trees located by the survey were very likely survivors of much larger numbers that had been planted and had suffered attacks by Microcyclus. When these trees were tapped, it was discovered that their yield was quite low, so low in fact that it was hardly more worthwhile to cultivate them than to tap wild trees. The reason for this disappointing result was only discovered later on: It happens that high latex yield and high resistance to Microcyclus are mutually exclusive characteristics of Hevea, at least in every specimen of the tree that has been collected up to the present. When the association between host and parasite was left to work itself out in its native habitat, the final result was an array of planted trees whose yield was unacceptably low for commercial exploitation.[22]

Moreover, the planting stock of Hevea available to Southeast Asian planters was already entering an extraordinary phase of improvement, further foreclosing efforts to cultivate in the Amazon low-yielding Hevea hardy enough to resist the South American Leaf Blight. The lead in this research was taken by scientists in the Netherlands East Indies. There were two specialized rubber experiment stations in Java and Sumatra by 1916, and eight by 1921. Well before P. J. S. Cramer's unsuccessful collection trip to the Amazon in 1913, Dutch researchers had embarked upon a program of rubber improvement. They had brought together at Buitenzorg the astounding total of 256 species of latex-yielding plants, including four species of *Hevea*. Tromp de Haas reported in 1909 that a tapping study had been carried out on the thirty-three trees at Buitenzorg grown from the seeds imported from Malaya in 1883. It had been discovered that the output of latex varied extremely from one tree to another; therefore, it was decided that seed selection and breeding might increase yields significantly.[23]

Buitenzorg thereupon undertook a vast survey of existing plantations to identify high-yielding trees. These source trees could not be multiplied through cuttings, because, as Kew had already found out, Hevea did not root reliably from cuttings. The simplest and quickest solution was to resort to planting seeds from these source trees. Such seeds, called *illegitimate* because their male parents were undeterminable, could not be expected to yield as abundantly as their female parents, however. The great height of the mature trees and the extremely low rate of success in self-fertilizing and cross-fertilizing the mother trees at first inhibited more scientific breeding. But there was practiced in some places a form of breeding in which one or two varieties of selected illegitimate seeds were planted in isolated groves, where controlled cross-fertilization might proceed.[24]

At the same time, experiments were undertaken in grafting buds from high-yielding mother trees on rootstocks established in the field. This procedure, more complicated than rooting cuttings directly or layering, might nevertheless make possible the rapid multiplication of high-yielding clones. It might also reduce the waiting time of six to ten years needed to confirm the outcome of breeding programs. Grafting trials began at Buitenzorg in 1910 under W. M. van Helten, with the assistance of two local planters. By 1916 they had worked out a commercially applicable method of bud grafting. Buds from a productive mother tree were inserted under a flap of bark incised near the base of a one-and-a-half-year-old Hevea seedling that had been planted directly in the field. Once the bud had thrown out a shoot, the rootstock seedling was lopped, permitting the budded clone to form the trunk and canopy of the grafted tree. Convincing evidence of the superiority of bud-grafted trees gradually accumulated. Further selections of parent stock were required, however, and the slump in rubber prices delayed application. It was not until the late 1920s that a significant number of bud-grafted trees was ready for commercial tapping.[25]

The new techniques made possible a considerable increase in yields. It was estimated that the planting of selected illegitimate seeds nearly doubled yields to an average of about 500 kilograms per hectare, and bud grafting superior clones could double them again, to about 1,000 kilograms. Within a few years, British planters in Malaya and Ceylon were beginning to imitate Dutch methods. In the meantime, Dutch plant researchers had also worked out optimal planting densities, devised a better tapping cut based on studies of latex vessel physiology, and introduced nitrogen-fixing ground covers as a substitute for clear weeding.

Dutch research was designed to make up for the lead in Hevea planting enjoyed by the British in Malaya as the result of H. N. Ridley's brilliant efforts. Paradoxically, much of the profit from their success was alienated, since quite a few of the Sumatran plantations were foreign-owned, many by British nationals, and much of the rubber grown in the Netherlands East Indies was exported via Singapore. British research in Malaya, once it got underway, was just as clearly designed to salvage the profitability of the large estates in their competition with emerging native smallholders. It happened that there was nothing in the cultivation of rubber trees that disqualified smallholders from attempting it, and their undervaluation of their family labor afforded them a competitive advantage. Therefore, once peasant proprietors had acquired some experience with rubber, they could grow it more cheaply than the estates. Although there may have been some difficulty in extending government technical assistance to smallholders, and estate owners may even have tried to reserve for themselves these services and the improved clones, nevertheless the area planted by native smallholders continued to grow, partly because they devised better practices independently of government agents.[26]

In Brazil, there was no comparable effort to investigate the problems of rubber cultivation. No plant specialists were sent from the adequately staffed agricultural and botanic research centers of Rio de Janeiro, Minas Gerais, or São Paulo. Jacques Huber, who began work at the Goeldi Museum in Belém in 1895, was the only researcher in the Amazon to interest himself in these questions. He planted a few trees at the museum and more at an experimental farm near Belém. His efforts were not sustained or efficacious, at least not until he visited the Southeast Asian plantations in 1911. Unfortunately, he died only three years later. His experimental farm, where as many as 30,000 trees were planted, operated only until 1916. In 1907, the state government of Pará established another experimental station at Igarapé-açu, 160 kilometers from Belém on the Bragança railway. A great sum was spent for its installations, £70,000 according to one account, but it was completely mismanaged. Federalized in 1912, it was also shut down by 1916.[27]

The scheme for the Economic Defense of Rubber, passed by the Brazilian Congress in 1912, included provision for seven experimental stations. Four of these were outside the range of Hevea, since they were intended to satisfy regional demands for studies of other native rubber-bearing plants like Hancornia. These stations were initiated by contracting foreign scientists, even before their locations were determined. Paul le Cointe, a French researcher who had been invited to head the station at Belém, learned upon his arrival that the plans for its establishment had been cancelled! He was then posted to Manaus, where he refused to accept what he considered an inappropriate site that had been chosen to satisfy local political interests. Finally, in 1916, all the stations were abolished, as falling revenues from rubber decided the government to liquidate all commitments to the sector.[28]

These failures were not symptomatic of a general incapacity of the Brazilian government to sponsor scientific research and extension services. At the time of the rubber debacle, Brazil was achieving considerable success in the identification of several tropical diseases, the eradication of yellow fever, the development and manufacture of snake venom antitoxins, the introduction of eucalyptus, and the modernization of agricultural practices. At the same time that Brazilian rubber gathering was in collapse, cacao was developing into another major plantation crop in Bahia. And food and raw material production for the domestic market was responding quite satisfactorily to increasing demand in the rapidly urbanizing coffee-growing southeast. Most notably, large-scale rice growing in Rio Grande do Sul was eliminating Brazil's need to import that staple.

The building of the Madeira-Mamoré railway and the laying of the Mato Grosso telegraph line demonstrated that the government was capable of organizing large-scale projects even in the remote interior of the country. Although the scale of the Economic Defense of Rubber was immensely beyond the capacities of the nation to execute, and although its conception was distorted by political favoritism, its failure was not proof that the government was incompetent to carry out a research and demonstration program of a size that would have been sufficient to induce private investors or smallholders to undertake rubber planting, had it been feasible at the time.[29]

The achievements of Dutch agricultural researchers in Java and Sumatra did not portend a permanent eclipse for Brazilian rubber cultivation, but it would be necessary for any future Brazilian rubber plantation enterprise, if it was to be competitive in the world market, to apply Dutch techniques. This did not seem to present any special difficulties. The Dutch advances were all applicable to the Brazilian setting. The results of their research were published and readily available. Indeed Huber and others in Brazil had already experimented with Malayan tapping knives and methods. Most important, the selected seeds and clonal budwood could be reimported into Brazil. There was no law against their export, and British and French planters did indeed make use of them in replanting their groves in Malaya and Cochin China.[30]

Nevertheless, there was a potential problem in the eventual import of clonal budwood from Asia: Since most of the trees that were overcome by the blight in Surinam and British Guiana had been grown from seeds imported from Ceylon, there was a strong possibility that all the Asian selections based on Wickham's collection were susceptible to the blight. This possibility had been increased by the practices of the Southeast Asian planters, who had quite naturally been systematically felling the trees on their estates that were low producers – that is, all those trees that were more likely to be blight-resistant.

As the groves in British Guiana and Surinam were ravaged by South American Leaf Blight, it was put forward there, in explanation of the failure of Hevea plantations, that labor costs were too high. The coincidence of declining rubber prices, brought about by the speculative over-planting in Malaya and Sumatra, contributed to this sensation, no doubt. Since the British and Dutch colonial authorities did not hesitate to import Asian workers to the Guianas and Trinidad, they could not claim, as did Brazilian authorities, that their work force was higher-priced than the coolies of Ceylon, Malaya, or Sumatra. Since Georgetown and Paramaribo continued to export other tropical crops, and since a sizable part of the work force continued to gather Balata rubber, an enterprise controlled by a local monopoly, there was apparently no absolute shortage of labor. The real labor problem, it would seem, was the decline in labor productivity that was directly the result of the blight. As many of the trees were killed off, and as the survivors proved poor yielders, laborers lost interest in a form of field work that was relatively unremunerative.[31]

The experiences of the planters of a few thousand hectares of Hevea along the coast north of the Brazilian border may not have been decisive in the minds of contemporary potential investors in Amazonian rubber plantations, yet the problem must have been carefully weighed. It was especially impressive that the disease had been investigated by some of the chief specialists available to the British and Dutch governments, some of them with considerable prior experience in Southeast Asian rubber plantations. Under what circumstances, then, would anyone venture to repeat the experience of Surinam and British Guiana? Was there any future for Brazilian cultivated rubber?

5

A jump in the dark, 1923–1940

In the early 1920s, as the result of the formation of a rubber cartel in Southeast Asia, Brazil again came under consideration as a possible site for large-scale planting. The seemingly insatiable demand of the United States market had stimulated a speculative wave of planting in Asia, leading to symptoms of oversupply as early as 1918. Rubber, still of limited application to warfare, had to be cut back in production and shipping space during World War I. By the end of hostilities, a vast new acreage then came into tapping age, exerting a powerful downward pressure on rubber prices. A voluntary plan to restrict output was tried without success in 1920, and prices continued to slump. By 1922, four out of five plantations in the British colonies were paying no dividends. A government-enforced restriction scheme was thereupon resorted to in Malaya and Ceylon, on recommendation of an official commission, called the Stevenson Committee. A surtax was imposed upon exports above a certain quantity, in hopes of raising the standard price to one shilling three pence a pound. The Dutch and French had been invited to take part in this cartel, but they refused, sensing that they might profit more by remaining outside it.[1]

The price of rubber quickly rose even higher than the cartel had envisioned, more because of extraordinary demand than the restrictions themselves. A renewed flood of rubber in the market was easily predictable, however; not only were the Dutch and French greatly increasing their acreage, but the Malayan and Ceylonese trees were sure to yield more after their enforced period of "rest." Nevertheless, the cartel was maintained. Above all, it was helping to increase the inflow of dollars into the British economy at a relatively small political cost, because by 1922, rubber consumption by British industry was less than a quarter that of the United States.[2]

The reaction of United States rubber manufacturers was on the whole subdued. Higher prices were unwelcome, but if they were more predictable, profits might yet be larger than before. Rubber recycling intensified. Two of the largest American companies, U.S. Rubber and Goodyear, had bought sizable estates in Malaya and Sumatra, and thus expected to benefit whether the cartel succeeded or failed. The most vocal opponent of the cartel, Harvey S. Fire-

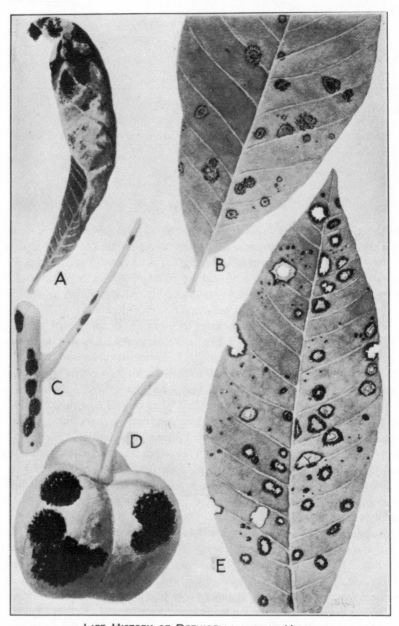

LIFE HISTORY OF DOTHIDELLA ULEI ON HEVEA

A, Fusicladium stage on a young leaf; B, pycnidial stage; C, infections on stem and petiole; D, infection of fruit; E, perithecial stage

Effects of South American Leaf Blight, from James Weir's USDA report. (Courtesy The New York Public Library Special Collections)

stone, founder of the Firestone Tire and Rubber Company, found himself isolated within the industry. In 1924, he adopted the same strategy as U.S. Rubber and Goodyear, taking an option on a failed Dunlop estate in Liberia.[3]

Within the United States government, Herbert Hoover, then secretary of commerce, led a more consequential rally against the British assault. He obtained from Congress an appropriation of $500,000 to investigate the possibilities of rubber cultivation in the United States–controlled Philippines and in the Western Hemisphere. The Department of Agriculture, however, was ill-prepared to convert this largesse into useful information. Although the department had *Hevea brasiliensis* in its collections since 1891, O. F. Cook, the head of its rubber crops section, for years insisted on the superiority of Castilla rubber. The department's preference had helped to stimulate United States investment in Castilla plantations in Central America and Mexico, a misjudgment doubly regrettable, since most of these projects proved to be swindles.[4]

It was necessary, therefore, to send forth teams of investigators to Central America and the Caribbean and to Brazil to discover what experience existed there of cultivated Hevea. The former team, led by John C. Treadwell, found trees dating from 1901 in Nicaragua and from 1903 in Haiti. At a single estate in Chiapas, 40–50 thousand trees had been planted between 1911 and 1915; and at Turrialba in Costa Rica, the United Fruit Company had started a plantation of Hevea on exhausted banana land in 1916. These and other scattered plantings suggested the practicality of new investments. South American Leaf Blight was not observed; Treadwell thought that its appearance was "not probable," and that the risk of its introduction could "be reduced to a minimum." Central America and the Caribbean emerged as the focus of the department's interest in future planting, partly out of fear of the blight and partly, no doubt, because the region was nearest to United States ports and supposedly politically docile. Nicaragua, Haiti, and the Dominican Republic were under U.S. military occupation at the time, and Cuba was officially a U.S. protectorate. The department quickly took over and enlarged a grove at Bayeux in Haiti, set up others in the Canal Zone and in Mexico, and encouraged cooperative plantings in Cuba, the Dominican Republic, and Puerto Rico.[5]

The Brazilian government was easily convinced of the desirability of collaboration with the joint expedition proposed by the Departments of Commerce and Agriculture to investigate the Amazon region. It contributed a steamboat and a counterpart team of four Brazilians, one of whom was João Geraldo Kuhlmann of the Botanical Garden of Rio de Janeiro.

The Amazon expeditions resulted in the publications of five detailed reports, including one written by the Brazilians. The leader of the Department of Agriculture team, Carl D. LaRue, a University of Michigan botanist with several years of experience on the U.S. Rubber Company's Sumatra plantation, was mainly interested in locating the best possible genetic material for future cultivation. He therefore wandered as far as Acre, Mato Grosso, and the Bolivian Bení region to view surviving wild groves. In Bolivia, LaRue collected seeds that were sent to Panama, but these appear not to have survived. His observations convinced him that Acre was most suitable for Hevea. He downplayed its inaccessibility, promoting it as a region "in which the white race can thrive." The leader of the Department of Commerce team, William L. Schurz, then commercial attaché at Rio de Janeiro, produced a separate regional study that emphasized the superiority of the lower Amazon, especially its southern tributaries, where good quality Hevea trees were native.[6]

Both Schurz and LaRue were aware of the failure of plantation Hevea in the Guianas and Trinidad and expressed concern over the harm that South American Leaf Blight might do to plantings in the Amazon. The blight was the subject of two separate reports to the Department of Agriculture. Robert Delafield Rands was sent to Trinidad and the Guianas to observe its ravages. He found that the blight had indeed caused the general abandonment of Hevea, and he expressed concern that it had reached Trinidad, beyond the natural range of the genus. A survey of all known pests and diseases of Hevea was produced by James R. Weir, a Forest Service employee with a doctorate in botany from Munich. He described Microcyclus as "without question the most serious leaf disease of *Hevea* in the American tropics" and predicted that the planting of rubber in close stands would provide ideal conditions for its propagation. Weir suggested various countermeasures; he did not, however, consider the blight an insuperable obstacle, but merely "a part of the overhead." He saw "no reason to believe that the diseases of Hevea encountered in the Amazon Valley cannot be successfully combatted if proper precautions before and after planting are taken." Nevertheless, he expressed a preference for planting the tree beyond its normal range, where infection might be reduced by sanitary measures and quarantine.[7]

Officials and businessmen in Brazil were much stirred by the evidence of U.S. determination to counter the British cartel. They did not doubt that they would be the beneficiaries of future U.S. investments in rubber, even though they were quite unclear about the form that such investments might take. Miguel Calmon, then minister of agriculture, was once again in a position to favor rubber development. He offered a waiver of import duties on rubber plantation equipment, a waiver of export taxes on planted rubber, and, most remarkable, permission to import Asian laborers. The governors of both the northern states also expressed their willingness to collaborate with foreign capital. Newspapers and forums such as the National Agricultural Society overflowed with welcome to potential investors.[8]

In the state of Bahia, which the U.S. expedition had briefly visited, probably at Miguel Calmon's request, an expansion in cacao planting was generating funds for further novelties. The surviving rubber trees at the state agricultural school were experimentally tapped, their seeds were gathered and distributed, and more seeds were brought in from the Amazon. State law 1876, passed in 1926, exempted cultivated rubber from export taxes, granted low freight rates, and offered a 50 percent discount on the purchase of state lands by persons proposing to plant rubber. Perhaps 100 thousand trees were planted during this surge of interest, most of them as shade for cacao.[9]

The results of the U.S. government's rubber investigations were not immediately published. Hoover allowed them to be conveyed confidentially to potential U.S. investors. LaRue visited Firestone's Washington offices even before writing his report for the Department of Agriculture. There he told Mark L. Felber to avoid the lower Amazon, where the dry season was too long and local specimens of Hevea unimpressive. Insisting on the virtues of Acre, he pointed out that Belém was full of idle river steamers and crews that could be had "for a song."[10]

Meanwhile, Brazil's case was being advanced in the United States by José Custódio Alves de Lima, a consular representative with influential connections. One of his letters, in April 1923, was directed to Henry Ford, who, he may have known, was also being approached by Harvey Firestone to collaborate in a riposte to the cartel. Late the next year, de Lima received the result of an experimental tapping in Bahia, 130 kilograms of rubber, which was certified in a New York laboratory to be of good quality. The best of this material de Lima sent to Ford. In July 1925, he was invited to Dearborn where he apprised Ford of the official favors that had been offered to prospective planters.[11]

Henry Ford was considering extending the self-sufficiency of his automobile production to the construction of his own tire plant. He therefore ordered W. E. McCullough to report on the advisability of operating rubber plantations. Had McCullough's recommendation, available by September 1925, been followed, the company would have saved a great deal of money. The current high prices, McCullough pointed out, were stimulating rubber planting "on a huge scale." He predicted, and was to be proved right within a year, well before Ford's plans were decided, that prices were sure to come down and stay down. He therefore concluded that Ford would do well to limit his stake in the rubber business to the opening of a purchasing office in the Amazon.[12]

In McCullough's estimation, Brazil was the most suitable site for a plantation, if Ford insisted on such a venture, because there land could be had cheaply and in large tracts. By then, Ford's incipient interest was the subject of rumor in Rio de Janeiro. Other potential investors were appearing in Belém, and one English syndicate, led by an American named Ernest S. Clark, had bought an estate. The occasion was ripe for a swindle. Jorge Dumont Villares, scion of an important coffee-growing family in São Paulo, secured from the state government of Pará options to some 2.4 million hectares of public land in seven different plots. In his selection of sites, he had the advice of none other than William L. Schurz, who also helped Villares to gain entrée to government and rubber company offices in the United States. In September 1926, Villares appeared in Akron, offering Firestone land at 50 cents an acre, and claiming that he had already sold 500,000 hectares.[13]

In Dearborn, Villares must have made contact with a Ford employee named W. L. Reeves Blakeley. Blakeley managed to obtain from Ford the assignment of surveying the lower Amazon for a possible plantation site. He was accompanied by Carl D. LaRue, who was to supply technical advice. The team was met in Belém by the ubiquitous Villares, who proceeded to accompany them up the Amazon. LaRue's commission, presented to him by Ford himself, was simply to "find a good area somewhere" to plant rubber. By then LaRue had been talked out of his notion that Acre was a practical site for commercial planting, and he had been made aware that the choice would have to be somewhere in the lower Amazon. Curiously, the Blakeley entourage made a beeline for one of the Villares concessions, an 80 kilometer stretch of the east bank of the lower Tapajós River, in the municipalities of Aveiros and Itaituba, spent one month traversing it, and returned to Dearborn, having visited no other site.[14]

LaRue's six-page report to Ford compliantly ruled out all other locations on the Tapajós, save the Villares concession. Herbert Hoover, primed with Schurz's planted rumors, also offered encouragement because he feared the option would be picked up by some European syndicate. These arguments were enough to convince Ford. He entered into negotiations immediately and the concession was granted 21 July 1927. Ford was cozened into paying Villares $125 thousand for land that the state of Pará might well have granted at no cost, had the approach been made directly. An inauspicious beginning, no doubt. More consequential was the lack of technical criteria in the selection of site. LaRue was able to point to impressive individual specimens of Hevea in the forest to bolster his choice, but he had failed to take into account factors that rendered the concession marginal for plantation production. Rainfall in this part of the valley was so highly seasonal that plant growth would be inhibited. The tract was hilly and therefore would be awkward for machines to cultivate and onerous for tappers to tend. Much of it was too sandy or leached for adequate plant nutrition, and not only was it a four-day sail upriver from Belém, the land lay beyond the reach of ocean-going transport for several months of the year.[15]

The Ford concession, soon to be known by its Brazilian popular appellation, Fordlandia, was at the outset buffeted by immense political storms. Its vastness – one million hectares – its fifty-year exemption from taxes, and its sweeping right of internal jurisdiction fueled nationalist sentiments and embarrassed the state government. Ford had committed himself to no more than the investment of approximately $1 million in the venture and the planting of a mere 1,200 hectares of rubber on this huge expanse. Furthermore, he was permitted to exploit whatever resources, timber or mineral, he pleased. Worse, one of Villares's associates, resenting Villares's refusal to share the proceeds of his coup, provided the Belém press with documentary evidence of the conspiracy, which included a commission for Governor Dionísio Bentes. To dissociate himself from the affair, Bentes began to obstruct Ford's operations. The obstructionism intensified when Bentes's opponent, Eurico de Freitas Valle, became governor. It ended only in July 1929, when Ford's personal emissary told Valle that the company was prepared to abandon the project.

In October 1930, a revolutionary movement overthrew the "Old Republic," and these initial difficulties were swept away. The new regime, ideologically opposed to the traditional elites that had been running each state as though it were sovereign, and driven by a need to develop new sources of revenue for the central government, was quite receptive to new enterprises, especially those that gave promise of industrial linkages. The new president, Getúlio Vargas, therefore confirmed the concession and interpreted doubtful clauses in the contract in favor of the Ford plantation.[16]

In December 1928, a company-owned freighter deposited at Fordlandia the components of an entire plantation nucleus, from diesel engines to nails and bolts. The American staff and their Brazilian workers immediately set to work to construct a small city, soon to be the third largest in the Amazon, complete with hospital, schools, cinema, water supply, electricity, docks, machine shops, and warehouses. Visitors never failed to marvel at this superb infrastructure, unmatchable for a thousand miles in any direction. The neatly aligned wooden bungalows, bunkhouses, general stores, and mess halls elicited praise from junketing Brazilian officials and went far to extract Ford from his early political difficulties.

Unfortunately, the laying out of rubber groves proceeded at a much less impressive pace. By the end of June 1929, the work force had only barely managed to complete the clearing and planting of the 400 hectares required under the terms of the concession. Over the next two years another meager 900 hectares were laid out. By comparison, 13,160 hectares were planted at the U.S. Rubber company's Sumatra plantation during its first three years at approximately the same cost. Apparently the clearing operation was slowed by the decision to remove merchantable timber before burning. When this practice was abandoned in 1933, planting increased, but only to 1,000 hectares. At that rate, planting the entire concession, a feat the Dutch and English had trembled to imagine, would require another thousand years.[17]

The critical factor in the development of the concession lay in the shortage of seed. From the beginning the Ford planners had followed LaRue's insistent and reiterated advice to seek seed in Acre and Mato Grosso. Raimundo Monteiro da Costa, an important rubber patrão and former member of the Brazilian counterpart team, had been contracted, shortly after the granting of the concession, to acquire 600,000 seeds on the upper Madeira. These had been planted in a temporary nursery at Parantins, just over the border in Amazonas.

James Weir, Mato Grosso, 1923, on the USDA expedition. (Courtesy The New York Public Library Special Collections)

It seems odd that this site was selected, since it put the company at the mercy of that state's government. Envious that Pará had been selected by Ford, Amazonas impounded the seedlings, even though they had originated outside its territory. The Ford staff was not in a position to obtain backing from Belém, and were put to a long legal battle to liberate this material. More important, only 100,000 of the seedlings survived; even if they had arrived in time, they would have been far fewer than required. The first year's planting therefore had to be done with 500,000 local seeds hurriedly collected and planted out of season. They proved lacking in vigor and had to be plowed under.[18]

Meanwhile, Ford's development costs were escalating. His expectation that timber sales would offset the initial investment in planting was shattered, along with the saw blades of the expensive sawmill included in the first shipment of equipment from Detroit. Ford's sawyers found it difficult to deal with the variety and hardness of the timber found on the estate, and the costs of transportation were found to be too high. These problems, like leaf blight, were well known to the U.S. Department of Agriculture, whose forestry reports were available for the Ford company's inspection. Ford suspected that there might be oil on his concession – Brazilian government explorers were prospecting in the region when LaRue and Schurz passed through. He invited Standard Oil to prospect on his land, but no oil was located and exploration ended by mid-1931. An inner tube factory was proposed for Belém, which it was thought might at first be supplied with wild rubber from the Tapajós region, but the gathering force of the depression cancelled this project. The plantation, which had counted on the earnings of Ford's Brazilian automobile assembly plant to supply much of its initial capital, was thrown back upon the resources of the home office.[19]

For the first five years of its existence, Fordlandia had no one resident on its staff, or even available as a consultant, with scientific training in tropical agriculture or practical experience in rubber planting. Several inexperienced managers succeeded each other until Archibald Johnston, of the Ford commercial office in Belém, was transferred to the plantation in October 1933. He seems to have had no agricultural experience either. Carl D. LaRue had not been given any further assignments by Ford. Possibly he was suspected to have participated knowingly in Villares's swindle. LaRue nevertheless sent an anguished note to Ford in 1930, expressing dismay that "things have not gone forward so well as they should have" at Fordlandia. This he felt reflected on his own reputation. Accordingly he offered his part-time services to the company as the most experienced person in the country. His letter, forwarded to Edsel Ford, was annotated "Do not think we would benefit any by using him" and filed.[20]

Not until mid-1932 did anyone in Dearborn begin to wonder if the plantation might profit from expert advice. A. M. Wibel encountered a reference to bud grafting, a technique by then fifteen years old in the Netherlands East Indies, and wrote to Harvey Firestone to find out if his Liberian plantation was employing it. He learned that it had indeed been in use since 1928. He informed W. E. Carnegie, of the accounting department, who wrote to Johnston, asking if the technique might not be tried. Johnston was under the impression that clones need not be grafted because Hevea branches, if merely stuck in the ground, "will take root almost without fail"! Only after considerable further encouragement was he brought to the point, at the end of December 1932, of asking for assistance in applying the technique, since there was no one in the Amazon who knew of it.[21]

The expert chosen by Ford was James R. Weir. Weir seems to have impressed the directors of the newly organized Rubber Research Institute of

Malaya with his remark in his survey of rubber diseases that the material on which the Southeast Asian plantations were based was quite likely highly susceptible. They had hired him, and there he was when R. H. McCarroll, a Ford employee sent to study the rubber market, passed through Kuala Lumpur in 1928. Weir complained of office routine and angled for a job with Ford. Unsuccessful, he soon found one to his liking directing plant research at the smaller of the two Goodyear plantations in Sumatra. Possibly as a result of the McCarroll contact, Ford hired Weir in January 1933. By March he had arrived at Fordlandia.[22]

Weir found nothing to praise. His initial report pointed to omissions of elementary estate management, including the failure to divide the plantings into numbered blocks and to destroy wild Hevea within a mile of the planting sites. His major recommendations, however, dealt with the principal issues of productivity and disease resistance. If the plantation were to succeed, its yields would have to approximate those of Southeast Asia. Selection for resistance to South American Leaf Blight would have to begin simultaneously, however, since it was already infesting some of the trees, and was sure to spread. He proposed a continuation of explorations throughout the valley for wild and planted specimens that might display both of these qualities. He suggested a visit to surviving plantings in the Guianas, where resistant specimens might supply seeds. The existing groves should be preserved and kept under observation for the possible appearance of high-yielding or resistant individuals. Much of this advice had already been proffered in LaRue's 1927 reports to Ford, which Weir had probably not been shown.[23]

Since there was no planting material at hand that could be identified as either high-yielding or resistent, there was nothing to bud graft. Weir announced that it would be necessary to import Southeast Asian clones. Their high productivity was guaranteed, and though they were extremely likely to be susceptible to leaf blight, if just one clone was found to be resistent, a great deal of time and effort would be saved. Weir was authorized to effect the transfer of this material personally. Late in 1933, he arrived at the Goodyear estate in Sumatra, where he selected 53 clones, packed as 2,046 budded stumps. These arrived at Fordlandia in mid-February 1934.[24]

Upon his return to Brazil, Weir made an astounding proposal. His valuable clonal material ought not to be planted at Fordlandia. Another site should be selected. He recommended a place called Belterra, on a 150 meter high plateau on the same bank of the Tapajós, 50 kilometers south of Santarém. Weir, like Wickham, believed that Hevea required well-drained upland soils to thrive, and he also believed that the richer the soil, the more resistant the trees would be to the leaf blight. His observations in 1923 had convinced him that upland sites inhibited the spread of the fungus, since they were windier and less subject to mists.[25]

By early 1934, Henry Ford had evidently lost interest in his Amazon adventure. Outlays at Fordlandia had been cut from $2 million in 1930 to $400 thousand in 1933. There was still no rubber to show for an investment that by then totaled nearly $7 million, nor prospect of any in the near future, given the slow growth of the trees. Although a second rubber cartel was forming, this time with the participation of the Dutch and French, the Roosevelt administration, itself inclined toward legitimizing cartels, was no longer encouraging the rubber companies to react. In spite of all this, Ford immediately authorized the execution of Weir's extraordinary plan. On 4 May 1934, a 281,500 hectare tract of the Fordlandia concession was traded for another of equal size at Belterra. The sawmill and the machine shop began to replicate the warehouses, dock, housing, schools, hospital, and the like, of Fordlandia.[26]

Johnston was pleased that the new tract was flat and could be reached year-round by cargo vessels from the United States, but he was upset that a considerable investment would have to be made in water supply. This plateau was considerably drier than Fordlandia, as LaRue had noted when he surveyed it in 1928. Nonetheless, Johnston pushed forward with the work. By the end of 1934, 1,053 hectares had been cleared and there were 5,000,000 seedlings in the nursery to serve as root stock. Weir meanwhile surveyed Fordlandia and "condemned" 703 hectares of trees planted on sandy soil. He ordered the discontinuance of planting at the first plantation and organized budwood nurseries for the grafting material. During 1935, bud grafting was taught to the staff and the cleared area was finally planted, slowly and with many replacements of seedlings.[27]

By this time, however, the disease that LaRue and Weir had been expecting began to appear at Fordlandia in epidemic form. South American Leaf Blight had been present from the start, but the first groves had been planted at abnormally wide distances, in order to satisfy the contracted minimum area; thus it had taken six years for the canopies to close and facilitate the movement of inoculum from one tree to the next. Weir described the attack in the older groves: "Practically all the branches of the trees throughout the estate but especially on the poorer sites terminate in naked stems. Each successive elongation of the shoot becomes smaller and smaller . . . with the result that it either dies back entirely with an attempt at lateral shoot development lower down or the growth impetus ceases altogether." At Belterra the rootstock nurseries were struck in April 1935. Weir knew of Stahel's use of Bordeaux mixture in Surinam, suggesting that in nurseries, at least, the disease could be contained. The plantation lacked spraying equipment, however, so early control attempts had little effect.[28]

Most important, the budwood nurseries at Fordlandia were also attacked. By the end of the year it was apparent that none of Weir's fifty-three Southeast Asian clones was immune, and none displayed any certain resistance. Weir warned that continuous control might have to be undertaken, a costly operation that might wipe out any potential profit. In any case, he concluded pessimistically that control might not be effective. Belterra, unlike Fordlandia, was level, which facilitated spraying. "Virulent tree diseases of universal distribution confined to a single host assuming epidemic proportions with every change of humidity and spreading directly from tree to tree, without some intermediate controllable stage, cannot be combatted at Fordlandia successfully or economically." He believed that most of the trees would survive, but the disease would continue to slow their development, adding more maintenance and interest charges to the costs of disease control. Already too many trees at Fordlandia had had to be replaced, imparting to the groves a ragtag appearance. It was unlikely that these groves would ever be profitably exploited.[29]

The failure of the Southeast Asian clones meant that a viable plantation operation was not immediately possible. It would require a minimum of ten years of selection and testing, and perhaps several more decades of breeding among the selections. Weir evidently had no taste for this. His 1936 report, which he described as a "bomb" thrown into the midst of the Ford executives, proposed reducing Fordlandia to a "skeleton force" and maintaining it as an experimental station where the motley collection of trees might be observed and employed in a program of selection and breeding. Contradicting the report he had written for the Department of Agriculture, he stated that "no rubber man would have gone to Brazil in the first place." The scientific operation he envisioned would have been of more use to the future Amazon economy than to the Ford Motor Company. Belterra was to be expanded no more than a few blocks a year, so that watch could be kept over the result and better clones substituted as they appeared. "The investment of capital in extensive planting under any other condition is not justified," he wrote. Weir suggested several other experimental directions, all of which would consume a great deal of time. The alternative was to abandon the Amazon entirely and plant rubber outside the natural range of Hevea and its parasites. "That way is still open," he declared. He recommended Central America.[30]

Weir's report infuriated Archibald Johnston, who had always wanted to expand rapidly and was pressing Dearborn to allow him to plant 2,000 hectares a year, up to 30,000 hectares. He believed the planting material that had been obtained in the Belém region was adequately resistant, and he disparaged the bud-grafting technique and the Southeast Asian clones. Johnston and Weir, apparently polar extremes in personality, intensely disliked each other and insisted on presenting Dearborn with their mutually contradictory plans. Johnston was delighted to receive a visit from W. N. Bangham, a former colleague of Weir in Sumatra, who by 1936 was working for Goodyear at their Central American estates. Bangham agreeably filed a report for Johnston that criticized Weir's work at every possible point and came out in favor of rapid expansion. He also showed Johnston a rather fawning letter he had received from Weir, containing criticisms of Johnston.[31]

Weir and Johnston nevertheless coexisted for one more year, during which Johnston laid out and bud grafted 700,000 trees at Belterra. He reported jubilantly in December that the new estate was "wonderfully free of all kinds of pest and the rubber is growing up in good shape, leaves are clean and there is very little disease of any kind." Weir meanwhile set up a research unit at Fordlandia where he organized several projects that were to be of critical importance for the future of rubber in Brazil. Since 1935, selections of resistant specimens had been made in the already planted groves. Since none of these appeared likely to prove high-yielding, a breeding program was set up to cross them with the best of the Southeast Asian clones. Weir also collected seeds of apparently resistant trees in British and Dutch Guiana. It was observed that wild specimens of *Hevea benthamiana*, *H. spruceana*, and *H. guianensis* seemed to be more resistant than *H. brasiliensis*. These were added to the breeding program and an expedition was sent to the Rio Negro to bring back more seeds of these species.[32]

Weir began in February 1937 to experiment with top grafting, a technique first tried ten years before in Java: A resistant clone was grafted on a high-yielding clone at a height of about two meters. Such a tree would thus be composed of three elements – a rootstock of unselected but better-than-average vigor, a high-yielding trunk that would form the tapping panel, and a resistant canopy. Weir thought this procedure "a jump in the dark." There was much about it that was problematic, including the practicality and cost of the grafting operation itself, but the technique was gradually improved.

Weir was assisted in these projects by Charles H. T. Townsend, Jr. His father, an American entomologist who had long resided in São Paulo, had been hired by Johnston in 1935 to examine and prescribe countermeasures against several species of insects that were attacking Hevea. The most important of the native pests was the mandarová moth (*Erynnis ello*), locally endemic on cultivated manioc plants. The larval stage of this moth attacked young leaves. Townsend identified others, including lace bug (fam. Tingidae, *Leptopharsa* sp.) and red mite (fam. Tetranychidae), to a total of twenty-three. In the next few years there were to be seasons in which pests were judged as damaging to the groves as leaf blight.[33]

In early January 1938, James D. Weir left Ford's employ, for reasons that are not clear. While still at Fordlandia, he had tried to obtain authorization for another researcher, requesting a senior scientist with experience. Johnston now asked the company to find a young man, specifically one innocent of Southeast Asian practices! Weir went on to seek employment with the U.S. government. The Department of State extracted information from him concerning Ford's operations but did not recommend him; he had a reputation for

Four-year-old Hevea at Fordlandia, 1934. The figure under the tree is probably Archibald Johnston. (Courtesy U.S. National Archives, Photographic Division)

being "cranky and conceited." Weir presented to the Brazilian foreign minister a plan to develop rubber in the Amazon, and in June 1940, he wrote Edsel Ford for permission to visit Belterra and Fordlandia, noting that his previous visit had been "frustrated." His request was denied. After the outbreak of war, Weir was hired by the Venezuelan government, but in 1943 he returned to his native Indiana, where he died at the age of 61.[34]

For the next two years Belterra experienced unusually dry weather. The trees, still young, did not yet present an unbroken canopy to the leaf blight. Yet it was soon observed in the groves, and the infestation was seen to be increasing. Johnston, nevertheless, saw no great danger. The disease finally appeared in epidemic form in 1940. The staff hastily shifted the bud-grafting crew to top grafting the susceptible Southeast Asian clones. The attack ceased only with the onset of the dry season. Dry weather was opportune, from that point of view, but it also slowed the development of the trees. Bangham paid another visit in late 1940. Congratulating Johnston that the "disturbing members of the staff had been removed," he told him that "splendid progress had been made during the last four years." The trees, he thought, were making "excellent growth" and he expected that leaf blight would not prove as serious as at Fordlandia. Belterra, he wrote Johnston, would eventually be competitive with Southeast Asia. He was dubious about top grafting, which had not been perfected and required repeated passes through the groves. In any case, Bangham thought it would not be needed at Belterra. He suggested to Johnston that test tapping be carried out at Fordlandia. He thought Townsend's estimate of 250,000 tappable trees was conservative.[35]

Bangham seems to have made a contribution to the breeding program by bringing some Goodyear clones with him. Townsend was continuing to seek more genetic material in wild groves. He made two more collecting trips to Acre, obtaining a total of 122 high-yielding selections. He confirmed the practicality of grafting canopies of *H. benthamiana*, *H. spruceana*, and *H. guianensis* on *H. brasiliensis* trunks, and advised large-scale trials in the field. Pollination experiments had begun in May 1939. Large scaffolds had to be built around the selected mother trees. Only a very small percentage of the laborious hand pollinations were successful, but his crew was achieving interspecific as well as intraspecific crosses.[36]

Belying Bangham's cheerful estimate, the blight returned in 1941, affecting 70 percent of the blocks with closed canopies. Approximately 60 percent of all new growth was destroyed and 14 percent of the mature blocks were killed outright. The top-grafted trees were surviving quite well, however. Experimental results showed top-grafted trees growing faster than controls. Therefore it was decided to graft another 3,200 hectares of Southeast Asian clones. Johnston by then had been promoted to a position at the Dearborn headquarters. He returned to survey the estates in October, and rued the day he had agreed to planting the Asian clones. He brought back photographs showing that the trees grown from seeds from the Belém area were much more vigorous. But he could not yet provide yield data demonstrating that they would be worth tapping.[37]

Some accounts of the Ford plantations ascribe their failures not to a mere fungus, but to labor problems. Labor problems are thought to have been as important or more important than the blight. The management of Fordlandia in its early years did experience considerable difficulty in attracting and maintaining a compliant and diligent labor force. In 1928 and 1929, there were riots that were supposedly ignited by the prejudices and inflexibility of one of the first managers in dealing with Brazilians. The resentments of the local workers may well have been real, and it is quite likely that Johnston's predecessor was tactless in his labor relations. It seems entirely possible, however, considering the hostility of the state government at the time and the manner in which local-level politics was played in Brazil in the "Old Republic," that *agents provocateurs* had been sent to circulate among the workers. In June

81

1930, the management ceded to Governor Valle the right to name the police delegate at Fordlandia. There was another "riot" in December 1930, but thereafter such incidents ceased.[38]

Ford was indeed operating in a region of very limited labor supply. The rubber boom had occupied some 150,000 workers, but many who survived that experience had returned to their native Northeast. By the late 1920s, there were perhaps 250,000 adult males in the rural areas of the entire Amazon basin, fewer than one for each sixteen square kilometers. The company's recruiters therefore encountered few sizable concentrations of potential workers within a reasonable distance of the estate. They ruled out the enlistment of tribal Indians, alleging an invincible prejudice of whites and mestizos against them. Frequently, householders rebuffed the recruiters because they were reluctant to divert any of their male members from subsistence or cash-earning activities they were already engaged in. The recruiters themselves avoided settlements where malaria was said to be endemic, fearing for Fordlandia's safety as well as their own. Indeed the poor health of potential workers, not any supposed inability to respond to wage incentives, was a major reason for turning down workers once they arrived at the estate. What was frequently diagnosed as laziness by outsiders was surely symptoms of malaria and parasites.[39]

Ford's recruiters complained that local political bosses hindered the enlistment of anyone who was a registered voter and who might be needed to guarantee their continuance in power. They discovered that in this remote region of Brazil, the municipal governments were still extracting corvée labor from landless workers, a practice that no doubt augmented the personal incomes of local authorities. Merchants involved in the gathering trade were just as loath to see their collectors depart; therefore, they frightened them with tales of the high cost of living at Fordlandia and the alacrity with which its employees were dismissed. Indeed, the merchants had the elements of a case against Ford, since the first demonstrations against work rules had been met with mass firings. Furthermore, the Ford managers expected prospective workers to pay their own way to the main gate and to find their own way home if the company's doctors found them unfit. The recruiters found that riverboat captains were raising prices when they heard their passengers were bound for Fordlandia. By 1932, the management was well aware of the complexities of labor recruitment, and turned this function over to local contractors, who thereafter generally provided a steady supply.[40]

William L. Schurz's careful study had reported that unskilled labor was paid twenty-five to thirty cents a day in the lower Amazon. The Amazon elite invariably insisted that rubber had been snatched from them because Southeast Asian labor was "slavish." On the contrary, by the late 1920s, labor on Malayan and Sumatran estates cost thirty-five to forty-five cents a day. Indeed, Custódio de Lima had regaled Henry Ford with tales of cheap Amazonian labor, but Ford replied expansively that he would pay five dollars a day if the workers proved efficient. Wage rates at Fordlandia were at first remarkably high: $1.50 to $1.65 a day, or $44 for monthly workers, rising to $55 after two month's experience. These rates were eventually brought closer to those prevailing in the region, but they remained two or three times those paid in Belém, where the work day was much longer than the eight hours required by Ford. Of equal value to the workers was the company's provision of free housing, potable water, electricity, schooling, and medical care, and close supervision of the concessionaires who operated retail stores on the property. President Getúlio Vargas visited Belterra's model community in October 1940, an event of some consequence, for Vargas, impressed by the vigor and health of the inhabitants, broadcast his praise of Ford's labor conditions over a national radio network.[41]

De Lima had transmitted to Ford the readiness of the government of Pará and of the federal government to import Asian labor if it should happen that enough workers could not be found in the Amazon and the Brazilian Northeast. This theme had been played by LaRue: "I know you will be permitted to import Chinese," he told the Firestone company in 1924, "A million Chinese in the rubber sections of Brazil would be a godsend to that country. And after Brazil saw what wonderful development came from the Chinese labor, that nation wouldn't ask expatriation of the coolies." Brazilian authorities, nevertheless, were clearly hoping for white immigrants. Only if that should prove impossible would they authorize Orientals, but then preferentially Japanese, of whom they had had some experience in São Paulo. The Ford manager tried to employ a few dozen British West Indians in 1929, an experiment that caused riots at Fordlandia and necessitated their sudden repatriation. These disturbances may also have been government-inspired: Brazilian official and unofficial immigration policy was at the time decidedly prejudiced against black immigration, and local authorities may well have regarded the formation of an English-speaking enclave in the Amazon as a potential strategic danger.[42]

But Ford never needed the thousands of Cearenses and Asians that had been promised him. The work force at the two estates numbered between 2,200 and 2,500 during most of the first decade. Johnston complained to visitors of labor shortages, and was inclined to view it as his principal problem, because he never ceased to propound a strategy of rapid expansion. His successor, Howard C. Deckard, however, found no lack of workers, actual or potential. On the occasion of Vargas's visit, for example, he failed to bring up the question of additional laborers. When questioned by Dearborn, he said that he had at the moment more than enough and was completing backlogged work. Indeed, he had not suffered any shortages over the two years he had been in charge. He expected in the long run that the children of his current work force represented the company's "best prospects." Deckard assured

Ford that if more workers were needed, he could "obtain them without much difficulty."[43]

The Ford company's labor problems cannot be regarded as a critical or even an important factor in its lack of profitability. The amount of conflict and labor turnover that Ford suffered on the Tapajós was certainly much less than it encountered in Detroit. Even Johnston complained more about J. R. Weir than about all his Brazilian employees put together. Nor were their labor problems any more complex or intractable than those of U.S. plantation operations in much more exotic locales. In Liberia by the mid-1930s, after considerable initial difficulties, including reliance on contractors who resorted to force, Firestone was paying 15,000 tribal workers the first cash wages they had ever seen, and no more than the going rate for west Africa at that. Surely an immensely greater difficulty for Ford than the turnover in labor was the fact that after thirteen years, an investment of almost $10.5 million, and the planting of 3,650,000 rubber trees, there was still almost nothing ready to tap![44]

Fordlandia and Belterra were the only large-scale rubber plantations established in the Western Hemisphere in response to the cartel. Ford's initial political difficulties apparently discouraged Michelin, Firestone, and Goodyear from serious consideration of investment in the Amazon. In Surinam, Gerold Stahel shifted his attention to rice cultivation, but he continued to observe the rubber trees that had not been felled. By 1927, he was suggesting to Dutch investors that Hevea might be practical, despite the continued lack of blight-resistant material. He thought it could be planted along the coast, since offshore winds inhibited development of conidia. This suggestion was not heeded, possibly because the Dutch were aware from experience in the East Indies that Hevea is subject to damage and delayed growth from strong winds.[45]

In 1928, Goodyear planted a small estate on Mindanao. The Philippines were unpromising, since labor was more expensive than in Malaya or Sumatra, and the Philippine legislature refused to waive the legal limit of 1,000 hectares on plantations, out of concern that the United States might renege on its pledge to grant independence if U.S. investments were to increase. For Goodyear, however, it was of interest that the Philippines remained outside the cartel. Goodyear assembled a large clone collection there and tried to improve labor productivity. In 1935, the company acquired 1,130 hectares of land in the Panama Canal Zone, probably under the stimulus of the second rubber cartel. Soon afterward, Goodyear bought 400 hectares in Costa Rica that in 1924 or 1925 had been planted to rubber by the United Fruit Company. To these properties Goodyear transferred its Southeast Asian clones. The disconcerted Goodyear staff found that South American Leaf Blight was already present, a thousand miles beyond the range of any native stand of Hevea. They were obliged to shift from a commercial to an experimental mode, and to begin a search for resistant material. That was the reason for Bangham's two visits to the Ford plantations, when an exchange of clones was arranged.[46]

In October 1936, James R. Weir visited Goodyear's Central American estates to select clones to bring back to Belterra. Possibly to repay Bangham's earlier snub in kind, he reported pessimistically on Goodyear's choice of terrain and planting methods. He believed that the leaf blight had long been present, introduced in a small thirty-year-old grove at Turrialba that Goodyear had also purchased, and then very likely spread by the staff itself. Weir's poor opinion of Goodyear's prospects was reaffirmed three years later by C. A. Pringle, one of Townsend's assistants, who reported that estate practices and the quality of labor was better at Belterra.[47]

Brazilian capital did not fill the breach opened by reluctant foreign capitalists. The formation of the second international rubber cartel awakened less response than had the first. In Bahia perhaps another 100,000 trees were planted in the late 1920s, and in São Paulo the state Agronomic Institute carried out some experimental planting at Ubatuba, on the coast. In the Amazon there were only two other plantations of note during the 1930s: a tract of 115,000 trees at Parintins, in Amazonas state, begun in 1931 by Japanese colonists, and a smaller tract near Manaus begun in 1935 by Cosme Ferreira Filho, a public advocate of rubber planting. Neither of these groves was properly tended. Brazilians clearly were not sanguine concerning the prospects of Brazilian rubber, planted or wild, even in a world market artificially supported.[48]

The Brazilian demand for rubber was quite small and did not increase during the 1930s. A study carried out for the Ministry of Labor, Industry, and Commerce calculated that imports of manufactured rubber products in all forms had declined from 8,891 tons in 1929 to 6,343 tons in 1937, while domestic manufacturers of rubber, already including some small Brazilian-owned tire and tube factories in Belém, Rio de Janeiro, and São Paulo, increased their consumption from only 544 to 2,759 tons during the same period. The shift to domestic manufacture was nevertheless clear. By 1940, Pirelli, Firestone, and Goodyear all had opened factories in São Paulo, and a Brazilian firm in Rio de Janeiro with technical assistance from Seiberling had also expanded its output. Together they nearly doubled the internal consumption of raw rubber.[49]

Vargas's government, with strong tendencies toward autarkical economic policies, favored manufacturing development and was alive to the necessity of satisfying the increased demand for raw materials that would result. The military command foresaw an expanded requirement for tires in case Brazil was drawn into the war. Nevertheless, they sensed no great urgency to shift production from the gathered to the planted product. There lingered the belief that wild rubber was superior to cultivated rubber, and it appeared feasible to intensify gathering activities. Paul LeCointe's estimate of 300 million wild trees was often cited to demonstrate that 60,000 or even 100,000 tons of wild rubber could be obtained, if transport for northeastern laborers could be arranged. A debate was carried on before the Federal Foreign Trade Council, Vargas's central planning agency, concerning the advisability of creating a national rubber institute. Such institutes – cartels in fact – had been created in coffee, sugar, and alcohol, pine logging, and cacao. The plan was combated and finally defeated by Amazon gathering interests, who seemed to resent government intervention, even if the purpose was mainly to raise domestic prices. They may also have suspected that the institute would have promoted the development of competitive plantations.[50]

The Ford plantations, then, remained the only significant attempt in Brazil to cultivate rubber. They represented an experiment on a vast scale, costly, blundering, and of uncertain promise. Brazilians were only vaguely aware of the struggle that had taken place there and the succession of trials that would yet have to be undertaken in order to determine the practicality of large-scale and competitive rubber planting in the presence of a virulent and apparently indomitable parasite. The market conditions of the interwar period had been extremely discouraging, restricting investment and clouding prospects for long-term development. Yet new economic forces were emerging, even as Brazil was drawn into the world conflict. Still more resources were being marshaled to be flung into the Amazon, to preserve the Ford estates and greatly intensify the search for solutions to the problem of leaf blight.

6

The battle for rubber, 1940–1945

The outbreak of war in Europe presented the industrial economy of the United States with daunting supply problems, of which rubber was the most critical. It had not been stockpiled, although some government officials had foreseen the shortage. It was discovered that U.S. chemical companies had no clear idea how synthetic rubber might be produced, since they had allowed themselves to be misled by their German cartel partners. A frantic search therefore began on several fronts to obtain the necessary supplies. One of these fronts was Brazil, where, it was suddenly recalled, Ford owned two vast rubber plantations and 300 million wild trees were waiting to be tapped, lacking only a remunerative price and American supervision. Thus a second wave of U.S. technical assistance, equipment, and capital engulfed the Amazon, this time in a deluge.

It was not until the German invasion of the Netherlands and France that measures to guarantee a rubber supply began to be taken. Suddenly the fate of the rubber-growing colonies was in doubt, given the evident interest of the Japanese imperialists in Southeast Asia and the much increased danger of German submarine warfare in the Atlantic. A Rubber Reserve Company was formed 28 June 1940 to buy rubber with a fund of $140 million provided by its parent agency, the Reconstruction Finance Corporation. The United States was consuming rubber at a rate of 50,000 tons a month, and was obliged to pay twenty cents a pound, since the international rubber cartel continued to restrict output and set prices.[1]

While the Rubber Reserve Company was attempting to accumulate a stock of rubber, the U.S. Department of Agriculture (USDA) sought a commission to investigate the possibility of increasing rubber cultivation in the Western Hemisphere. A meeting called by Agriculture Secretary Henry Wallace on 10 May 1940 brought together his technical staff, State Department representatives, and the heads of several rubber companies. It was decided to carry out a field survey and establish cooperating experimental stations in several countries. This survey, for which Congress provided $500,000, was to be more than a reprise of the interrupted program of the early 1920s. By now it was clear that rubber planting in the Western Hemisphere would require selection and breeding for disease resistance, a program that would require at least twenty years to bear fruit. It would appear that within the USDA, scientific activists were planning a long-term presence in tropical America. Taking advantage of the sense of emergency current in the administration, they were laying the groundwork for what might indeed be a brilliant coup, with potentially huge consequences for the international trade balance and military security of the United States.[2]

The calculation behind this expensive venture was that South American Leaf Blight would eventually reach Southeast Asia. If in the meantime the USDA could develop clones that combined high resistance with high productivity, then rubber plantations in the Western Hemisphere would enjoy a very considerable advantage. The United States would in such a case no longer be at the mercy of a British- and Dutch-controlled cartel. Instead, assuming that Latin America would be even more securely within its sphere of influence after the war, the United States would have every prospect of controlling the market itself.

The task of rubber investigations was assigned within the USDA to the Bureau of Plant Industry, which established a headquarters at Goodyear's plantation at Turrialba, Costa Rica. Other stations were opened or reactivated at Los Diamantes, near Goodyear's other experimental plantation in Costa Rica; at Marfranc, in Haiti; at United Fruit's experimental station at Tela, in Honduras; at Tezonapa, in Vera Cruz, Mexico; at Iquitos, Tingo María and Oromina, in Peru; and at Goodyear's plantation in the Canal Zone. Survey teams were sent to Central America and the Caribbean and to Colombia, Peru, and Bolivia. Their immediate purpose was to locate surviving planted stands of rubber, observe the conditions of the remnant trade in wild Castilla and other sorts of rubber, and collect seeds and seedlings of promising specimens of Hevea.

In October 1940, Elmer W. Brandes was sent by the Department of Agriculture to Rio de Janeiro, where he signed an agreement with Alvaro Fagundes, representing the Brazilian Ministry of Agriculture, authorizing the operation of a survey team in Brazil and the establishment of an experimental nursery at Belém, on the grounds of the Agronomic Institute of the North (IAN). This institute, under the Ministry of Agriculture, had been formed only the year before. Present at the negotiation was Felisberto Cardoso de Camargo, a graduate of the University of Florida School of Agiculture and an expert in citrus, soon to be appointed the IAN's director. The Ford plantations agreed to collaborate in this operation by providing the IAN with the clones Ford had obtained from Southeast Asia and the upper Amazon and with the hybrids resulting from their breeding program.

The Ministry of Agriculture agreed to an exchange of Hevea materials on a very large scale. The Americans had at their disposal a considerable stock of clonal seeds and budwood that Goodyear had just shipped to its Panama and Costa Rica stations from its Philippine plantation. Walter E. Klippert, of the Goodyear company, had already negotiated directly with the IAN for the exchange of some of this material. The Americans also had prospects of obtaining Southeast Asian clones from Firestone's Liberian plantation. These materials they proposed to trade for a share of whatever selections their own plant investigators, accompanied by Brazilian specialists, might make in the upper Amazon.

The Brazilian government, in signing this and other agreements, such as that which permitted the construction of United States air bases on its territory, was embarking on a perilous course. In November 1937, Getúlio Vargas, seeking to maintain himself in power, had carried out a coup d'état with army support. The new regime, called *Estado Novo*, in imitation of European Fascist experiments, was nationalist, authoritarian, and corporativist. In regard to economic matters, it was even more *dirigiste* than Vargas's prior administration. His generals were clearly pro-Axis, and there was a domestic Fascist movement that had tried to overthrow Vargas and had nearly succeeded. The Estado Novo nevertheless reluctantly subordinated itself to United States demands in the hope that it might be permitted to survive a war that it calculated the Allies would win. Even so, its acceptance of U.S. interference was conditional and ran counter to deep nationalist sensibilities.

Collaboration with Brazil and with the director of the Belém station was of primary importance to the USDA researchers. They were convinced that in the territory of Acre and in the northern part of Mato Grosso they would find trees combining superior productivity and resistance to the South American Leaf Blight that would make possible the restoration of Western Hemisphere rubber to the world market. They required as well a testing ground for resistance to the blight, situated within the zone in which it was epidemic. The export of Ford materials, furthermore, would also require the acquiescence of the Brazilians, especially if it was to be carried out on a large and continuing scale.[3]

The project was nearly done in, however, by news coming out of Bolivia concerning the activities of the team sent to that country. It was led by Carl D. LaRue, who had gotten leave from his post at the University of Michigan. LaRue had entered Bolivia with the intention of exporting Hevea budwood for use at Turrialba. Bolivia lacked entirely facilities that might have provided even the appearance of exchange; therefore, it is not clear on what grounds the USDA expected the Bolivians to collaborate. LaRue wrote Brandes that he had obtained from the Bolivian minister of the treasury oral permission to collect and export the material, but that he was told to draw up a written agreement with Napoleón Solares, a senator and the manager of the largest rubber export house, Suárez Hermanos. Solares invited LaRue to visit his wild rubber groves, apparently under the impression that LaRue represented

American interests that were preparing to invest in Bolivian plantations. When LaRue pressed him instead for written permission to collect, Solares at first declared himself without authority to do so, and then he denounced LaRue publicly.[4]

LaRue had been instructed to cross the border at Acre when his mission in Bolivia was completed, in order to take up the direction of the Brazilian rubber survey. Brandes, realizing that LaRue's presence would fatally compromise the USDA, sent him to Central America instead, whence he was soon returned to Michigan. Very likely LaRue had been trapped in an imbroglio whose intent had been to embarrass the United States, yet Brandes thought it worthwhile to lecture him on the proper attitude to adopt in eliciting the co-operation of local officials. He should have been "scornful of what *they* have and concentrate on telling them the virtues of the high-yielding clones *we* have to offer. That was the course I took in Rio." Brandes hastened to limit the damage the faux pas would cause when it became known in Brazil. He would, in his future correspondence with Brazilian authorities, "emphasize that collections of budwood (or seeds) for planting in the country are uppermost in our minds. We have permission to remove such material from the country, but certainly that feature should not be given more than passing mention if it is necessary to mention it at all."[5]

Much damage had already been done, however. Bolivia sent Solares to Brazil as ambassador, a platform from which he expounded to the press his opinion that the Americans had found a variety of Hevea resistant to the leaf blight and had wanted to smuggle it out of Bolivia. The Bolivian Congress, annoyed by the LaRue incident, had already passed a law against the export of rubber seeds. The Brazilian press carried on a furious campaign against the survey teams. In South America the Wickham myth had evidently inspired even more profound feelings than in England or Asia.[6]

C. B. Manifold, who took LaRue's place as head of the survey in Brazil, tried hard to mollify the newspapers. He issued press releases that claimed that "there was no occasion for fear or concern," since "everything is being done fairly and for their interests" and with "the full and enthusiastic support of the officials of the Brazilian government." Manifold seemed to be unaware that the press might be expressing in fact the veiled animosity of the Estado Novo. He explained that it was necessary to locate Hevea trees that might be high-yielding and resistant, but then he went on to assert that the United States already possessed Southeast Asian clones that were five times as productive as ordinary trees and that research stations outside Brazil had already found strains of Hevea that were resistant, leaving the reader to wonder what further use there was to collecting more seed in Brazil.[7]

More effective in calming doubts about American intentions was the dispatch by the USDA to Belém, on 5 February 1941, of 204,000 seeds and 200 budded stumps of Southeast Asian clones from Panama, part of the Goodyear collection brought from the Philippines. The delivery was carried out ostentatiously on three army air force bomber aircraft. In return the IAN provided 1.5 tons of unselected rubber seeds, suitable for use as rootstock in order, as Brandes disingenuously put it, "to establish nurseries on which a superior budwood can be multiplied for Brazil." Goodyear had already sent 204,000 clonal seeds to the IAN in November, in exchange for the potentially much more valuable Ford selections. In March the USDA sent another 500 budded stumps, this time in return for five tons of Belém seed. The rubber exchange, for good or ill, had begun.[8]

No matter what the interpretation that U.S. propaganda put upon these exchanges, or what the Brazilian public might have made of them, Brandes was quite explicit in his instructions to Manifold in Belém: "The Philippine clonal seed are of course only for our investigational program." He intended, in other words, that the "donated" clonal material be subjected in Belém to tests for resistance to the leaf blight, in order to evaluate its utility for planting in Panama and Costa Rica. Reciprocity with the Brazilians was thus not exactly symmetrical.[9]

This attitude may have derived from the sense Brandes and Manifold had acquired of the limited readiness of their Brazilian counterparts to accept American direction. Manifold was reporting to Brandes that Camargo lacked control over his assistants at the IAN and that the authorities at higher levels were entirely uncooperative. He was plagued with supernumeraries sent him by Brazilian authorities who were technically unprepared but eager to partake in the potential profits from what they thought were American plans to invest in more plantations. Those Brazilians who were competent suffered their government's indifference, and even medical neglect, so that those accompanying one American team all came down with malaria and typhoid and had to drop out. The Brazilian staff at the IAN, Manifold reported on 12 January 1941, encouraged him to send most of the collections to Turrialba, since nothing had yet been done to prepare nurseries. Manifold said they were "disgusted and ashamed of their government." His own feeling was that the Brazilians were "only friendly on the surface," and "only want to get something out of us."[10]

The apparent preference of the Americans for Central American rubber development may also have derived from the close and growing collaboration of the USDA field workers with the Goodyear company. Several of them had had earlier experience on the Goodyear plantations in Malaya, Sumatra, and the Philippines, and Goodyear had already clearly made its commitment to Central America. The Ford plantations were by comparison remote from these interlocking professional relationships and, it was probably easy for the first survey teams to observe, not at all as promising places for their own future employment. In 1942, the USDA stationed a former Goodyear employee, Lawrence A. Beery, Jr., at Belterra to advise Townsend and his assistants.

Later writings by USDA personnel seem to credit Beery for work that had been well under way at Belterra and Fordlandia before his arrival.

Meanwhile, Manifold and his assistants were collecting seeds and seedlings in wild groves in the Acre territory and Mato Grosso. This was slow and not very productive work, because seed fall occurred at different seasons in different localities, the crop varied unpredictably, and seeds were quickly eaten by animals. The search for seeds of high-yielding trees was probably frustrated in part by the leaf blight. Since Microcyclus attacks flowers as well as leaves, seed output of high-yielding trees, which are also the least resistant, is relatively low, other factors being equal. The Americans, of course, were hoping to find what had never yet been found – mother trees that were resistant as well as high yielders of rubber – yet they were under pressure to return quickly and were not able to make careful ecological observations.[11]

Nevertheless small collections of promising material were sent to Belém. These remittances, which included species of Hevea other than *H. brasiliensis*, were divided up, some to be planted at Belém, some for forwarding to Turrialba. The Secretariat of Agriculture of the state of Amazonas also generously contributed seeds of *H. spruceana*, half a ton of which was sent to Turrialba. In September the more resistant of the Ford selections were brought to Belém from Belterra. In October and November Belém received some 800,000 seeds, by way of the USDA quarantine station at Coconut Grove, Florida. This was half of a shipment of fourteen Southeast Asian clone combinations from the Firestone plantation in Liberia.

All these materials were planted at the IAN by U.S. agronomists and their Brazilian collaborators. By early 1942 there were more than a million seedlings undergoing trials there. The Americans noted the appearance of leaf blight among the new plantings as early as March 1941. Unharmed seedlings were deliberately infected in order to test their resistance. Several hundred of them at first appeared promising, and it was thought that a number of the clones were sufficiently resistant for commercial planting. By the end of 1942, however, it was evident that none of the Goodyear selections was resistant in Belém. With more dismay it was noted that clones that showed high resistance in Brazil were not proving resistant in Central America. Even some of the Ford selections, resistant at Belterra, were susceptible at Belém. It began to be suspected that undetected environmental differences or variability in the pathogen were the causes, and that field trials might consequently be much more costly and time-consuming. At Turrialba, Michael H. Langford reported, as though it were a novelty not already noted long before in Surinam, that seedlings could be protected in the nursery by spraying Bordeaux mixture.[12]

With the entrance of the United States into the war on 7 December 1941, and the simultaneous Japanese attacks on the rubber colonies of the British, French, and Dutch, the long-range efforts of the Bureau of Plant Industry were overshadowed by the immediate need for rubber. Despite considerable advances in the chemistry of artificial rubbers in other countries, notably in the Soviet Union and Germany, almost no artificial rubber was yet being produced in the United States. Furthermore, the characteristics of the artificial product, which was optimistically but inappropriately called synthetic, were such that for most applications it was necessary to blend it with natural rubber. The stockpile of rubber accumulated at the beginning of the war was therefore rapidly dwindling. The British government, after the entrance of the United States into the war, agreed to a rubber pool that made available to the latter a portion of the output of the plantations still in British hands in Ceylon and India. But this supply, along with the output of the Liberian property of the Firestone company, was expected to amount to no more than 115,000 tons a year, less than 10 percent of projected wartime requirements.[13]

Attention therefore shifted to wild rubber, which might conceivably be restored to the level of output of the boom years, or even beyond. The Rubber Reserve Company, meanwhile renamed the Rubber Development Corporation (RDC), was not optimistic about the prospects for such a project, yet it was obliged to press forward. The survey team that reported from Brazil early in 1941 guessed that there might be 200 million wild Hevea trees in the Amazon valley, with a potential yield of 667,000 tons a year, but they thought that, in practical terms, 100,000 tons might be extracted. It was hard to say how much investment might be necessary in order to achieve that goal, however. More tappers would have to be brought into the region, and more supplies would have to be injected into supply channels. An output of 100,000 tons a year implied, according to the survey's optimistic calculation, 100,000 tappers, to be drawn most probably from the arid and impoverished northeast, as in the days of the boom. It could be foreseen that so large and rapid an inflow of labor implied further investment in river craft, receiving stations, food storage depots, and medical facilities.[14]

The Brazilian government broke relations with the Axis powers on 28 January 1942. It had already instituted a system of preferences in behalf of domestic rubber manufacturers who supplied essential auto and truck tire replacements and it had taken control of all rubber sales. On 3 March 1942, Brazil entered into an agreement with the United States government to participate in a joint effort to increase rubber output. This agreement was similar to others signed by the United States with the other rubber-producing countries in the Western Hemisphere. Brazil was to export its rubber exclusively to the United States for a period of five years at a minimum price set at first at thirty-nine cents a pound, later raised to forty-five cents, with a bonus of up to thirty cents a pound for deliveries over 10,000 tons. The Brazilians were required to ship only what was in excess of their own requirements and they were to receive financial and material assistance in providing the infrastructure needed to expand the trade.[15]

A series of new organizations was created to stimulate expansion. The centerpiece was the Rubber Credit Bank in which the RDC bought a minority interest. The bank was to exercise a monopoly in the finance and operation of the trade. Other government agencies were to enlist tappers, expand transport, increase food supply, and provide medical assistance. General direction was invested, on the Brazilian side, in a Commission to Control the Washington Accords and in the Office of the Coordinator of Economic Mobilization. On the American side, the RDC moved in more personnel to offices in Manaus, Belém, and Rio de Janeiro. The Office of the Coordinator of Inter-American Affairs financed the food supply and medical functions of the Brazilian agencies and detailed personnel to participate in those operations. The U.S. embassy in Rio de Janeiro exercised an overall, albeit indirect, supervision.

The RDC officers were immediately confronted by the realities of the rubber trade. The survey team had described for them the patron system, which remained intact from the days of the boom: Commercial forwarders, or aviadores, in Belém and Manaus sent foodstuffs, tools, kerosene, and weapons to the patron. The patron sold these to his work force on credit and bought the rubber they gathered, discounting his advances. He shipped the rubber downriver to his aviador, who in turn discounted his own advances. The typical patron, who by now had come to be known by the more elegant term *seringalista*, was more often an absentee landlord residing in Manaus than a simple storekeeper, and often he was the owner of numerous wild groves. The typical seringueiro, the survey team found, was paid 3 cruzeiros, or 15 cents, per kilogram, while his storekeeper, or those whom he represented, received 1.25 cruzeiros, or 6.25 cents. Prices of supplies at the seringalista's store, however, were set so as to leave the tapper with nothing in his pocket at the end of the season. The tapper was prohibited, as part of the agreement under which he was engaged, from selling his rubber to other dealers, and the storekeeper often employed gunmen to enforce that agreement and discourage runaways.[16]

In Manaus and Belém the Americans encountered the elite of the trade, a small number of aviadores of whom the principal was a Syrian immigrant named Chamié, a person not inclined to sacrifice his business interests to the war effort. In fact, he was said to be hoarding 8,000 tons of rubber on the expectation that the ceiling price would eventually be raised. Frank Nattier, Jr., of the Office of the Coordinator of Inter-American Affairs, commented that Chamié's opponents were nearly all men exactly like him who merely wanted to take his place, "The methods, the quarrels and the manner of thinking of these people are fantastic. The situation in all respects resembles a musical comedy, except in the deadly seriousness of its implications."[17]

The RDC, presuming that higher pay to the tappers would stimulate them to bring in more rubber, attempted to bypass this system. It promised to pay prices that were nearly triple those paid by the seringalistas. W. E. Klippert, by now working for the RDC in Costa Rica, used this strategy among the Castilla gatherers and quintupled their output. But in the Amazon the RDC was obliged to provide the tappers with supplies as well, since the seringalistas simply increased the prices they charged in their stores in order to sop up the tappers' new purchasing power. The RDC did not dispose of sufficient river craft to provide supplies, however, and thus the rubber supply, after a year of operations on the river, fell far short of expectations. The RDC reported 24,000 tons produced in all the Amazon countries in 1943, 5,000 tons more than the year before, but of this amount only 10,000 tons were shipped to the United States, an increase of only 3,000 tons.[18]

The embassy at last decided that the only hope of increasing exports was to collaborate with the satraps who controlled the trade; in mid-October 1943, it made this recommendation to the secretary of state. While admitting that "No darker picture exists anywhere of what in more progressive societies we choose to call corruption and exploitation," nevertheless, it had been a mistake to ignore "the established society, with its century-old tentacles stretching up all the thousands of tributaries." The intermediaries had "sabotaged even our wisest efforts." What was necessary then, was to turn the entire system "back to the Brazilians" and let them bring the rubber to the docks.[19]

The RDC could not avoid this solution, since it was showing no result and was mired in confusion. Its offices spread chaotically across Manaus and Belém, staffed with personnel whose functions were undefined. It was unable to account for money it had spent, nor could it hide one colossal blunder. Persuaded by an interested party that more rubber would be forthcoming from the tappers if the RDC found a market for the Brazil nuts they gathered in the off-season, it had purchased the 1942 crop for a million dollars. It had then been unable to find transport for the nuts, and finally had to sell them locally, realizing only $75,000! A letter by a Commerce Department functionary to Jesse Jones, the director of the Reconstruction Finance Corporation, still the RDC's parent organization, described its operations as "the worst example of bad planning, misinformed policies, lack of experienced administration and disorganization I have seen in 22 years of Latin American observations."[20]

The new policy failed to unleash the productive forces of the Amazon. Total output in the region (including Peru, Colombia, and Bolivia) increased in 1944 by no more than 6,000 tons – only a thousand tons greater than the increase of the year before – for a total of just 30,000 tons. Some of this had emerged from hoarded stocks, most probably. The aviadores were quite uninterested in increasing output when the same or better profit rate might be made by keeping rubber scarce and by absorbing all the additional income available from the higher prices and the increased stock of trade goods the Americans were willing to provide. The Rubber Credit Bank was quite unable to enforce its regulation specifying that the gatherers were to receive at least 60 percent of the price paid the seringalista, nor was it able to inspect prices paid for foodstuffs in the seringalistas' general stores. Field technicians of the RDC reported that the workers were forced in consequence to shift from tapping to hunting and fishing in order to survive.[21]

The services established to provide labor, transport, and medical care, and the RDC itself, had been reduced to the status of auxiliaries in a battle whose outcome was now depressingly obvious. The Brazilian government in February 1943 turned the recruitment of tappers from outside the region into a quasimilitary operation, contracting them for two years, paying advances and promising family allowances, and furnishing transportation. The conditions in transit were vile; the medical services supposedly for their benefit were largely applied in Manaus, Belém, and lesser towns; the delivery of supplies was ineffectual; and the family allowances were delayed or unpaid. Total immigration of tappers was inadequately recorded, but has been estimated at 32,000. It is likely that many of these laborers lingered only briefly in the wild groves and some never reached them at all, at best replacing local workers who had shifted from some other employment into rubber gathering.[22]

Manifold's survey team had not overlooked the small planted stands of Hevea scattered along the lower reaches of the Amazon, and the RDC technicians made constant efforts to revive them. Their estimates of the number of these groves ranged up to 2,000. On the lower Tapajós alone, near the Ford plantations, there were some 450, containing 375,000 trees. It had been the habit of smallholders to tap only when prices were high, thus the trees had been neglected for several years. In general, output from these trees was very low, not surprisingly, since as survivors of leaf blight, they were evidently resistant. Their yields were so low, in fact, that smallholders usually departed for the wild rubber groves and left their families in charge of the these low-yielding stands. The high price of rubber nevertheless encouraged constant planting during the war; on the lower Tapajós, at least 100,000 more trees appeared.[23]

Interestingly, some smallholders devised independently a planting technique that had already been employed by Javanese peasants who were, like the Amazonians, practicants of slash-and-burn farming in highland areas. Hevea seeds were planted, two or three to a clump, among the household subsistence crops in the customary burned clearings. When the field was abandoned after three years, the rubber trees were left to shade out weed growth and form a stand that had involved little extra effort to create. This procedure, the Americans observed, did not allow enough head start for the trees, and they recommended eliminating the less successful of the seedlings in each clump, in order to stimulate the growth of the most vigorous. The smallholdings were suffering low yields, they thought, partly because seed was unselected, locations had been chosen that were too dry, too wet, or sandy, and cultivation had been inadequate. But they also saw that the stands were affected by leaf blight, which had seriously retarded their growth.[24]

Of the larger commercial plantations, most of them dating from the collapse of the rubber boom, none was restored to production. The 115,000–tree stand at Parintins, planted by Japanese colonists in 1931, was taken over by the government of the state of Amazonas, which appears to have been unable to operate it. Reports suggest that the trees may have been so unproductive that tapping was uneconomic.[25]

The Ford plantations received waves of observers from the RDC and the USDA who watched the leaf blight ravage the groves. Felisberto Camargo recalled that he was "desolate" to see on his visit in late 1942, what he thought were millions of trees "dying from top to bottom in a fearful manner." The rains were exceptionally heavy that year, and Townsend's assistant, J. A. Zilles, reported that some blocks would have to be entirely replanted. In 1942, the rains were again heavy and another epidemic occurred; new foliage in most of the areas that had not been top grafted was lost. By then Townsend and Johnston were committed to top grafting. In the 1941 season, clone gardens had been greatly expanded and enough material was produced to graft 322,000 trees by March of the following year. By the end of March 1943, another 820,000 trees had been grafted. Top grafting then went on continuously, reaching as many as 400,000 trees a month through the end of 1945. This furious pace was necessary because the first attempt at grafting was successful no more than half the time. On trees that had to be lopped before grafting to prevent the spread of infection, the initial rate of success was much lower.[26]

The leaf blight struck again in 1944 and 1945. By then it was becoming apparent that some of the canopy clones chosen for resistence were proving susceptible. The grafts made with *Hevea guianensis* and *H. spruceana* appeared more promising, but some of them showed susceptibility to a *Phytophthora* leaf blight. And the Ford staff could not yet be sure that rubber from these grafts would be of commercial quality. These repeated setbacks finally convinced even Archibald Johnston that new plantings would have to be limited until the breeding experiments had produced clones combining high resistance and competitive yields. The laborious work of cross-pollination therefore was pressed forward: Sixty thousand hand pollinations were carried out in the 1943 season alone. But the trees thus produced could not yet provide yield data.[27]

Meanwhile, rubber tapping had begun on the older groves at Fordlandia. This rubber cost a remarkably high thirty-five cents a pound, taking only operating expenses into account, yet the RDC's price table made it worthwhile to proceed. In 1941 at Fordlandia, some 171,000 trees had come into production, along with 36,000 at Belterra. The combined output of these trees, 63,636 kilograms, implies an extremely inadequate 75 kilograms per hectare. Three years later, there were only 260,000 trees in tap on the two estates. Yield had risen to 103,619 kilograms, or 110 kilograms per hectare at Fordlandia and 170 kilograms at Belterra. In Sumatra, even peasant smallholders achieved better than twice that amount by the 1930s. Worse yet, only 10 percent of the trees were even then available to tap. Johnston continued to lament the lack of additional labor, but had he obtained all he could use, no more than another 50,000 trees were in condition to be worked. Again, it is clear that the supply of labor was not the limiting factor in Ford's continuing difficulties.[28]

Field technicians of the RDC were sent to Bahia to examine the potential for expanding exports of Mangabeira and Maniçoba rubbers. There they were told of the Hevea trees that had been planted in the panhandle of South Bahia at various times since 1909. They were led to believe by Dr. Heitor Cordeiro, of the Cacao Institute at Ilhéus, that there were as many as two million Hevea trees in the region, all of them ready to tap; but an initial survey by Michael Polli in late September 1942 suggested that no more than 400,000 trees were tappable. Still, even that figure might represent 1,000 or even 2,000 tons of rubber, and southern Bahia was accessible, less fever-ridden, and endowed with a sizable labor force. The Belém experimental station was notified, and sent one of its staff to assist with tapping methods. C. B. Manifold carried out a more careful study of existing groves and found that there were, in fact, fewer than 80,000 tappable trees.[29]

Polli had observed leaf blight, and it soon became evident that it was a serious limitation in Bahia. Indeed, several of the field technicians reported that they had never seen blight so intense in the Amazon. Conditions for the spread of the fungus were apparently ideal in the 1943 and 1944 seasons, so that the Americans were presented with the spectacle of plantations almost completely defoliated, sometimes three times in the space of six months. Nevertheless, in scattered locations the disease did not appear, and very small stands, of 150 or fewer, were often spared. Yields, it was observed, did not decline as much as might be expected from the extreme loss of foliage, possibly because tapping was very conservative and was interrupted in order to gather seeds for sale to other planters. Seed sales began to boom as other landowners once again waxed enthusiastic about the long-term prospects of rubber in the region.[30]

The small amount of rubber forthcoming from these groves was shipped to São Paulo. Partial data suggests that only thirty-five kilograms per hectare was being obtained by late 1943. The Americans advised against planting any material except resistant selections from Belém or Belterra, but nurseries were formed, nevertheless, with seeds fallen from local trees. The Americans considered much of this work, including that of Cordeiro, incompetently and hastily done, and they kept their distance from it. They limited themselves to demonstrating tapping methods and the use of rubber presses, suggesting the use of sprays to control the blight in nurseries, and looking for blight-resistant specimens in the producing groves.[31]

In British Guiana there were 64,000 trees still standing of the groves planted before World War I. The RDC sent a field technician there as well, since the rubber agreement with the British government had placed its Western Hemisphere colonies within the American sphere. Neither American nor British agricultural reports mention leaf blight during the war years. Instead, the principal limitation on output was considered to be the low productivity of the inexperienced tappers. Output per tapper reached 520 kilograms, about the same as that of wild rubber gatherers. Exports of Hevea rubber from British Guiana reached 130 tons, then declined to 99 tons in 1946, averaging 283 kilograms per hectare. Trinidadian export data indicates that rubber production peaked there in 1946 at 225 tons, but yield rates are not available, and it is not clear whether other kinds of rubber were included in the data. In neither of these colonies did the high wartime price of rubber stimulate new planting. In Surinam there was no revival either in production or in planting.[32]

In Belém the USDA researchers carried on with little supervision from the RDC or the IAN. The RDC was not interested in long-term projects that offered no prospect of an immediate increase in rubber output, even though it recognized that the program might be useful in cementing Brazilian collaboration. Felisberto Camargo, director of the IAN, was the Brazilian government's designated rubber specialist, yet he felt it necessary to divert most of his efforts to strengthening his own position within the bureaucracy.

Camargo spent most of 1942 obtaining permission to establish field stations at Porto Velho, Rio Branco, and Cametá where, among other projects, rubber clones might be given local trials. In order to amass a large quantity of budding stock for those stations, he opposed any planting at Belém at all that year. Camargo worked even harder to achieve autonomy for the IAN from the Ministry of Agriculture, a goal he realized partially in January 1943 through a decree that attached the institute directly to the cabinet of the ministry and reserved to it the responsibility for the development of rubber nationwide. On the other hand, Camargo expended a good deal of his political strength by supporting the RDC's attempt to eliminate middlemen in the wild gathering trade, a stand that earned him the hatred of the aviadores of Belém. These activities further alienated the Americans at the IAN, who considered them a waste of Camargo's energies.[33]

The USDA researchers meanwhile continued to send seeds, supposedly for rootstock, to Central America, a total of more than 1.3 million in the first months of 1942, and their survey teams under Karl Butler and James Baldwin continued to collect promising materials in Acre and other remote gathering areas. They were especially concerned to make selections adapted to dry seasons and to the higher, cooler climates of Central America. Elmer W. Brandes told Camargo that the increased wartime river traffic represented "the greatest opportunity of a lifetime" to collect new genetic material. He pointed out that the Ford selections were based on too limited a population, and that even if a few clones were to prove highly resistant as well as high-yielding, they would lack "adaptibility to the divergent soils and climatic conditions of" – as he preferred to put it to Camargo – "the Amazon Valley." For this reason Brandes proposed that Camargo accept two more botanists to help with collecting, Russell Seibert and Carl Grassl, experienced scientists and, he hastened to assure Camargo, long-established Americans, despite their German surnames.[34]

Brandes waited in vain for authorization from the Ministry of Agriculture. Camargo had been seriously embarrassed by the activities of the American teams already in the field. His opponents in Belém had obtained mailing bags that Baldwin, without permission from Camargo, had ordered printed with labels encouraging Amazon inhabitants to send rubber seeds to the IAN. The Americans did not understand how bitter were Brazilian regional rivalries or how conveniently the rubber collection program might be used to intensify them. Camargo was not an Amazonian, but a native of São Paulo. His political support had come up to that moment from President Vargas and from the interior territories and states, who saw Camargo's field stations as a means of spreading agriculture throughout the valley and reducing the commercial monopoly of Belém. Camargo was therefore obliged to cover himself by complaining directly to the minister of agriculture and to the coordinator of economic mobilization. He thereby alienated the U.S. embassy, which reported to Washington condescendingly on Camargo's "real or fancied grievances," doubted his "executive ability," and concluded that there was "little prospect of important constructive accomplishments at IAN in the near future."[35]

Despite Camargo's efforts, the outcome of this episode was a decree-law, published 21 July 1943, which prohibited the remittance of seeds or seedlings of Hevea anywhere outside of the Amazon valley without the prior authorization of the Ministry of Agriculture. The ministry enforced this law in accord with regional sensibilities. When Brandes pointed out to Alvaro Fagundes, in Rio de Janeiro, the extreme susceptibility of the southern Bahian plantations to leaf blight and suggested the advisability of sending them some of the Belém selections, he was not attended to. R. D. Rands, writing Manifold from Washington in December 1944, attributed this resistance to Camargo, but, in fact, the matter was out of his hands. Only in 1945 did Camargo manage to obtain an amended decree-law that devolved upon the IAN the authority to permit the transit of Hevea materials through the Amazon or out of it. There is much evidence to show that Camargo, throughout the war, remained convinced of the need for exchanges and confident in the genuineness of American reciprocity. He continued to offer them seeds and even encouraged Baldwin to go on with his collecting.[36]

At the same time that he confronted the scandal over Baldwin's mailing bags, Camargo was obliged to fend off an attack by none other than Valentim Bouças, the director of the Brazilian Commission to Control the Washington

Accords. Bouças, in his business magazine, the *Observador Econômico e Financeiro*, denigrated the entire selection and breeding program at the IAN. Basing his complaints on misreadings of the American reports of the early 1920s, he claimed that there was no leaf blight problem, that Ford's difficulties had been caused by mistaken site selection, and that the IAN should immediately begin forming nurseries to permit large-scale planting.[37]

Camargo easily countered these arguments and alleged that the animus behind them was his refusal to support government financing of rubber plantings by speculators to whom it mattered little if the seedlings lived or died. He pointed out that the Ford selections were already planted in Central America: If Brazil abandoned the research program, it would fall irretrievably behind in the race to develop commercially viable clones. Camargo could not resist responding intemperately to the prestigious and powerful Bouças, but Camargo did defend forcefully his principal thesis, which was that there was no point in planting Hevea rubber until clones could be developed that combined high resistance to South American Leaf Blight with yields that were equal to those of the newest and best of the Southeast Asian clones.[38]

Bouças was interviewed by a group of American journalists who were treated to a tour of the Amazon by the RDC in October 1943. They learned of his reputation for using public offices to promote his business interests. His advocacy of a moderate ceiling price for raw rubber was apparently not unrelated to his directorship of Goodyear's Brazilian subsidiary. Since there was no ceiling price on the tires Goodyear and Firestone sold abroad, they were reaping wonderful profits on their exports, which had grown to $1.8 million in 1943, ten times the value of two years before. The Goodyear company was represented in the Rubber Credit Bank as well, since one of its employees, Edward Long, occupied a place on the bank's board of directors, as a nominee of the RDC. Douglas H. Allen, head of the RDC, was for obvious reasons Bouças's main ally in holding down the price of raw rubber. Felisberto Camargo, the journalists reported, meanwhile had come around to advocating a reduced presence of the Americans in the trade and a higher price for rubber, as a way of stimulating the seringalistas to intensify operations and to pass some of their income on to the tappers. One or two of the American reporters were able to perceive the conflicts of interests inherent in these positions.[39]

All of the reporters were charmed by Camargo's ebullience and drive and impressed by his political courage. Camargo's long-range plan for Amazon rubber planting did indeed presuppose considerable courage. He called for nothing less than the downfall of the seringalistas and the creation of a class of cash-cropping smallholders. The scarcity of labor in the Amazon rendered plantation agriculture inevitably too costly to compete with Southeast Asia, he claimed. Furthermore, in Southeast Asia itself, the plantations were being outsold by peasant smallholders by the 1930s. Only the preferential supply of selected seed and budwood to the plantations had saved them from collapse.

In the Amazon, however, a Brazilian peasantry, once settled on lands most appropriate for Hevea and provided with superior genetic material by the IAN, might yet outsell their Malayan and Javanese counterparts. What was needed was to organize smallholding colonies, on which the smallholders would be assisted to carry on subsistence farming while they developed rubber groves and other cash crops.[40]

Central to this scheme was a selection and breeding program to create clones combining high productivity and high resistance. Camargo regarded the double grafting carried out at Belterra as unproved and excessively costly, and apparently he thought it too difficult to teach smallholders. He complained bitterly that there were still professional agriculturalists in the Amazon who refused to admit the gravity of the leaf blight. These he regarded as demagogues; above all, he insisted, it was necessary to proceed scientifically if the Amazon was to expand its economic base. The IAN's work would benefit the entire national economy if the price of Brazilian cultivated rubber could be made competitive in the world market. Camargo disparaged the option of a small protected domestic market. Brazilian industry and industrial consumers would be at an extreme disadvantage if truck and auto tires cost more in Brazil than in Argentina. On the contrary, he insisted, Brazil should seek to reduce the raw material costs of Brazilian rubber manufactures so as to enhance their overseas sales. Camargo's recommendations were sensible and his view of the future was realistic. Clearly, his suggestions also implied a strategic and expanding role for the research institution he headed.

Camargo pursued even further his visions of social and economic reconstruction in a last report to Vargas, dated 4 July 1945, which was never published. In it he called for rubber cultivation on a vast scale, vast enough to make Brazil a major supplier in the world market. He complained that the Rubber Credit Bank had not received to date a single loan request to plant rubber. He had challenged the Commercial Association of Manaus to assess their members to pay for the formation of rubber plantations, but they had proved unwilling. This demonstrated to Camargo that the "semi-feudal" economic system of the Amazon was incapable of installing rational agriculture. He therefore expounded his plan for government-sponsored smallholding, on a "collectivist" basis. He pointed to the Argentine colonization scheme in Misiones as a model. Taking into consideration numerous factors in rubber growing, he thought Rondônia the area of highest priority in which to begin such a colonization effort. To fund this project he advocated an income tax, deficit financing, and the commitment of 3 percent of federal revenues to the Amazon region.[41]

Camargo's memorandum scrambled together ideas then seemingly in political ascendancy. It was a plan, he admitted, more "geopolitical and military than agronomic," yet it bristled with data on clone yields, soils, and climatic conditions. It must have bewildered Vargas and his advisors, who could not have given it serious attention, beleaguered as they were by a reawakening liberal democratic opposition. The U.S. embassy, which obtained a copy of the plan, may have been alarmed at Camargo's characterization of the colonization scheme as "collectivist," yet the RDC and USDA technicians had consistently expressed their preference for smallholding and their revulsion for the seringalistas and aviadores. They thought large-scale plantations valuable mainly in the initial phase, principally for their demonstration effect, as training camps for prospective peasant proprietors. To some degree they may have been expressing an ideological preference that suffused the USDA under the populist Secretary of Agriculture Wallace, but those among them who had been employees of the Goodyear plantations in Sumatra and Malaya may well have drawn their own conclusions concerning the long-term social and economic advantages of peasant rubber growers.[42]

One of the Americans on the IAN staff provided a detached description of the smallholding plan. Norman Bakkedahl, on loan from the Bureau of Standards, managed the IAN rubber-testing laboratory. He explained that the government was to assign public land in five-hectare plots to colonists "who show good intentions." The government would finance the planting of 400 trees on each plot, which would leave sufficient land for subsistence crops. The colonists would be paid a small salary as long as they continued to cultivate the trees. If the trees were brought to maturity, the government would transfer title to the colonists. At the predicted postwar world price, the 400-tree grove would provide an income of $600 a year, eight times the average earnings of tappers in wild groves.[43]

The jaunt of the American journalists and an inspection tour by Senator Hugh Butler, a Nebraska Republican, in November 1943, caused enough scandal in Washington to force the RDC to change its course. In February 1944, the buying price of raw rubber was increased to 60 cents a pound, and many of the auxiliary services operated by the RDC were reduced or canceled. The supply of natural rubber from the Amazon was not improved by these actions. Brazilian rubber exports to the United States in the last year of the war did not increase above the 11,973 tons achieved in 1944. Natural rubber supply, despite the rapid development of synthetic substitutes and draconian measures of conservation, remained problematic, and constituted, according to a report of the special director of rubber programs in June 1945, "the most serious single obstacle to the attainment of 1946 production objectives."[44]

At Belterra, the American reporters had been told by Archibald Johnston that gathered rubber was costing the RDC $500 a pound, a little joke that Senator Butler was literal enough to take seriously. The corporation did indeed engineer failures of nearly that magnitude in Haiti, where it planted African Cryptostegia vines: Only 5.5 tons were harvested at a total cost of $7 million. In the southwestern United States, the RDC planted 34,000 hectares of Guayule (*Parthenium argentatum*), a desert shrub native to the region that yielded good quality rubber, but at a considerably higher cost than Hevea. No more than 200 tons of it was ever harvested, at a reported cost of $100 a pound.[45]

An audit of the accounts of the Brazilian office of the RDC in June 1945 revealed that its costs had exceeded income by $9.1 million since the beginning of its operations. These accounts do not seem to have included the expenses of the aviation service operated by the RDC through 1944, which amounted to $14.5 million. In addition, some $4 million of funds of the Office of the Coordinator of Inter-American Affairs were spent for public health services by late 1943: By war's end this expense may have amounted to $8 million. Adding up these charges, which probably fall short of reality, the rubber obtained from Brazil from mid-1942 to mid-1945 seems to have cost from 90 cents to $1.05 a pound. The RDC experiment demonstrated, if nothing else, that the aviadores and seringalistas could swindle the Americans as easily as they did their benighted tappers, and that even with an incentive four or five times that of the world price, they would not appreciably increase their output.[46]

More significant than the financial losses, as N. P. Alves Pinto has pointed out, was the reprieve granted the archaic and reactionary system of credit and distribution. The infusion of government funds, he notes, was a new and critical element in the revival of the gathering system. And its revival had cost many lives. It is impossible to say how many – this uncertainty is an aspect of the tragedy. The disappearance of workers drafted for rubber tapping was an issue raised in the federal Constituent Congress upon the fall of the Vargas dictatorship. It was estimated that 17,000 to 20,000 had not returned, a loss greater than that of the Brazilian expeditionary force that had fought in Italy. Lamentably, few American newspapers commented on the Brazilian inquiry or suggested that the United States bore any responsibility to help rescue the survivors of the "battle for rubber."[47]

Government intervention in the Amazon had at least one solid achievement to its credit. American and Brazilian funds, on a modest scale, had been applied to the solution of the problem of cultivation. The IAN continued to lay out experimental plots of Hevea during the final year of the war. A mixed staff of Brazilians and Americans produced 600,000 seedlings in 1944, and provided budwood for the substations at Porto Velho, Cametá, and Rio Branco. Collaboration with Belterra continued strong in the exchange and testing of clones. In addition to large-scale trials of Asian and Ford-developed clones, the IAN proceeded with crosses of material brought in by USDA collectors from Acre and Mato Grosso, and carried forward other lines of investigation. The American contribution to this effort cost the Bureau of Plant Industry some $50,000 a year.[48]

The Ford plantations had made at least as much progress. They had developed techniques of top grafting that were practical and effective, they had observed and made selections from a large collection of Hevea materials that they had obtained from diverse points in the Amazon basin, and they had carried out a first generation of crosses between these resistant materials and their Southeast Asian clones. Their four years of commercial tapping had demonstrated that top-grafted trees, including interspecific grafts, yielded latex that did coagulate and was of adequate quality, although they could not tell if the low yields might be caused in part by the influence of the canopy clones. The plantation had been a training ground for many of the small farmers who planted groves in the valley of the Tapajós and for many wild rubber tappers who spread the use of the Southeast Asian tapping knife far and wide.[49]

But the Ford presence in the Amazon was not to outlast the battle for rubber. The company once again sought a buyer for the properties. Goodyear apparently displayed some interest, but Ford withdrew its offer. In November 1945, the Ford board of directors decided to turn the plantations over to the Brazilian government for the sum of five million cruzeiros ($250,000), the amount Ford owed its workers under Brazilian laws concerning severance pay. It has been estimated that the two plantations had cost the company more than $20 million, although company accounts suggest that total expenditures to the end of December 1945, when the transfer was completed, amounted to no more than $12.8 million. The report of that month showed that the assets of the plantations came to $9,948,872. This may be exaggerated, since Johnston, just two years before, had valued them at $6,412,524.[50]

The basis for Ford's decision is not directly known, but it is clear that the company was abandoning its quest for vertical integration and already had sold off its tire plant. Furthermore, Ford was experiencing considerable financial difficulties and was selling off other unprofitable properties. The plantations were producing only 115 tons of rubber by 1945, about 2 percent of what the company had a right to expect from its 3.2 million trees. At the price the United States was paying for rubber, the plantation would not meet its current expenses unless at least 450 tons were sold, and the accords under which the subsidized price was offered would soon expire. Probably the directors were also concerned that natural rubber would in the near future face heavy competition from synthetics.[51]

In later years Ford's failure was explained in various ways. It was for some authors hard to believe that the great Henry Ford would have failed had he really wished to succeed. The size of his investment, committed only after the collapse of the first cartel, is sufficient response to that argument. Some Brazilian nationalists claimed that he was the victim of sabotage, practiced by technicians in the hire of the British-led cartel. Nothing in the documentation, however, suggests that the numerous errors committed by the staff were the result of character flaws graver than ignorance and willfulness. The scarcity or supposed fickleness of the workers has been mentioned by authors who were unaware of the presence of Microcyclus, or thought it relatively unimportant. The unproductiveness of the plantations was nevertheless apparent to the company: To cover its embarrassment it told its employees, near the end of the line, that the plantations had been "established as experimental stations, where pioneering would be done in the development of high-yielding, disease-resistant rubber trees."[52]

Had that been in fact their purpose, it might be said that the plantations had performed quite creditably. An immense and complex task had been well begun. Belterra and Fordlandia, with their small and largely self-taught staff, were the most advanced outposts of knowledge and practice of rubber cultivation in tropical America. Their clones, unproved as they were, nevertheless were the most valuable asset by far of those turned over to the Brazilian government. The carefully staked-out trial gardens, and those at the IAN, might yet form the basis for rational cultivation in the presence of South American Leaf Blight. But many more years of experiments were evidently necessary before that problem could be considered solved.*

There was now, however, a new obstacle in the path of further research in Brazil. The elite of the century-old, inefficient, and inhuman gathering system had been resuscitated by the United States and Brazilian governments at an enormous cost in resources and human suffering. They were now to set their faces against the rationalization of rubber production, no matter what additional waste of resources or continued suffering might ensue. Furthermore,

---

*It is impossible to avoid comparisons between the Ford plantations and the Jari estate, the work of Daniel K. Ludwig, an American shipping and mining billionaire. Jari was a 1.6 million hectare estate located along the river of the same name, near the mouth of the Amazon. In 1967, Ludwig initiated a forestry project there, on the expectation that a world paper pulp shortage was developing. Ludwig also engaged in rice cultivation in the river floodplain, exploited kaolin deposits, and planned to mine bauxite that was found on the property. By 1981, Ludwig had spent almost a billion dollars, three times his original estimate, and still had no prospect of steady profits. Unable to obtain more credit, he was finally obliged to sell out to Brazilian interests. Ludwig's failure has been attributed to various difficulties, but not to a labor problem. Ludwig paid the local minimum wage to a work force that reached 13,500, and experienced no shortage, although his turnover was very high because he did not provide sufficient housing. There were important ecological problems, but plant parasites do not appear to have been critical. All the tree species planted at Jari were exotics and escaped serious damage. The rice varieties that were introduced, though attacked by local diseases, were from the beginning subjected to constant supervision and replacement. There were ecological problems of other kinds, principally poor soil conditions, but they were not insoluble, given the technical capacity of Ludwig's staff and the equipment at their disposal. Instead, Jari's failure appears to derive from Ludwig's haste and eccentric managerial practices, and from political conflicts that arose out of his secrecy and lack of respect for Brazilian sensibilities. Although the Brazilian government, as an extraordinary measure, had guaranteed his foreign loans, he refused to consider buying his equipment in Brazil. Added to this, he proposed to will Jari to a medical foundation in Switzerland. These explanations are no more than conjectural, however. Jari, a project at least ten times costlier than Fordlandia and Belterra, deserves a monograph in its own right. See Norman Gall, "Ludwig's Amazon Empire," *Forbes* (14 May 1979): 127–44; Gwen Kinkead, "Trouble in D. K. Ludwig's Jungle," *Fortune* (20 April 1981): 102–17.

the postwar market for natural rubber was extremely uncertain; it was foreseeable only that the market would be much different from that of the 1920s and 1930s. With prospects for natural rubber so clouded, the costs of sustaining so long-range a project seemed onerous indeed.

7

Administrative discontinuities, 1946–1961

At war's end it was foreseen by everyone in the rubber trade that Brazilian wild rubber would quickly be driven from the world market. All that prevented its immediate elimination were the Washington Accords, which guaranteed Brazil's sales at double the world price through June 1947. It appeared that the Southeast Asian plantations would soon be producing at greater than prewar capacity, since they had suffered little damage and their trees were more mature and rested. With lower prices imminent, there were attempts to reconstitute the prewar cartel and official British efforts to support the price of its colonial product. Natural rubber producers, however, now confronted an immensely threatening competition from artificial elastomers. By mid-1946 general-purpose synthetic rubber was being offered in the United States at a price somewhat lower than natural rubber. Although natural rubber offered superior elasticity and resistance to heat and friction, it was supposed that improvements in the chemistry of artificial rubbers would be forthcoming, thereby diminishing further the prospects of rubber growers.[1]

Meanwhile in Brazil, all of the rubber that had been planted during the war was unselected or was susceptible to South American Leaf Blight. The researchers at Belém and Belterra were still far from a solution to the blight problem. It was therefore apparent that Brazilian cultivated rubber would be no more competitive than the gathered product.

The world market was of declining relevance to Brazil, however, because the domestic rubber situation was entirely transformed. The tire factories installed in São Paulo just before the outbreak of war had proved essential to maintaining the growth of the Brazilian economy in the midst of extreme shortages. Nearly a quarter of a million tire-consuming vehicles were registered in Brazil, mainly trucks and buses. By war's end, despite limitations on the allocation of the raw material, Goodyear, Firestone, and several domestically owned companies, notably Pneus Brasil, were producing more than a half million tires a year. The elimination of controls portended a rapid increase in the scale of the industry. Already in 1946, rubber manufacturers consumed 45 percent of domestic output.[2]

Unidentified employee observes seedlings in nursery at Firestone Camamu Plantation, 1956. (Courtesy Firestone Tire and Rubber Company)

But domestic output of natural rubber would come to an end if the wartime price guarantee were to expire and imported synthetic rubber were to invade the market. Rubber gatherers could not be expected to continue to tap wild trees at prices that would yield a loss. For the Brazilian government, the ruin of the gathering trade would have important political and economic consequences. Rubber gathering employed a frontier population that would otherwise surely wander off to the towns, leaving the national borders unoccupied. Furthermore, gathered rubber was available immediately, not in ten years, and funds invested in it, though inefficiently applied, bore returns within a single season. Dismantle the trade, and unemployment would increase in the Amazon by tens of thousands. Year after year the authorities who allocated federal funds to the Amazon were to face the same dilemma: whether to divert development capital that might provide future high levels of regional income

109

to the support of an archaic economic system whose maintenance might prevent immediate collapse.

The political system, furthermore, was being restored to liberal constitutionalism. A national congress was once again in session. Issues such as rubber policy would no longer be decided exclusively in the offices of technocrats, but in public debate in which political interests might compromise economic goals, and in which economic programs might be transformed into electoral payoffs. When in 1951, Getulio Vargas was reinstalled in the presidency with the electoral support of urban wage workers, populist and nationalist sentiments were introduced into political debate. Land redistribution, the expropriation of the petroleum industry, and other reformist proposals began indirectly to influence rubber development planning.

In 1946, the lagging growth in the domestic supply of natural rubber was alarming the rubber manufacturers of São Paulo. They persuaded the government to call a conference that, they hoped, would recommend the immediate abrogation of the Washington Accords so that the manufacturers might begin to import synthetic rubbers at the market price. Firmo Dutra, head of the Rubber Credit Bank, was named chairman of this National Rubber Conference, held at Rio de Janeiro in July. Artfully, he led the representatives of the rubber-gathering trade in parrying the manufacturers' onslaught. They demanded the continuation of minimum prices – 18.00 cruzeiros to the seringalistas and 24.60 cruzeiros to the aviadores, both subject to periodic revision. Minimum prices should remain in force, they insisted, until the Amazon infrastructure of transport and supply might be adequately developed. In return for this concession, the rubber manufacturers were to be allowed complete protection for their products in the domestic market. Finally, the government was asked to monopolize the purchase of rubber and to stockpile amounts that exceeded manufacturers' requirements.[3]

These proposals, embodied in Law 86, dated 8 September 1947, guaranteed the survival of the archaic rubber-gathering system and, not incidentally, of the Rubber Credit Bank, at an immense cost to Brazil, not all of which was foreseen in the debates. It was even attempted to shift part of the burden to the wild rubber tappers, whose impending loss of employment the delegates had alleged to be the justification for minimum prices for themselves. With many an indignant exclamation, representatives of the gathering trade, including José Negreiros Ferreira of the Association of Employers of the Wild Rubber Industry and Octávio José da Costa of the Association of Seringalistas of Mato Grosso, tried to abolish the minimum price that had been granted the tappers during the war at the insistence of the Rubber Development Corporation. A minimum price to the tappers, they claimed, compromised their constitutionally guaranteed right to work!

To the consumers of rubber – the rest of society, in fact, since rubber tires were a factor in the price of everything transported by motor vehicle, including foodstuffs and city workers – the representatives of the wild rubber trade alleged that their claim to assistance was no different from that of the sugar and cotton growers, who provided raw materials for large-scale domestic industries. The inapplicability of this analogy did not escape the manufacturers, who would certainly suffer a narrowed market for their output because of the price supports. The manufacturers pointed out that they were being asked to pay three times the price that natural rubber from Southeast Asia would cost them, delivered to Santos. They succeeded, with some added pressure on Congress, in limiting the promised support to a three-year period.[4]

The most severe price that Brazil would pay for turning over national rubber policy to a regional elite was the abandonment of rubber planting. The conference did not explicitly propose such a measure. That would have revealed too much about its intentions. It did vote a recommendation in favor of "intensive cultivation," and another in favor of colonization. But these were pious declarations, passed without debate and lacking the essential clauses concerning funding and administration. The delegates displayed their hostility to the rubber research program by suggesting that the Agronomic Institute of the North (IAN) be "transferred" to Belterra. Such a move would have written off five years of breeding and selection in Belém.[5]

Felisberto Cardoso de Camargo was a delegate at the conference, and it was doubtless he who kept this recommendation from reaching the floor for a vote. Camargo was unable to gain a serious hearing for his colonization schemes, apparently, expending what little political capital he possessed in the struggle between manufacturers and wild rubber dealers by demanding a minimum price for concentrated latex in line with that to be paid for raw rubber. In this effort he was seeking to protect the IAN's market. Although the Ford staff had succeeded in coagulating rubber at Belterra, the IAN was encountering difficulty in replicating this feat. Concentrated latex was therefore all it had to sell. Unfortunately, the rubber manufacturers had less use for this product and Camargo incurred their wrath by insisting on, and obtaining with the support of the Amazon delegates, 24.30 cruzeiros per liter.[6]

The IAN was able to survive in the face of the rubber gatherers' hostility partly because it continued to enjoy a subsidy of about $50,000 a year from the United States. At war's end a few USDA field technicians were left at their posts at the IAN at Belém and Belterra. The U.S. government had decided to deemphasize its cooperative field investigations in natural rubber, but it was not quite ready to abandon them. Although its policy shifted to the perfecting of synthetic rubber, that goal was not yet in sight. The uncertain future of the Southeast Asian colonial empires suggested a need to stockpile natural rubber, a policy that the Goodyear company sought to turn to its advantage by promoting "living stockpiles," by which it meant plantations in the Western Hemisphere. That company's preference continued to center on Central America, even though its tire factory in São Paulo continued to expand.[7]

The staff of the IAN tried gamely to bring the former Ford estates to commercial viability. They were under pressure to demonstrate "as a question of patriotism," as one newspaper put it, that Brazilians "possess the qualities to continue a work initiated by foreigners, despite the pessimistic talk of the locals." The trees at Fordlandia were regarded from the first as too damaged or unproductive to justify much effort. The top grafting at Belterra, however, had saved some 70 percent of the high-yielding Southeast Asian trees. Costs were reduced as much as possible; the staff informed R. D. Rands in 1948 that Belterra would be in the black when a half million trees could be tapped. That goal was reached only in 1952, but yield appears to have amounted to only 162 kilograms per hectare. Two years later yield had risen to 208 kilograms, far too little to support the immense infrastructure set in place by Ford. Yield seems to have fallen in later years, as less promising trees were tapped. The peak of production appears to have been reached in 1959, when 566 tons of dry rubber was obtained, and perhaps a million trees were tapped of the original 2.7 million. Many blocks were simply being abandoned, as poor yields were verified. No more rubber was planted except for experiments.[8]

Belterra's breeding programs were now directed by Charles H. Townsend, Jr., son of the entomologist hired by Archibald Johnston. Townsend, on the USDA payroll, had been asked by Camargo to remain. He did not regard top grafting as a viable solution to the problem of leaf blight. He estimated that it tripled the cost of a single-grafted tree, obliging an increase in the size of budwood gardens and requiring skilled labor to drag stepladders innumerable times through the groves. Furthermore, he believed it delayed growth to maturity, tying up capital still longer and extending the period during which the floor of the grove was sunlit, obliging additional weeding. He also suspected that the low yields might be partly the result of some physiological influence upon the trunk clones by the clones employed as the crown component.

Camargo had pointed out that the Ford estates' clone collection was their most valuable asset. He had suggested at the time the estates were transferred, that it might also be the most salable product, though he ruled out permitting Ford to sell clones, as "contrary to the interest of the country." Now these same clones might yet retrieve Brazil's fortunes. Townsend pressed forward with the laborious task of hand pollination, hoping to breed stock that would combine high yield and resistance. The first generation of crosses between the apparently resistant Ford selections and high-yielding Asian clones proved disappointingly unproductive. They were therefore back-crossed with Asian clones in the expectation that resistance would breed true while yield could be improved. *Hevea pauciflora* and *H. spruceana* were added to the breeding program, since *H. benthamiana* had proved hardly more resistant than *H.*

brasiliensis. Since Hevea cannot be tapped before the seventh year, even tentative conclusions from these experiments awaited the early 1960s.[9]

Curiously, these breeding experiments proceeded with no more genetic material than that already accumulated at Belterra and Belém, even though it was recognized as insufficient and not very promising. The last collecting expedition, along the Rondônia telegraph line, took place sometime in 1945. The collected seeds were planted directly in a grove at the IAN substation in Porto Velho. Unfortunately, these trees, occupying almost 84 hectares, were nearly all destroyed in 1950 in a fire caused by an outdoor barbecue. None of the survivors proved productive.[10]

Meanwhile, in Southeast Asia, the rubber research centers were reopened. Early in 1948, at the Rubber Research Institute of Malaya (RRIM) at Kuala Lumpur, fears revived over potential invasion by Microcyclus, now that commercial airline connections were reducing travel time to a matter of days. R. A. Alston, ranking the fungus with the potato blight and coffee rust in destructiveness, pointed out that the Ford and Goodyear plantations and the estates in the Guianas that it had ruined had been based on Southeast Asian clones; therefore Malaya and the rest of the region were extremely vulnerable. Although it might be unlikely that the conidial stage could survive such a journey, he thought that the perithecia and ascospores might, citing the reports of J. R. Weir and M. H. Langford. Alston warned that the chances of such an invasion depended on luck and that "no one knows what the odds are." He recommended, at a conference in Singapore in 1949, that plant import regulations be strengthened in all the rubber-producing countries, that all plant shipments to Malaya be subject to quarantine, and that no further imports of rubber planting material be permitted, except under the control of the RRIM.[11]

The RRIM began to undertake experiments in emergency eradication, in the event the fungus appeared. It was decided to spray a mixture of fungicides and defoliants over affected areas. The conviction grew, however, that it would be wise to import the resistant Ford and IAN clones. An exchange was carried out in 1951, Malaya receiving seventeen clones. Ceylon carried out a separate exchange in 1953, the same year in which the Indonesian research centers began to recognize the potential problem. The RRIM discovered that the productivity of the Brazilian clones was considerably below that of the best Southeast Asian clones; thus a breeding program would have to be undertaken. At a meeting of rubber specialists at Bogor in 1954, W. N. Bangham, by then back at work at Goodyear's Sumatran estates, described the problems experienced in Central America and at Belterra. He thought top grafting inadvisable and recommended another breeding program. The researchers adopted this proposal, with full understanding that they were committing themselves to many years of effort.[12]

At Belém the IAN, which was undertaking studies of a number of plant and tree crops besides rubber, was encountering great difficulty in securing steady funding. Its total budget amounted to three million cruzeiros, about $160,000, around 1948. Camargo had proposed an Amazon development fund to be allocated 3 percent of federal revenues. This fund, embodied in Article 199 of the Constitution of 1946, was to remain in operation for a term of twenty years. Congress, however, debated for seven years how the fund was to be spent before authorizing a Superintendency of the Economic Valorization Plan of the Amazon (SPVEA) in 1953. Camargo meanwhile obtained a grant from the Rubber Credit Bank to set up more experimental nurseries. He also sought funds, unsuccessfully, from an ephemeral UNESCO (United Nations Educational, Scientific, and Cultural Organization) program called the International Institute of the Hylean Amazon and from a federal development plan known as SALTE.[13]

In the meantime, the rubber situation was becoming critical. The Rubber Credit Bank foundered under the cost of storing unneeded rubber and lacked funds to buy more rubber at the established price. The gathering trade consequently withheld rubber from market, causing severe supply problems in the industrial south. Two more rubber conferences were held in 1948 and 1949 at which the gathering trade, in the absence of manufacturers' delegates, and led by Octávio Meira, Firmo Dutra's successor at the Bank, demanded that the government monopoly set up under Law 86 be made permanent. The gatherers insisted that the bank avoid competing with aviadores in financing the trade, and that it be allocated funds sufficient to buy all the rubber offered for sale at the full price guaranteed by the law. Foreseeing the exhaustion of government stocks within a few years as domestic demand increased, they suggested that the bank buy additional rubber from neighboring countries and sell it at the same price charged for domestic rubber.[14]

The conference delegates intensified their attack on rubber cultivation. They demanded that the bank be prohibited from diverting funds to activities that might compete with gathering and that the IAN, one-third of whose budget was provided by the bank, be cut off from further funding. Belterra, which they feared might yet achieve a sizable output, they wanted divided into lots and sold off. The delegates also opposed plantations outside the Amazon, demanding that the Decree-Law of 1943, limiting the transfer of planting materials out of the region, be rigorously enforced. Cosme Ferreira Filho, who became a spokesman of the gathering trade after an unsuccessful attempt at planting rubber, claimed to regret the failures of cultivation in the Amazon, but insisted that the wild rubber trade, if infused with more funds, would increase output. There were, he claimed, millions of trees that still had not been tapped. New techniques might be applied and rubber seedlings might be planted within the rubber trails.[15]

Congress did not cut off funding to the IAN, although the Rubber Credit Bank did indeed stop payments for the IAN nurseries. The rest of the gathering traders' demands were met. The Rubber Credit Bank, renamed the Amazon Credit Bank (BCA) in 1950, continued unfailingly to interpret the best interests of the Amazon in behalf of the gathering trade. By 1951, less than 5 percent of its 526 million cruzeiros in resources had been made available for agricultural loans of any kind. The rest was funding wild rubber.[16]

The Brazilian army, which had campaigned in Italy and had certainly observed that mobility was the essence of modern warfare, seems not to have participated, oddly enough, in the policy debate that made inevitable an insufficient supply of domestic rubber. Apparently the army considered the survival of the gathering trade more important. The seringalistas evoked effectively the image of a vast hinterland, populated only by the tappers, that would fall undefended to Brazil's neighbors, or perhaps to imperialist powers, if the price of rubber were not supported. In May 1951 at the Army Staff School, Felisberto Camargo assailed the "champions of routine" who made use of "the most cunning of resources and defenses, professing a great social consciousness or exalting national integrity as a veil under which to carry on the most irrational exploitation of man and natural resources." He outlined once again his colonization scheme, likening it this time to a "military occupation development," rather than to collectivism, but the army appears to have doubted Camargo's competence to achieve the results he claimed were possible.[17]

The increase in Brazilian imports of motor vehicles in the first postwar years led to the next stage of the crisis. In both 1949 and 1950 demand for replacement tires grew by more than 16 percent. But Amazon rubber gatherers, underfunded despite all the favors granted them, and the tappers, once again exploited to the point of inanition, were incapable of rising to the challenge. Output slumped from 32,930 tons in 1947 to 18,619 tons in 1950. Inevitably, the Brazilian government had to authorize importation. The first shipment, 400 tons of Malayan rubber, arrived at Santos in May 1951. The press was outraged. Brazil, the native habitat of Hevea, was now importing rubber from the very countries that had made off with it, exactly seventy-five years before.[18]

This disturbing vulnerability appeared at an embarrassing moment: Brazil was experiencing a growing trade deficit, $197 million in 1951 alone. The price of natural rubber had tripled in two years because of the insurrection in Malaya and the Korean War. That first cargo of imported rubber cost over a half million dollars, and another 5,000 tons was delivered before the year was out. Camargo predicted that by the end of the decade, Brazil would have imported 72,000 tons of rubber, at a cost of more than $60 million. Nor would the development of synthetic rubber resolve the problem, because Brazil, lacking adequate petroleum deposits, would end by importing the raw materials for that industry as well.[19]

On the other hand, the shock produced by the need to import rubber might

115

be therapeutic: From now on a refusal to confront the situation, Camargo warned, would be paid for in dollars and sterling. A rubber-planting program large enough to satisfy the demand foreseeable by the end of the decade could be paid for in cruzeiros, the equivalent of just $25 million. In fact, prospective Brazilian rubber growers were potentially in a more favorable position than before. Now that rubber demand had been entirely internalized, explained Cássio Fonseca, secretary of the Executive Commission for Rubber Defense that had been set up to administer the rubber monopoly, the uncertainties of the world market need no longer rule investment decisions. The government could guarantee a secure and steadily growing market at regulated prices. What was principally necessary was long-term credit at interest rates lower than those prevailing. Fonseca suggested that the rubber imports might provide the needed funds: Let the Amazon Credit Bank sell the rubber at the same high price it guaranteed the gathering trade, and lend the proceeds to prospective rubber planters, charging no more than 4 percent interest, repayable in twelve years.[20]

Camargo's smallholding scheme began to receive more serious attention from the federal government in the year following the first rubber imports. It was the centerpiece of a Technical Conference on the Economic Valorization of the Amazon, at which Camargo proposed planting thirty million trees in government-sponsored colonies over a ten-year period, at a cost, following Townsend's estimates, of 65 million cruzeiros ($1.6 million) a year. This would have amounted to 10 percent of the funds not yet appropriated under Article 199. The lots would be turned over to the colonists once the trees reached tappable size. The Finance Committee of the Senate reported favorably on this scheme, partly because it recognized that private investors had not entered the field, even though, as it imagined, the technical problems had been solved.[21]

But Camargo was not to put his plan into effect. In 1952, he was elevated to the directorship of the National Service of Agronomic Research in Rio de Janeiro. It is not clear whether he owed his promotion to the reelection of his friend Getúlio Vargas, or to the enmity of the gathering trade, seizing the opportunity to remove him from the Amazon. His successors at the IAN, in any case, did not possess the qualities he had specified for the director of his rubber-planting scheme: "the absolute confidence of the President of the Republic" and, if possible, of the president's party, "to prevent his sub-directors being importuned by local politicians and by those involved in the rubber gathering trade." His office ought not to be subordinate to any agency involved with the gathering trade, in order to avoid its "absorption, derailment, demoralization or the annulment of its efforts." Camargo had not left behind a team committed to rubber research. Over the next few years the budget for rubber studies was cut and the clones amassed by USDA collectors were lost through neglect.[22]

In 1956, Belterra was removed from the IAN's control and turned over to an agency of the Ministry of Agriculture. The tapping program continued to expand for a few more years, but K. G. MacIndoe, a visiting Firestone rubber specialist, described Belterra as "a ghost plantation, depressing to one looking for a successful commercial enterprise." Townsend went on with his experiments, testing a third generation of back-crosses to high-yielding oriental clones. He was discovering, however, that the resistance of the third generation was unacceptably reduced. The qualities that determined resistance, whatever they were, were not only incompatible with high productivity; they were, most likely, also determined by more than one set of genes, so that continued crosses strayed further from the desired characters. MacIndoe remarked that Townsend's work "had lost direction," and he doubted the accuracy of his data.[23]

The programs of the Bureau of Plant Industry were also in danger of losing their way. The BPI was spending more than $300,000 a year at its several research stations, a not insubstantial sum that Elmer W. Brandes, still head of the rubber program, was at pains to justify. Since congressional appropriations committees rhetorically favored small farmers, he could emphasize the need for a breeding program to develop clones suitable for their use. It was presumed that smallholders would not be competent to carry out top grafting successfully, thus Brandes was able to represent the breeding program as necessary to smallholder participation. Critics, however, dredged up the wartime disasters of Cryptostegia and Guayule planting, and suggested that it was really Goodyear's future plantations that were being made viable at government expense. At the end of the Korean War, however, Western Hemisphere rubber sourcing no longer seemed urgent, and funding for research became more precarious. It was transferred to the Point Four technical assistance program and extinguished in 1956.[24]

The shock of natural rubber imports galvanized a number of rubber-growing schemes from one end of Brazil to the other. The Ministry of Agriculture invited William MacKinnon and R. D. Rands, of the USDA, and Mario Bocquet, of the Rubber Research Institute of Indochina, to tour the rubber areas and offer advice. MacKinnon and Rands proposed a five-year development plan to plant 37,000 hectares. In Amapá the territorial government and the National Institute for Immigration and Colonization (INIC) sponsored a number of smallholding colonies in which rubber was to be planted with IAN materials and technical assistance. Highly optimistic references to these colonies were included in official reports for the next few years. It was stated that three million trees were planted. In fact some of the colonies did not even exist. Of the 300,000 trees that may have been planted, very few received the necessary base or top grafts. An investigative team learned that the colonists were not given the assistance promised, and that they accepted the seedlings only to obtain larger plots. The colonists were therefore abandoning the rubber, and were growing food crops for sale to nearby manganese mining centers.[25]

In the cacao zone of southern Bahia, the director of the newly founded Agronomic Institute of the East (IAL), Renato G. Martins, invited the minister of agriculture and a congressional delegation to survey the one million rubber trees said to be growing in the region. They found that the Mocambo estate at Uruçuca, where Hevea had first been planted in the 1920s to shade cacao, had suffered relatively less than other rubber plantings during the wartime leaf blight epidemics, and had been the only estate to expand rubber cultivation after the war. Another 30,000 trees had been planted there and a small factory had been installed to produce rubber gloves.[26]

Martins managed to obtain clones from the IAN at Belém, a triumph since this could not be achieved during the war, although it may have added to Camargo's political difficulties. More clones came from the USDA experimental station at Turrialba, and two USDA field technicians were sent to assist with planting. Martins personally accompanied to São Paulo a truck shipment of three tons of Bahia rubber, a gesture that won him a great deal of favorable press comment. He did not fail to extoll to reporters southern Bahia's well-developed infrastructure and trained work force, both developed by the cacao trade. Smallholding colonists were taking up Hevea, with the encouragement of two other state officials, Oswaldo Bastos de Menezes and Antônio Lemos Maia, who had set up a nursery at Ituberá. A meeting of northeastern bishops recommended government assistance for rubber planting, as a means of helping smallholders, and the Bank of Brazil and INIC provided credit and free seedlings. Enthusiasm continued strong during the 1950s, despite yields that seem to have amounted to no more than 100 or 200 kilograms per hectare. Perhaps as many as three million trees were planted in southern Bahia during this period of renewed interest.

The Amazon Credit Bank (BCA), by then under the direction of Gabriel Hermes, took up Cássio Fonseca's recommendation. With considerable resources suddenly available through the resale of imported rubber, it offered fully financed loans for the planting of Hevea at 4 percent interest – a negative rate in real terms – with repayment of the principal to begin only after six years. It sought to organize a rubber planting service in the Amazon and established fifty-nine rubber seedling nurseries on the properties of planters who had been given rubber loans. These may have been, in fact, the only farmers who attempted to grow rubber under this program, since the BCA recorded only 1,104 hectares planted by 1953. This would have amounted to no more than 400,000 trees, at a cost of eight million cruzeiros, an insignificant effort compared to the bank's profit that year of 300 to 400 million cruzeiros.[27]

The newly created SPVEA, directed by A. C. Ferreira Reis, decided in 1955 to carry out the MacKinnon and Rands proposal to plant 37,000 hectares. The SPVEA would make available 127 million cruzeiros ($1.7 million) in farm credit through the BCA. It proposed that state and territorial governments in the Amazon spend concurrently another 146 million cruzeiros ($1.9 million) for nurseries. Actual disbursements were far less. What came to be called Projeto Borracha spent in 1957 only eight million cruzeiros of SPVEA and BCA funds. The SPVEA, for lack of sufficient collaboration from the state governments, perhaps, paid for the nurseries itself. In 1957 it was reported that the nurseries had distributed only 200,000 grafted stumps, sufficient stock for no more than 500 hectares.[28]

This work was extended in 1958, when an accord was reached among the SPVEA, the IAN, and other government agencies and the Brazil–United States Agricultural Technical Office (ETA). The latter was funded by the U.S. government's Point Four technical assistance program. The accord, called ETA Project 54, was supposed to stimulate, through extension services, the planting of 2,000 hectares a year for five years, a modest enough goal, which depended on pledges of 341 million cruzeiros ($2.3 million). The ETA's rubber specialist was Charles Townsend, who had transferred to the Rio office of Point Four. After four years, ETA Project 54 had 116 workers in the field and 160 hectares in nurseries, but no more than 2,200 hectares had been planted. The Ministry of Agriculture had reduced the viability of the accord by insisting that most of the extension efforts be diverted to wild groves, where seringueiros were to be taught the use of Southeast Asian tapping methods. It was also alleged that the BCA was at fault, having underfinanced collaborating planters and delayed their advances.

Projeto Borracha in 1956 initiated a smallholder colony at Guamá, 20 kilometers south of Belém. This was directed by INIC, which settled some 200 Japanese immigrants and national colonists there. Each smallholder was required to plant 2,000 rubber trees. The colony's director, doubting the resistance of clones so far developed and the yields of Southeast Asian clones under local conditions, simply planted directly in the field, 10 seeds in each hole, 6,500 seeds per hectare. His idea was to carry out a trial on plantation scale, in the hope that one tree in twenty would prove resistant and moderately high-yielding. The colonists, wary of planting rubber, delayed carrying out this phase of the project. By 1958, they were combating South American Leaf Blight (SALB). Apparently SPVEA's funding was erratic and the colonists soon found themselves on their own. Titles were not to be turned over to them until their rubber was mature, a precaution to ensure that they would tend their trees to tappable size, but it prevented them from offering their plots as security for bank loans. The SPVEA and its associates appear to have lost interest in the project, and the remaining colonists shifted to annual crops.[29]

Rather than salvage the Guamá colony, the IAN, with ETA Project 54 funding, in 1959 started another at Itacoatiara, 150 kilometers east of Manaus. Although much like earlier colonies based on Camargo's model, it was

119

more directly inspired by smallholding plans in French Africa that had been studied by the IAN's new director, Rubens Rodrigues Lima. It contained seventy-seven lots, each of fifteen hectares, five of which were reserved for rubber. A selection of Ford and IAN clones was planted as budded stumps or base grafted in the field. As at Guamá, the plots were not to be ceded to the colonists until they had paid them off in rubber deliveries. Until then, it appears, the colonists were not assigned specific plots to work. The colony developed normally until the fifth year, when the ETA Project 54 office suffered a reduction in funds channeled through the Ministry of Finance. It was decided to turn the colony over to the state of Amazonas and sell off the lots. ETA Project 54 itself limped on through 1961, having distributed planting material for no more than 1,500 hectares.[30]

The rubber imports focused attention on the largest consumers, the tire manufacturers, now including Pirelli as well as Firestone and Goodyear. R. D. Rands and William MacKinnon suggested to Minister of Agriculture João Cleophas that these companies be asked to participate in rubber development. The minister asked the companies to organize a corporation to promote the establishment of plantations in the Amazon and, as a short-range project, to collaborate with the Brazilian government in an agency reminiscent of the RDC, investing in river craft and introducing labor and supplies. Firestone and Goodyear were opposed to such a venture, but they were already participants in the government's projected synthetic rubber plant, a position they did not want to jeopardize. They therefore agreed early in 1952 to survey the rubber-producing areas, with Pirelli and government technicians. The survey report, written by Theodor Hoedt, of Pirelli, Bert Vipond, of Firestone, and Walter Klippert, of Goodyear, avoided any mention of a role for large-scale plantations. Instead it extolled rubber smallholdings and even proposed improving the efficiency of the wild rubber trails, which, they fancied, might double their output with no added input of labor simply by improving tapping methods. They suggested laying out nurseries in Acre and Mato Grosso to encourage the seringalistas to replace their trails gradually with planted groves.[31]

The tire companies were not to be let off so easily. In the midst of their expedition, the survey team was already hearing rumors of a decree that was indeed signed even before their report was submitted: Henceforth the rubber companies were to devote 20 percent of their net profits to the planting of rubber, or suffer the loss of their rubber import quota. The companies struggled against this measure, which they considered unconstitutional. Firestone negotiated a compromise: It would undertake to plant 1,200 hectares in return for canceling the decree. Goodyear and Pirelli then agreed in turn to plant the same area. With this settled, a new decree was announced in April 1954, permitting the companies to satisfy the earlier decree through the submission of plans acceptable to the Ministry of Agriculture, thus extricating the government from a position that many within it had considered extreme. By this time there were two more foreign tire companies on the scene, Dunlop and General, who made the same commitment as the others. The only modern tire company in Brazil that was domestically owned, Pneus Brasil in São Paulo, was at the time undergoing management difficulties and it failed, apparently without ever having participated in this agreement.[32]

The companies set out to buy land. None was interested in heading up the Amazon, lacking in infrasructure and remote from the factories. Walter E. Klippert, the Goodyear surveyor, thought the labor supply upriver "poor and inadequate." Ignoring the problem of leaf blight, he preferred to plant where rainfall and humidity were high and constant, on a 4,450 hectare property lying a hundred kilometers to the east of Belém along the Bragança railway. A sawmill had once operated there, and sugar and rice had been planted. Secondary forest had taken over and there had been a return to logging and to manioc planting. Klippert thought the terrain suitable despite its sandy soil because it was flat, and therefore appropriate for mechanical cultivation. Theodor Hoedt, a great admirer of Goodyear technology, recommended that Pirelli buy 7,590 hectares in the same area, on a site adjoining the IAN colony on the Guamá River.[33]

Firestone, influenced partly by Keith Truettner, one of the USDA field technicians assigned to Bahia, decided to buy in that state a property 9,580 hectares in extent, occupying parts of the municipalities of Camamu and Ituberá, where there were many small properties already cultivating some rubber. That site, interestingly enough, had been visited by the 1923 USDA survey team. They had ruled it out for plantation development, however, because of its hilly terrain. Dunlop and General joined Firestone in Bahia, both of them locating in the municipality of Una, near the IAL.[34]

Firestone proposed an experimental operation. The company thought that rubber would prove profitable, if only because the government was sure to continue to support prices. However, it was not at all sure that the leaf blight problem was resolved. The clones developed at Belterra and Belém were apparently both resistant and moderately high-yielding, but that could only be established empirically. The Firestone technicians were quite pessimistic about the viability of top grafting as an alternative, and did not base their early planting on this technique.[35]

Firestone hoped that a successful plantation would encourage smallholders to take up rubber planting, as had happened in Liberia. The company therefore provided a moderate amount of free planting materials and advice to its neighbors. In part an ideological preference for smallholding, this strategy also reflected a self-interested desire to promote a class of farmers that might be able to afford to buy trucks and tires and, above all, shoulder a responsibility that Firestone preferred to avoid. The tire companies were not at the outset keen to undertake this project, even though they possessed the requisite experience and resources. Oddly, a nationalist current within the Vargas gov-

121

ernment was in effect obliging the foreign tire companies to integrate vertically, a practice decidedly antinationalistic. The companies were reluctant, in part because they opposed on principle governmental attempts to channel their profits, and partly because they feared the leaf blight.[36]

Events were to vindicate the tire companies' caution. Firestone seems to have expended the most money and effort. By 1959, its estate had cost more than $1.8 million. Its early planting was not on contour, but aligned east and west, probably to allow prevailing winds to ventilate the rows as a defense against SALB. This strategy created a problem of erosion that proved impractical to resolve through terracing. It had not been realized, furthermore, that a lateritic hardpan underlay the estate. On the hilltops, where it lay exposed, it would be impossible to plant. Attempts to do so amused local farmers, who expressed ironic admiration for the Americans' persistence.

Lacking budding materials, Firestone was not able to base graft during the first three years, a sign that there had been excessive haste. The Firestone manager also experienced difficulty in obtaining Belterra clones for his estate, at least until early 1959, for lack of cooperation from the IAN. Another Firestone rubber specialist brought in clonal material from the company's experimental grove in Guatemala, but some of it was confiscated by Brazilian customs! It was therefore necessary in the 1956 to 1959 plantings to use, for the most part, Firestone Liberian clones and Southeast Asian clones, both of which required top grafting. This work, carried out with great misgiving, achieved only 50 percent success. Among other misfortunes, birds delighted in perching on the newly budded branches and repeatedly snapped them off. SALB was present by 1959 and required constant spraying of nurseries and budwood gardens. A survey by the manager in 1960 showed only 19 percent of the trees attaining expected growth levels.[37]

At Marathon, the Goodyear estate, unselected seeds from Belterra had been planted directly in sandy fields and had been base grafted with a variety of presumably resistant Belterra and IAN clones and also with a variety of Southeast Asian clones. The latter were then top grafted with resistant crowns, a costly procedure because it was undertaken unadvisedly during the dry season. All these clones were placed randomly within blocks, a practice generally condemned by specialists, and a source of difficulties when SALB began to attack the estate, as it soon did. According to Firestone's manager, who visited the estate in 1959, Marathon had "nice bungalows, good warehouses, fine roads and beautifully lying land, *but* they have very very poor rubber trees."[38]

Although Pirelli had selected better soils, its problems were grave. Planting began there in 1956, and by 1957 there were 190 hectares. The top-grafting program was unsuccessful, however, and by this time SALB was already appearing. It was necessary therefore to uproot 150 hectares and start again. By 1960 there were 420 hectares planted, but the nurseries had to be sprayed daily, and a crew of twenty men was kept constantly busy replacing trees.

The 1957 planting had to be uprooted, because of slow growth. All three of the larger estates, in fact, had to uproot and replant. In five years the three companies had spent 342 million cruzeiros (approximately $3.4 million), but had planted just 1,766 hectares. After another five years, with continuous replanting, disillusionment with supposedly resistant clones, and further uprooting, they still had not achieved the area promised the Ministry of Agriculture in 1954.[39]

It is not possible to sustain the claim that this work was undertaken in a spirit of resistance to the decree that had brought it about. Firestone records demonstrate the intention to make its plantation a paying proposition, and to overcome even the most dismaying setbacks. Goodyear and Firestone drew liberally on their stock of talents and experience gained from a worldwide network of plantations. The managers in the field, undoubtedly concerned for their own careers, struggled heroically to bring their rubber to tappable size, and achieved continued funding from their home offices by revealing to them as little as possible of their distress. They shared their information among themselves, with the other tire companies, with small planters, and with the IAN and IAL. Goodyear and Firestone came to see their Brazilian plantations as an opportunity to further their research into plant breeding and defense. The Firestone Liberian plantation conducted its own investigations into resistance to SALB, parallel with the RRIM program, and tried to carry out field trials of its selections in Bahia. Although some nationalists thought that there was some sort of conspiracy among the foreign tire companies in favor of their African or Asian plantations, this does not appear to be the case.[40]

The first rubber imports inspired efforts at experimental plantings in the industrial state of São Paulo. Although no one remembered it, the first proposal to plant rubber there was made in 1872 by João Martins da Silva Coutinho, the same man who had carried the idea to Paris in 1867. The trees planted in 1915 at Gavião Peixoto, near Araraquara, had not only survived, demonstrating that Hevea could grow more than twenty degrees from the equator, they had also been multiplied by their enthusiastic owner, Colonel José Procópio de Araujo Ferraz, so that there were 30,000 of them shading his coffee. More rubber trees were to be found along the coast, some planted in 1922 from seeds obtained from the colonel, others planted after 1932 by Carlos Arnaldo Krug, of the Agronomic Institute of Campinas (IAC). In 1940, federal extension agents rediscovered the colonel's trees and planted their seeds in various places across the state. This initiative was brought to an end by complaints from the ever-zealous gathering trade, but not before seeds were delivered to the IAC and to other experimental stations at Ribeirão Prêto and Pindorama. These trees were mature by 1950 and available to supply seed for hundreds of thousands of rootstock seedlings.[41]

In 1951, João Ferreira da Cunha, who headed the tropical plant section of the IAC, approached the trade associations of the rubber manufacturers for funding of an experimental station. He was not at the time optimistic regarding the prospects of rubber on the cool plateau, where coffee trees had found so favorable a habitat, but instead wished to site the station at Santos, on the warmer Paulista coast. That region had experienced a modest boom in banana exporting in the 1930s, but the war had ruined the trade and a new source of income would be welcomed. R. D. Rands and William MacKinnon visited da Cunha on their Brazilian tour. They expressed the opinion that the cooler weather of São Paulo would retard growth, but believed that if the region should prove inhospitable to SALB, this might be a relatively unimportant drawback. They agreed that it would be worthwhile to establish nurseries on the coast, and thought that they might supply seedlings to Bahia and other places afflicted with blight. On the other hand they were not entirely sure that the littoral would remain blight free, since they had already seen it appear in quite temperate regions of Central America. Despite the uncertainties, Rands and MacKinnon recommended that São Paulo be included in the national rubber planting scheme that they proposed to the Ministry of Agriculture.[42]

The rubber survey report of Hoedt, Vipond, and Klippert reviewed respectfully the IAC's studies of the coastal plain, which demonstrated that its soils and rainfall were adequate for rubber. They agreed that it might be advisable to undertake pilot plantings, but they doubted that growth rates and yields would prove satisfactory in a region experiencing a distinct winter season and annual average temperatures six degrees Celsius below the optimum for Hevea. They therefore discouraged their companies from establishing plantations there.[43]

It was Felisberto Camargo who obtained selected seeds for the initial IAC plantings. He approached Firestone, which shipped 100,000 Southeast Asian seeds from its Liberian plantation. He may also have taken IAN clones with him when he departed the IAN and passed these to the IAC. The IAC experimental substation at Ubatuba possessed more than seventy clones of varied provenances. The largest stock of improved seed immediately available, however, was that from Firestone, consisting of illegitimate crosses of just two Indonesian clones, Tj1 and Tj16. These were offered to cooperating farmers along the coast. After five years, however, no more than 100,000 seedlings for rootstock had been distributed, and it appears that only a small proportion of these, perhaps a third, were later bud grafted.[44]

With the installation in 1956 of the energetic Jânio Quadros in the governorship of São Paulo, these tentative efforts were given direction and funding. A rubber study commission was formed within the Secretariat of Agriculture that recommended that the state itself undertake experimental plantings, since farmers had proven reluctant. A Rubber Expansion Service (SES) and a Rubber Cultivation Development Fund were established. Competent and diligent IAC technicians carried out soil studies and visited the USDA station at Turrialba and the IAN in Belém. The Institute for Technological Research at the University of São Paulo undertook studies of rubber samples collected in the field by the IAC, work they had been doing for the rubber manufacturers since the war. High expectations were expressed in the press, which pointed to the state's efficient transport network, its bustling internal market, its effective extension services, and its "enlightened and responsive" planters. The hope was also expressed that rubber might improve the economy of the relatively backward coast.[45]

Early in 1957, some forty nurseries were set up on cooperating farms in order to make superior planting material available on a large scale. Almost half of these farms belonged to immigrant Japanese smallholders, some of whom engaged in tea planting in the area of Registro, intermediate in altitude between the coast and the plateau. Seedlings, according to the plan, were to be delivered at cost, with no repayment for seven years, and no interest charge. No other incentive was offered, but none was thought necessary. The SES budget amounted to 42 million cruzeiros ($262,000) during its first two years. One million rootstock seedlings were raised in the nurseries of the cooperating farms, and most of them appear to have been planted, in a variety of environmental conditions throughout the state. By 1958, bud-grafting material was also being made available. Plans for 1959 and 1960 involved the planting of another 1.5 million seedlings.

In June 1958, the Rubber Cultivation Development Fund signed an agreement with the ETA in Rio de Janeiro. This agreement, denominated ETA Project 50, provided for assistance in training specialists and in obtaining more Southeast Asian clones for local trials. In São Paulo the agreement was supervised by João Jacob Hoelz. More clones were obtained through this fund from Bahia and Belém as well.[46]

Felisberto Camargo remained marginal to this enterprise, even though he was a Paulista and was once employed by the IAC. In 1958, however, after leaving the National Service of Agronomic Research, he was invited by the secretary of agriculture of São Paulo to assess the state's potential. He delivered a report that in general confirmed the soundness of the measures the SES had so far taken. He recalled that he had for years favored the planting of rubber in the Amazon, where climatic factors were ideal, and where it was in the national interest that the regional economy expand its base, but "lamentably the directors of the economic policy of the Amazon, blinded by the feudalism of the wild trade, continue to be dominated by the idea of forest extraction." If São Paulo's rubber factories were ever to obtain sufficient raw material, therefore, rubber would have to be planted within its borders. It could be taken as a political given that the internal price of rubber would continue to be supported for another ten to twenty years. Rubber produced in the state might be expected to yield perhaps 30 percent less than in Bahia; therefore, it was essential to offset this disadvantage by obtaining the most productive clones available, most importantly the new RRIM series 500 and 600.[47]

Camargo did not think that SALB could be excluded from São Paulo over the long run or be assumed to present no danger. Unfortunately, however, clones that combined resistance and productivity were not yet available. Belém and Belterra, he stated, still had to carry out "an enormous series" of experiments before they would have any clones to offer. In the meantime, São Paulo should plant the Southeast Asian clones. He advised against base grafting, recommending instead that the high-yielding clone seedlings be replanted directly in the field and top grafted with a resistant canopy. Although there was some danger in further imports of clones from Central America, the Amazon, and Bahia, he recommended that it be permitted. If the government did not carry them out with sanitary safeguards, then private parties surely would with no safeguards at all.

Camargo was alert, as usual, to the political context. In São Paulo it would be necessary to provide a rationale for rubber development that would attract the coffee growers. He therefore made sure to suggest that rubber was an appropriate tree crop for exhausted coffee lands, and that coffee planters should be given priority in the distribution of rubber credit. Knowing that the gathering trade would certainly thwart an approach to the Ministry of Agriculture, he entered into correspondence with the director of the Brazilian Coffee Institute, controlled by Paulistas, in order to obtain large shipments of Southeast Asian clones at preferential exchange rates. Camargo further recommended that Dunlop, which had not yet installed its plantation, be invited to São Paulo. Dunlop, he pointed out, possessed all the new RRIM clones on its Malayan estates.

As Camargo suspected, Microcyclus was not long in reaching São Paulo. It was first observed in a nursery at Sete Barros, near Registro, in February 1960. Soon it was attacking groves all along the coast. Planters complained, justifiably, that they had not been given sufficient warning of the damage the blight might do. Fungicides had not been recommended or distributed. On the plateau, SALB incidence appears to have been quite low and limited to sites that were low-lying and excessively humid. Many of the plantings were too small and scattered, however, to have offered much of a target. Even so, planters grew discouraged and withdrew from the program because they were encountering difficulties in carrying out the necessary bud grafting, and the state-organized nurseries lacked sufficient replacement materials.[48]

An effort was made to procure resistant materials for top grafting and to initiate a local program of selection and breeding. Camargo himself returned to Belém to acquire clones from the IAN and from the Goodyear plantation. The IAN refused to release its own material or to allow Goodyear's to be sent. Only through the intercession of the governor of São Paulo were the clones finally obtained. By then, however, Paulista planters had lost interest in the program, even though they received compensation for their losses. The nurseries were unable to sell their seedlings and began to give them away.

126

Even before the fungus appeared, the SES had been extinguished, for reasons that are not clear. The Development Fund was abolished in April 1960. ETA Project 50 limped along through December 1961, engaging in further grafting and planting experiments. Some of the groves on the plateau were probably uprooted; others survived, very possibly never having been grafted at all. Thus a promising program was abandoned, without having undergone a rigorous trial.[49]

Thus the 1950s drew to a close with no solution of the problem of rubber cultivation in sight. The development of a domestic tire industry had brought on a greatly enlarged demand for rubber. The rubber-gathering trade had insisted on trying to monopolize that market, but it was entirely unsuccessful in accompanying its growth, even under conditions of a government-run cartel. The consequent need to import natural and synthetic rubber excited a great deal of planning. Four centers of agricultural experimentation accepted the challenge, several government agencies took it upon themselves to draw up plans, and numerous farmers had been encouraged to plant.

As one congressman protested, "So many people to take care of rubber in this country and still there isn't any rubber!" Rubber schemes, characterized as "lyrical" by Alfredo Wisniewski, an IAN scientist, had followed one after the other. Invariably they were underfunded or mismanaged. Many were undermined by persons attracted by the chance to gorge on government largesse. Those initiated in São Paulo and Bahia were combated by Amazon politicians ferociously defending their own region. Rubber was "a right that pertains to us, traditionally and above all because rubber cultivation is one of the most useful tools for reviving the regional economy," said Cosme Ferreira Filho. "We must save. . . the Amazon from being deliberately despoiled of its natural right to maintain internal hegemony in the production of rubber." The transfer of sugar to the northeast during the colonial period should serve, he thundered, "as an unforgettable warning." And yet these claims were undermined by the rubber gathering trade, which remained as opposed to cultivation in the Amazon as it was to cultivation in Bahia.[50]

Only on the plantations of the multinational rubber companies, especially the Firestone estate, was Hevea given a rigorous and unremitting trial under the supervision of rubber technicians whose experience in the field was immense. Evidently they had all chosen their sites too hastily, and had made other mistakes in the development of their groves. But these were not fatal errors, and the companies displayed a will to overcome them. What they all discovered very quickly was that their biggest problem was going to be Microcyclus, and that some means of controlling it would have to be found before reasonable yields and profits could be secured.

8

Complete perplexity, 1961–1972

Under Juscelino Kubitschek, elected president of Brazil in 1956, the federal government had given little support to natural rubber development. Kubitschek's planners had included a goal of 70,000 hectares of planted rubber in his Target Program, but they had demonstrated no commitment to carrying it out. The bias of central planning in the 1950s and 1960s was clearly in favor of industry over agriculture, and agricultural research and development was neglected. Thus a 1958 meeting convoked by the Ministry of Agriculture, in effect the fourth rubber conference, was not followed by any new allocation of funds, but marked the beginning of a decade of relative neglect of natural rubber.

Kubitschek sought instead to close the growing gap between supply and demand by installing a synthetic rubber plant. Planning for the facility had begun at the time of the first natural rubber imports in 1951. Suspended for several years, it was taken up again when Kubitschek initiated his drive to create a Brazilian motor vehicle industry. The tire companies, confronted by a much enlarged demand, were petitioning to import synthetic elastomers, by then lower in cost than natural rubber. The government, impelled by a need to conserve foreign exchange, abolished the Amazon Credit Bank's monopoly of synthetic imports and negotiated with the tire companies the proportion of synthetics they might employ in their products. It then authorized the construction of a styrene-butadiene plant of 40,000 tons capacity in the Rio de Janeiro suburb of Duque de Caxias. This plant, known by the acronym FABOR, was funded largely by Goodyear and Firestone.[1]

This first synthetic rubber factory in Latin America economized some of the foreign exchange that Brazil was spending on the importation of this raw material, and by increasing the proportion of synthetic rubber used in tires and tubes, it reduced imports of natural rubber to just 2,000 tons by 1965. In that year a second plant, COPERBO, was inaugurated by the government of the northeastern state of Pernambuco. Brazilian policymakers, like Cássio Fonseca, vice-chairman of the Rubber Defense Executive Commission, were nevertheless uneasy. Synthetic rubber seemed altogether the wrong solution.

Felisberto Camargo, Director of the Agricultural Institute of the North, Belém. (Courtesy José Geraldo Camargo)

It absorbed scarce capital inputs and imported a technology that would have to be paid for in dollars and that was soon obsolete. The FABOR plant represented a further penetration of the sector by the multinationals. Both FABOR and COPERBO, which at first converted sugarcane-based alcohol into polybutadiene but soon switched to petroleum feedstocks, had to be supplied with imported crude oil derivatives. All that had been gained was a breathing space, during which a solution to the natural rubber question might yet be formulated.

Unfortunately, the moment, from the political point of view, was not opportune. Constitutional government was in crisis from 1961 onward, and rubber policy fell into incoherence and neglect for the rest of the decade. Jânio Quadros, Kubitschek's successor in office, was critical of the favoritism toward the gathering trade evidenced by the Amazon Credit Bank and he accused the Rubber Defense Executive Commission of a lack of dynamism in promoting cultivation. He created a fund for that purpose and endowed it with a 10 percent tax on rubber imports. As he had done in São Paulo, he nominated a study group to propose a new agency to carry out rubber development. The SPVEA, by then wholly lacking credibility in the field, nevertheless obligingly came forward with a proposal to create such an organization, grandiloquently christened "Heveabrás," to plant 50,000 hectares at a yearly cost of 700 million cruzeiros ($2.2 million), from a variety of funding sources. All

129

of this came to naught when, a few months later, Quadros resigned the presidency.[2]

For his substitute, vice-president João Goulart, guaranteeing an adequate rubber supply was a matter of low priority, compared to maintaining his shaky hold on office. His nationalist followers, nevertheless, imposed a sort of direction on his administration. They were indignant that government favors had made possible the foreign companies' monopoly of the tire sector. Somehow, the spokesmen of the rubber-gathering trade were able to portray themselves to this group as selfless defenders of Brazil's frontiers against imperialist covetousness, betrayed by their own government in their struggles against the multinationals. Since it was the rubber-gathering elite who had principally opposed the installation of the foreign-controlled FABOR plant, they shone in the eyes of the populist nationalists, who overlooked their treatment of the seringueiros and were apparently unaware of their obstruction of rubber cultivation. The sympathy garnered by the gathering trade helped it to gain redress of the losses it had suffered in 1960 and 1961, when inflation had eroded the minimum price that rubber manufacturers were obliged to pay for their raw material.[3]

Predictably, the abundant and reliable domestic synthetic rubber was even more attractive after these price increases, and natural rubber began to lose still more customers. With the near elimination of imported rubber by 1965, and the inauguration of the COPERBO plant, another crisis was clearly upon the sector. Meanwhile, the populist Goulart had been overthrown in a military coup. The generals saw themselves not only as the nation's last line of defense against communism, but also as the saviors of its economy. They would sweep away corruption and deputize their technocratic favorites in the civil bureaucracy to remove hindrances to the free play of the market. A series of measures was taken to galvanize the Amazon region: The Amazon Credit Bank was turned into a regional development bank and renamed Bank of Amazônia (BASA), and in place of the ineffectual SPVEA a new planning agency was created, called the Superintendency of the Amazon (SUDAM). Among their responsibilities were the rationalization of the rubber sector and the supervision of a program of extremely generous tax incentives for new investments in the region.[4]

Rubber policy was taken in hand by the Ministry of Planning. Foreseeing an oversupply of rubber, both at home and abroad, the ministry sought to control the market in order to broaden demand and prevent the collapse of wild and plantation producers. In January 1967, Congress, in accord with the ministry's proposals, passed law 5227. It imposed on Brazilian rubber producers a draconian plan to abolish government purchases and to eliminate the domestic subsidy within five years. Indeed that was already on the way to accomplishment – since the coup, the minimum price had been raised at less than half the rate of inflation. The Rubber Defense Executive Commission, renamed the National Rubber Council (CNB), would continue to oversee prices. A Superintendency of Rubber (SUDHEVEA) was created to take over the strategic rubber stock, formed at the time of the Indonesian crisis of 1966, and to certify the origin of rubber offered for sale. It was to collect a 5 percent tax (soon to be known by its acronym, TORMB) on all elastomers, natural and synthetic. Part of the revenues thus obtained was to be turned over to BASA for loans to rubber planters. SUDHEVEA would also carry out market studies and review government and private plans to develop rubber. Finally, the law revoked the 1954 decree that had compelled the tire companies to invest in rubber plantations, apparently out of a fear that they might eventually dominate both natural and synthetic sources of supply.[5]

Law 5227 was not devoid of compassion for regional interests. SUDAM was ordered to plan for the diversification and improved productivity of the Amazon economy, and BASA was to accord priority to the Amazon in the financing of rubber planting. Rubber was defined as broadly as possible, so as to awaken once again among northeasterners the hope that their commercially unimportant native Hancornia, Sapium, and Manihot plants might be eligible for government loans. But these gestures hardly offset the threat to cancel the price subsidy within five years. An end to subsidies would obliterate an activity that seemed on the verge of extinction. From the late 1940s to the early 1960s, income from rubber gathering had fallen from 8 percent to 5 percent of the regional economy of the Amazon. Even so, extractive activities in general, including tin ore and gold prospecting, the hunting of pelts, and the gathering of Brazil nuts, still occupied 60 percent of the regional labor force. Rubber was a key element in sustaining these other survival stratagems, because it was government funded.[6]

The tattered legion of seringalistas and aviadores assembled for one more political battle. In 1967, the Chamber of Deputies appointed an investigative committee, chaired by Deputy Cid Sampaio, of the Northeastern state of Pernambuco. Sampaio was representing the COPERBO plant, which was unable to operate profitably on alcohol feedstocks without a heavy government subsidy, and was encountering consumer resistance for its product among the tire manufacturers. Thus a coalition of northeastern and Amazon interests was determined to impress upon the public consciousness yet again the image of a vast wilderness, preserved for the nation through the persistence of a handful of brave, unaided frontiersmen, whose only livelihood was rubber. Vehemently, representatives of the gathering trade, such as Guilherme Zaire, seringalista and Acre state deputy; Alpertino Lopes, president of the Chamber of Commerce of Rondônia; and Manuel Miranda Sobrinho, aviador of Belém, demanded their share of the pie. If rubber was anachronistically produced, so was corn, sugar, and every other crop. "Why choose us for victims?" asked

Samuel Benchimol, an economist from Manaus. If Brazilian internal prices had to be equated with the world market, why not start, he suggested, with the automobile industry![7]

Felisberto Camargo raged against this travesty of economic logic. In his testimony he called for an end to the "criminal policy of trying to maintain, through legal dispositions inspired by demagogy, the standards of an obsolete extractive regime." But Sampaio called to the witness stand a parade of government employees who admitted to the committee that all the rubber planting schemes so far undertaken had been failures, and that all current plans, even if their outcomes were any different, were on a scale much inferior to Brazil's future needs.

The rubber manufacturers, insisting on the validity of Law 5227, demanded that the Congress "admit the extinction of forest extraction" and authorize still more synthetic factories. They wanted the government price, furthermore, to be based on the cost of planted, not wild, rubber. In vain: On 21 June 1968, Congress passed another rubber law, number 5459, entirely contrary to that of the year before. Now the TORMB was to be raised high enough to equalize the prices of imported plantation rubber and wild rubber. In part this reversal reflected the restored importance of wild rubber in the light of rapid growth in demand, which, by 1968, had risen beyond the capacity of the synthetic plants. The 20,000–30,000 tons the gathering trade might achieve was once again of use in reducing imports. Nelson Prado Alves Pinto notes that the military, convinced of the strategic necessity of occupying the border areas, was planning a vast survey of the region's resources and the building of a network of penetration highways, including the Trans-Amazon. The gatherers might be enlisted in these schemes; therefore, they were to be afforded the means to remain in place.[8]

The new law, nevertheless, contained the means for a much more intensive attack on the problem of rubber cultivation. In 1968, the difference in price between domestic and imported rubber amounted to 2.60 cruzeiros per kilogram. This implied that the TORMB would accumulate a fund of 31 to 36 million cruzeiros ($8.1 to $9.4 million) a year, enough to expand enormously rubber research and technical and financial assistance to rubber planters. SUDAM had already unveiled a project that it had inherited from SPVEA. That agency had developed in collaboration with ETA Project 54 a five-year plan to plant two million trees on cooperators' demonstation plots and to finance the planting of another eight million trees on private lands. The committee thought this project, which SUDAM called the Amazon Rubber Cultivation Project (PROHEVEA), "entirely utopian" with the funds SUDAM then had at its disposal, but it recommended that with the added resources the new law provided, it could and should be doubled.[9]

Cássio Fonseca, head of the new CNB, was, however, quite unwilling to make any such commitment of TORMB funds. He doubted the practicality of

PROHEVEA in the absence of adequately staffed technical agencies and urged that such be established. A study group was set up by SUDHEVEA to evaluate the capacities of agencies then involved in rubber and to refine the PROHEVEA project. This group, called the Executive Group of the Rubber Plan (GEPLASE), confirmed, in effect, Fonseca's suspicions regarding the scarcity of trained personnel to undertake rubber development, yet it also insisted that Brazil needed to plant 100,000 hectares and should do so within five years. GEPLASE was followed by an expanded study, called the National Rubber Plan, which reviewed the situation of natural rubber development quite thoroughly, endorsing the planting of 100,000 hectares, but timorously stretching this program out over twenty years.[10]

In 1971, Fonseca resigned his directorship of the CNB, opening a breach through which the TORMB fund might be raided by the gathering trade. Executive decree-law 1200, emitted 28 December 1971, authorized an enlarged natural rubber reserve and permitted the fund to be used to finance wild rubber. This was not the gatherers' only counterattack. They were undoubtedly the source of the proposal included in several of SUDAM's reports to fund the planting of Hevea in existing wild rubber groves, an impractical scheme that would have been the equivalent of unencumbered grants to the seringalistas. Amazon deputies also criticized the recommendations of GEPLASE and the PNB to allocate to southern Bahia and São Paulo a part of the rubber development funding. Indeed, Cid Sampaio even sought to have the cultivation of rubber outside the Amazon entirely prohibited![11]

GEPLASE identified South American Leaf Blight as the "principal restraint on the establishment of rubber cultivation" in Brazil and the "limiting factor" in most of the area in which it might be planted. "It is a matter of extreme gravity, permanent, difficult to solve, and it demands many concentrated efforts to get it under control." Of these, the principal was to develop clones that would be resistant as well as productive.[12]

Unfortunately, there was no longer in Brazil a single qualified researcher assigned full-time to the problem of leaf blight. In Belém, the IAN, renamed the Institute for Agricultural Research and Experimentation of the North (IPEAN), had relegated rubber to a low priority. The IPEAN was assisting usefully in the acclimatization of rice, jute, pepper, and African oil palm, all of which were becoming important regional crops. But rubber remained a frustrating puzzle and a political problem, and was being ignored. Much of the material collected by Ford and the USDA had been lost or mislabeled with the transfers of managerial control at Fordlandia, Belterra, and the IAN. Townsend's crosses were by then hopelessly outdated, in any case, since their high-yielding components were clones that in Southeast Asia had long been replaced with a new and more productive generation. Only one collecting expedition was carried out during this decade, to Rondônia in 1962, and samples were taken from just fifty-seven mother trees. Eurico Pinheiro, of the crop science section, carried forward selection and breeding experiments with two assistants, while teaching part-time at the Faculty of Agricultural Sciences of Pará (FCAP). He had shifted the program largely to crosses with *Hevea pauciflora*, as crosses with other species of the genus had been found to lose resistance. Several hundred outcrosses and backcrosses were being subject to field trials each year. Whether this generation of clones would offer high yields while preserving their apparent resistance, it was not yet possible to determine.[13]

At the Agronomic Institute of Campinas (IAC) in São Paulo, Luiz Octávio Teixeira Mendes, once employed by Felisberto Camargo at the IAN, obtained research funds to investigate a novel approach he had first suggested in 1942. Mendes noted that the Rubber Research Institute of Malaya (RRIM) had applied colchicine, a compound used to induce polyploids, that is, plants with multiple sets of chromosomes, to Hevea and had observed enlarged sieve tubes. He decided, therefore, to subject resistant but low-yielding clones to this procedure, hoping that high-yielding polyploid clones might thus be artificially and quickly derived. These experiments were the only important ones in Brazil outside of IPEAN; the GEPLASE survey found that none of the other agricultural research centers was carrying on significant work, and that even Pinheiro and Mendes had published extremely little concerning the results of their labors.[14]

Meanwhile, at the Firestone estates in Liberia and at the RRIM, the resistant clonal material obtained through exchanges with the IAN in the early 1950s had been crossed with high-yielding Southeast Asian clones. The Firestone crosses were sent for tests of resistance to leaf blight to Firestone's plantation at Camamu, and to its experimental station at Finca Clavellinas in Guatemala. RRIM selections were sent for similar field trials to a research unit installed at the University of the West Indies in Trinidad. In Guatemala, Firestone possessed resistant clones found in the Madre de Dios region of Peru in the late 1940s. When all were found to be low-yielding, they were crossed with Southeast Asian clones. The results of the trials of these crosses were disappointing. By the late 1960s, it was clear that the crosses lacked resistance. Thus the Malaysian and Liberian researchers, with far greater resources and experience than their Brazilian colleagues, had had no better luck. In Asia and Africa, calls for vigilance against a potential invasion of Microcyclus reached a higher pitch.[15]

In the light of these trials and the earlier performance of Fordlandia and Belterra clones – which lost their supposed resistance when transferred to the Goodyear, Pirelli, and Firestone estates – it seemed that conservative evaluations of the newer planting materials were in order. It could not yet be determined whether this loss was due to local environmental conditions or to the evolution of newer strains of the pathogen. Michael H. Langford's studies of races of Microcyclus at Turrialba, carried forward by Kenneth R. Langdon and John W. Miller of the University of Florida, suggested that the fungus would eventually adapt to the hybrid clones. Furthermore, it seemed quite likely that the clones produced by further backcrossing would display the same loss of resistance that Townsend had experienced, presumably because resistance depended on more than one gene. As for the polyploids, Mendes was finding it difficult to obtain in them characteristics that were exclusively desirable. Anatomical and cytological studies of Hevea were still lacking, but it was suspected that it was already a tetraploid, possessing thirty-six chromosomes in the diploid state; therefore, colchicine doubling might not result in increased latex capacity.[16]

Nevertheless, the public statements of rubber researchers suggested that the leaf blight problem had been overcome. In 1965, ETA Project 54 claimed that IPEAN now had resistant clones "capable of rivalling in productivity those selected in the Orient," thus rubber planting, once highly risky, was "economically guaranteed." Pinheiro wrote in 1968 that the institute's new series of clones "are the equivalent in productivity to several of the Oriental clones, and unlike the latter do not present susceptibility to leaf blight." GEPLASE asserted "no doubt remains that already satisfactory results have been obtained" in breeding and reported respectfully on Mendes's experiments. Congress, in recommending large-scale planting with vastly increased funding, clearly counted on the accuracy of these statements. Deputy Cid Sampaio informed Congress that "today the clones selected by IPEAN, if they are not immune to the disease, present a resistance which, according to its technicians, makes possible economic cultivation of Hevea."[17]

Because none of the clones that had so far been bred could in fact be recommended with reasonable certainty, top grafting continued to be suggested as a means of preserving Southeast Asian clones from leaf blight. At the USDA station at Turrialba, it had been found that the low-yielding crown did depress somewhat the productivity of the top-grafted trunk, but that the effect was lessened if the graft was attached higher up. Unfortunately, the use of stepladders slowed down the work and made it more expensive. The RRIM discovered that the rate of success in top grafting could be appreciably raised by grafting on branches that were still green. Top grafting permitted the tire companies' estates to import the newest and most productive of the postwar Southeast Asian clones, such as RRIM 600, but their managers were still quite wary of an expensive technique that delayed tapping by two years, increased wind damage, and produced groves of ragged appearance and uneven output. At Belterra, the site of the largest experiment ever carried out in top grafting, curiously no studies were made of resulting yields or side effects.[18]

The third line of approach to the problem of leaf blight was that of chemical control. The copper- or sulphur-based fungicides that had proved effective in Central America could not be used in groves of mature trees. Copper is an oxidizing agent that impedes the coagulation of the latex, and sulphur, which is, of course, employed in the vulcanizing process, also reacts with the rubber molecules. By 1960, new fungicides, such as Dithane, Cercobin, and Parzate, had appeared on the market. They were imported, however, and were therefore very costly to apply. Alfonso Wisniewski, head of the IPEAN, waxed quite vehement when questioned by the Sampaio committee concerning the practicality of chemical control of leaf blight. "If I had to plant a rubber grove, thinking I would combat it with fungicides, I'd stop believing in rubber." If high-yielding and resistant clones could not be found, he said, "then it would be better to say no more about rubber trees."[19]

No doubt he had in mind as well the difficulties of applying the fungicide to mature trees, twenty or thirty meters in height. In Malaya various kinds of sprayers were being tried, but all were either underpowered or too ponderous to draw through the groves. Archibald Johnston had suggested aerial spraying at Belterra as early as 1942, and had tried to get budget authorization for an airplane. He believed Fordlandia was too hilly for aerial spraying to work, but that Belterra would be ideal for this form of control. He was told that Belterra's overhead was already too high to support further heavy expenditures, and the matter was ignored by the Brazilian managers thereafter. But Johnston's suggestion was potentially valuable. It was taken up again before the Sampaio committee by C. J. Huding, manager of the Goodyear estate. He stated, however, that aerial dusting was practicable only on a very large scale, therefore rubber planting would have to be carried out on estates of a minimum of 10,000 hectares.[20]

Meanwhile, at the Cacao Research Center (CEPEC) of the Bahian Cacao Development Commission, located at Itabuna, another sort of aerial control measure was under consideration. G. R. Manço, who had been studying the timing of leaf fall in Hevea, noticed that different clones of Hevea, or trees of the same clone in different sites, shed their leaves at different times, thus preserving over the course of the dry season the more virulent conidial form of the fungus. He read, however, the proposal of the RRIM to spray herbicides from the air in Malaya in the event of an invasion by Microcyclus and conceived the idea that the trees might be sprayed with herbicides just before the onset of the dry season, thus extending and regularizing the period of leaflessness, and thereby reducing the inoculum available to infect the next year's vulnerable leaflets. This theory was given initial tests at the CEPEC nursery in 1969 and 1970.[21]

In the 1960s, federal and state agricultural extension services had almost no experience with rubber. ETA Project 54 had been conceived as a coordinated program through which extension might be provided farmers, with credit from BASA and a supply of reliable clones from the IPEAN. But by 1966 that project had come to nothing. Of the four million seedlings raised, it may be that no more than a half million were distributed. In 1967, PROHEVEA, the successor program, took over its surviving nurseries and budwood gardens and proceeded to expand them and to lay out model plots on the lands of farmer cooperators. More than 200 of these plots were planned, each twenty hectares in size, with a total potential yield of 6,000 tons of rubber. More important, these models were supposed to demonstrate to neighboring farmers that rubber could be profitably grown with existing clones and techniques.[22]

Of the seedlings distributed by ETA Project 54, it may be that few were ever planted, since field inspection was in fact rare. According to the pungent testimony of Samuel Benchimol, who enrolled in the program, the extension agents gave such inappropriate or contradictory advice that farmers were uprooting the plants in despair. The colony at Itacoatiara, supposedly closely supervised by IPEAN, turned out to be as unproductive as the rest; half of it was later lost in a fire. PROHEVEA's planting program fell behind schedule. GEPLASE found that by the end of 1969, hardly a quarter of the planned planting had been carried out. Worse, the demonstration plots were in ''dismaying'' condition: Many were sited on inappropriate soils, or were so improperly or negligently maintained that nearby farmers who had planted rubber were refusing to follow IPEAN instructions. Others, no doubt, had decided not to plant rubber at all.[23]

Some observers believed that the critical factor in the failure of the official colonies and in the abandonment of the privately planted groves was the inability or unwillingness of BASA to supply credit. The bank's terms for rubber loans appeared generous: 60 percent of costs up to 75,800 cruzeiros ($238) per hectare in 1961, interest at 7.5 percent per year, and no repayment for seven years. In fact, extremely few rubber loans were made and installments were repeatedly delayed. Over and over, the complaint was heard from farmers that they had acquired seedlings from IPEAN or from extension agents, planted them, applied to the bank, and never received approval. Possibly BASA's managers were simply trying to avoid loans that would inevitably produce losses. Given Brazil's rate of inflation, these were negative interest loans of astonishing generosity.[24]

And what of the government-run Belterra and Fordlandia estates? Had they contributed to the production of natural rubber? The new agency created by the Ministry of Agriculture to supervise the former Ford plantations was called the Rural Establishment of the Tapajós (ERT). Its output gradually slumped as the work force and the trees aged and employment on the estate became part of a political spoils system. During the Goulart administration the ERT was shifted to the federal land reform agency, a sign that it was planned to subdivide the estates into lots and distribute them to the workers. This did not occur, but the resident population and the payroll continued to grow. Although another 165 hectares were planted after 1964, four years later the state of abandonment was far advanced. Only 180,000 trees were in tap, and only 300 of the 1,200 persons on the payroll were engaged in tapping. Yield estimates were conflicting, but output may have amounted to less than 200 tons, and it was all latex concentrate since the resident technicians still could not achieve coagulation.[25]

Cid Sampaio's investigating committee was anguished to learn of the incompetence and opportunism to which the properties had been subjected. Its president, Deputy Hélio Gueiros, treated his colleagues to a melancholy soliloquy: "I'm coming to the conclusion that, unhappily, matters in Brazil in government hands simply don't work. An establishment with 1.7 [*sic*] million planted trees can't be exploited because exploitation is uneconomic. Where are we headed? Out in Acre, on the upper Perús or on the upper Juru, a wild grove survives one way or another. The government owns a grove that's planted, near a place that has air service and it's not exploited because it's uneconomic. It seems incredible. Is there no escape from bureaucracy? Can't this estate be given to someone to plant? Get a *seringueiro* and say to him: I won't pay you anything; this is a grove like any other; how many trees can you tap? A thousand? Here, here's a thousand. Tap them and give the Establishment 10 percent. It's not possible that for a lack of a market for latex, we can't make rubber in a grove a short distance from Santarém, when they make rubber in Acre, on the upper Guaporé. It's unbelievable. . . .After all, here we are four years under what might be called a strong government, and we have plenty of decree-laws and institutional acts. And the speaker is not an opposition deputy, but it seems as though our efforts are useless."[26]

In 1969, the ERT was abolished, possibly because of the committee's revelations. The estates were turned over to the Pará office of the federal agricultural extension agency, which seems to have managed, at least for a time, to restore output to earlier, but still very modest, levels. In 1969, it was reported that with a small increase in the work force, 420,000 trees were being tapped; latex obtained that year may have been the equivalent of 380 tons of dry rubber, implying a yield of 270 kilograms per hectare. By then, however, the weeds were growing as tall as the rubber trees in the unkempt groves, whose recuperation was coming to seem an extremely unlikely undertaking.[27]

In São Paulo not all the Hevea planted during the official campaign of the late 1950s had been uprooted; indeed, some further planting may have been carried out. In 1969, it was estimated that there were 700,000 to 800,000 trees in the state, but more than half of them were on the littoral and were much damaged by leaf blight. Some of the trees on the highland plateau, however, were ready to tap by 1966, and a few latex processing plants were accordingly installed. Yield reports were provided by only two of these properties, both in the municipality of Colina. Only half of their nine- to ten-year-old base-grafted trees were ready to tap, and yields on the two properties amounted to 200 and 338 kilograms per hectare. These were disappointing results. There were few farmers who seemed to be taking the trouble to tap their trees. Some of those who did were tapping too intensively, perhaps with the intention of maximizing their immediate return before uprooting them. Nevertheless, the IAC continued to advise the state's farmers that the planting of Hevea was practical, that leaf blight had never been found on the plateau, and therefore susceptible high-yielding clones could be planted. The IAC reported varying theoretical yields up to an astounding 2,000 kilograms per hectare in its experimental groves.[28]

The estates owned by the multinational corporations were faring no better. In Mato Grosso, in the municipality of Porto dos Gaúchos, 700 kilometers north of Cuiabá, a private land development called Colonization of Northwest Mato Grosso (CONOMALI), had been founded in 1955 by a company headquartered in Rio Grande do Sul. Its colonists began planting rubber, and within four years there were half a million Hevea trees on their lots. This effort attracted German investors, who paid for the planting of another 1.5 to 2.0 million trees. CONOMALI was thus almost as large an undertaking as Belterra. And it appears to have been well conceived and executed; the planting was done with base-grafted Fordlandia and IAN clones. Nevertheless, as the groves reached maturity in 1968, and their canopies became a solid mass, leaf blight struck. According to the GEPLASE report, the groves would have to be top grafted under the same emergency conditions that had prevailed at Belterra twenty-five years before.[29]

The tire companies, even though they had been released from their obligation to plant rubber, all maintained their plantations. But they were unable to show a profit, as the manager of the Goodyear estate informed Deputy Cid Sampaio, because of the ravages of Microcyclus. Asked why the company had not engaged in experimentation, the manager replied glumly that the whole estate was an experiment: By 1968, Goodyear had tried out 600 clones, without finding any sufficiently resistant. Blight, and attempts at double grafting, delayed tapping by three to six years and obliged constant replanting. Goodyear had invested $2.5 million, achieving yields of only 210 kilograms per hectare and an output of only 70 tons a year, worth, at the subsidized domestic price, the equivalent in cruzeiros of less than $70,000. Dunlop's estate was apparently experiencing even lower yields. The Pirelli estate had to top graft all its clones in 1968, after several attacks of SALB. The next year its manager still had no rubber to ship. Firestone's output, 436 kilograms per hectare, was the best of all the companies, but fell far short of its Liberian yields. Had the tire companies been able to equal Southeast Asian plantation standards of 1,200 to 1,400 kilograms per hectare, together they would have been supplying Brazil with more than 6,000 tons of rubber.[30]

Firestone, which had bought out the General Tire Company factory in Rio de Janeiro, was the only company forging ahead with new groves. It had systematically replanted areas that had not been laid out originally on contours. Its managers had found top grafting extremely costly and preferred to replace clones that proved susceptible. Nearly half of the Camamu estate had been thus replanted. Although it was taking part in the company's coordinated breeding and testing program centered at Firestone's Liberian estate, nearly all of its planting was of Ford and IAN clones, principally Fx 25. By 1968, unfortunately, this clone's resistance had broken down; 153 hectares were badly affected and would have to be replanted. It was suspected that new races of Microcyclus were emerging. In 1969, the estate was also struck by the mandarová caterpillar, and 700 hectares were reported destroyed.[31]

With continued replanting, yields at Camamu by 1971 had reportedly reached 825 kilograms per hectare, and the company was planning a much larger planting program of 600 hectares a year. But leaf blight struck again the following year and yields began to fall off. Top grafting had to be carried out on even newer clones, since they also seemed to be losing their resistance.[32]

The Sampaio committee gave little credence to the explanations offered by the tire companies' plantation managers. True enough, their presentations had eschewed overtones of pessimism that might have put their competence in question. Deputy Sampaio therefore felt free to insist on his own explanation for the companies' lack of success: It was deliberate! They preferred, he claimed, to import rubber from their plantations abroad and to this end they were manipulating international prices. This seems illogical, since they surely would have profited more by selling as much domestically grown rubber as possible at the protected domestic price. In any case, they denied that any of their rubber came from their plantations in Africa or Southeast Asia, a denial supported by Cássio Fonseca.[33]

Rubber planting was nevertheless spreading in southern Bahia partly because of the presence of Firestone and Dunlop. In 1960, Governor Juracy Magalhães decreed a Rubber Expansion Service, budgeted at fifty million cruzeiros ($250,000). Even though this agency was never effectively installed, the National Development Bank provided a number of loans. Several hundred farmers undertook Hevea planting eagerly, principally at Camamu and Una, where Firestone and the IAL, renamed the Institute for Agricultural Research and Experimentation of the East (IPEAL), were distributing seeds and seedlings. A local landowner, Manuel Pereira de Almeida, planted 400,000 trees and helped found a smallholding colony. Since Hevea was less demanding of the soil than cacao, farmers put rubber on their less productive lands. By 1964, there were 8.1 million trees in southern Bahia, 5.1 million of them at Una, Camamu, and Ituberá. Only 1.6 million were ready to be tapped, evidence that more than half of the Hevea planted during the 1950s had been abandoned. Of the young trees, most were base grafted, indicating that extension services had reached most of the farmers. It was believed that as much as 300 tons of rubber was sold. Still, this was equivalent to an insignificant fifty-five kilograms per hectare.[34]

The rush to plant rubber in southern Bahia had resulted in an excessive reliance on the Fx 25 clone. Half the new acreage had been planted in it.

Microcyclus again appeared in epidemic form in 1964, attacking Fx 25 and two other Brazilian clones, Fx 3810 and IAN 717. The anomaly of clones unharmed on one plantation suffering severe damage on neighboring estates was widespread. Planters who had supposed their lands beyond the reach of the leaf blight and who had therefore planted Southeast Asian clones were obliged hastily to top graft. Worse, some of the clones more resistant to Microcyclus were struck by another quite dangerous fungus, *Phytophthora palmivora*, a parasite common in the cacao groves. CEPEC researchers had to recommend that the older susceptible trees be tapped to exhaustion and removed and that those under three years old be top grafted. This was a very considerable loss, and farmers who had planted in an access of enthusiasm grew quite discouraged. The rate of rubber planting, 7.5 million trees from 1960 to 1963, declined to 1.7 million over the next four years.[35]

Still, by 1967, the rubber plantations of southern Bahia contained 11.7 million trees. If all these were to come into production, and a very modest output of a half ton per hectare was achieved, the region's output would nearly equal that of the wild rubber groves. Cid Sampaio therefore lectured representatives of the CNB and BASA on the "imprudence" of offering credit to Bahian rubber growers. They assured him that they were making loans only to plantations in being, lest they collapse, but BASA would provide no funds for further expansion and the state banks would not be authorized to do so. Unfortunately, they explained, they lacked the authority to prevent private banks from lending money for rubber.[36]

Thus representatives of the gathering trade persisted in their persecution of still-experimental rubber cultivation, as their own business languished and unemployment in their region increased. Between 1950 and 1970, the labor force of the Amazon states and territories doubled, to about 1.7 million. Of these workers, barely 300,000 were fully employed. It has been claimed, in regard to earlier times, that labor scarcity or the failure of rural workers to respond to wage incentives had ruined attempts at rubber planting. As improbable as those arguments were even in regard to the past, they could certainly no longer be advanced. The "economically active" proportion of the Amazon population was in decline – from 31.5 to 28.9 percent between 1950 and 1970, and the cities of the Amazon were swelling with tens of thousands of desperate indigents.[37]

Wild rubber tapping was becoming less and less attractive to the rural poor as their seringalista patrons fell so far into debt that BASA would no longer extend further credit. In 1960, the minimum wage in the region amounted to 2,400 cruzeiros ($12) a month. Five years later, payments to tappers in Acre and Rondônia, the most productive regions, amounted to the equivalent of $15 a month, a fictitious improvement, considering the capacity of the seringalistas to rig prices in their stores. It was noted that tappers who managed to obtain a positive balance in their account were departing the wild rubber trade.

What this implied for attempts to improve productivity in the wild stands may be imagined. Despite these realities, representatives of the gathering trade continued to ascribe Southeast Asia's price advantage to servile, underpaid labor.[38]

But the threat to wild rubber from domestic rubber plantations was still far from real. Certainly the maneuvers of the gathering trade had made it difficult for the government to shift resources into rational cultivation. Insufficient funding of rubber research resulted in poorly grounded advice and ineffective planning. As one deputy complained before the Sampaio committee, "The testimony. . .suggests that there is complete perplexity in the face of the rubber problem. These various agencies, only after being called here before this investigating committee did they take any steps to plan their work or set their goals." The result was that potential planters were losing confidence in the claims of the rubber developers. "This is just a way of attracting the investor, of getting everyone excited," exclaimed Samuel Benchimol, referring to IPEAN's prediction that trees would be ready to tap in six to eight years. As one observer noted, the farmers complained that lack of credit obliged them to abandon their rubber groves, but these same groves sometimes adjoined plots of pepper plants that were beautifully tended.[39]

In contrast to the stagnation of the Amazon economy, the Brazilian industrial heartland was during these same years expanding vertiginously. The years 1968 to 1973 were those of the "Brazilian Miracle," with economic growth rates close to 10 percent a year. The demand for rubber was inevitably growing at an even faster rate. But natural rubber output, wild and planted, remained below 25,000 tons. The gap was filled partly by an increase in natural rubber imports – 1973 was the first year that the importation of natural rubber, 36,600 tons, surpassed domestic production.

More ominously, Brazil was becoming excessively dependent on synthetic rubber, which grew from 65 percent to 75 percent of total rubber consumption, one of the highest ratios in the world, and entirely anomalous among industrializing tropical countries. The expansion of synthetic capacity was certainly the fastest response to the crisis of supply, and it was one of a number of industrial achievements of the 1960s. But synthetic rubber depended on imported raw materials and technology, and the means of payment of imported inputs were extremely limited. This was the Brazilian economy's principal point of vulnerability. It was perfectly sensible, therefore, to press on with the search for a solution to the problem of cultivated rubber. Unfortunately, another decade of effort had been plagued by budget shortages, cross-purposes, and incompetence.

Brazilian rubber development in the 1960s was so fitful that it is hard to discern the depressive effect of leaf blight in all of those endeavors. Had it not been operative, however, and had farmers in Bahia and the Amazon been achieving 1,000 kilograms of rubber per hectare, then the presence or absence of bank credit or extension agents would have been a secondary matter. (Indeed, since bankers and agricultural technicians are attracted to successful crops, a reasonable yield would have multiplied their attentions.) These same farmers were successfully growing, under identical or less favorable financial and technical conditions, pepper, cacao, sisal, and other crops for nonsubsidized prices in the competitive world market. Overall, Brazilian farmers in the decade before 1966 raised food production by 74 percent and export crop production by 146 percent. It is important to emphasize this point, since the mass of government-generated documentation might induce the sensation that it was bureaucrats, rather than farmers, who were producing crops. It is also important to emphasize it, lest the reader gather the impression that the Brazilian farm sector was generally incompetent or unresponsive to demand.[40]

Rubber, however, was exceptional. Under the prevailing ecological conditions, it could not be made to grow profitably. The experience of the multinational tire companies in the 1960s, more than the scattered domestic efforts, provides abundant proof of this thesis. Experienced American, English, and Dutch rubber technicians, backed with the money of some of the world's largest rubber manufacturing and plantation companies, had failed quite independently of the vagaries of Brazilian politics, bureaucracy, and culture. No humans, of any nationality, had yet found a solution to the problem of a fungal plant disease whose only saving grace was that it had not yet managed to cross oceans.

9

Economically guaranteed, 1973–1986

The formation of an international oil cartel at the end of 1973 transformed the Brazilian rubber situation and gave rise to a decade of feverish effort to resolve the problem of natural rubber. The country's excessive reliance on synthetic rubber appeared more inappropriate than ever, in view of that industry's dependence on imported petroleum. Therefore considerable resources were suddenly marshaled to carry out a vast program of scientific and practical research, extension services, and farm credit. Brazil appeared to be at last ready to do whatever was necessary to conquer the leaf blight, after years of irresolution and cross-purposes.

Natural rubber's competitiveness seemed much enhanced, and Brazilians reflected on markets abroad that they might yet recapture were they to succeed in cultivating Hevea. Despite the appearance of new kinds of synthetic rubbers, planted rubber continued to be preferred for certain applications and retained nearly a third of world demand through the early 1970s. Meanwhile, Brazil's modest supply of wild rubber was in decline. The development schemes initiated along the Trans-Amazon highway were converting once-remote rain forest into ranches and farms. Many seringueiros were abandoning their underpaid occupation and joining those projects, or else departing for casual employment in the cities. Natural rubber output, which had averaged 24,500 tons from 1971 to 1973, fell to an average 19,400 tons from 1974 to 1976. It seemed that less time was left to devise practical means of cultivation than had been supposed.[1]

The oil crisis forced the government to assist farmers who might reduce the balance of payments gap, either by exporting food crops or by producing raw materials like rubber, which substituted for imports. This assistance took the form of cheap and abundant credit. The Bank of Amazônia (BASA) was only one of several agencies used to funnel credit to rural areas as a way of offsetting in part the favoritism to the cities inherent in the industrialization program. The flow of agricultural credit through these agencies multiplied five times during the 1970s, twice as fast as farm output itself. By the end of the decade, total farm credit equaled 85 percent of the net value of farm output.

Other inputs into the farm sector were similarly expanded. Even though more than half of domestic fertilizer consumption was imported, fertilizer use, which had quadrupled in the 1960s, quadrupled again, to four million tons, in the 1970s.[2]

The rubber sector enjoyed two additional advantages. Planted rubber continued to be sold at the same subsidized price as wild rubber – two to three times the world price, and it was backed by a large and growing single-purpose fund. The TORMB (Tax for the Organization and Regulation of the Rubber Market) surcharge on natural and synthetic rubber imports by the early 1970s amounted to more than $25 million a year, guaranteeing SUD-HEVEA (Superintendency of Rubber) the commanding position in rubber policy. Originally designed to administer the rubber stocks and price controls, SUDHEVEA was subordinate to the Ministry of Industry and Commerce, a sign that it had been expected to deal in elastomers as industrial raw materials. Indeed up to then its success had been limited to developing synthetic rubber. That orientation, however, and its location in Brasília, provided the agency a degree of objectivity in its relations with the gathering trade that SUDAM and BASA had found impossible.[3]

With the appointment of Mário Lima to the directorship, SUDHEVEA began to make aggressive use of TORMB funds. In July 1972, it was given charge of a new scheme, dubbed PROBOR. This was to provide 7 percent, full-funding loans for the planting of 18,000 hectares of rubber. Repayment was waived for eight years, until tapping might begin, and farmers were assured that if through no fault of theirs they did not achieve the yields promised by PROBOR, their loans would be canceled. Part of the fund was made available for the "recuperation" of another 5,000 hectares of existing groves. Eligibility was originally to be limited to the Amazon region, but Bahia was finally included in the program. The main novelty of PROBOR, compared to its many failed predecessors, consisted in the availability of the promised funds.[4]

In 1977, Stésio Henri Guitton, Mário Lima's successor as superintendent, initiated a much larger plan, called PROBOR 2, calling for 120,000 hectares to be planted within five years. In addition, 10,000 hectares of planted groves and 10,000 hectares of wild groves were to be recuperated. This program was expected to afford Brazil self-sufficiency in rubber. It was budgeted at $202 million, including $114 million for the planted groves. Again, full financing and 7 percent interest rates were offered, for groves up to 100 hectares. Even before PROBOR 2 was completed, SUDHEVEA unveiled PROBOR 3, which was to plant 250,000 hectares, enough to provide a huge surplus for export. This plan, begun in late 1982, also furnished loans to develop commercial nurseries, to recuperate another 6,000 hectares of planted groves, and to maintain cultivation of 5,000 hectares of PROBOR 1 plantings.[5]

The decision had been made to throw a great deal of money at the rubber problem, in the belief that only an intensive effort could succeed. But these ambitious programs fell much behind schedule. By the early 1970s, there was among farmers considerable suspicion of government assertions that rubber was "a sure investment." Loans were given under PROBOR 1 for 18,000 hectares – a process that took seven years – but only 13,538 of these hectares were planted. Twelve years after the start of the program, only 1,850 hectares were in production. By 1984, only 83,333 hectares had been planted under PROBOR 2, and only 20,882 hectares under PROBOR 3. And these official figures overestimated the true situation, since loans were constantly being written off for noncompliance.[6]

It appears that as many as half of the PROBOR 2 projects were abandoned, even before the appearance of South American Leaf Blight (SALB). Seven percent interest was a gift, with inflation over 20 percent, and inspection by local officers of BASA was spotty at best. It was therefore tempting to use the credits for other purposes, and many people did. Others failed because of mismanagement or simply because, with the steep increase in inflation, the funds disbursed were too low to cover expenses. SUDHEVEA seemed to view this poor performance as an inevitable cost of rapid expansion in a field still technically immature. In 1983, its director, José Cesário Menezes de Barros, who himself had planted a small grove near Manaus and astonishingly allowed it to fail for lack of proper maintenance, referred to PROBOR 1 as having "assumed the character of a pilot program." Nevertheless, if only a third of the area under the three programs were to come into operation and achieve yields of 700 kilograms per hectare, by 1990 that would more than satisfy projected domestic demand.[7]

SUDHEVEA also paid for technical and social assistance to rubber growers. It supported field services of the Brazilian Technical and Rural Extension Enterprise, an agency of the Ministry of Agriculture that was reorganized in 1973, and field services of similar agencies at the state level. Several hundred extension agents received special training in rubber. SUDHEVEA subsidized social service agencies to provide cheap foodstuffs, basic education, and medical care to rubber gatherers and small farmers. This was carried out on a large scale: 320 schools and 220 clinics were functioning by 1982. Brazilian specialists had long complained that the rubber problem constituted a vicious circle – a lobby of successful rubber farmers was necessary to maintain government support for planted rubber, but there could be no successful rubber farmers without government aid. SUDHEVEA was aware of the difficulty, having reported in 1982 that PROBOR 3 had fallen behind because "an interested public had not yet been identified." The superintendency therefore fostered associations of tappers and smallholders not only to disseminate technical information, but also to strengthen its political support.[8]

Under PROBOR 1 some $4.7 million was directed toward basic and applied research. Existing research programs at the time were not merely stagnant, but shrinking. In 1974, Eurico Pinheiro departed IPEAN, and the remaining projects there and at Belterra suffered further "administrative discontinuity." But in 1976, the central research agency that rubber specialists had long recommended was at last set up under the Brazilian Agricultural Research Enterprise (EMBRAPA) of the Ministry of Agriculture. It was named the National Center for Rubber and Oil Palm Research (CNPSD) and located at Manaus. A National Rubber Research Program was initiated, with funding in 1980 of about $1.0 million a year. By 1982, the CNPSD was spending $4.3 million a year at Manaus and its subordinate research units, an impressive sum compared with the Rubber Research Institute of Malaysia (RRIM), the most advanced in the world, which spent $13.6 million that year. The World Bank, which was coming to see rubber as a viable smallholder's crop in the Amazon, made some funds available to EMBRAPA, and some local counterpart funds were applied through sixteen research institutions that received grants from EMBRAPA to study rubber. Altogether, more than a hundred researchers were engaged in at least 150 projects.[9]

The CNPSD and its Rubber Research Program were as plagued with problems in their initial stages as PROBOR. Most of the new staff lacked sufficient scientific training as well as experience with rubber. They were left to choose their lines of research without central direction from Manaus, and their choices were not necessarily the most valid. Of the cooperating stations, Bahia's Cacao Research Center seems to have been most ready to absorb the additional funding. Its competent staff had already helped raise the yields of cacao, another tree crop often locally grown in consortium with rubber and exhibiting some of the same problems. SUDHEVEA, which joined the International Rubber Research and Development Board (IRRDB) in 1980, was attempting to overcome the gap in experience by widening its contacts and effecting exchanges of personnel with the research centers of Southeast Asia.[10]

With the sudden infusion of funds derived from sales of imported elastomers, the CNPSD and its subsidiary research centers were at last able to attack the critical question of leaf blight on a broad front. New concepts and techniques, evolved elsewhere during the decade of the 1960s, were introduced and haltingly applied. The central problem of breeding for resistance was most transformed by these advances. The South African plant pathologist, J. E. van der Plank, had elaborated upon a concept of resistance consisting of two forms, vertical and horizontal. Vertical resistance was based upon a single gene or a few genes. It was effective against a single strain or race of a pathogen, but it conferred no resistance against other races. Horizontal resistance, on the other hand, was the result of accumulated smaller advantages over a pathogen, based on a large number of genes. It was likely to provide only partial resistance, but it was effective over the whole range of genetic variation of which a pathogen was capable. This conception was further developed by R. A. Robinson and others, who described host-pathogen relationships as systems and suggested that breeding should aim to stabilize them.[11]

Plant breeders preferred selecting for vertical resistance because it was easier and the result was often spectacular. But this form of resistance, effective in the case of annual plants, which might be bred periodically to keep abreast of genetic adaptations in the pathogen, was not likely to protect tree crops, which took many years to reach maturity and had to be preserved through several decades of growing seasons from such adaptations. Rubber planters had certainly witnessed the phenomenon in Brazil. One lamented "the incredible capacity" of Microcyclus "to adapt to the most diverse clones, principally when the area planted to a given clone reaches large proportions." Although only three studies had ever been carried out to identify races of Microcyclus, it seemed quite likely that there were more than the four that had been found, and it was suspected that the fungus produced new races very readily.[12]

It was becoming clear, therefore, that efforts since the 1930s to obtain resistant Hevea clones had been largely misdirected. K. H. Chee's research at the RRIM station at the University of the West Indies in Trinidad showed that the resistance that had so far been achieved in Hevea expressed itself in a hypersensitive reaction that was not favorable for leaf survival. In 1977, Alfonso Wisniewski, once director of the IPEAN, declared pessimistically that "a labor of genetic improvement spanning these past 35 years to select or create a clone of Hevea resistant to the pathogen has, in truth, achieved results, if not discouraging, at least of little significance."[13]

Brazilian plant breeders would have to begin their task anew. This time the quest would be for plants displaying moderate resistance and possessing a high degree of genetic variability in comparison to already collected specimens. Thus a breeding program might obtain clones that accumulated a large number of minor characteristics, controlled by many genes, each possessing some quality resistant to leaf blight. The gene controlling the timing of leaf fall was one of these. Others might be those controlling rapidity of leaf maturation, which might shorten the most dangerous period of vulnerability, and uprightness of leaf position and waxiness of leaf surface, both of which might more readily shed moisture and, therefore, inoculum.[14]

The prospect of beginning anew, however, was daunting. A program of selection for horizontal resistance might put off a solution to the problem of leaf blight for another thirty years. As P. R. Wycherley once wrote, "The generations of Hevea still march closely with the generations of men who produced them." In order to compress the "generations of Hevea," Brazilian plant specialists initiated a review of existing tests for early detection of productivity and attempted to discover indicators of other desirable physiological characteristics. They also sought means of inducing precocious flowering, so as to be able to breed at shorter intervals. Since already developed clones in different locations displayed great variability in disease resistance, carefully coordinated replication of clone development trials at numerous field stations would be unavoidable. Furthermore, the leaf blight pathogen itself would have to be studied, especially its epidemiology, the sources of its virulence, and its genetic variability.[15]

The material for a new breeding program was abundantly at hand. Clones that had fallen out of favor because their levels of resistance were deemed inferior might be reconsidered. It was suggested that abandoned groves and nurseries should be searched for survivors presenting interesting forms of genetic variability. Two species of *Hevea* that had been overlooked, *H. camporum* and *H. camargoana*, were brought into the program. They were dwarfs that gave promise of precocity, cheaper chemical control, and possibly higher productivity. Wisniewski even suggested that the breeding program should be based not on *H. brasiliensis*, but on *H. benthamiana*, *H. guianensis*, and *H. pauciflora*, all of which seemed to offer horizontal resistance. His chemical analyses showed that the rubber derived from these species was not inferior, even though specimens normally encountered in the wild were much less productive than *H. brasiliensis*. He reasoned that it would be less time-consuming to look for higher-yielding specimens of these species than to breed resistance in productive clones of *H. brasiliensis*.[16]

The strategy pioneered at Campinas by Luiz Octávio Teixeira Mendes, polyploidization of less productive but resistant clones, was taken up by other experimenters. Mendes published papers showing that several of his treated clones yielded three times as much as those untreated, without losing any degree of resistance. It was suggested that the larger, thicker leaves of these polyploids might also enable them to mature more rapidly and resist drought. Yet these initial clones presented other characteristics that seemed to disqualify them for commercial use: Their bark did not renew, and latex flow was not continuous.[17]

Although a great deal of breeding stock was available, the new strategy implied a need for much more. The key to horizontal resistance was a large pool of genetic variability. However, with the sudden increase in funding, collections could be undertaken more readily, and the resulting selections could be guaranteed the necessary custodial care. In 1972 and 1973, joint expeditions were sent to the upper Acre region by the IPEAN, FCAP, and IPEAL. Some eighty mother trees pointed out by seringueiros as highly productive were chosen.[18]

These collectors returned with alarming news: The native wild groves where they found their selections were being sold to well-financed prospective ranchers with the encouragement of the Brazilian government, which was eager to develop the northwestern Amazon. The wild groves were especially coveted because they were more likely to possess secure titles, dating back in many cases to the turn of the century. Seringalistas were proving only too happy to sell out and take their cash to the cities, their tappers were moving on to

149

Bolivia, and the groves were being burned and cleared and sown to pasture.[19]

In 1974, the Brazilian government permitted an international expedition, jointly sponsored by the CNPSD and the Institute for Rubber Research in Africa (IRCA), a branch of the French Rubber Institute. It is not clear what advantage the Brazilians sought from this collaboration, but the French had lost their plantations in Vietnam and Kampuchea and were beginning anew in the Ivory Coast, where they lacked breeding stock. The expedition brought back some sixty clones from Acre and Rondônia. The French participants were disappointed that the Brazilians were still exclusively concerned with collecting seeds of high productivity and were overlooking the opportunity to collect from trees exhibiting other genetic factors. They believed, in any case, that the seringueiros reported productivity unreliably. By 1976, the CNPSD was capable of mounting its own collecting expeditions on an annual basis. Some forty to sixty selections were soon being multiplied each year at Porto Velho and Rio Branco as well as at Manaus.[20]

A much larger international exchange was about to be proposed. At the RRIM in Kuala Lumpur, breeders were dismayed to find that their latest generation of clones were little more productive than those initiated just before World War II. In 1978, the best clone was still RRIM 600. Apparently the potentially profitable permutations derivable from the Wickham selection were approaching an end. Furthermore, one hundred years after the arrival of Hevea in Southeast Asia, local pathogens were becoming more attracted to the intruder. Most alarming, an increase could be seen in the incidence of leaf diseases. *Oidium heveae* and *Glomerella cingulata*, observable since the earliest commercial plantings, had spread their range and were attacking more intensely. Newer diseases were appearing, most notably *Phytophthora botryosa*, which was first described in 1969. Possibly the programs that had bred higher yields had also bred out resistance or had selected against these pathogens. In this circumstance, the Brazilian clones at hand were more closely examined. Unfortunately there was little correlation between resistances to South American Leaf Blight and the Southeast Asian diseases, and IAN 873 proved the only promising clone that the RRIM had so far obtained.[21]

Southeast Asian specialists were growing increasingly anxious concerning the potential destructiveness of SALB, should it reach their part of the world. Jet aircraft schedules were reducing travel time to the point that an invasion even of the conidial stage was possible. Liberia had abolished direct international flights from Brazil, no doubt at the insistence of the Firestone plantations, whose front gate was not far from that country's international airport. Firestone had already put much effort into the search for clones both resistant and high-yielding, but that struggle had yet to begin seriously in Southeast Asia. While Firestone had been able to work with its own Peruvian selections, the Malaysians had only the clones that Ford and the USDA had selected forty years before.[22]

These problems were broached at Southeast Asian rubber conferences beginning in 1975. International collaboration was called for to document all existing resistant material, exchange it, screen it in infected areas, and distribute it worldwide. A mission sent to South America to seek collaboration was told by SUDHEVEA that such an expedition would be admitted if it benefitted Brazil equally and provided opportunities for training CNPSD researchers. Although the IRRDB envisaged collections in all the Amazon countries where the genus *Hevea* was native, its failure to obtain outside funding obliged it to limit collection to *H. brasiliensis*, within the borders of Brazil. It was agreed that three mixed teams would be organized, that the results would be equally divided, and that Brazil would receive the newest RRIM clones and training from that center's experts.[23]

The expeditions, sent out early in 1981 to Acre, Rondônia, and Mato Grosso, returned with 64,723 seeds and 1,160 seedlings, about the same quantity that Henry Wickham and Robert Cross had obtained all by themselves, but for a considerably higher price – $240,000. The seeds were a good deal fresher, however, so that the RRIM, which got three-quarters of the IRRDB share of the seeds, was able to report 14,600 seedlings safely in its nurseries the next year, and the other recipient, the IRCA at Abidjan, germinated another 3,300. Some 13,000 survived at Manaus. Rubber plant breeders had thus, at one stroke, multiplied several times the available genetic material. The maintenance of these seedlings to maturity would cost the IRRDB a further $250,000 each year, modest enough in comparison to many other public expenditures, but of immense importance to the future economies of the participating countries.[24]

These exchanges may not have been the only ones carried out in the recent past. The meeting of the IRRDB in Brazil in 1980 presented Southeast Asian breeders the chance to observe the new clones that the CNPSD had collected on its own, and, it is said, to make off with some of them. On another occasion, it was reported that foreign "tourists" were allowed onto the CNPSD grounds on a Saturday by a gatekeeper, and they pilfered seeds of the prized dwarf species. The informal pocketing of specimens, which increases the danger of the transfer of pathogens, is a practice that continues, it seems, despite official sanctions, out of competitiveness and, perhaps, sheer hubris.[25]

The new selections kept at Manaus displayed a satisfactory genetic variability, but all proved quite susceptible to leaf blight and to another leaf fungus, *Thanatephorus cucumeris*. The IRRDB kept another part of the bargain by sending experts to Brazil from several of its affiliated Asian research centers. The RRIM field station at Trinidad was closed, and K. H. Chee, its principal researcher, was sent to CEPEC in Bahia, in the hope that the Brazilian government might permit the RRIM to field test the susceptibility of its new clones at that site, which evidently offered ideal conditions for the development of Microcyclus. This hope was dimmed by the sudden refusal of the Malaysian government to permit the export to Brazil of selected clones of African oil palm. Brazil, which had certainly yielded more than it had received in the Germplasm 1981 expedition, in retaliation suspended further rubber exchanges.[26]

The great delay in obtaining clones that could be, in good conscience, recommended for commercial planting obliged planters to study more carefully the practicability of top grafting with resistant clones. The technique remained experimental because it added a disconcerting number of variables to an already risky business. Numerous clones were found to be incompatible with those employed as canopies, and barely enough experience had been accumulated to make choices of canopy clones that would be reliably horizontally resistant to SALB. Most of those chosen were *H. pauciflora*, and these proved especially vulnerable to Phytophthora disease. The top-grafted trees were set back two years in growth, but that cost could be reduced by adopting the practice, developed in Malaysia, of nursery production of tall base-grafted seedlings in plastic bags.[27]

It was coming to be admitted that the canopy did have a physiological effect on the tapping panel, but, surprisingly, some of the interrelationships appeared to increase yield. Observations were beginning to be made to locate more such relationships. A wider range of clones was being tried as canopies, including species such as *H. rigidifolia* that were still more resistant than *H. pauciflora*. A few planters, observing that their top-grafted trees reached tapping size faster than the rest, calculated that top grafting cost on balance less than fungicidal treatment, at least in areas where no clones were resistant to leaf blight, and when the grafting was done systematically and not as an emergency measure. If top grafting influenced the trunk clone for the worse, it mattered little, decided Brian Avery-Jones at the Goodyear estate, since the Southeast Asian clones were far more productive to begin with.[28]

The problematic outcomes of other strategies of leaf blight control led to a greater emphasis on chemical control and delivery systems. In 1971, for the first time in Brazil, aerial dusting was attempted experimentally by CEPEC. The next year the Pirelli plantation at Belém tried it as well, desisting abruptly when initial results appeared unsatisfactory. In southern Bahia, however, several of the estate owners persisted, and when an especially severe epidemic of SALB broke out in 1973–4, CEPEC was compelled to expend funds on a Special Program of Hevea Leaf Blight Control. Some 4,000 hectares were sprayed that year, employing fixed-wing aircraft and a helicopter, at a cost of about $100,000.[29]

These first attempts appear not to have increased yields. Fixed-wing aircraft were abandoned, since only helicopters could be effectively maneuvered over the broken hill country typical of the region. Timing and coordination of dusting were more carefully executed; more effective combinations of fungicides, including Benomyl, Mancozeb, Triadimefon, and Cercobin, were devised; and oil and surface-spreading agents were partially substituted for water as a vehicle. Nevertheless, numerous passes, between six and ten each season, were necessary in order to reduce inoculum noticeably. Clones that were crosses with *H. benthamiana* were found to benefit less from applications of fungicides, even at weekly intervals, because their leaf fall was too irregular. Studies in 1978 and 1979 of sixteen treated estates showed increases in output of between 8 and 19 percent; nevertheless, in those two years production of all estates, treated and untreated, rose 21 percent. In 1978, although 5,776 hectares were sprayed, it cost $940,000, or 31 percent of the total value of all rubber produced in Bahia. The aerial dusting program was then cut back in cost and size – planters were made to share expenses and farmers with small or isolated groves were no longer serviced – and another delivery system began to be tested.[30]

This new system was the thermal fogger, a tractor-trailer mounted machine that sprayed a hot water vapor. The fogger afforded a much higher reach than pressure sprayers, up to thirty meters, and the vapor enveloped the leaves, instead of merely washing their upper surface. A fogger could treat fifteen hectares a day. The Firestone manager ordered one in 1970, and by 1974 there were a number of imported thermal foggers in the region. Use of this equipment cost only 40 percent as much as aerial spraying, and it was much more applicable to estates of all sizes. By 1984 a Brazilian-made fogger was being tested, promising further cost reductions, and techniques of application were being improved. Thermal fogging offered perhaps the most promising immediate return on investment, and some planters began to rely on this method to the exclusion of other solutions.[31]

Another novel strategy emerged during the 1970s, that of *climatic escape*. Most of the commercial planting in Brazil had been deliberately located within the native range of Hevea, or in places with similar climate, thereby providing ideal conditions for the spread of leaf blight. J. R. Weir's decision to transfer the Ford operations to Belterra, on the other hand, was in part based on the hope that the windiness and relative dryness of that plateau would be unfavorable to the formation of the dew that served as a vehicle for the spread of conidia. The planting of rubber in the highlands of São Paulo twenty years earlier had also foreshadowed the new approach. There the average temperature minima were so low that they were offered as the reason why Mycrocyclus had not appeared on surviving trees that were surveyed. Clearly climatic escape might permit the employment of high-yielding Southeast Asian clones without the expense of either top grafting or thermal fogging.

The first tentative proposal that plantings should be shifted to areas too dry for the reproduction of the fungus appeared in SUDHEVEA's abortive National Rubber Plan of 1970. In 1972, IPEAN presented a map showing certain areas of the Amazon, including Belém where Pirelli and Goodyear had their estates, as too wet for successful planting. In 1976, planting in dry regions was proposed by V. H. Figueiredo Moraes and A. C. Candeira Valois, as one of several promising strategies. They claimed that "the rubber tree is more plastic in its hydric requirements than the pathogens which attack its leaves." This opinion was supported by observations made by Eurico Pinheiro of a 2.5 hectare grove that had been planted at Açailândia, Maranhão, in 1967 and abandoned three years later. The region experienced a water deficit of almost 350 millimeters a year and a six-month-long dry season. The grove, acquired by FCAP in 1978, contained a collection of twenty-five susceptible Belterra clones by then large enough to tap. Their yield was estimated at an astounding 2,000 kilograms per hectare. Furthermore, they were free of leaf blight, and an attempt to inoculate them with the fungus was unsuccessful.[32]

With the initiation of PROBOR 3, planting in escape zones was declared eligible for funding. Experiments in Hevea cultivation were begun at the Center for Agricultural Research of the Cerrado, near Brasília, a station responsible for the development of that quarter of Brazilian territory invested with poor, aluminum-toxified soils covered with scrub savanna and experiencing high water deficits. There it was found that dry winds caused severe stress to the plant, necessitating wind breaks and irrigation. Although clones resistant to leaf blight apparently were not required since the disease was not observed, it was decided that it would be necessary to select for drought resistance. The costs of these preliminaries, it might be imagined, might easily outrun those needed to combat leaf blight.[33]

Even in less harsh climates, such as Açailândia, however, it seemed that escape might prove ultimately impractical. In Malaysia and India it was the common opinion that yield was positively correlated with rainfall, although there was little scientific data in support. Indeed the French collectors in the joint expedition of 1974 were surprised to find highly productive Hevea in parts of Mato Grosso with a five-month dry season. At the time, oddly enough, their Brazilian colleagues displayed slight interest in the genetic resource that such trees represented. Still more significant, the collectors found that the trees in those seasonally dry regions were also infested with Microcyclus, putting in question the thesis that the fungus was less adaptable than the tree. At Açailândia, *Thanatephorus cucumeris*, in other habitats much less destructive, was causing intense defoliation on all the trees. Then, five years after the first observations, Microcyclus made its appearance in a newly formed nursery.[34]

The dramatic increase in funding at CNPSD and the other centers made possible the pursuit of numerous other lines of research, of lower priority but each potentially contributory to strengthening planted rubber against leaf blight: for example, the identification of micronutrients that could strengthen plant vigor, improve resistance, and possibly shorten immaturity. The interplanting of field crops was taken up once again, since smallholders were unlikely to attempt rubber cultivation unless their lands yielded a steady income. And studies were undertaken of a parasitic fungus, *Calcarisporium*, which attacks *Microcyclus*.[35]

The plantations of the foreign tire companies were at first relegated to a marginal role in the programs traced out by SUDHEVEA. They were not eligible for financing under PROBOR 1 and 2, and were not integrated into the research programs or extension services. There was, according to A. G. Lund, Firestone's president, considerable fear that rubber planting "might wind up in the hands" of the foreign tire companies if any important amount of government assistance were made available to them. This was perhaps somewhat short sighted, since these estates were continuing to accumulate a storehouse of practical information, of more use in the short run than the more basic work of the research stations. The tire companies nevertheless persisted, partly because the government was requiring them to compound their products with a certain amount of domestic natural rubber, a requirement that their plantations might help them meet.[36]

In 1973, nearly twenty years after the inauguration of the Firestone estate at Camamu, only 1,212 of its 3,239 hectares were in production. The management, despite the high cost of what had so far been accomplished, persuaded the Akron headquarters to expand to 6,000 hectares, the entire surface of the property that seemed appropriate for rubber. The acquisition of two more estates of 10,000 hectares each was given some thought, in order to provide a projected 30 percent of Firestone's Brazilian raw material requirements by the early 1980s. One of the sites considered was along the Araguaia River, land that had fallen to the company in payment of a debt. This was turned down after SUDHEVEA refused to help finance the expansion. The planting program at Camamu was, nevertheless, completed on schedule. Newer clones had been used, including some of the supposedly resistant clones developed at Firestone's Liberian estate.[37]

By 1976, the new clones were also attacked by the blight, forcing the managers to turn to thermal foggers and, once again, to top grafting. Apparently a constant replanting effort was carried on, as certain clones were judged beyond salvage. This made it possible for the estate to report quite high yields, relative to other Bahian estates. Its 1981 output of 702 kilograms per hectare was, nevertheless, 150 kilograms below that reported a decade earlier. And its area of tappable trees had risen during the same period to 1,659 hectares, an increase of just 445 hectares. Its 1,409 workers were apparently producing only 500 kilograms each, lower than many wild gatherers were able to achieve at no capital investment at all. The blame for this cannot be laid on incompetence. Firestone was at the time operating 53,000 hectares of estate rubber in four countries. At its Liberian estate, output was 1,579 kilograms per hectare, 4,593 kilograms per worker. The company was competitively supplying the U.S. market with some 40 percent of that country's latex demand. Visiting specialist R. L. Wastie, who was told by the manager that SALB reduced yields at Camamu by 50 percent, considered the estate "one of the best maintained I saw anywhere."[38]

But Firestone soon after entered a phase of financial retrenchment, and sought buyers for several of its divisions, including its Bahian estate. After attempting to pass ownership to a Brazilian-owned company, it sold in 1983 to Michelin. That company was newly arrived in Brazil, producing truck tires in São Paulo. It had started a 4,000–hectare plantation at Rondonópolis, Mato Grosso do Sul, a zone of escape, where it seemed to be experiencing difficulties. Camamu was apparently of interest to Michelin for the experience of its staff. Thus a thirty-year-old experiment came abruptly to an uncertain transition.[39]

Goodyear owned six vast plantations in Malaysia and Indonesia. Their operations were necessarily cost-effective, since they sold their rubber not to Goodyear rubber factories but in the competitive world market. In 1974, the company's estate near Belém lost $200,000 on somewhat over 1,000 hectares of tappable trees that yielded only 150 kilograms per hectare. The next year a new manager, Brian Avery-Jones, was able to avoid an operating loss, and judging that rubber could be profitable in Brazil as long as the government maintained a guaranteed price, he persuaded the company to add gradually to its plantings, a project that came to receive some SUDAM financing. He decided part of the problem was the estate's poor, sandy, aluminum-toxified soils, so acid that they prevented nitrogen fixation by cover crops. Within a few years his yields doubled. Even so, yields and output per worker remained about a fifth of those of the Goodyear Southeast Asian estates. In 1983, Avery-Jones directed the installation of a new plantation of 5,000 hectares in consortium with a subsidiary of the National Credit Bank. This was located at Santa Teresinha, in Mato Grosso, a zone of escape.[40]

During the 1970s Pirelli became the leading tire producer in Brazil. It absorbed the facilities of the Goodrich, Tropical, and Dunlop companies, including the plantation of the latter at Una, Bahia. In 1974, Pirelli's rubber plantings at Fazenda Uriboca, near Belém, amounted to 809 hectares. Its yield was lower than that of Firestone or Goodyear, and local conditions appear to have caused it even more trouble with leaf blight. For these reasons, it appears, it did not expand. The rubber plantation acquired from Dunlop apparently suffered even more serious problems and was sold to Brazilian interests. Pirelli, nevertheless, wanted to keep its hand in the plantation business, just in case technical solutions were found. The company's tire and cable factories therefore continued to buy Uriboca's small output.[41]

In southern Bahia, despite severe difficulties with leaf blight, the area planted to rubber grew more or less constantly from 1973 onward. In that year, some 15,200 hectares were counted; by 1981 there were 26,500 hectares. There was, at the same time, a slight tendency for the number of rubber properties to decline, from 912 to 894. Rubber planting was becoming more capital-intensive, and credit and PROMASE assistance was not being directed to very small farmers. Output increased, according to surveys that took into account unofficial as well as officially sanctioned sales, from 1,913 tons in 1973 to 6,287 tons in 1981, suggesting that yields over the same period nearly doubled, but only up to 460 kilograms per hectare.[42]

The modest expansion of rubber in southern Bahia was occurring because local farmers considered rubber suitable for planting on land marginal for cacao, a crop more valuable than rubber per unit of land, but more demanding of soil nutrients. It was substantially the result as well of government price, credit, and spraying subsidies. A survey taken just before PROBOR 1 got under way, of fifty-eight of the better-managed farms, representing nearly 30 percent of total area in rubber, showed that they had not been covering their variable costs, even at the government-supported price. PROBOR credit was not problem-free, however. It often arrived late, and until 1975 it was not corrected for inflation. Furthermore, it was not being made available in Bahia in quantity sufficient to satisfy demand, even though the region was undoubtedly best prepared to absorb it. Less than a third of Bahian rubber planters enjoyed PROBOR loans.[43]

The most dramatic expansion of rubber planting, however, took place in the northwestern border region of Acre, Rondônia, and northern Mato Grosso, where vast government-sponsored colonization schemes were attracting hundreds of thousands of rural migrants, mostly southerners, but also significant numbers of former seringueiros. Most of these areas were planted in corn, bananas, and rice, but tree crops were favored by the government for reasons of ecological stability as well as export income. Hevea was programmed as a crop suitable to shade cacao and coffee. SUDHEVEA moved into the area by 1976, and by 1983 had approved projects totaling 24,000 hectares, mostly in small plots. But less than half this area was in fact planted, judging from a report on one of the subprojects for smallholders that the Acre state government sponsored. Reluctant colonists had to be persuaded to try planting rubber, they were then given inappropriate advice, and then forced to wait for credit installments. By 1982 it was reported from Acre that leaf blight infestation was "general." The only means of preventing such costly errors would be clone testing and selection in every colony, for observation over several years prior to the approval of loans. SUDHEVEA was not inclined to so conservative a policy, however.[44]

The state of Espírito Santo drew SUDHEVEA's attention when it was reported that two small groves of Hevea planted in the municipality of Viana in 1960 and 1962 were free of Microcyclus and were yielding at a theoretical rate of more than 1,000 kilograms per hectare. One of the two groves was the work, originally, of the state Secretariat of Agriculture, but no account had been kept of its progress. This estimate was quickly revised upward in a series of perfunctory papers by the state agricultural research center, to 1,500, 1,790, and then 2,000 kilograms per hectare. Espírito Santo had suffered the loss of much of its coffee acreage, uprooted in a federal program designed to improve coffee productivity by eradicating aging and low-yielding trees. Many small-holders were consequently drifting into the cities for lack of an alternative cash crop for their hilly and highly eroded farms. Possibly this circumstance inspired a roseate evaluation of the state's rubber-growing potential. In any event, Espírito Santo was approved for inclusion of 9,000 hectares in PRO-BOR 2. A nursery was installed and seedlings were offered, although there was no sound basis on which to recommend one clone over another.[45]

Although little further study was undertaken of the progress of the planting, it was claimed that all of Espírito Santo represented a zone of escape from SALB, and few limits were proposed to planting anywhere in the state. Nevertheless, when a distinguished foreign visitor was escorted through one of the groves in Viana, and he remarked to another foreign visitor, a phyto-pathologist, that he had never seen *Microcyclus ulei*, the latter immediately pointed some out to him. "But I thought there was none here!" he exclaimed. "Yes," the other replied, "that's what they tell you."[46]

Along the Amazon River, where, since the 1940s, so many rubber development schemes had been proclaimed, a few installed, and all dissipated, PROBOR 1 called forth yet a few more. In 1973, the state government of Pará, whose Secretariat of Agriculture was then directed by Eurico Pinheiro, announced that rubber planting was "economically guaranteed," and "one of the most profitable agricultural undertakings for the Amazon region," and proposed to plant 20,000 hectares over five years at a total cost to maturity of 309 million cruzeiros (nearly $50 million). The areas approved for planting were near Belém. Curiously, an IPEAN report of the year before had marked this region inappropriate for rubber. In 1978, the government of Amazonas founded a rubber-planting colony at Itacoatiara. There 200 families were to plant 1,000 hectares, with partial funding from SUDHEVEA. It is not clear to what degree either of these plans was realized; in any case, by the early 1980s there was no sign of them. The director of the latter project, Imar Cezar Araujo, was later put in charge of the CNPSD.[47]

It may be that some of the private rubber-planting ventures that SUD-HEVEA funded in the Amazon would eventually be successful, but by the mid-1980s the only trees that had reached production were those of a number of smallholders who, without any government funding, had long been casu-ally tapping wild trees and just as casually planting unselected seeds in small groves as a supplement to subsistence farming. A survey of 233 such groves at Santarém, near the old Ford plantations, where the largest concentrations of them stood, found that they supplied 221 tons a year. But the survey also showed that yield averaged the equivalent of only 147 kilograms per hectare, and that the owners judged only 45 percent of the trees worth tapping. Very likely, output per worker was no better than in the wild groves.[48]

The PROBOR funds had also been offered to seringalistas to recuperate their wild groves. In 1977, SUDHEVEA claimed that 13,648 of them had been recuperated, even though wild rubber output had continued to fall. Very likely, nearly all those funds had been diverted to projects such as the Manaus free trade zone. But extension agents were beginning to reach some of the groves, introducing Southeast Asian plantation techniques. One of these was the application of Ethrel or vegetable oil substitutes to the tapping panel to promote latex flow. Another was acidic coagulation of latex in the collecting cup. Coagulated rubber could be pressed dry and sold at a higher price than the rubber that had been "smoked" over fire. Coagulation saved the tapper much time and effort and enabled him to extend his collection into the rainy season. Efforts to see to it that seringueiros received government-decreed minimum prices may also have been somewhat more effective, since credit could be withheld from excessively exploitative seringalistas. These measures helped raise wild rubber output from 1976 to 1985 by 15,000 tons, despite the loss of many groves. This was a modest increase, compared to Brazil's needs, perhaps, yet it was more than triple that of cultivated rubber during the same period. Unfortunately, the quality of the wild rubber was deteriorating as greater amounts reached the market. The technical specifications of the tire factories were meanwhile rising, placing the gathering trade again in danger of extinction.[49]

The vast former Ford estates continued more or less intact, though invaded by several thousand squatters who were encouraged by the federal land reform and colonization agency, INCRA, in a sort of "inter-ministerial claim-jumping," as one observer put it. There was little reason to deny the property to settlers who might make practical use of it, since it was producing precious little rubber. The trees at Belterra were, by 1980, more than thirty-five years old. Of the two million surviving in the tangle of second-growth forest in which they were engulfed, only 10 percent were still being tapped. Yield was down to 200 tons a year, mostly in the form of latex, the equivalent of 300 kilograms per hectare. The estate was no longer supplying clones for the market, although ragged clone gardens persisted under the direction of the federal extension agency. Belterra, where the pleasant, screened wooden bungalows raised so long ago by the energetic Archie Johnston still stood under shade trees grown thick and tall, had fallen victim to a genial, mindless populism. It operated perpetually at a loss, the workers unmanaged, the managers directionless, and the final stage of a return to primeval forest was already discernable.[50]

In São Paulo, a few of the rubber groves planted during the brief surge of government interest, circa 1960, continued to develop, and specialists from the Biological Institute and the Agronomic Institute of Campinas continued to inspect them. Leaf blight was slight in the highlands, even though it could be found year round at Registro. Test tapping of three of the highland plantations, between 1969 and 1973, yielded an average 526 kilograms per hectare. And even at Ubatuba on the littoral, where infestation had been heavy in 1960 and 1961, one grove was reported at 437 kilograms per hectare. Experimental results are higher than commercial yields; nevertheless, they were submitted, in 1975, to a newly formed task force within the Secretariat of Agriculture whose assignment was to confect, in response to the announcement of PROBOR 1, a rubber development plan. Seedling nurseries were once again set up and a "state of euphoria" seized diehard and prospective rubber planters when SUDHEVEA was sent the petition to include São Paulo in PROBOR 1. But the petition was rejected.[51]

SUDHEVEA inserted a clause in PROBOR 2, admitting the possibility of loans to other "nontraditional" regions besides Espírito Santo, at the discretion of the National Rubber Council. But the prospect of Sao Paulo growing rubber inflamed the sensibilities of Amazon congressmen perhaps more than any other. Much worse in their eyes than the loss of "their" cacao to Bahia, had been the loss of "their" coffee to São Paulo. That transfer had made possible that state's rise to wealth and power within the federation. A second loss to that state would be intolerable. PROBOR money could not be awarded to the overbearing Paulistas. Although Paulista agricultural specialists reported more than ninety groves in production with more than 190,000 producing trees, and wondrous theoretical yields of up to 1,500 kilograms per hectare in these groves, most of which had received minimal cultivation for twenty years, their claims clashed with SUDHEVEA data, which indicated that the state produced just 167 tons that year, and thus only 265 kilograms per hectare. Once again SUDHEVEA remained unconvinced, and São Paulo remained outside PROBOR 2.[52]

There was still little evidence to show that São Paulo's cold winters would not prove as damaging to the growth of Hevea as the leaf blight from which it was supposedly a safe haven. Contradictorally, the Paulista rubber specialists who were promoting the planting of rubber in the highland region were also recommending that it be planted once again on the littoral, where they said it could be handily controlled with fungicides and thermal foggers. But if chemical control was adequate protection against leaf blight, then why plant so far south at all, where climatic conditions were evidently suboptimal? In any case, more immediately a handicap to rubber development in the state was the high price of adequate farm land. The dense, affluent population and diversified industrial plant of São Paulo raised land values and offered alternate agricultural opportunities with potentially greater profitability, such as sugarcane and citrus.[53]

Beginning with PROBOR 3, however, SUDHEVEA appeared to have decided to resolve the problem of Amazon intransigence by spreading rubber cultivation over an immense area. Besides the Amazon, Espírito Santo, and Bahia, projects were approved in the northeastern state of Pernambuco, the interior states of Minas Gerais, Goiás, and Mato Grosso do Sul, the coastal state of Rio de Janeiro, and, finally and most liberally, in São Paulo. While it was politically shrewd to extend credit to farmers in several states, the expansion also obeyed a certain logic. It was mostly by chance, and stubborn human will, that Hevea had been implanted in a single non-Amazonian state. The same, or perhaps better, climate and soils stretched from Rio Grande do Norte in the north to Rio de Janeiro in the south. The tree might also find safety in a region of highly seasonal rainfall in the interior, if the concept of escape proved valid. Once again, however, a large-scale experiment was being undertaken under the patronage of an incautious bureaucracy that professed to see no practical obstacles.[54]

This experiment, furthermore, would require many years of uninterrupted funding if self-sufficiency was to be achieved, and that continuity was endangered. The higher world demand for natural rubber, predicted as a consequence of higher oil prices, failed to materialize in the late 1970s. Instead, rubber slumped, along with most other commodities, as the global economy proved unable to absorb higher energy costs. The Southeast Asian rubber producers formed a desperate, largely unsuccessful cartel of their own in 1980. Hope evaporated for a Brazilian invasion of a market turned much more competitive and bleak. Meanwhile, the capacity of the Brazilian government to continue to support such programs as SUDHEVEA was severely strained. Brazil had contracted huge loans abroad in order to produce more electricity and exportable minerals as the means of reducing its huge bills for imported oil. Now these loans were coming due under conditions of high international interest rates, and federal expenditures had to be reduced. In 1984, therefore, PROBOR was cut back drastically. By 1986, SUDHEVEA itself was coming under scrutiny, and it was predicted that many of its functionaries would be dismissed.[55]

Brazilian farmers, large and small, had shown scant interest in planting rubber, despite promotional efforts by SUDHEVEA and other agencies. Many estate owners had evidently diverted their rubber loans to other purposes. Smallholders, even in the vicinity of producing estates, evidently preferred to plant other crops. Clearly, neither group was confident that rubber could be grown profitably. For estate owners, this signified that even if they could protect their groves against leaf blight long enough to bring it into production, there was no market for such a property. Since, in practical business terms, a major reason for planting and tending a tree crop through seven unproductive years was the potential capital gain, the general lack of faith in rubber planting was a decisive obstacle to its rapid expansion. For the smallholder, the difficulties in managing a susceptible crop were daunting. They would have to learn grafting techniques and would have to rely on government assistance that in their experience had not proved reliable or trustworthy. Why not plant crops they were familiar with and could manage on their own?[56]

Finally, the generous fund over which SUDHEVEA presided, as solid as it appeared, might yet evanesce. The growth in Brazilian demand for natural rubber, and the continued incapacity of Brazilian suppliers to satisfy that demand were, in the foreseeable future, the twin determinants of the fund's quantum. And yet, paradoxically, the survival of the wild rubber trade was essential to the maintenance of that fund. The TORMB tax was designed to raise the price of imported rubber to that of domestic rubber, to guarantee the survival of the gathering trade. But suppose other misfortunes should befall the trade? Suppose those last groves should finally be torched to make way for pastures, or suppose the last of the seringalistas should finally go out of business, then what would be the political necessity of the tax? It could easily be imagined that the high tariff on Southeast Asian rubber might then be lowered to some reasonable rate, to satisfy the considerable pressure of Brazilian rubber products manufacturers. Brazilian rubber planters could not survive such a reverse.

More than one hundred and ten years after Henry Wickham filled a few straw baskets with the seeds of the rubber tree, and more than eighty after Ernst Ule found on a leaflet of Hevea the fungus that came to bear his name, a practical solution to that fateful parasitical relationship had not quite been found. Nevertheless, a degree of optimism might be at last justified. More private as well as public money was invested in rubber in the last decade than ever before; planted rubber, which twenty years earlier had contributed an insignificant proportion of Brazil's output, was providing more than 20 percent by the mid-1980s; and a much broader and more intensive research effort had been mounted to understand and overcome the leaf blight once and for all.

Conclusion

Suppose Brazil had never lost its near monopoly of natural rubber. Suppose that Hevea, like Castilla, had grown poorly in the gardens of Peradeniya and Penang and that in Brazil there had been found some corner, like southern Bahia in the case of cacao, where Hevea might flourish while its parasites languished. What impact upon the economy of Brazil would rubber then have had? Instead of relying heavily on a single crop, coffee, whose sluggish market was the bane of Brazilian policy makers, Brazilian exports would have soared. By the 1920s, little Malaya, which also sold tin as well as rubber, was exporting more to the United States than Brazil. Rubber, while not impervious to the economic cycle, would have immensely fortified Brazil's finances, its capacity to import, and its possibilities of capital accumulation. In recent years Brazil has industrialized, and demand for rubber has swelled. Had planted rubber in the meantime succeeded, those industries would have economized, since 1951 when the first purchases became necessary, 1.5 million tons of imported elastomers, worth some $2.2 billion.[1]

Brazil, more than one hundred and thirty years after the first proposals to cultivate rubber, is only beginning to produce significant amounts of it, at heavily subsidized prices. Of the 405,000 tons of elastomers that Brazil's industries consumed in 1985, only 2 percent was planted rubber.

Thus did a fungus deflect the course of a nation's history. And yet, of course, it is not the case, nor is it the thesis of this book, that it was the fungus itself that prevented rubber cultivation. Rather, it was human ignorance of a means to prevent or attenuate fungus attacks that rendered rubber cultivation uneconomic. This is a thesis, furthermore, that does not originate with the author, as should by now be clear. Every rubber specialist and everyone who has attempted to cultivate rubber is aware that Microcyclus has always been the limiting factor in the cultivation of rubber in the New World tropics. When northern Europe's potatoes were invaded by *Phytophthora infestans* in the 1840s, human ignorance was more profound: It was still a matter of furious debate whether the fungus was the cause of the plants' destruction or merely a result of some other evil. To rubber plant researchers their problem

163

has always been clearly defined, even though the solutions have been difficult and costly to envision and execute.

To those not employed in tropical agricultural research, the problem has nevertheless always been much obscured. Brazilians, who possess collectively the admirable trait of daring to express openly their self-doubts, have traditionally examined themselves for character flaws to account for their failure to cultivate rubber. In 1971, Paulo de Tarso Alvim, who, as director of CEPEC, quite likely suffered extreme exposure to the Amazonian litany of despair, recited it for an audience of agricultural experts: "Was it lack of interest or lack of initiative of the region's inhabitants? Was it the lack of vision of its governors? Was the Amazon backwoodsman inferior to the African black, to the native of Malaysia, or even to the mestizo northeasterner who implanted cacao farming in Bahia, bringing seeds from the Amazon itself? Would the economic situation of the region be different if our country were the colony of the *gringo*, like Malaya and Africa when rubber and cacao were introduced there?"[2]

The record provides much evidence of a preference on the part of those responsible for rubber development to avoid or to obfuscate the real nature of the problem. No doubt there are perfectly good theoretical reasons to account for the ungrounded optimism of managers in large organizations, public and private. Certainly practical ones are easy to identify. Many of the pioneers of rubber development in Brazil deceived themselves well enough as long as they could, then spent their later lives, embittered, self-justifying, or trying to dissociate themselves from that part of their careers.[3]

But self-flagellation is entirely out of place in a country that has for at least fifty years been experiencing economic development faster than the industrialized and scientifically well endowed world. Indeed, Brazil's economy has been growing since 1960 at a rate of nearly 5 percent annually, on a per capita basis, one of the fastest in the world. And during the same period of time its agricultural output has been growing at a rate of 4 percent per capita, again one of the fastest rates in the world. The Amazon region has participated in this growth, including the successful introduction of exotics such as Nelore cattle, pepper, jute, rice, and African oil palm, and, even more remarkably, the domestication of several native species – Malva (*Urena lobata*), Sorva (*Couma utilis*), Guaraná (*Paullinia cupana* var. *sorbilis*), Açaízeiro (*Euterpe oleracea*), and, still experimentally, the Pará nut tree (*Bertholletia excelsa*).

Indeed, the Ministry of Agriculture, the National Research Center, and the Brazilian Society for the Advancement of Science have initiated programs to rationalize the process of selecting exotic and native species for domestication, proposing, in the case of African oil palm, hybridization between exotics and natives. Alvim's research center is one of several that have displayed extraordinary capacity to improve crop plants and their cultivation, including cacao, which in twenty-five years has been brought to three times its former yields. In any case, it is not possible to attribute to the particular failings of Brazilian scientific, administrative, or entrepreneurial elites the delay in discovering effective countermeasures against the virulent fungus; in none of the multinational tire company plantations and in none of the research centers in the New World tropics, or indeed in any other part of the world, have more effective solutions to the problem of Microcyclus yet been devised or applied.[4]

The reader will have observed the considerable obstacles that were raised by the rubber-gathering trade to rubber planting, and may consequently prefer a political explanation for the failure of rubber cultivation. But the circumstances out of which that opposition developed must be kept in mind. It is clear that some seringalistas did themselves attempt to plant rubber but were unsuccessful at it. Indeed, Cosme Ferreira, one of the chief spokesmen for the gathering trade, was one of those who had tried and failed. Had it proved easy to plant Hevea, the seringalistas obviously would have converted themselves into planters and therefore into defenders of cultivation. Had even a few of them managed to extract a profit from cultivated rubber, surely some of it would have been devoted to political lobbying in behalf of rubber research and development.

This is not to suggest that the political history of rubber cultivation is inconsequential. On the contrary, political reactions to the frustrations of rubber development helped to shape its course, as this study has, the author fervently hopes, made clear. Consider, for example, the curious paradox of official rubber supports. If the government had not set a domestic price for natural rubber several times that of the world price at the insistence of the gathering trade, then Brazilian farmers would never have been persuaded to plant it, and the means would have been entirely lacking to fund a rubber research program. Such interactions are to be expected in any historical situation, whether an ecological limiting factor is present or not; to claim otherwise would be to demand deterministic explanations, and that is possible neither in human affairs nor in biology.[5]

On the other hand, it has been argued here that the demographic and social factors that have frequently been put forward as responsible for the failure of cultivated rubber in Brazil were not in fact of much significance. The claim that the scarcity of population or the unwillingness of the existing population to serve as wage laborers inhibited the formation of a plantation system is invalid not only because it does not seem to fit the facts, but also because, if it applied, no plantation system could have developed anywhere in the tropical world. The essence of plantation systems in nearly every instance has been, first, an exotic crop, and second, an exotic work force. In any case, the supposed scarcity and reluctance of the native work force was certainly overcome with the passage of time, and on the lower Amazon for many years there has been no lack of underemployed and willing recruits to either plantations or government-sponsored colonies.

In the Brazilian popular imagination the removal of Hevea seeds to Southeast Asia continues to be resented, and to be regarded as a tremendous economic loss. But this is another paradox, as well as a misapprehension. Brazil might well be worse off had no rubber plantations ever been planted in that quarter of the world. The problem of South American Leaf Blight might not have been resolved any sooner, and in such a case, Brazil would have lacked a convenient overseas source of natural rubber for its own industries. Indeed, the entire world's economy would have evolved in quite different ways, and most of them, it may be assumed, would have been less favorable to Brazil's development. This line of thought has not checked the occasional asinine speculation that Brazil might have benefited from sabotage of the Southeast Asian rubber plantations through the deliberate introduction of Microcyclus. It is indeed possible that the RRIM has been aware of such speculations and that its efforts to obtain or breed resistant clones has been to some degree motivated by fear of a deliberate introduction.[6]

The Southeast Asian and African rubber-producing countries have always taken seriously the possibility of invasion by the fungus, and it is in part to that wariness that Brazilian researchers owe what collaboration they have so far received from their colleagues in those regions. Yet the same lack of symmetry persists in regard to that collaboration as it did to USDA collaboration during and after World War II. The world market for natural rubber has been depressed for twenty years and more. It is not in the interest of the present exporting countries that Brazil should achieve a level of competitiveness so formidable that it might invade the world market. Yet that is SUD-HEVEA's announced goal. It would be very convenient if Brazilian research centers could obtain from their Southeast Asian counterparts the scientific expertise needed to defeat leaf blight, but up to now reciprocity has been limited. Southeast Asian centers are eager to dispatch specialists to Brazil, thus are cadres formed who can identify SALB and who have observed preventive measures. It remains to be seen, however, whether the immensely valuable genetic materials that Brazil has dispatched to Africa and Southeast Asia will result in clones that will be worth planting in Brazil.

Another Brazilian conception, widespread though not quite as popular as formerly, that the multinational tire companies, which have operated the largest and most important rubber plantations in their country, have themselves sabotaged rubber development, seems to be quite far from reality. Whatever the disadvantages of turning over much of the rubber sector to foreign companies, and one must suppose there are many, the rubber companies have tried as hard as they could to grow rubber as well as they knew how. Certainly they acted under duress, but they also were provided ample opportunity to profit from rubber if they were successful, and they have consequently sought to expand their plantations from time to time, even in the absence of government decrees.

The Amazon region has appeared lately in the world press almost exclusively in the context of forest destruction and cultural extinction. Notices of the region frequently offer a backward, nostalgic glance to the great age of the rubber boom, but they make no mention of current programs to implant cultivated rubber. Indeed, SUDHEVEA's efforts to succor surviving seringueiros and to convince other government agencies and large-scale private developers of the advantages of rubber have been, in comparison to all those other projects, of small proportions. Although scattered rubber groves are being laid out along frontier penetration roads, they cannot be considered a cause of that vast and ill-considered program of devastation. If all the rubber planned under PROBOR 1, 2, and 3 were finally to be planted, it could all fit within a thirty-five kilometer radius of Belém, and that, quite surely, would be the most logical place for it, not the Acre frontier.

The struggle of humans to protect from pests and parasites the plants that they have chosen to cultivate must have begun with cultivation itself. As plants were grown in ever larger masses, their enemies swarmed, and pests and diseases came to represent a larger and uncontrollable cost of production. When crops became not merely articles of subsistence and barter, but of commercial exchange, the stakes were raised, since entire economies depended on guaranteed supplies. The advantage lay with producers whose local environmental conditions favored the crop over its diseases. In the tropics this usually meant that exotic crops, escaped from their parasites, grew more vigorously and profitably. Scientific farming intervened, seemingly decisively, to maintain crops even in the presence of their enemies. But biocides that ward off parasites and pests and the fertilizers that fortify plant defenses add to costs. Parasite-free plants are still cheaper to raise. Thus Brazilian scientists must go on looking for means of defense against Microcyclus. In the long run, it is possible that Brazil's disadvantage will lessen. In Southeast Asia native insects and fungi may be acquiring a taste for Hevea, and Microcyclus may at last reach that region of the world. And the same drive to destroy the Amazon forest that is rendering the gathering trade extinct may also eliminate native reservoirs of the inoculum, along with native genetic resources of Hevea.[7]

The Brazilian effort to conquer the redoubtable fungus continues to be worth the cost. Despite the imponderables of the world rubber market, there are signs in Brazil's favor. Malaysian and Indonesian small farmers are abandoning their groves to plant African oil palm and other crops. Synthetic rubber may in the long run be once again beset by higher oil prices, and butadiene in the shorter run may suffer restrictions in its uses, since it is suspected of

Conclusion

carcinogenic properties. Brazil is in much the same situation as India and China, both of which are pressing forward with Hevea planting, to conserve their oil reserves and to utilize most efficiently their factors of production. Meanwhile *Microcyclus ulei*, a great frustrator of human hopes and desires, remains a formidable challenge to human intelligence and patience and skill.

Appendix

Table 1. *Exports of natural rubbers, Brazil, 1827–1934*

Year		Metric tons	Year	Metric tons
1827–31	(avg.)	69	1911	26,908
1832–35/6	(avg.)	122	1912	31,133
1836/7–40/1	(avg.)	251	1913	26,676
1841/2–45/6	(avg.)	203	1914	24,688
1846/7–50/1	(avg.)	638	1915	25,890
1851/2–55/6	(avg.)	1,544	1916	23,189
1856/7–60/1	(avg.)	1,470	1917	25,031
1861/2–65/6	(avg.)	2,295	1918	16,685
1866/7–70/1	(avg.)	3,558	1919	24,481
1871/2–75/6	(avg.)	4,274	1920	17,365
1876/7–80/1	(avg.)	9,133	1921	12,839
1881/2–85/6	(avg.)	7,842	1922	14,619
1886/7–90	(avg.)	9,386	1923	13,249
1891–95	(avg.)	14,939	1924	15,879
1896–1900	(avg.)	16,537	1925	17,329
1901		22,265	1926	17,128
1902		21,080	1927	19,261
1903		23,352	1928	13,861
1904		23,461	1929	14,625
1905		26,059	1930	10,409
1906		24,789	1931	9,293
1907		26,866	1932	4,582
1908		28,129	1933	6,960
1909		28,734	1934	8,209
1910		28,380		

Notice that the table includes rubbers of all species, including Castilla, which amounted to 10–15 percent of rubber exports in times of high prices.

Notice also that rubber exports may have included rubbers from Peru, Bolivia, and Colombia on occasion, and that exports were probably not exactly equivalent to production in a given year.

Source: Derived from *Anuário Estatístico: Mercado Nacional* (SUDHEVEA) 15 (January–December 1981): 46. These figures are lower than those of the Brazilian customs reports, which are the data most often transcribed in secondary studies of Brazilian rubber. Customs, however, reported gross weight rather than dry weight, which is the standard now in use. SUDHEVEA therefore reduced the gross figures by 22.5 percent, to account for water loss, impurities, and frauds. SUDHEVEA considered a further correction, of 10–15 percent, necessary because the customs reports until 1942 included, under the heading of rubber, nonelastic materials such as Balata, Sorva, Chicle, and so on. The figures above have included that correction, at a more conservative 5 percent.

Appendix

Table 2. *Rubber production, imports and exports, Brazil, 1935–1986*

	Production (metric tons)			Exports (metric tons)		Imports (metric tons)	
	NR Total	NR Planted	SR	NR	SR	NR	SR
1935	11,285	564	—	9,108	—	—	—
1936	12,185	609	—	9,753	—	—	—
1937	13,847	694	—	10,891	—	—	—
1938	11,905	595	—	8,882	—	—	—
1939	13,788	695	—	8,732	—	—	—
1940	13,364	571	—	8,713	—	—	—
1941	15,480	837	—	7,903	—	—	—
1942	18,846	1,159	—	9,458	—	—	—
1943	21,457	1,278	—	10,931	—	—	—
1944	21,357	1,172	—	11,973	—	—	—
1945	25,051	1,368	—	12,522	—	—	—
1946	22,080	1,246e	—	7,365	—	—	—
1947	24,678	1,408e	—	7,076	—	—	—
1948	20,000	1,206e	—	—	—	—	—
1949	21,300	1,303	—	—	—	—	—
1950	18,619	1,256e	—	1	—	—	—
1951	21,411	1,340	—	—	—	5,400	—
1952	26,666	1,604	—	—	—	10,800	—
1953	25,500	1,575	—	—	—	400	—
1954	22,500	1,471	—	—	—	15,900	—
1955	21,911	1,551	—	—	—	21,633	446
1956	24,224	1,677	—	—	—	5,331	580
1957	24,462	1,704	—	—	—	14,063	1,963
1958	21,135	1,538	—	—	—	19,784	2,158
1959	21,738	1,653	—	—	—	29,100	10,344
1960	23,462	1,738	—	—	—	24,331	17,417
1961	22,736	1,529	—	—	—	20,039	23,436
1962	21,741	na	15,990	—	—	19,603	17,654
1963	20,205	na	29,959	—	1,454	20,979	9,215
1964	28,323	na	32,496	—	5,101	10,028	14,048
1965	29,290	na	38,691	—	7,049	1,854	9,747
1966	24,347	na	54,216	110	10,945	11,595	11,275
1967	21,494	na	51,541	400	6,093	4,763	11,210
1968	22,958	na	58,856	—	1,317	12,891	17,933
1969	23,950	na	61,670	—	2,621	10,231	14,137
1970	24,976	na	75,459	—	—	11,224	15,644
1971	24,231	na	78,174	—	33	22,139	27,558
1972	25,818	3,658	94,581	—	462	18,422	28,775
1973	23,402	4,496	125,620	—	848	36,595	51,266
1974	18,606	3,123	155,161	—	1,102	36,527	40,337
1975	19,348	3,771	128,848	—	2,119	42,240	26,863
1976	20,298	4,104	164,384	—	963	50,481	22,650
1977	22,560	4,148	188,148	—	309	47,495	25,279
1978	23,708	4,672	206,073	—	6,725	56,244	31,716
1979	24,959	5,258	223,797	—	13,679	51,654	34,116
1980	27,813	5,600e	249,116	—	13,434	56,200	46,054
1981	30,257	7,000e	222,871	—	28,227	44,464	24,838

170

Table 2. (*cont.*)

	Production (metric tons)			Exports (metric tons)		Imports (metric tons)	
	NR Total	NR Planted	SR	NR	SR	NR	SR
1982	32,795	7,500e	228,142	—	46,224	38,099	34,749
1983	35,220	8,000e	220,920	—	40,050	35,194	34,560
1984	36,006	8,500e	258,392	—	53,277	59,233	33,974
1985	40,371	9,000e	265,940	—	41,656	60,224	38,995

na = not available
e = estimated
NR = natural rubber
SR = synthetic rubber
Tonnages of natural rubber are dry weight.
Production of planted natural rubber up to 1979 was derived from reports of production in areas outside the natural habitat of Hevea, plus production on the Ford and multinational tire company estates, plus 5 percent of reported wild output. From 1980 onward, 1,000 tons a year have been added to SUDHEVEA estimates.
Exports and imports do not include those in the form of manufactured goods. Imports are overstated, since they are derived from import license requests, which may not have resulted in all cases in imports.
Up to the 1970s, the official sources do not agree precisely. The data above therefore represent a selection of official sources.
Sources: Brazil, SUDHEVEA, *Anuário estatístico: Mercado da borracha, 1980, 1981, 1985*; Brazil, SUDHEVEA, *Relatório de atividades, 1976, 1982, 1984*; International Rubber Study Group, *World Rubber Statistics Handbook, vol. 2, 1965–1980* (London, 1984); Comissão Executiva de Defesa da Borracha, *Anuário de estatística e informações* 18 (1965); Océlio Medeiros, *A margem do planejamento da Amazônia*, 2d ed. (Rio de Janeiro, 1948); Joint Brazil–U.S. Economic Development Commission, *Technical Studies* (Washington, DC, n.d.); *Rubber Statistical Bulletin 38 (August, December 1986)*.

Notes

Introduction

1 See Carl Sauer, *Agricultural Origins and Dispersals* (Cambridge, MA, 1969) and Alfred Crosby, *The Columbian Exchange; Biological and Cultural Consequences of 1492* (Westport, CT, 1972).
2 See Charles S. Elton, *Ecology of Invasions of Animals and Plants* (London, 1958).

1 Prometheus in reverse, 1855–1876

1 Carlos Teschauer, *Avifauna e flora nos costumes, superstições e lendas brasileiras e americanas* (Porto Alegre, 1925), pp. 162–4, 173–4.
2 William Lewis Herndon and Lardner Gibbon, *Exploration of the Valley of the Amazon*, 2 vols. (Washington, DC, 1853), 1:285, 330–1; William H. Edwards, *A Voyage up the River Amazon, Including a Residence at Para* (New York, 1847), pp. 220–1; Roberto Santos, *História econômica da Amazônia, 1800–1920* (São Paulo, 1980), p. 50.
3 Richard Evans Schultes has written an authoritative "History of Taxonomic Studies in Hevea," in P. Smit and R. J. Ch. V. Ter Laage, eds., *Essays in Biohistory and Other Contributions* (Utrecht, 1970), pp. 229–93; see also Auguste Chevalier, "Les premiers découvreurs des espèces du genre *Hevea* et les plus anciens spécimens d'*Hevea's* conservés dans les herbiers du Muséum de Paris," *Revue de Botanique Appliquée et d'Agriculture Tropicale* 16 (August 1936): 616–24. Condamine also published a notice sent him from French Guiana by François Fresneau, purportedly describing the Seringa tree. The drawing that accompanied his notice, however, shows that he was misled. See Charles Marie de la Condamine, "Mémoire sur une résine élastique, nouvellement découverte à Cayenne par M. Fresneau," *Mémoires de l'Académie Royale des Sciences* (1751): 319–33. Other relevant sources on Hevea include Schultes, "Wild *Hevea*: An Untapped Source of Germplasm," *Journal of the Rubber Research Institute of Sri Lanka* 54, pt. 1, no. 1 (1977): 227–57; Adolfo Ducke, "Novas contribuições para o conhecimento das seringueiras da Amazônia brasileira," *Boletim Técnico do Instituto Agronômico do Norte*, no. 10 (28 December 1946); Francisco de Assis Castro, "Manejo silvicultural em seringais nativos, na microregião Alto Purus-Acre," *Acta Amazônica* 9 (December 1979): 629–32; P. R. Wycherley, "Rubber: *Hevea brasiliensis* (Eu-

phorbiaceae),'' in Norman W. Simmonds, ed., *Evolution of Crop Plants* (London, 1976), pp. 77–9. *Hevea* is monoecious, it has male and female flowers on the same tree.

4 George Bentham, "On the North Brazilian Euphorbiaceae in the Collections of Mr. Spruce," *Hooker's Journal of Botany* 6 (December 1854): 363–77; Richard Spruce, "Note on the India Rubber of the Amazon," *Hooker's Journal of Botany* 7 (July 1855): 193–6. See also Spruce's notes published posthumously by A. R. Wallace, *Notes of a Botanist on the Amazon and Andes*, 2 vols. (New York, 1908); Henry Bates, *Naturalist on the River Amazon*, 2 vols. (London, 1863); Wallace, *A Narrative of Travels on the Amazon and Rio Negro* (London, 1889). Wallace's collection was lost in a shipwreck.

5 João Martins da Silva Coutinho, *Relatorio apresentado ao illmo. e exmo. snr. Dr. Manuel Clementino Carneiro da Cunha* (Manaus, 1861); and *Breve noticia sobre a extração da salsa e da seringueira* (Manaus, 1863), cited by Arthur Cezar Ferreira Reis, *O processo histórico da economia amazonense* (Rio de Janeiro, 1944), 77–8. Auguste F. M. Glaziou, the Swiss landscaper of Rio de Janeiro's parks, is credited with planting the rubber trees there, but Museum director Ladislau Netto may have been involved. See Netto's *Apontamentos relativos á botanica applicada no Brasil* (Rio de Janeiro, 1871), with comments by Charles Naudin, pp. 17–21. Glaziou sent herbarium specimens to Kew in 1872; see João Martins da Silva Coutinho, "Gommes, resines, et gommes-résines," *Exposition Universelle de 1867 à Paris, Rapports du Jury International* 6 (1868): 139–72.

6 Collins, "On the Commercial Kinds of India Rubber or Caoutchouc," *Journal of Botany* 6 (January 1868): 2–22; and "On India-Rubber, Its History, Commerce and Supply," *Journal of the Royal Society of Arts* 18 (17 December 1869): 81–93.

7 Donovan Williams, "Clements Robert Markham and the Introduction of the Cinchona Tree into British India, 1861," *Geographical Journal* 128 (December 1962): 431–42; Daniel Headrick, *Tools of Empire* (New York, 1981); Clements R. Markham, *Peruvian Bark, A Popular Account* (London, 1880). A version that awards Markham little credit is Lucile Brockway, *Science and Colonial Expansion* (New York, 1979), pp. 103–39.

8 Markham, "The Cultivation of Caoutchouc-Yielding Trees in British India," *Journal of the Royal Society of Arts* 24 (7 April 1876): 475–81; Hancock was present at the lectures of Collins and Markham at the Royal Society of the Arts.

9 Markham, *Peruvian Bark*, p. 441; idem, "The Cultivation"; Minute Paper, Revenue Forests Department, 4 September 1872, India Office London Records Centre, Revenue Forests Home Correspondence, 1872–1878, L/E/2/34 [hereafter IOLRC]. *Report on the Caoutchouc of Commerce* (London, 1872). R. Little, M.D., Singapore, n.d., enclosure to George Ord, governor of Straits Settlements, to Lord Kimberley, 26 July 1873, IOLRC.

10 M. E. Grant Duff to undersecretary of state for foreign affairs, 10 May 1873, IOLRC; Henry A. Wickham to Joseph D. Hooker, Fazenda Piririma, Santarém, 22 March 1872; Inwards Book, 1873–1877, 19 April 1873, Royal Botanic Gardens-Kew [hereafter RBG-K]. Wickham sent more miscellaneous specimens on 14 May and 8 September 1873.

11 James Collins to undersecretary of state for India, Deptford, 10 April and 13 May 1878 and Minute Paper, unsigned, 4 June 1873, IOLRC; Markham to Hooker, London, 2 June 1873, RBG-K, Misc. Corresp. India Office, Caoutchouc 1.

12 See *Report of the Royal Botanic Gardens, Calcutta, 1875–76*, cited by Thomas Petch, "Notes on the History of the Plantation Rubber Industry in the East," *Annals of the Royal Botanic Gardens, Peradeniya* 5 (1911–1914): 439; Outwards Book, 1869–1881, 22 September 1873, RBG-K; Collins to undersecretary, 10 April and 13 May 1878; Collins to Markham, Deptford, 10 March 1873. Markham mentions the 1873 shipment in "The Cultivation," p. 480. G. King, superintendent of the Royal Botanic Gardens, Calcutta, to assistant secretary, Government of Bengal, 3 February and 30 November 1874; Minute Paper, unsigned, 10 April 1878; Markham [to undersecretary of state for India], 15 April 1878; James Collins to undersecretary of state for India, 13 May 1878; all in IOLRC.

13 Wickham to Hooker, 15 July 1873, RBG-K, Hooker Corresp. Wickham's life has been sketched by Edward V. Lane in a series of remarkable articles: "The Life and Work of Sir Henry Wickham," *India Rubber Journal* 126 (5, 12, 19, 26 December 1953) and 127 (2, 9, 19, 23, 30 January 1954). Also see his "Sir Henry Wickham: British Pioneer; a Brief Summary of the Life Story of the British Pioneer," *Rubber Age* 73 (August 1953), 649–56. Wickham's book was *Rough Notes of a Journey through the Wilderness from Trinidad to Para, Brazil* (London, 1872).

14 Wickham to Hooker, Santarém, 22 March 1872, RBG-K, Hooker Corresp. Lane's account, which was based partly on Violet's diaries, provides many of these details. See also J. T. Baldwin, "David B. Riker and *Hevea brasiliensis*; the Taking of Rubber Seeds out of the Amazon," *Economic Botany* 22 (October–December, 1968): 383–4. For a view of life in Santarém at the time, see Herbert H. Smith, *Brazil, The Amazons and the Coast* (New York, 1879), pp. 127–30.

15 T. S. Green to G. Buckley Mathew, minister to Brazil, Belém, 8 April 1873, Public Records Office [hereafter PRO], FO 128/99; Green to Earl Granville, Belém, 29 September 1873, PRO, FO 13/492; Wickham to Green, Santarém, 5 November 1873, PRO, FO 13/492; Wickham to Hooker, Santarém, 8 November 1873, RBG-K, Caoutchouc 1. It seems to have been generally believed that the Hevea seed was very perishable; see the note of the director of the Peredeniya Garden to the Ceylon government, 19 July 1873, copy, IOLRC. Green to Earl Granville, Belém, 15 December 1873, PRO, FO 13/492.

16 Markham to Hooker, India Office, 20 July 1874, RBG-K, Caoutchouc, 1; Wickham to Hooker, Piquiatuba, 15 October 1874, RBG-K, Caoutchouc 1; Markham to Hooker, India Office, 7 October 1874, RBG-K, Caoutchouc 1; Foreign Office to Green, 3 November 1874, PRO, FO 13/501; Minute Paper, 4 December 1874, signed Markham, IOLRC; Markham to Hooker, India Office, 4 December 1874, RBG-K, Caoutchouc 1.

17 Minute Paper, 9 June 1874, signed Markham, IOLRC; Minute Paper, 2 July 1874, IOLRC; Foreign Office to Green, 3 July 1874, draft, PRO, FO 13/501; Green to Earl of Derby, Belém, 3 September 1874, IOLRC; Green to Louis Mallet, Belém, 6 May 1875, IOLRC.

18 Reference Paper, Store Department, 6 July 1875, IOLRC; Reference Paper, Aud-

itor, 7 July 1875, IOLRC; Reference Paper, Store Department, 21 July 1875, IOLRC; Charles F. Gahan to Hooker, India House, 16 July 1875, RBG-K, Caoutchouc 1; List of Dispatches Received at the British Consulate of Para during 1875, 22 October 1875, PRO, FO 13/521.

19 Wickham to Hooker, Santarém, 18 April 1875, RBG-K, Caoutchouc 1; Minute Paper, 9 September 1875, initialed Markham, IOLRC; Wickham to Hooker, Santarém, 29 January 1876, RBG-K, Caoutchouc 1. According to J. O. Pereira de Carvalho, seed fall in the region is March to April: "Fenologia de espécies florestais de potencial econômico que ocorrem na Floresta Nacional do Tapajós," *CPATU-Boletim de Pesquisa*, no. 20 (December 1980): 1–10.

20 Wickham to Hooker, Ceringal [*sic*], Rio Tapajós, 6 March 1876, RBG-K, Caoutchouc 1; Baldwin, "David B. Riker," pp. 383–4; E. V. Lane, "The Life" (26 December 1953): 6; Wickham, "The Introduction and Cultivation of the Hevea in India," *India-Rubber and Gutta-Percha Trades Journal* 23 (20 January 1902): 81; Wickham to director, Kew, London, 7 November 1906, RBG-K, Misc. Reports, Brazil, Balata Gum and Rubber, 1877–1908 (Wickham was annoyed that a Kew publication on rubber had failed to mention his name); Wickham, *On the Plantation, Cultivation, and Curing of Para Indian Rubber* (London, 1908), pp. 48, 52–3. There is an interesting exchange between Jacques Huber and Wickham in Huber, "Rubber Trees and Wild Rubber Reserves of the Amazon," in International Rubber Congress, 2, London, 1911, *The Rubber Industry* (London, [1911?]), pp. 87–8, 91. On Wickham's efforts at self-promotion at the congress, see Amando Mendes, *Amazônia econômica* (Rio de Janeiro, [1942?]), p. 20.

21 Wickham, *On the Plantation*, pp. 48, 52–3.

22 Ibid., pp. 53–4.

23 Michael Hall, assistant keeper of maritime history, Merseyside Maritime Museum, letters to author, 20 June, 17 August 1984; Antonio Loureiro, *Amazônia – 10,000 anos* (Manaus, 1982); Paul Walle, *Au pays de l'or noir: le caoutchouc du Brésil*, 2d ed. (Paris, 1909), p. 75; Thomas Shipton Green, "Para," *Reports from Her Majesty's Consuls on the Manufacture, Commerce, etc. of their Consular districts, 1876, part 4* (London, 1876), p. 1125.

24 C. Barrington Brown and William Lidstone, *Fifteen Thousand Miles on the Amazon and its Tributaries* (London, 1878), p. 125; Santos, *História econômica da Amazônia*, p. 58; Domingos Soares Ferreira Penna, *A região occidental da Provincia do Pará* (Belem, 1869), p. 89; Barão do Marajó [José Coelho da Gama e Abreu], *As regiões amazonicas* (Lisbon, 1896), p. 368. See also Norma Guilhon, *Os confederados em Santarém* (Belém, 1979), p. 137.

25 Wickham, *On the Plantation*, p. 54; Petch, "Notes on the History," p. 440.

26 Brown and Lidstone met the Baron, who was head of the Conservative Party in Santarém, *Fifteen Thousand*, p. 119; see also Pará, Instituto Histórico e Geográfico do Pará, *Catalogo da primeira serie de uma galeria historica* (Belém, 1918), n.p.; Rodolfo Smith de Vasconcellos, *Archivo nobiliarchico brasileiro* (Lausanne, 1918). For Ulrich's name, see *Manual do empregado de Fazenda; Colecção de actos legislativos e executivos expedidos pelo Ministerio de Fazenda em 1876* (Rio de Janeiro, 1877), p. 265 (the author is indebted to Nancy Naro and Raquel Froes de Fonseca for this citation).

27 *Regulamento das Alfandegas e Mesas de Rendas, annotado por Eleuterio Augusto*

de Athayde (Rio de Janeiro, 1866), p. 247. This regulation was put in effect by Decree 2647, 19 September 1860.

28 René Bouvier, *Le caoutchouc: brillante et dramatique histoire de l'hévéa* (Paris, 1947), p. 63; see *The World* (London), 16 August 1876, for an example of press releases. P. R. Wycherley is one of many rubber specialists who have pointed out that there was no law in Brazil at the time against the export of rubber seed; see his "Introduction of Hevea to the Orient," *The Planter* 44 (March, 1944): 1–11.

29 O. Labroy and V. Cayla, *A borracha no Brasil, relatorio apresentado ao Exmo. Snr. Dr. Pedro de Toledo* (Rio de Janeiro, 1913), p. 42; Herbert H. Smith, *Brazil: The Amazons and the Coast* (New York, 1879), pp. 127–8.

30 Paul le Cointe inspired this chapter's title: He called Wickham "Prométhée d'un nouveau genre," *L'Amazonie brésilienne* (Paris, 1922), 1:343. Wickham's quote was cited by Lane, "The Life" (19 December 1953): 20. One of the latest to pay homage to the Wickham myth is Jonathan Kandell, who reports in his study of the Amazon that Wickham "smuggled" his seeds, *Passage through El Dorado* (New York, 1984), pp. 103–4.

31 Santos, *História econômica da Amazônia*, pp. 230n, 232. See Warren Dean, "Forest Conservation in Southeastern Brazil, 1900–1950," *Environmental Review* 9 (Spring 1985): 54–69.

32 Santos, *História econômica da Amazônia*, p. 269. On the hundred-year-long effort of Portuguese colonial authorities to transfer Asian species to Brazil, see Luis Ferrand de Almeida, "Aclimatação de plantas do Oriente no Brasil," *Revista Portuguesa de História* 15 (1975): 339–481. *Report on the Progress and Condition of the Royal Gardens at Kew, 1876* (London, 1877), p. 10; Mea Allen, *The Hookers of Kew* (London, 1967), p. 230; "The Brazil-Nut Tree in Singapore," *Gardens Bulletin* (Straits Settlements), 2 (5 August 1921): 435; India Office records note many introductions of exotics, IOLRC, Revenue Forests Home Correspondence, 1872–1878, L/E/2/5.

33 Arthur Cezar Ferreira Reis, "O Jardim Botânico de Belém," *Boletim do Museu Nacional, Botânica*, n.s., no. 7 (27 September 1946). Ferreira Reis bases his account of the 1797 caper on documents that also reported that the French spices had come from Portuguese Timor via Ile de France and Réunion! Anon., "Como vmce. se encarrega pelo amor á Nação" [Belém?, 1816], ms., John Carter Brown Library, Providence, RI, Codex Port 7. Another version concerns Luiz d'Abreu, held captive in Cayenne in 1813. He escaped with seeds of numerous species, including camphor, nutmeg, avocado, clove, and sago palm; see "Botanico," *Revista Agricola*, no. 3 (April 1870): 41–4. Auguste de Saint-Hilaire, *Voyage dans le District des diamans et sur le littoral du Brésil* (Paris, 1833), 2:278n.

34 F. Albuquerque, "Os primeiros cultivadores de quina no Brasil," *Chacaras e quintais* 8 (15 December 1914): 4–8, 11; see also A. J. de Sampaio, "O tricentenario da quina," *Revista Nacional da Educação* 1 (July, 1933): 1–10.

35 Manuel Barata, *A antiga produção e exportação do Pará* (Belém, 1915), pp. 13–16 (Barata's source was Palheta's request, in the Pará archives, for Indian slaves to tend his seedlings.); A. d'Escragnolle Taunay, *Pequena história do café* (Rio de Janeiro, 1945), p. 23. Richard Evans Schultes has alluded to the contradiction discussed in this paragraph; see his "The Odyssey of the Cultivated Rubber Tree," *Endeavor*, n.s., 1, nos. 3–4 (1977): 133–7.

2 Awaiting developments, 1876–1906

1 "R. Irwin Lynch," *Journal of the Kew Guild* 4, no. 32 (1925): 341–2; *Report on the Progress and Condition of the Royal Gardens at Kew, 1876* (London, 1877), 8–9; Inwards Book, 1873–1877, 14 June 1876, Royal Botanic Gardens-Kew [hereafter RBG-K]; Unsigned memorandum, 7 July 1876, RBG-K, Misc. Corresp., India Office, Caoutchouc 1; Joseph D. Hooker to Louis Mallet, Kew, 7 July 1876, India Office London Records Centre, Revenue Forests Home Correspondence, 1872–1878, L/E/2/34 [hereafter IOLRC]: This is the only document that provides a different figure, 60,000. Hooker to Clements R. Markham, 24 June 1876, IOLRC; Reference paper, 22 July 1876, IOLRC.

2 Inwards Book, 1873–1877, 9 June, (arrival by mail?), 22 June 1876, RBG-K; Henry A. Wickham to Hooker, London, 26 July and 1 August 1876, RBG-K, Hooker Corresp.; Wickham to Hooker, 18 April 1875, RBG-K, Caoutchouc 1; Markham to Hooker, India Office, 19 and 21 July 1876, RBG-K, Caoutchouc 1.

3 Minute paper, 23 August 1876, signed by Markham, IOLRC; Outwards Book, 1869–1881, 18 September 1876, RBG-K. Wickham to Hooker, Queensland, 18 February 1877, and Wickham to Hooker, Lewisham, 5 February 1885, both RBG-K, Hooker Corresp.; *Report on the Progress, 1877,* p. 17; *Report on the Progress, 1880,* p. 48.

4 Clements R. Markham, *Report of the Geographical Department of the India Office, 1867–1877* (London, 1877); Donovan Williams, "Clements Robert Markham and the Introduction of the Cinchona Tree into British India, 1861," *Geographical Journal* 128 (December 1962): 431–42; D. Williams, "Clements Robert Markham and the Geographical Department of the India Office, 1867–1877," *Geographical Journal* 134 (September 1968): 343–52.

5 Outwards Book, 1869–1881, 9 August 1876; Thiselton-Dyer to George Hamilton, Kew, 12 August and 15 September 1876; Markham to Thiselton-Dyer, India Office, 18 September 1876; Markham to Thiselton-Dyer, Botherham, 31 December 1876; all RBG-K, Caoutchouc 1.

6 Minute paper, 16 February 1876, signed by Markham, IOLRC; Markham to Hooker, India Office, 1 April 1876, RBG-K, Caoutchouc 1.

7 Robert Cross, *Report on the Investigation and Collecting of Plants and Seeds of the India Rubber Trees of Para and Ceara and Balsam of Copaiba* (London, 1877); T. J. Shipton Green to earl of Derby, Belém, 16 October 1876, Public Record Office, FO 13/521. Cross also acknowledged Green's "best assistance."

8 Inwards Book, 1873–1877, 25 November 1876, RBG-K. Markham to W. Thiselton-Dyer, Eccleston Square, 21 November 1876; Louis Mallet to Hooker, India Office, 29 November 1876; Markham to Thiselton-Dyer, India Office, 10 October 1876; William Bull to Thiselton-Dyer, Chelsea, 11 May 1877; all RBG-K, Caoutchouc 1. "Report on the Progress of the Ceara Scrap-Rubber Tree at Kew," 30 January 1877, RBG-K, Caoutchouc 2. *Report on the Progress, 1877,* p. 15.

9 Outwards Book, 1869–1881, entries 11 August to 1 November 1876, 30 November 1876, 11 June to 27 September 1877, RBG-K; J. M. H., "Distribution of Rubber Plants from Kew," *Bulletin of Miscellaneous Information, Kew* [hereafter *BMI-K*], no. 3 (1907): 103–5; Memorandum entitled "Hevea brasiliensis," RBG-K, Caoutchouc 1.

10 Henry N. Ridley to Turrill, Kew, 8 July 1959, RBG-K, Biographical File (Wickham); Thomas Petch, "Notes on the History of the Plantation Rubber Industry of the East," *Annals of the Royal Botanic Gardens, Peradeniya* 5, pt. 7 (September 1914): 444; Ridley, "Evolution of the Rubber Industry," *Proceedings of the Institution of the Rubber Industry* 2, no. 4 (1955): 116.

11 Ridley, *Report on the Progress, 1876*, p. 9; *Report on the Progress, 1877*, p. 16; Ridley, "History of the Evolution of the Cultivated Rubber Industry," *Bulletin of the Rubber Grower's Association* 10 (January 1928): 45–9; Ridley, *The Story of the Rubber Industry* (London, 1912), p. 7; Petch, "Notes," p. 440; Adamson to colonial secretary, letter copy, 30 October 1876, IOLRC. Considering all the inquiries that were directed to Kew on this subject, it seems odd that the India Office's records were never searched.

12 David Prain, "The Introduction of Para Rubber to Buitenzorg," *BMI-K*, no. 11 (1914): 162–5; W. T. Thiselton-Dyer, "Para Rubber," *BMI-K*, no. 142 (October 1898): 253; Petch, "Notes," p. 441n; Thiselton-Dyer to Mallet, Kew, 8 September 1877, IOLRC; Thiselton-Dyer to George Hamilton, Kew, 23 February 1878, IOLRC.

13 Petch, "Notes," p. 459; see also P. R. Wycherley, "The Singapore Botanic Gardens and Rubber in Malaya," *Gardens Bulletin, Singapore* 17 (5 December 1959): 176.

14 Robert Cross, "The American India Rubber Trees at Nilambur" in A. M. and J. Ferguson, *India Rubber and Gutta Percha* (Colombo, 1882), pp. 96–9; Petch, "Notes," p. 518, mentions that the director of Peradeniya as late as 1899 preferred Castilla, long after local planters had abandoned it. *Ficus elastica*, by the way, is the common indoor ornamental rubber plant.

15 Robert Cross, *Report on the Investigation*, p. 7; Wickham, "Report," transcribed in A. M. and J. Ferguson, *India Rubber*, p. 99–102; Wickham to Thistleton-Dyer, London, 4 September 1901, RBG-K, Caoutchouc 1; [Ridley], "Para Rubber in the Botanic Gardens, Singapore," *Agricultural Bulletin of the Straits Settlements and Federated Malay States* [hereafter *ABSSFMS*] 2 (January 1903): 1–2. Markham made no mention of Wickham (or Collins) at all in his book on cinchona and rubber, *Peruvian Bark* (London, 1880).

16 Henry Trimen to director of Kew, 26 August 1887, RBG-K, Caoutchouc 1; Thiselton-Dyer, "Para Rubber," pp. 257–8, citing Willis; Petch, "Notes," pp. 489–92, 495, 466–7.

17 "Selected Papers from the Kew Bulletin, III – Rubber," *BMI-K*, add. ser., 7 (1906): 75–6.

18 J. W. Purseglove, "Ridley, Malaya's Greatest Naturalist," *Malayan Nature Journal* 10 (December 1955): 43–55; Ridley, "Early Days of Rubber," *Journal of Heredity* 19 (November 1928): 485–7; Ridley, "Historical Notes on the Rubber Industry," *ABSSFMS* 9 (June 1910): 205, 206; Ridley, "Evolution of the Rubber Industry," pp. 115–16; James C. Jackson, *Planters and Speculators; Chinese and European Agricultural Enterprise in Malaya, 1786–1921* (Kuala Lumpur, 1968), p. 215. Edward V. Lane, "The Life and Work of Sir Henry Wickham," *India Rubber Journal* 127 (30 January 1954): 7–8. O. D. Gallagher, "Rubber Pioneer in his Hundredth Year," *The Observer* (20 June 1955), p. 11, mentions that Ridley was awarded £800 upon retirement; Wickham's prizes totaled £16,000, provided

for the most part by two Americans: Quincy Tucker, of the U.S. Rubber Manufacturers Association, and Edgar B. Davis, a retired rubber company executive and oil millionaire.

19 Wycherley, "The Singapore Botanic Gardens," pp. 178–9; Colin Barlow, *The Natural Rubber Industry* (Kuala Lumpur, 1978), p. 21; Petch, "Notes," pp. 498–9. Wickham provided further advice on rubber growing in later years; some of it, very possibly cadged from Ridley, eventually proved correct. By 1908, he decided to cash in on his assumed expertise in rubber planting by promoting special rubber-curing equipment of his own design that turned out to be ineffective. He also promoted in 1919 the collection of oil-bearing Piqui (*Caryocar*) seeds out of Brazil. These were planted in Malaya, but it was decided at the time that the tree was insufficiently productive to be commercially viable. It now appears, however, that the tree's potential multiple uses may yet result in its cultivation. Wickham to director of Kew, London, 11 August 1906, RBG-K, Jequié, Maniçoba and General, 1879–1913; D. Prain to A. W. Copeland, Kew, 15 March 1907, RBG-K, Malaya, Rubber, 1852–1908; Lane, "The Life," (30 January 1954): 7–8. *The New York Botanical Garden* [Newsletter] 18 (Winter 1985): 4.

20 Ridley, "The History and Development of Agriculture in the Malay Peninsula," *ABSSFMS* 4 (August 1905): 299; Ridley to director of Kew Gardens, Singapore, 20 October 1897, RBG-K, Misc. Reports, 6.21, Malaya Rubber, 1852–1908; Petch, "Notes," pp. 469–72; Jackson, *Planters and Speculators*, p. 214.

21 John Ferguson, "On the Cultivation of the India-Rubber Trees of South America," *Transactions of the Royal Scottish Arboricultural Society* 10 (1883): 108; R. L. Proudlock, *Report on the Trees at Nilambur and at Calicut, South Malabar* (Madras, 1908), pp. 40–1, 46–7; Outwards Book, 1869–1881, 30 August 1876, RBG-K; C. van der Giessen and F. W. Ostendorf, "The Oldest Hevea Trees in Java," *Chronica Naturae* 104 (July 1948): 197–200; P. van Romburgh, "Geweekte gewassen in den cultuurtuin te Tjikeumeuh," in *'S Lands Plantentuin te Buitenzorg* (Djakarta, 1892); P. van Romburgh, *Les plantes à caoutchouc et à gutta-percha cultivées aux Indes Néerlandaises* (Djakarta, 1903). A. J. Ultée characterized the donation to Buitenzorg as "great generosity," *Onze Koloniale Landbouw, IV, Caoutchouc*, 3d ed. (Haarlem, 1921), p. 7. A Kew librarian suggested, facetiously, that the director was unaware that Java was not in the British Empire. Lucile Brockway supposes Kew's plant exchanges derived from a sense of solidarity as expressed in the phrase "white man's burden," *Science and Colonial Expansion: The Role of the British Royal Botanic Gardens* (New York, 1979), pp. 119, 120. On the Dutch, see Pieter Honig and Frans Verdoorn, eds., *Science and Scientists in the Netherlands Indies* (New York, 1945), pp. 181–207.

22 Petch, "Notes," pp. 466–7, 470; F. G. Spring, "Vitality of Rubber Seeds," *ABSSFMS* 1 (February 1912): 1–4; Thiselton-Dyer, "Para Rubber," p. 245; Ridley, "On the Introduction of Para Rubber to the Straits," *ABSSFMS* 4 (October 1905): 390–1; Ridley, "Exporting Seeds of Rubber," *ABSSFMS* 5 (January 1906): 1. Of course, Wickham had carried out a sort of selection for long-lived seeds, and perhaps that was a factor in later higher survival rates. See also Marinus J. Dijkman, *Hevea; Thirty Years of Research in the Far East* (Coral Gables, FL, 1951), pp. 13, 43.

23 J. P. William and Brothers, *Hevea Brasiliensis (Para Rubber), New Product Cir-*

cular, no. 30, 2d issue (1 June 1899). A later issue, dated 1906, contains the information concerning Hawaii.

24 Ferguson and Ferguson, *India Rubber*, p. 82; Petch, "Notes," p. 442; H. K. Rutherford, Ceylon Tea Plantations, to director of Kew, London, 12 May 1897, RBG-K, Ceylon, Rubber, 1880–1908.

25 Petch, "Notes," pp. 442–3; Ridley, *The Story of the Rubber Industry* (London, 1912), p. 10; Wu Tee-jin, "H. N. Ridley," in Singapore, Research Institute of Economic Plants in the Tropics, *H. N. Ridley, 1855–1956*, vol. 1 of *Developers of the Rubber Industry of Singapore and Malaysia* (Singapore, 1969), n.p.

26 Eugène Poisson, "Informations et renseignements: Brésil et Antilles," *Revue Coloniale* 3 (22 December 1898): 1–2; Isaac Henry Burkill, *A Dictionary of the Economic Products of the Malay Peninsula* (Kuala Lumpur, 1966), 1:1169; "Cultivation of Hevea in the Belgian Congo," *International Rubber Journal* 62, (13 August 1921): 23; J. Orton Kerby, *An American Consul in Brazil* (New York, 1911), pp. 275–80. R. A. Alston, "Memorandum on South American Leaf Blight of Rubber," RRIM, Ref. D.37/1 (P.1269/48), Kuala Lumpur, 17 May 1948, Malaysian Rubber Producers Research Association Library, Brickendonbury, Herts.

27 J. A. Mendes, *Extracção e futuro da borracha no valle do Amazonas* (Belém, 1910), p. 151: A ton of dry seeds sold for £10, and there were 350,000 dry seeds to the ton, but only 280,000 new (or boiled) seeds to the ton. On rubber seeds as fish bait, see International Rubber Research and Development Board, IRRDB Project for the Identification, Collection and Establishment of Hevea Materials from South America, *Report of the Preliminary Mission to South America* ([Brickendonbury, Herts.], 1978), p. 8.

28 *India Rubber and Gutta-Percha Journal* (8 October 1884), n.p.; Brazil, Ministério de Agricultura, *Legislação Florestal* (Rio de Janeiro, 1935), 2:9, 10.

29 René Bouvier, *Le caoutchouc* (Paris, 1947), p. 72; André Crémazy, *L'hévéaculture en Indochine* (Paris, 1927), p. 18; P. J. S. Cramer to director of Kew, Buitenzorg, 20 May 1914, RBG-K, Museums, Hevea File; T. A. Tengwall, "History of Rubber Cultivation and Research in the Netherlands East Indies," in Honig and Verdoorn, eds., *Science and Scientists*, p. 344; O. de Vries, et al., *Selection of Hevea in Java* (Bandoeng, 1929), pp. 4–5; F. Summers, *The Improvement of Yield in Hevea brasiliensis* (Singapore, 1930), pp. 143–4. On the Dutch transfer of cinchona, see A. Groothoff, *Onze Koloniale Landbouw, III, De Kinacultuur*, 2d ed. (Haarlem, 1915), pp. 7–18.

30 Cramer, *De cultuur van Hevea* (Amsterdam, 1910); Cramer, "Wild Rubber and Selection," in International Rubber Congress and Exhibition, Djakarta, 1914, *Rubber Recueil* (Amsterdam, 1914), pp. 13–32; Ernst Ule, *Kautschukgewinnung und Kautschukhandel am Amazonenstrome* (Berlin, [1906]); "On the Selection of *Hevea brasiliensis*," *BMI-K*, no. 4 (1920): 114; Cramer to director of Kew, 20 May 1914, RBG-K, Caoutchouc 1; J. G. Bouychou, "The Origins of the Far East Rubber Tree; I – Introduction and Distribution," *Revue Générale de Caoutchouc* 33 (August 1956): 730–5. On the superiority of upriver rubber, see R. E. Schultes, "The History of Taxonomic Studies in Hevea," in P. Smit and R. C. Ch. V. ter Laage, eds., *Essays in Biohistory and Other Contributions* (Utrecht, 1970), pp. 245–6.

31 On the organization of the Kew network, see Brockway, *Science and Colonial Expansion*, pp. 79–83.

3 Production and folklore, 1876–1910

1 Cássio Fonseca, "Uma comédia de erros; a borracha natural no Brasil," *Elastômeros* 4 (May–June 1980): 23.

2 Paul le Cointe, *L'Amazonie brésilienne* (Paris, 1922), 1:420.

3 It was possible to exploit the Indians for labor while at the same time massacring them. This was revealed to have been carried out by a British-owned company in the Peruvian Amazon. Such a policy, of course, could achieve profitability only over a short period, and may well have failed to recover the company's initial costs. See W. E. Hardenburg, *The Putumayo, the Devil's Paradise* (London, 1912).

4 On the labor system, see Barbara Weinstein, *The Amazon Rubber Boom, 1850–1920* (Stanford, CA, 1983), pp. 15–20.

5 Auguste Plane, *L'Amazonie* (Paris, 1903), pp. 38, 39; capital estimates are from Roberto Santos, *História econômica da Amazônia* (Rio de Janeiro, 1980), pp. 149–53; Alberto Moreira, *A borracha na Amazonia* (Rio de Janeiro, 1912), pp. 20–21, 35; and Brazil, Comissão da Exposição Internacional de Borracha de New York, *Brazil the Land of Rubber* (New York, 1912), p. 27.

6 Santos, *História*, p. 90, compares immigration figures; cf. Charles L. Temple, *Brazil; Report on the State of Amazonas*, Great Britain, Foreign Office, Diplomatic and Consular Reports, misc. ser. no. 530 (London, 1900), p. 30. For Malaya, see James C. Jackson, *Planters and Speculators; Chinese and European Agricultural Enterprise in Malaya, 1786–1921* (Kuala Lumpur, 1968), pp. 227, 239.

7 George E. Church, "The Acre Territory and the Caoutchouc Region of South-Western Amazonia," *Geographical Journal* 23 (May 1904): 597; le Cointe, *L'Amazonie brésilienne*, 1:328, citing Euclides da Cunha.

8 Plane, *L'Amazonie*, p. 43; José Amando Mendes, *Extracção e futuro da borracha no vale do Amazonas* (Belém, 1910), p. 29. Araujo Lima opined that the advantage was with the seringueiro, who usually did not repay his advances and could not be held to them, *A situação economica do Amazonas, especialmente em face das pretensões americanas* (Rio de Janeiro, 1923), pp. 19–20.

9 Plane, *L'Amazonie*, p. 38.

10 Gustavo Schuch de Capanema, "Agricultura; fragmentos do relatorio dos commissarios brasileiros á Exposição Universal de Paris em 1855," *Arquivos da Palestra Scientifica do Rio de Janeiro*, 1 (1858): 171; Antônio Gonçalves Dias, "Exposicão Universal em Paris: Relatorio da Commissão Brazileira," *Revista Brasileira* 1 (1858): 324–5; Franz Keller-Leuzinger, *The Amazon and Madeira Rivers* (London, 1874), p. 117; Robert Cross, *Report on the Investigation and Collection of Plants and Seeds of the India Rubber Trees of Para and Ceara and Balsam of Copaiba, 29 March 1877* (Edinburgh, 1877).

11 M. A. Pimenta Bueno, *Industria extractiva: a borracha; considerações* (Rio de Janeiro, 1882), pp. 5–6, 7, 9; Brazil, Câmara de Deputados, *Politica economica; defesa da borracha, 1906–1914*, Documentos Parlamentares, no. 41 (Rio de Janeiro, 1915), pp. 93–4; André Rebouças, *Agricultura nacional* (Rio de Janeiro, 1883), p. 54. For an angry riposte to Pimenta Bueno's claim that wild rubber

would soon be exhausted, see *A borracha; breves reflexões oppostas pelo Diario de Grão Pará ás considerações do snr. commendador M. A. Pimenta Bueno* (Belém, 1882).

12 João Barbosa Rodrigues, *As heveas ou seringueiras; informações* (Rio de Janeiro, 1900), pp. 30–1.

13 Amazon Steam Navigation Company, Limited, *The Great River, Notes on the Amazon* (London, 1904), p. 87; Ernesto Mattoso, *Album do Estado do Pará, oito anos do governo (1901–1909)* (Paris, 1908), pp. 182–9; see also Wenceslau Bello, "Extracção de borracha," in Centro Industrial do Brasil, *Brasil, suas riquezas naturais, suas industrias* (Rio de Janeiro, 1907), 2:13; H. Vasconcellos, "Brazilian Rubber and Trade Interests with Great Britain," in D. Spence, ed., *Lectures on India Rubber* (London, 1909), pp. 47–9.

14 "Selected Papers from the Kew Bulletin, 3, Rubber," *Bulletin of Miscellaneous Information, Kew*, add. ser., 7 (1906): 113–14, 116–17.

15 Brazil, Câmara de Deputados, *Politica economica*, pp. 7–67; reprinted as Miguel Calmon du Pin e Almeida, *Producção e commercio de borracha; parecer da Commissão de Agricultura* (Rio de Janeiro, 1906).

16 João Nogueira da Mata, *Biografia da borracha* (Manaus, n.d.), p. 81; Guilherme Catramby, *A cultura da seringueira; publicação feita por ordem de. . . Antonio Constantino Nery, Governador do Estado* (Manaus, 1907).

17 Jacques Huber, *A seringueira. . . conselhos praticos para a sua cultura racional* (Belém, 1907).

18 Wickham, "Report," transcribed in A. M. and J. Ferguson, *India Rubber and Gutta Percha, Being a Compilation of all the Available Information Respecting the Trees Yielding these Articles of Commerce and their Cultivation* (Colombo, 1882), p. 111. Antônio Francisco de Paula Souza reported no cultivation as of 1865, *Elementos de estatistica, comprehendendo a theoria da sciencia* (Rio de Janeiro, 1865), 2:134. Brazil, Comissão Brasileira Junto à Missão Norteamericana de Estudos do Valle do Amazonas, *Relatorio* (Rio de Janeiro, 1924), p. 431; Costa Miranda, *A situação da borracha* (Rio de Janeiro, 1927), p. 14; U.S. Bureau of Foreign and Domestic Commerce, *Special Consular Reports* 6 (1891–1892): 382; Brazil, Commission Representing the Empire of Brazil at the Universal Exposition of 1876, Philadelphia, *L'Empire du Brésil à l'Exposition Universelle de 1876 à Philadelphie* (Rio de Janeiro, 1876), p. 460; *O Liberal* (Belém), 4 July 1976, 2o. Caderno; le Cointe, *L'Amazonie brésilienne*, 1:414; A. C. Tavares Bastos, *O vale do Amazonas*, 2d ed. (São Paulo, 1937), p. 208; Howard and Ralph Wolf, *Rubber; a Story of Glory and Greed* (New York, 1936), p. 155; José Manuel Pereira da Silva, *Novas industrias; processos praticos da cultura da seringueira, mangabeira, maniçoba e copahyba* (São Paulo, 1899), pp. 8, 21; Brazil, Serviço de Inspecção e Defesa Agricolas, *Questionarios sobre as condições da agricultura dos municipios do Estado do Amazonas* (Rio de Janeiro, 1913). Pará state law 336, of 20 March 1896, provided prizes for planting various crops, including rubber.

19 Loren G. Polhamus, *Rubber: Botany, Cultivation and Utilization* (London, 1962), p. 62; Plínio de Carvalho, *A seringueira do Amazonas (Hevea brasiliensis) pode ser cultivada em todas as terras ferteis do Brasil* (São Paulo, 1911), n.p.; Plane, *L'Amazonie*, p. 204; le Cointe, *L'Amazonie brésilienne*, 1:357; Ernst Ule, *Kaut-*

schukgewinnung und Kautschukhandel am Amazonenstrome (Berlin, [1906?]), p. 69; Jacob Cohen, *A seringueira; considerações oportunas, história da minha cooperação profissional durante 33 anos, 1910 a 1943* (Belém, 1945), p. 9.

20 Brazil, Comissão da Exposição Internacional de Borracha de New York, *Brazil, the Land of Rubber*, p. 46.

21 Congresso Commercial, Industrial e Agricola, 1, Manaus, 1910, *Annaes* (Manaus, 1910). Among its recommendations was the setting up of a government colony at Itacoatiara, the first of many such proposals. Barbara Weinstein discusses 1909 law and conference, *The Amazon Rubber Boom*, pp. 220, 225–6. On results, J. Huber, "The Present and Future of the Native Hevea Rubber Industry," in International Rubber Congress, 4, London, 1914, *The Rubber Industry* (London, 1915): 377–84; F. Pasquier, "La culture de l'arbre à caoutchouc de plantation au Brésil," *Revue Universelle des Mines, de la Metallurgie*, ser. 4, t. 33, 1er. trimestre (1911): 9–16; Cohen, *A seringueira*, p. 9. Huber, "Rubber Trees and Wild Rubber Reserves of the Amazon," in International Rubber Congress, pp. 87–98; Huber, *Relatorio sobre o estado actual da cultura da Hevea brasiliensis nos principaes paizes de produção do Oriente* (Belém, 1912).

22 Economic Defense of Rubber debate in Brazil, Câmara de Deputados, *Politica economica*; see discussions in Roberto Santos, *História econômica da Amazônia*, pp. 253–5; and Nelson Prado Alves Pinto, *Política da borracha no Brasil; a falência da borracha vegetal* (São Paulo, 1984), pp. 45, 48–9.

23 Brazil, Câmara de Deputados, *Politica economica*, p. 217, Quadro 29; Weinstein, *The Amazon*, p. 272.

24 Optimistic versions for foreign consumption included A. J. Carneiro de Souza, *Rubber in Brazil* (Rio de Janeiro, 1913); and Armand Ledent, *L'organisation agricole au Brésil* (Anvers, 1913). Manuel Lobato, *O valle do Amazonas e o problema da borracha* (New York, 1912), p. 63; "The Rubber Crisis in Brazil," *India Rubber World* 50 (1 April 1914): 342.

25 Gow, Wilson and Stanton, Ltd., *Rubber Producing Companies (Capitalized in Sterling)* (London, 1912); Brazilian Rubber Trust, Ltd., *The Para Rubber of Brazil* (London, 1910); C. E. Akers, *Report on the Amazon Valley, Its Rubber Industry and Other Resources* (London, 1912), p. 24; Glenn D. Babcock, *History of the United States Rubber Company* (Bloomington, IN, 1966), pp. 83–8; Ana Célia Castro, *As empresas estrangeiras no Brasil, 1860–1913* (Rio de Janeiro, 1979), pp. 79, 119.

26 Brazil, Comissão Brasileira Junto à Missão Norteamericana, *Relatorio*, pp. 238, 245, 254, 256; Carl D. La Rue, *The Hevea Rubber Tree in the Amazon Valley* (Washington, DC, 1926), p. 41; J. Virgolino de Alencar, *O Acre de hoje e de amanhan* (Rio de Janeiro, 1917), a report presented to the Sociedade Nacional de Agricultura in 1916. Alencar's grove and many others were found by the U. S. Department of Agriculture's surveys during World War II. See also Brazil, Ministério de Agricultura, Indústria e Comércio, Directoria do Serviço de Inspecção e Fomento Agricolas, *Aspectos da economia rural brasileira* (Rio de Janeiro, 1922), pp. 79–83. Jean-Claude Bernardet found an advertisement in the São Paulo press of 1921 for a documentary motion picture film entitled "A cultura da borracha no Brasil," see his *Filmografia do cinema brasileiro, 1900–1935* (São Paulo, 1979).

27 On transfer of cacau to Bahia in 1677, see Manuel Barata, *A antiga producção e*

exportação do Pará; estudo historico-economico (Belém, 1915), p. 11. There are somewhat conflicting reports on early planting in Bahia in Gregório Bondar, *A seringueira do Pará (Hevea brasiliensis) no Estado da Bahia* (Salvador, 1926); V. A. Argollo Ferrão, *Cultura da seringueira Hevea brasiliensis no estado da Bahia* (Salvador, 1926); Luiz A. de C. Carvalho, "História pouco conhecida da borracha natural brasileira," *O Jornal* (Manaus), 25–31 May 1981. On efforts in Rio de Janeiro, see Sociedade Nacional de Agricultura, *Plantas produtoras de borracha* (Rio de Janeiro, 1908); Guilherme Catramby, *A borracha no estado de Rio de Janeiro* (Rio de Janeiro, 1913); Alberto Pereira da Silva, *A industria da borracha no estado do Rio de Janeiro* (Rio de Janeiro, 1913).

28 Weinstein, *The Amazon*, pp. 258–66; Weinstein, "The Persistence of Pre-Capitalist Relations of Production in a Tropical Export Economy," in Michael Hanagan and Charles Stephenson, eds., *Workers and Industrialization: Comparative Studies of Class Formation and Worker Militancy* (Westport, CT, 1984). José Verissimo de Matos averred that if the work force and elite were incapable of agriculture, then a "curious regression" had taken place, since the area had once been a prosperous farm region: *Interesses da Amazonia* (Rio de Janeiro, 1915), pp. 25–6. John Melby's explanation, that the Amazon had simply fallen behind in the race and could not catch up, seems to ignore the Netherlands East Indies and Cochin China. "Rubber River: An Account of the Rise and Collapse of the Amazon Boom," *Hispanic American Historical Review* 22 (August 1942): 463.

29 de Souza, Lecture at annual meeting of the Sociedade Brasileira pelo Progresso da Ciência, Belém, 7 July 1983.

30 James Collins, "On India-Rubber, Its History, Commerce and Supply," *Journal of the Society of Arts* 18 (17 December 1869): 81–93.

31 Colin Barlow, *The Natural Rubber Industry* (Kuala Lumpur, 1978), pp. 41–4; on the Netherlands East Indies, see John A. Fowler, *Plantation Rubber in the Netherlands East Indies and British Malaya* (Washington, DC, 1922), pp. 8–9.

32 Temple, "Report on the State of Amazonas," in Great Britain, Foreign Office, Diplomatic and Consular Reports, misc. ser., no. 530 (4 June 1900); Henri Coudreau, *Les Français en Amazonie* (Paris, 1887), pp. 75–8.

33 Huber, "The Progress of the Rubber Industry in Para," in International Rubber Congress, 2, London, 1911, *The Rubber Industry* (London, 1911), p. 8; Akers, *Report*, p. 84; "The Rubber Crisis in Brazil," *India Rubber World* 50 (1 April 1914): 347.

34 La Rue, *The Hevea Rubber Tree*, pp. 39–41.

35 Pereira, speech reprinted in Brazil, Câmara de Deputados, *Politica economica*, p. 215.

4 The reason why, 1904–1923

1 "Rubber Cultivation in Trinidad and Tobago, Report of the Special Committee of the Board of Agriculture," *Bulletin of the Board of Agriculture, Trinidad and Tobago* [hereafter *BBATT*] 16, pt. 3 (1917): 95–104; Trinidad and Tobago, Department of Agriculture, *Rubber, Trinidad and Tobago* (Port-of-Spain, 1911); J. T. Baldwin, Jr., "Library Notes Made in Trinidad on Hevea," *Economic Botany* 23 (January–March 1969): 20–1; Richard A. Howard and Dulcie A. Powell, "The

Introduction of Rubber-Producing Species in the West Indies," *Economic Botany* 17 (October–December 1963): 338–45; W. T. Thiselton-Dyer, "Para Rubber," *Bulletin of Miscellaneous Information, Kew*, no. 142 (October 1898): 275.

2 Thiselton-Dyer, p. 276; Daniel Morris, "Rubber Planting in the West Indies," in D. Spence, ed., *Lectures on India Rubber* (London, 1909), pp. 109–10; Edgar Beckett, "Rubber," *Timehri: The Journal of the Royal Agricultural and Commercial Society of British Guiana*, 3d ser., 1 (1911): 37–41; Walter Egerton, "British Guiana and the Problem of its Development," *Journal of the Royal Society of Arts* 66 (7 June 1918): 465; J. B. Harrison and F. A. Stockdale, *Rubber and Balata in British Guiana* (Georgetown, 1911), pp. 4–5; F. A. Stockdale, "Lecture on the West Indies," in International Rubber Congress, London, 1911, *The Rubber Industry* (London, 1911), pp. 69–72; C. K. Bancroft, "Report on the South American Leaf Disease of the Para Rubber Tree," *Journal of the Board of Agriculture of British Guiana* [hereafter *JBABG*] 10 (October 1916): 13.

3 A. W. Drost, *Para Rubber Culture in Surinam* (Amsterdam, 1911), pp. 3, 7, 9, 11, 25, 28–9, 31; Baldwin, "Library Notes," p. 22; Bancroft, "Report," p. 13. Authorities in French Guiana appear to have been very slow in introducing Hevea; it may have begun only after 1922, and then on a very modest scale; see Leon Jacob, "La Guyane," in *Les colonies françaises d'Amérique* (Paris, 1924), pp. 108, 109; French Guiana, *Annuaire de la Guyane Française* (n.p., 1914).

4 Harrison and Stockdale, *Rubber and Balata*, pp. 6, 8, 9, 11–16; Bancroft, "Report," pp. 13–15.

5 Harrison and Stockdale, *Rubber and Balata*, p. 20; "Rubber," *JBABG* 10 (January 1917): 81–2; Howard and Powell, *Rubber-Producing Species*, p. 345; "Hevea Rubber Cultivation and Curing at Non Pareil Estate, Sangre Grande, Trinidad," *BBATT* 14, pt. 4 (1915): 118–19; "Exports of Agricultural and Forest Products," *JBABG* 11 (October 1918) and 12 (October 1919); "Rubber Cultivation in Trinidad," *BBATT*, p. 97; "Balata and Rubber Enterprises in the Guianas," *India Rubber World* 60 (1 June 1919): 518–19.

6 Jacques Huber, *A seringueira: conselhos practicos para a sua cultura racional* (Belem, 1907), p. 41; A. E. van Hall de Jonge, "Bladziekte in de Heveas," *Bulletin Department van den Landbouw in Suriname* [hereafter *BDLS*], no. 24 (April 1910): 2. Van Hall may have been reporting Target Leaf Spot, caused by *Thanetephorus cucumeris*.

7 Drost, *Para Rubber*, pp. 24–5; J. Kuyper, "Eine Heveablattkrankheit in Surinam," *Recueil des Travaux Botaniques Néerlandais* 8, no. 3–4 (1911): 371–9; J. Kuyper, "Een *Fusicladium-Ziekte* op Hevea," *BDLS*, no. 28 (September 1912): 371–9; E. Griffon and A. Maublanc, "Sur quelques champignons parasites des plantes tropicales," *Bulletin Trimestriel de la Société Mycologique de France* 29, no. 2 (1913): 244–6, 250; Paul Hennings, "Fungi Amazonici, II, a cl. Ernesto Ule collecti" *Hedwigia* 43, no. 6 (1904): 254; Hennings, "Ueber die auf Hevea-Arten bisher beobachteten parasitischen Pilze," *Notizblatt des Königlichen Botanischen Gartens und Museums zu Berlin* 4 (15 April 1904): 133–8; Victor Cayla, "Maladies cryptogamiques des feuilles de l'Hevea en Amérique," *Journal d'Agriculture Tropicale* 13, no. 144 (1913): 186–8.

8 Cayla, "Maladies," p. 188; François Vincens, "Contribution à l'étude des maladies de l'*Hevea brasiliensis* dans la vallée de l'Amazone," *Bulletin de la Société*

de Pathologie Végétale de France 2 (August 1915): 11–13; O. Labroy, *A borracha no Brasil* (Rio de Janeiro, 1913), p. 82; Thomas Petch, "Leaf Diseases of Hevea," *Tropical Agriculturist* 42 (April 1914): 268–9.

9 Bancroft, "Report," pp. 20–1; Paul Holliday, *South American Leaf Blight (Microcyclus ulei) of Hevea Brasiliensis* (Kew, Surrey, England, 1970), pp. 2–4. See also Ian K. Ross, *Biology of the Fungi* (New York, 1979), pp. 94–120; G. C. Ainsworth, et al., *The Fungi, an Advanced Treatise* (New York, 1973), 4A:175; and E. Muller and J. A. von Arx, "Die Gattungen den didymosporen Pyrenomyceten," *Beiträgen zur Kryptogammenflora der Schweiz* 11, no. 2 (1962): 373–4. See also "South American Leaf Blight of Rubber," *Planter's Bulletin of the RRIM*, no. 127 (July 1973). According to P. Holliday, the pycnospores are not infective, therefore, they play no role in the spread of the disease.

10 Gerold Stahel, "De Zuid-Amerikansche Hevea Bladziekte, Veroorzaacht door Melanopsammis ulei nov. gen. (= Dothidella ulei P. Hennings)," *BDLS*, no. 34 (June 1917): 5–8; Stahel, "De Zuid-Amerikanische Hevea-Bladziekte op de Rubberplantage der Lawa Caoutchouc Compagnie," *West Indië Landbouwkundig Tijdschrift* 4 (1919): 63–4. Muller and von Arx, "Die Gattungen," pp. 373–4: There are eleven species of the genus, three of which are South American, but no other attacks Euphorbiaceae.

11 Stahel, "De Zuid-Amerikansche" (1917), p. 11; Bancroft, "Report," pp. 16, 19; "Rubber," *JBABG*, 81–2; J. B. Rorer, "The South American Hevea Leaf Disease," *BBATT* 16, pt. 3 (1917): 128–9; C. K. Bancroft, "The Leaf Disease of Rubber," *JBABG* 10 (January 1917): 93–5.

12 Keng Hoi Chee, "The Suitability of Environmental Conditions in Asia for the Spread of South American Leaf Blight of Hevea Rubber," *Planter* 56 (November 1980): 445, 448; Jacques Huber, "The Present and Future of the Native Hevea Rubber Industry," in International Rubber Conference, 4, London, 1914, *The Rubber Industry* (London, 1915), p. 380; Thomas Petch, *The Physiology and Diseases of Hevea brasiliensis* (London, 1911), p. 169; Stahel, "De Zuid-Amerikansche" (1917), p. 68.

13 Huber, "The Present," pp. 377–84; Robert Delafield Rands, *South American Leaf Disease of Para Rubber*, U.S. Department of Agriculture Bulletin, no. 1286 (Washington, DC, 1924), pp. 8, 12.

14 Cayla, "Maladies," p. 186; Thomas Petch, *The Diseases and Pests of the Rubber Tree* (London, 1921), p. 80.

15 British Guiana, Department of Agriculture, *British Guiana Agricultural Industries, 1918* ([Georgetown, 1918]); Great Britain, *Colonial Reports – Annual, British Guiana Report for 1919 [to] 1935* (London, 1921–1936); "Balata and Rubber Enterprises," and "Rubber Cultivation in Trinidad," both in Trinidad and Tobago, Department of Agriculture, *Report[s], 1919–1929* (Port-of-Spain, 1921–1930); "Exports of Agricultural and Forest Products," *JBABG* 11–20 (October 1916–October 1927); series continued in *Agricultural Journal of British Guiana* 3–5 (December 1930–December 1934). British Guiana, Department of Science and Agriculture, *Report, 1920* (Georgetown, 1921), pp. 3, 14, 15. Great Britain, Foreign Office, Historical Section, *Dutch Guiana*, Handbook no. 136 (London, 1920), p. 48; *De Vraagboek; Almanak voor Suriname, 1928* (n.p., n.d.), pp. 157–8.

16 Paul le Cointe, *L'Amazonie brésilienne* (Paris, 1922), 1:353.

17 Bancroft, "The Leaf Disease," p. 97; William A. Orton, "Botanical Problems of American Tropical Agriculture," *Bulletin of the Torrey Botanical Club* 53 (1926–7): 69.

18 Voon Phin Keong, *Western Rubber Planting Enterprise in Southeast Asia, 1876–1921* (Kuala Lumpur, 1976), pp. 15–16. It is of interest to note that English botanists in Malaya also tried to acclimatize the Brazil, or Para, nut (*Bertholletia excelsa*), but were unsuccessful, apparently because no pollinating agents were available from among the local insect population: J. Lambourne, *The Brazil Nut in Malaya*, Department of Agriculture, Straits Settlements and Federated Malay States, gen. ser., no. 2 (Kuala Lumpur, March 1930). On probabilistic explanation in biology, see Ernst Mayr, *The Growth of Biological Thought* (Cambridge, MA, 1982), pp. 37–43. An interesting ecological relationship of Hevea came to the author's attention at the experimental station at Manaus. At the base of the petiole of the Hevea leaf, there is a nectary at which ants feed. Probably they protect the leaves against leaf-cutting ants. The author has found no reference to the nectaries in Southeast Asian literature. Possibly they are not visited by ants there, or if they are, there is no defensive function for them to perform.

19 Stahel, "De Zuid-Amerikansche" (1919), p. 64; W. N. C. Belgrave, "Notes on the South American Leaf Disease of Rubber," *Agricultural Bulletin of the Federated Malay States* 9 (1921): 179–83.

20 Jacques Huber, *Relatorio sobre o estado actual da cultura da Hevea brasiliensis nos principaes paizes de produção do Oriente* (Belem, 1912), p. 100; Colin Barlow, *The Natural Rubber Industry* (Kuala Lumpur, 1978), p. 112.

21 W. T. Thiselton-Dyer, "Para Rubber," p. 271; Herbert Wright, "Rubber Cultivation (With Special Reference to Parts of the British Empire)," *Journal of the Royal Society of Arts* 55 (26 April 1907): 614–43; Petch, *The Diseases*, pp. 77–81; A. J. Ultée, *Onze Koloniale Landbouw, 4, Caoutchouc,* 3d ed. (Haarlem, 1921), p. 44; John A. Fowler, *Plantation Rubber in the Netherlands East Indies and British Malaya* (Washington, DC, 1922); T. A. Tengwall, "History of Rubber Cultivation and Research in the Netherlands Indies," in Pieter Honig and Frans Verdoorn, eds., *Science and Scientists in the Netherlands Indies* (New York, 1945), p. 347; Marinus J. Dijkman, *Hevea, Thirty Years of Rubber Research in the Far East* (Coral Gables, FL, 1951), pp. 228–9; H. N. Whitford, *Report on Plantation Rubber in the Middle East* (New York, 1931), p. 16.

22 William L. Schurz, *Rubber Production in the Amazon Valley* (Washington, DC, 1925), pp. 45, 46; Conferência Técnica sobre a Valorização Econômica da Amazônia, *Valorização econômica da Amazônia; subsídios para seu planejamento* (Rio de Janeiro, 1954), p. 29; Alfredo Kingo Oyama Homma, et al., "Estrutura produtiva de seringais no município de Santarém, PA," *CPATU, Circular Técnico, No. 3* (Belém, 1980); Charles Wagley, *Amazon Town* (New York, 1953), p. 89. It has recently been claimed that the physiological basis for the dichotomous relationship of resistance and productivity lies in the limited capacity of Hevea to absorb potassium, apparently essential both to the synthesis of latex and certain phytoalexins that supposedly confer resistance: See Afonso Celso Candeira Valois, "Expressão de caracteres em seringueira e obtenção de clones produtivos e resis-

tentes ao mal-das-folhas," *Pesquisa Agropecuária Brasileira* 18 (September 1983): 1016.

23 C. Daubanton, *An Enumeration of the Latexproducing Plants Cultivated in the Botanical gardens of Buitenzorg, Java* (Bogor, 1914); Tromp de Haas, "The Valuation of Para Rubber Trees by a Chemical Method," in D. Spence, ed., *Lectures on India Rubber* (London, 1909), p. 173; Dijkman, *Hevea*, p. 13.

24 Dijkman, ibid.; Tengwall, "History of Rubber," p. 347–8; Otto de Vries, et al., *Selection of Hevea in Java* (Bandung, 1929), pp. 6–12; John A. Fowler, *Plantation Rubber*, p. 2; W. Vischer, "Bud Grafting Results," *The Planter* 1 (July 1921): 63–71; J. G. J. A. Maas, "The Vegetative Propagation of *Hevea Brasiliensis*," *Tropical Agriculturist* 54 (January 1920): 2–6; A. C. Tutein-Nolthenius, "Bud Grafting of Rubber," *Tropical Agriculturist* 58 (April 1922): 192–6.

25 W. M. van Helten, "Het oculeeren van Hevea," *Archiev voor de Rubber Cultuur* 2 (May 1918): 187–95, and (September 1918): 637–8; L. Tas, *Vegetatieve Vermenigvuldiging bij Hevea brasiliensis* (Jakarta, 1921). See also Ultée, *Onze Koloniale*, pp. 22–4.

26 Peter Tamas Bauer makes much of the refusal of colonial Malayan officials to provide smallholders with services, *The Rubber Industry, a Study in Competition and Monopoly* (Cambridge, 1948), pp. 211–12, 254–62, 280–1; an opposite version is found in R. D. Rands, "Hevea Rubber Culture in Latin America," in Frans Verdoorn, *Plants and Plant Science in Latin America* (Waltham, MA, 1945), p. 84, citing *Bergcultures* (June 1941), pp. 783–97. Frederick Summers, *The Improvement of Yield in Hevea Brasiliensis* (Singapore, 1930).

27 *Boletim da Superintendencia da Borracha* 1 (31 July 1913), decrees on experiment stations; le Cointe, *L'Amazonie*, 1:411; Jacob Cohen, *A seringueira; considerações oportunas, história da minha cooperação durante 33 anos, 1910–1943* (Belém, 1945), pp. 29–31; Charles E. Akers, *Report on the Amazon Valley* (London, 1912), p. 25.

28 le Cointe, *L'Amazonie*, 1:411.

29 Nancy Stepan, *Beginnings of Brazilian Science* (New York, 1976), pp. 105–33, deals with medical research and public health efforts.

30 Carl D. La Rue made this point in 1923: See *The Hevea Rubber Tree in the Amazon Valley*, U.S. Department of Agriculture Bulletin, no. 1422 (Washington, DC, 1926), p. 38; Summers, *The Improvement*, p. 53.

31 "Hevea in British Guiana," *Tropical Agriculturist* 58 (January 1920): 9; R. D. Rands, *South American Leaf Disease of Para Rubber*, p. 8.

5 A jump in the dark, 1923–1940

1 Great Britain, Committee upon the Present Rubber Situation in British Colonies and Protectorates, "Report," and "Supplementary Report," in *Parliamentary Papers and Accounts*, 1922, 16:5–13 and Session 2, 2:135. An important study of rubber restriction schemes is P. T. Bauer, *The Rubber Industry, A Study in Competition and Monopoly* (Cambridge, MA, 1948).

2 "Less Opposition to Rubber Plan of the British," *Journal of Commerce and Commercial Bulletin* (16 April 1923).

3 K. E. Knorr, *World Rubber and its Regulation* (Stanford, CA, 1945), pp. 90–8; Howard and Ralph Wolf, *Rubber, A Story of Glory and Greed* (New York, 1936), pp. 240–1. Goodyear's plantation produced 12 percent of its rubber, U.S. Rubber plantations produced 20 percent. U.S. Tariff Commission, *Crude rubber, a Brief Summary* (Washington, DC, 1940), p. 15.

4 U.S. Congress, House, *Investigating Sources of Crude Rubber and Compiling Foreign-Trade Statistics*, 67th Cong., 4th sess., 15 February 1923, H. Doc. 578. For Department of Agriculture interest in rubber, see a collection of sources brought together by Loren G. Polhamus, "Contributions on Rubber from Various Offices of the U.S. Department of Agriculture," bound file dated 1937, 2 vols., National Agricultural Library, Beltsville, MD. On scandals, see J. Fred Rippy, *Latin America and the Industrial Age* (New York, 1944), pp. 166–87; and Rippy, "Some Rubber-Planting Fiascos in Tropical America," *Inter-American Economic Affairs* 10 (Summer 1956): 3–24.

5 John C. Treadwell, et al., *Possibilities for Para Rubber Production in Northern Tropical America*, U.S. Bureau of Foreign and Domestic Commerce, Trade Promotion Series, no. 40 (Washington, DC, 1926), pp. 14–15. There were also reports on Asian rubber in the same series: David M. Figart, *The Plantation Rubber Industry in the Middle East*, no. 2 (Washington, DC, 1925); and Charles F. Vance, *Possibilities for Para Rubber Production in the Philippine Islands*, no. 17 (Washington, 1925). The Philippines government refused to waive its 1,000 acre limit on plantation size, fearing that American investment would lead to a cancellation of the promised independence.

6 Carl D. LaRue, *The Hevea Rubber Tree in the Amazon Valley*, U.S. Department of Agriculture Bulletin, no. 1422 (Washington, DC, 1926), pp. 44–6; Brazil, Ministério de Agricultura, Commissão Brasileira Junto á Missão Official Norteamericana de Estudos do Vale do Amazonas, *Relatorio* (Rio de Janeiro, 1924); William L. Schurz, *Rubber Production in the Amazon Valley* (Washington, DC, 1925).

7 Robert Delafield Rands, *South American Leaf Disease of Para Rubber*, U.S. Department of Agriculture Bulletin, no. 1286 (Washington, DC, 1924); James R. Weir, *A Pathological Survey of the Para Rubber Tree (Hevea Brasiliensis) in the Amazon Valley*, U.S. Department of Agriculture Bulletin, no. 1380 (Washington, DC, 1926), p. 33. John H. Barnhart, *Biographical Notes upon Botanists* (New York, 1965), 3:473.

8 *Jornal do Brasil*, 29 March and 23 June 1923; José Custódio Alves de Lima, *Recordações de homens e cousas do meu tempo* (Rio de Janeiro, 1926), pp. 219–22; Brazil, Ministério de Agricultura, *Relatorio*, pp. 11–16; Araujo Lima, *A situação do Amazonas, especialmente em face das pretensões americanas; conferencia na Sociedade Nacional de Agricultura em 19 de julho de 1923* (Rio de Janeiro, 1923). Also, on Asians see Roberto Santos, *História econômica da Amazônia* (São Paulo, 1980), p. 253; Brazil, Câmara dos Deputados, *Politica economica; defesa da borracha* (Rio de Janeiro, 1915), p. 422.

9 V. A. Argollo Ferrão, *Cultura da seringueira Hevea brasiliensis no estado da Bahia* (Salvador, 1926), pp. 5–6; Gregorio Bondar, *A seringueira do Pará (Hevea brasiliensis) no Estado da Bahia* (Salvador, 1926), pp. 4–6; Bahia, *Lei, decreto e*

regulamento sobre favores a plantio da "Hevea-brasiliensis" na Bahia (Salvador, 1927), law 1876, 21 July 1926.

10 Barry Machado, "Farquahar and Ford in Brazil: Studies in Business Expansion and Foreign Policy" (Ph.D. diss. in history, Northwestern University, 1975): This chapter has benefited considerably from consultation of this excellent study. Felber to Firestone, Washington, 17 March 1924, Firestone Tire and Rubber Company Archives, Akron, OH [hereafter FTRC-A], AA/D-65, box 26.

11 de Lima, *Recordações*, pp. 219–22, 373–4; Ferrão, *Cultura*, pp. 5–6; Bondar, *A seringueira do Pará*, pp. 4–5; Mira Wilkins and Frank E. Hill, *American Business Abroad; Ford on Six Continents* (Detroit, 1964), p. 165; Allan Nevins and Frank E. Hill, *Ford, Expansion and Challenge, 1915–1933* (New York, 1957), pp. 234–5.

12 W. E. McCullough to C. W. Avery, Dearborn, 14 September 1925, Henry Ford Museum and Archives, Dearborn, MI [hereafter HFMA-D], C. W. Avery Papers.

13 Edwin V. Morgan, U.S. ambassador to secretary of state, Rio de Janeiro, 31 July 1925, U.S. National Archives, Washington, DC, Record Group 166, Foreign Agricultural Relations Reports, Brazil [hereafter RG 166-FAR], 1911–1938, 5-65; S. G. Carkhuff to H. S. Firestone, Akron, 7 September 1926, FTRC-A, AA/D-65, box 26; and another approach, G. D. Martin, Firestone Plantations Company, to H. S. Firestone, Akron, 24 January 1928, FTRC-A, AA/L205; Edward C. Holden, U.S. vice consul, to Department of State, Belém, 12 April 1927, RG 166-FAR, 1911–1938, 5-65.

14 C. D. LaRue, "Reminiscences," HFMA-D.

15 Machado traces the machinations of the Villares group in detail, "Farquahar and Ford," pp. 284–94; C. D. LaRue, "A Report of an Exploration of the Tapajós Valley," [Dearborn, April 1927], HFMA-D, 74-1, Fordlandia. Ford was simultaneously matching Firestone's $93,500 to fund Thomas Edison's research in latex-bearing plants that might be grown in the United States. This work did not have a successful result and was abandoned when Edison died in 1931. Matthew Josephson, *Edison* (New York, 1959), pp. 470–4.

16 João Nogueira da Mata, *Biografia da borracha* (Manaus, n.d.), p. 110; Companhia Ford Industrial do Brasil, "Estatutos e principaes documentos relativos á concessão feita pelo Estado do Pará," n.p., n.d., U.S. National Archives, Washington, DC, Record Group 54, Bureau of Plant Industry, Field Crops Research Branch, Brazil [hereafter RG 54-BPI], 731. This paragraph and the next is based on Machado, "Farquahar and Ford," pp. 327–37, 342–59, 366–7, 374. See also Howard and Ralph Wolf, *Rubber*, pp. 239, 266.

17 Archibald Johnston to J. R. Rogge, [Fordlandia], 24 April 1933, HFMA-D, 390-86; Glenn T. Babcock, *History of the United States Rubber Company* (Bloomington, IN, 1966), p. 87; "Statement of Increase in Advances to Companhia Ford Industrial do Brasil as Shown by Ford Motor Company General Ledger," HFMA-D, 74-17, Yearly Budgets from 1933; "Ford's Rubberplantages," *Indische Mercuur* 51 (28 March 1928): 242–3.

18 LaRue, "Suggestions Concerning Planting Material for the Tapajós Plantations," [Dearborn, May 1927?], HFMA-D, 74-1; Roy Carr to R. H. McCarroll, Santarém,

22 September 1928, HFMA-D, 64-1; Carr to McCarroll, Fordlandia, 3 April 1929; Machado, "Farquahar and Ford," p. 346.

19 Machado, "Farquahar and Ford," pp. 374, 381; Vice Consul George E. Seltzer, Manaus, "Annual Report," 30 October 1926, and Vice Consul James A. Roth, "Report of the Lumber Industry of Amazonas," 3 March 1924, both in RG 166-FAR, Forestry Reports, entry 3, box 531; Brazil, Ministério de Agricultura, *Relatorio*, p. 259; Sorenson to Perini, Dearborn, 16 April 1930, HFMA-D, 38-64; "Data-Boa Vista and São Paulo, Proposed 1000 Tire Plant," HFMA-D, 74-16; A. Johnston to A. M. Wibel, Belém, 7 May 1931, HFMA-D, 390-86. Wibel, "Reminiscences," HFMA-D.

20 LaRue to C. J. Craig, treasurer, Ford Motor Company, n.p., 18 October 1930, HFMA-D, 534-1. The author is indebted to Prof. Barry Machado for this reference. In his "Reminiscences" LaRue mentioned recommending a Dutch technician to Ford, who turned him down because he thought him too expensive at $20,000 a year. It pained LaRue that his original work in bud grafting had been kept secret by his employer, U.S. Rubber, and that the report published by his assistant, Donkersloot, and subsequent reports by the Dutch had not awarded him credit for that work.

21 Harvey Firestone to A. M. Wibel, n.p., 17 July 1932; Johnston to Carnegie, [Fordlandia?], 16 September 1932; Johnston to Wibel, Belém, 31 December 1932, all in HFMA-D, 390-86. See also P. T. Bauer, *The Rubber Industry, A Study in Competition and Monopoly* (Cambridge, MA, 1948), pp. 262–3.

22 James R. Weir to McCarroll, Kuala Lumpur, 17 June and 16 November 1928, HFMA-D, accession missing. LaRue recalled in his "Reminiscences" that it was he who had hired Weir for the 1923 government survey.

23 Weir, "Preliminary Statement on the Agricultural Situation at Boa Vista," Fordlandia, 31 March 1933, HFMA-D, 390-86. See also LaRue, "Recommendations for Development of Rubber Plantation on the Tapajos River," [Dearborn, April–May 1927?], HFMA-D, 744-1.

24 Howard C. Deckard, "Report," Fall 1970, RG 166-FAR, acc. 3326, box 92; "Mr. J. R. Weir," [Dearborn?], 18 December 1935, HFMA-D, 390-86; A. Johnston, "Visit to Far Eastern Plantations," Singapore, 30 March 1936, HFMA-D, 74-13. One of the first acts of the second rubber cartel was to prohibit export of improved clones!

25 Weir's opinions are foreshadowed in his article "The South American Leaf Disease of Hevea and its Control," *Rubber Age* 21 (25 June 1927): 293–4, 300.

26 Machado, "Farquahar and Ford," p. 394; Contract of Exchange (Permuta), RG 54-BPI, Brazil, 731.

27 "Budgrafting History," n.p., 18 December 1935, HFMA-D, 390–86; Weir to R. I. Roberge, "Departmental Communication," n.p., 24 May 1935, HFMA-D, 390-86.

28 Weir to Roberge, 24 May 1935, HFMA-D, 390-86; Weir, "General Report on Rubber Planting Activities in Brazil, Season 1934–35," Dearborn, 1935, HFMA-D, 134-4.

29 This and the next paragraph from Weir, "Report on the Plantation Work in Brazil and Recommendations, 1936," Fordlandia, 20 April 1936, with cover letter to

Roberge, same date, and Weir to Johnston, Fordlandia, 20 January 1936, all in HFMA-D, 390-86.

30 O. de Vries, et al., mention early top grafting in *Selection of Hevea in Java* (Bandung, 1929), p. 14.

31 Roberge to Johnston, Dearborn, 10 August 1934, HFMA-D, 74-17; Johnston to Roberge, Fordlandia, 3 September 1936, HFMA-D, 390-86; Bangham, "Report of Conditions on the Plantations of the Companhia Ford Industrial do Brasil," Fordlandia, 18 June 1936, HFMA-D, 74-15; Johnston to Wibel, Fordlandia, 1 July 1936, HFMA-D, 134-4; Weir to Bangham, Edinburg, IN, 25 May 1936, HFMA-D, 74-15.

32 Wilkins and Hill, *American Business Abroad*, p. 178; [Weir], Companhia Ford Industrial do Brasil, Research Department, "General Outline of Work," Edinburgh, IN, 28 June 1937, and Weir, "Report of the Research Department for October, November, December, 1937," Edinburgh, IN, 1 January 1938, both in HFMA-D, 74-12, Rubber Research.

33 Johnston to Wibel, Belém, 4 March 1935, HFMA-D, accession missing. It is not clear at what date Townsend's son, of the same name, came into the company's employ. It appears that the elder Townsend, then sixty-nine years old, was first hired in 1932, see Personnel Photos, HFMA-D, 74-8. C. H. T. Townsend, "Insect Census of Fordlandia," Fordlandia, 29 March 1935, HFMA-D, accession not copied. Townsend began applying a biological control to lace bugs – a parasitic fungus, *Hirsutella verticillioides* – that "worked very well," "Research Department Report for January 1943," n.p., n.d., HFMA-D, 74-5.

34 Wibel to J. J. Blandin, [Dearborn], 9 January 1938, HFMA-D, 390-86; Gibson B. Smith, "Rubber for Americans: The Search for an Adequate Supply of Rubber and the Politics of Strategic Materials" (Ph.D. diss. in history, Bryn Mawr, 1972), p. 145; Johnston to Wibel, Fordlandia, 1 July 1938, HFMA-D, 74-15, W. N. Bangham; Machado, "Farquhar and Ford," p. 409; Weir to Ford, New York, 20 June 1940, HFMA-D, 74-17, Clones. Boyd Gill, "Hoosier Played an Important Part in American Rubber Tree Cultivation," *Indianapolis Star* [1943?], in clipping file, Indiana State Library. In this interview Weir made only the barest possible reference to his Ford work.

35 Johnston, "Plantation Report," [Dearborn?], 11 January 1942, HFMA-D, 6-376; "Reports," for the months of February, April, May, June, November, 1940, Belterra, 1940, HFMA-D, 74-12. Bangham to Johnston, and attached report, San José, Costa Rica, 29 December 1940, HFMA-D, 74-17. Bangham, well regarded as a rubber specialist, was also thought difficult to deal with: See B. O. Vipond to B. H. Larrabee, Akron, OH, 13 March 1952, FTRC-A, Plantations Companies, 1952, box 67.

36 Johnston to Roberge, Belterra, 21 August 1939, HFMA-D, 74-17; Townsend to Johnston, Fordlandia, 2 January 1940, HFMA-D, 74-12. "Report," for the month of May, 1939, Fordlandia, 1939, HFMA-D, 74-5.

37 Johnston, "Plantation Report," (see note 35). H. C. Deckard to C. E. Sorenson, Belterra, 4 June 1941, HFMA-D, accession not copied; J. A. Zilles to H. C. Deckard, Belterra, 15 September 1941, HFMA-D, 74-17, Budgrafting.

38 Howard and Ralph Wolf, *Rubber*, pp. 269–70; Machado, "Farquhar and Ford," p. 364.

39 Files marked "Recruiting Amazon," 1929–1931, HFMA-D, 74-17.

40 Schurz, *Rubber Production*, pp. 89–90; de Lima, *Recordações*, p. 374; Companhia Ford Industrial do Brasil, "Salary and Wage Schedule," n.p., 6 August 1930, HFMA, 38-64. "Re Activities of Companhia Ford Industrial do Brasil," U.S. Consulate, Belém, 31 May 1938, RG 166-FAR, 1911–1938, 5-65.

41 Valentim Bouças, speech delivered to U.S. journalists, Rio de Janeiro, 29 October 1943, (original in English), transcription, RG 166-FAR, acc. 3326, box 92; Treadwell, et al., *Possibilities for Para Rubber Production*, p. 18; H. N. Whitford, *Report on Plantation Rubber in the Middle East* (New York, 1931), pp. 57–65, 181; "President's Visit," HFMA-D, 74-12.

42 Mark L. Felber to Harvey S. Firestone, Washington, 17 March 1924, FTRC-A, AA/D-65, box 26; Inácio Batista de Moura and Paulo Eleuthério, *A Amazonia do futuro; visita feita ao extremo norte do Brasil* (Belém, 1926), p. 56; LaRue, *The Hevea Rubber Tree*, pp. 36–7; Howard and Ralph Wolf, *Rubber*, p. 269.

43 Sílvio Meira, *Belterra, sua situação jurídica* (Belém, 1949); A. Johnston, "Plantation Report," [Dearborn?], 11 June 1942, HFMA-D, 6-376; Gastão Cruls, "Impressões de uma visita à Companhia Ford Industrial do Brasil," *Revista Brasileira de Geografia* 1 (October–December 1939): 14; Deckard to Johnston, Belterra, 1 November 1940, and Braunstein to Edsel Ford, 17 October 1940, both in HFMA-D, 74-12. Jay Walker, U.S. consul, to secretary of state, Belém, 5 August 1941, Strictly Confidential, RG 166-FAR, acc. 5, box 21. Bangham's report also stated that the company had more labor than it needed, 1940, HFMA-D, 74-17. See also Machado, "Farquahar and Ford," pp. 416–17: Roberge proposed Portuguese workers, and the U.S. State Department obligingly sent word to U.S. consuls in Portugal and the Brazilian government even more obligingly doubled its immigration quota!

44 Howard and Ralph Wolf reported a contemporaneous 100 percent labor turnover at Goodyear's Akron factory, *Rubber*, pp. 437–9, see also pp. 261–2; C. M. Wilson points out similarities in labor relations, *Trees and Test Tubes* (New York, 1943), p. 114.

45 Stahel, "De rubbercultuur en de Zuid-Amerikansche Heveabladziekte in Suriname," *Indische Mercuur* 50 (24 August 1927): 623; E. B. Fairweather, "Trees Recover from Leaf Disease," *Rubber Age* 20 (25 January 1927): 395–6; G. Lems, "Verleden, heden en toekomst van de rubbercultuur en Suriname," *Surinaamse Landbouw* 11 (1963): 19–26.

46 Walter N. Bangham, "Rubber Returns to Latin America," in C. M. Wilson, ed., *New Crops for the New World* (New York, 1945), pp. 81–4; Hugh Allen, *Rubber and the Goodyear Plantations* (Akron, OH, n.d.), pp. 10–11, 32; Howard and Ralph Wolf, *Rubber*, p. 246; Bangham, "Plantation Rubber in the New World," *Economic Botany* 1 (April–June 1947): 217–18.

47 Weir to R. I. Roberge, Cristobal, CZ, 23 and 25 October 1936, and Pringle to Johnston, n.p., 18 January 1939, both in HFMA-D, 390-86.

48 Harold E. Guston to E. B. Hamill, Manaus, 24 April 1943, RG 166-FAR, Technical Collaboration, box 2; Companhia Nipponica de Plantação do Brasil, Report of the Board of Directors, Belém, 1938, 1939, 1940, HFMA-D, 74-13, Japanese Company Data. Other plantation crops were successfully developed by Japanese colonists in the 1930s, notably cotton and vegetable oils.

49 Ladário de Castro, "Borracha do Amazonas," *Boletim do Ministerio de Trabalho, Industria e Comercio* [hereafter *BMTIC*] 5 (September 1938): 149–53. On Ford's manufacturing survey, see Machado, "Farquahar and Ford," pp. 403–7; R. I. Roberge, "Situation on Local Rubber Factories in Brazil," n.p., October 1935, and Roberge to Harvey S. Firestone, Dearborn, 19 December 1935, both in HFMA-D, 390-86. J. H. Rudeberg to J. W. T., São Paulo, 20 June 1940, FTRC-A, Subsidiaries, São Paulo, box 4.

50 C. E. Nabuco de Araujo, "The Brazilian Rubber Industry," *International Rubber World* 104 (1 April 1941): 35–8, 50; Lobato Filho, *O problema da borracha* (Belém, 1940), pp. 5–10; Anibal Porto, *O problema da borracha brasileira* (Rio de Janeiro, 1939), pp. 8–15, 47; Firmo Dutra, "O histórico da borracha e seus problemas," *Estudos Brasileiros* 4 (March–April 1940): 516–38; Ladário de Carvalho, "A borracha nacional e suas possibilidades economicas," *BMTIC* 4 (January 1938): 162–3. Decree law 300 was announced 24 February 1938, offering special incentives for foreign rubber investments on the same scale as Ford, to no avail. See José Amando Mendes, *Amazônia econômica*, 2d ed., (Rio de Janeiro, 1942), pp. 8–11, 51–4, 101–4, 191–3.

6 The battle for rubber, 1940–1945

1 This and next paragraphs derived from Herbert Feis, *Seen from EA: Three International Episodes* (New York, 1947), pp. 3–90; Jesse H. Jones, *Fifty Billion Dollars* (New York, 1951), pp. 396–400; U.S. Tariff Commission, *Crude Rubber; A Brief Summary of the Current Situation* (Washington, DC, 1940), pp. 15, 27, 34; E. W. Brandes, et al., *Cooperative Inter-American Plantation Rubber Development* (Washington, DC, 1946); E. N. Bressman, "Rubber Production in the Western Hemisphere," *Inter American Quarterly* 3 (January 1941): 52–60; Guenther Reimann, *Patents for Hitler* (New York, 1942), pp. 158–201; R. D. Rands and L. G. Polhamus, *Progress Report on the Cooperative Hevea Rubber Development Program in Latin America* (Washington, DC, 1955), pp. 32–4; Gibson B. Smith, "Rubber for Americans: The Search for an Adequate Supply of Rubber and the Politics of Strategic Materials" (Ph.D. diss. in history, Bryn Mawr, 1972), pp. 146–9. See also R. F. Chalk, "The United States and the International Struggle for Rubber, 1914–1941" (Ph.D. diss. in history, University of Wisconsin, 1970) and Douglas H. Allen and Francis Adams Truslow, *Summarized History of the Operations of Rubber Development Corporation and its Predecessor, Rubber Reserve Company* (New York, 1948). For United States–Brazilian relations during the war, see Frank McCann, *The Brazilian-American Alliance* (Princeton, NJ, 1973), and R. A. Humphreys, *Latin America and the Second World War* (London, 1981–2), 1:136–44 and 2:59–85.

2 E. W. Brandes, "Rubber on the Rebound – East to West," *Agriculture in the Americas* [hereafter *Agr. Amer.*] 1 (April 1941): 6. This was a publicity organ of the Foreign Agricultural Relations Branch of the U.S. Department of Agriculture (USDA). Archibald Johnston took notes on the Wallace meeting: Johnston to Edsel Ford, n.p., 10 May 1940, Henry Ford Museum and Archives, Dearborn, MI [hereafter HFMA-D], 74-12, Sale of Plantation. For Bureau of Plant Industry organization, see USDA, Bureau of Plant Industry, *Directory of Organization and Field*

Activities (Beltsville, MD, 1945). See also R. D. Rands, "Hevea Rubber Culture in Latin America, Problems and Procedures," in Frans Verdoorn, *Plants and Plant Science in Latin America* (Waltham, MA, 1945), pp 183–99.

3 T. D. Mallery, "Rubber Studies Begin," *Agr. Amer.* 1 (December 1941): 5–6.

4 LaRue to Brandes, Cachuela Esperanza, 20 November 1940, and LaRue to Brandes, La Paz, 19 October 1940, both in U.S. National Archives, Washington, DC, Record Group 54, Bureau of Plant Industry, Field Crops Research Branch, Brazil [hereafter RG 54-BPI], box 729. See also "The Reminiscences of Mr. Carl D. LaRue," 21 January 1955, HFMA-D.

5 Brandes to LaRue, Washington, DC, 29 November and 6 December 1940, RG 54-BPI, box 729.

6 William C. Burdett, chargé d'affaires ad interim, to secretary of state, Rio de Janeiro, 23 December 1940, U.S. National Archives, Washington, DC, Record Group 166, Foreign Agricultural Relations Reports, Brazil [hereafter RG 166-FAR], 1939–1941, box 19.

7 "A Combined Brazilian-American Commission Studies Rubber at Porto Velho," 16 January 1941, RG 54-BPI, box 729.

8 "Bombers Carry Rubber Seeds," *Agr. Amer.* 1 (March 1941): 15.

9 Loren G. Polhamus, "War Speeds the Rubber Project," *Agr. Amer.* 2 (February 1942): n.p.; Brandes to Manifold, Washington, DC, 1 February 1941, RG 54-BPI, box 729; Walter E. Klippert, *Reflections of a Rubber Planter* (New York, 1972), pp. 90–2.

10 Manifold to Brandes, Porto Velho, 12 January 1941, and Manifold to Brandes, Manaus, 3 February 1941, both in RG 54-BPI, box 729; Luiz Caetano de Oliveira Cabral to Mello Moraes, director of the Centro Nacional de Pesquisas Agronômicas, n.p., n.d., RG 166-FAR, 1939–1941, box 19.

11 T. D. Mallery to Brandes, Belém, 8 April and 30 June 1941, Brandes to Mallery, Washington, DC, 10 May 1941, all in RG 54-BPI, box 729; report of plan to collect seeds, in folder marked "Brazil Correspondence," noted "rec'd May 16 [1941] at Belém, J. D. M[allery]," also in same file "From Bangham's letter of April 12 [1941] to Rands" RG 54-BPI, box 730; Hans G. Sorenson, "[Rubber Investigations] Research Line Project no. RI-1-1-2, Propagation and Distribution of Recommended Clones to Cooperating Countries, Agencies and Individuals, Progress Report for the Year Ending June 30, 1942," Belém, n.d., RG 54-BPI, box 731; "Rubber Survey Report Amazon Valley in Brazil," n.p., n.d. (Draft copy 1, with corrections, probably mid-March 1941), RG 54-BPI, box 730; Polhamus, "War Speeds Project," n.p. Firestone may have collaborated in order to be able to count on assistance from Goodyear and the USDA should Firestone decide to set up Western Hemisphere plantations itself. See "Isolation of Leaf-Blight Resistant and Superior-Yielding Clones from Firestone Clonal Seed," n.p., n.d., copy marked "rec. May 16 [1941] at Belém, J. D. M.," RG 54-BPI, box 731.

12 Karl D. Butler, "Rubber Investigations, Research Line Project no. RI-1-1-1, Control of Leaf Blight, Progress Report for the Fiscal Year Ending June 30, 1942," Belém, n.d., RG 54-BPI, box 731; Rands, "Hevea Rubber Culture," pp. 188–9; Butler, "Relative resistance of Hevea Seedlings. . . up to Dec. 1942," HFMA-D,

74–17; M. H. Langford, *Fungicidal Control of South American Leaf Blight of Hevea Rubber Trees*, USDA Circular no. 686 (Washington, DC, 1943).

13 G. Douglas James, "History of Rubber During the Second World War," n.p., n.d., mimeo., Malayan Rubber Producers Research Center Library.

14 U.S. Special Committee to Study the Rubber Situation, *Report of the Rubber Survey Committee* (Washington, DC, 1942), p. 10.

15 Nelson Prado Alves Pinto, *Política da borracha no Brasil* (São Paulo, 1984), pp. 92–3, 100; Frank McCann, *The Brazilian-American Alliance* (Princeton, NJ, 1973), pp. 267–8, 388.

16 "Rubber Survey Report." Two excellent sources of data on the rubber trade are a letter [J. Caldwell King] to Nelson Rockefeller, n.p., n.d. [circa May 1942], and a report, "Rubber Survey in Amazon by Messrs. King, Rohlfing, and Fernandez, February/May 1940" (carried out for the Johnson and Johnson Company), both among Philip H. Williams papers, Mudd Library, Princeton University [hereafter PHW-P], box 8.

17 Frank E. Nattier, Jr., to coordinator of inter-American affairs, attention Robbins and Bressman, memorandum CO no. 747, Rio de Janeiro, 19 March 1942, RG 54-BPI, box 730.

18 Klippert, *Reflections*, pp. 111–12; Rubber Reserve Corporation, *Report on the Rubber Program, 1940–1945* (Washington, DC, 1945); John H. Burns, vice-consul, to secretary of state, "Transmission of Comparative Statistics," Belém, 7 February 1944, RG 54-BPI, box 729.

19 W. N. Walmsley, Jr., "Amazon Rubber Program," enclosed in letter, Walter J. Donnelly, counselor of Embassy for Economic Affairs, to secretary of state, Rio de Janeiro, 18 October 1943, U.S. National Archives, Washington, DC, Record Group 234, Reconstruction Finance Corporation, Brazil [hereafter RG 234-RFC], 271, box 28.

20 Henry W. Ryan and John Caswell, special assistants to the rubber director, "Confidential Report on Brazilian Rubber for the Rubber Director," March 8–April 20, 1943, and William LaVarre to Jones, n.p., 23 April 1943, both in RG 234-RFC, 271, box 28. See also Jesse H. Jones, *Fifty Billion Dollars*, pp. 418–27.

21 Rubber Reserve Corporation, *Report*. Brazilian export data are too low, since much Brazilian rubber was smuggled to Peru, where export taxes were much lower. The RDC therefore grouped together all Amazon basin exports. Francis C. Rebelo, assistant field technician, "Special Report on the Xapuri Municipality, Seringueiros versus Seringalistas," Rio Branco, 15 September 1944, RG 166-FAR, Technical Collaboration, box 1; Alves Pinto, *Política da borracha*, pp. 96–7. See also Edward C. Higbee, "Of Man and the Amazon," *Geographical Journal* 41 (July 1951): 402–3.

22 Alves Pinto, *Política*, pp. 98–9, citing Almir de Almeida, *Contribuição à história administrativa do Brasil* (Rio de Janeiro, 1950), 2:48; Almeida's figure is in rough agreement with RDC estimates: Edward D. McLaughlin, consul, to secretary of state, Belém, 16 March 1943, and Walter W. Hoffman, consul, "Migration from Ceará to the Amazon," n.p., 18 April 1944, both in RG 166-FAR, box 96.

23 Bruce V. Worth and John D. O'Neil, field technicians, RDC, "Report on the Rio Tapajoz, December 3, 1942–March 3, 1943," n.p., n.d., RG 166-FAR, Tech.

Collab., box 3; Harold E. Gustin, senior technician, to E. B. Hamill, senior technician, "Memorandum: Inspection Trip to Seringais in Baixo Amazonas: Costa de Amatary and Furo de Ramos," Manaus, 26 April 1943, and Gustin and João da Silva, assistant technician, "Technician's First General Report on Rubber Production in Baixo Amazonas," Manaus, 30 October 1943, both in RG 166-FAR, Tech., Collab., boxes 3 and 2, respectively; H. Pease and B. Worth, "Territorio do Acre," Rio Branco, 22 June 1942, PHW-P, box 6.

24 "Rubber Survey Report"; F. Bruce Lamb, field technician, "Progress Report on Lower Rio Tapajós," Manaus, 19 June 1944, RG 166-FAR, Tech. Collab., box 3. T. A. Tengwall, "History of Rubber Cultivation and Research in the Netherlands Indies," in Pieter Honig and Frans Verdoorn, eds., *Science and Scientists in the Netherlands Indies* (New York, 1945), p. 350.

25 "Rubber Survey Report"; Gustin to Hamill, Manaus, 24 April 1943, RG 166-FAR, Tech. Collab., box 2; Harry C. Haines, field technician, to C. Homer McDuff, "Progress Report #3 on Baixo Amazonas Area (25 July–19 August)," 24 September 1945, PHW-P, box 5.

26 Camargo to Stallard, Belém, 1 December 1944, HFMA-D, 134-4; "Plantation Report[s] for the Month[s] of January 1942–December 1943," HFMA-D, 74-12; "Belterra Monthly Progress Report[s]," April 1941–December 1945, HFMA-D, 74-5; [A. Johnston], "Belterra Estate," n.p., 8 November 1943, HFMA-D, 74-13; Lawrence A. Beery, Jr., "Ford Hevea Topworking Clones; Resistant and Semi-Resistant to South American Leaf Blight (Dothidella ulei)," n.p., 17 February 1945, HFMA-D, 74-5(?).

27 "Plantation Report[s] for the Month[s] of January 1944–December 1945," HFMA-D, 74-5; "Observation of a Trip to Belterra and Fordlandia from April 24 to May 4 1942," RG 54-BPI, box 730; Stallard to Johnston, Belterra, 9 October 1942, HFMA-D, 74-17, Bud Grafting.

28 Data from "Plantation Reports" and "Monthly Progress Reports"; also [Johnston], "Belterra Estate"; Worth and O'Neil, "Report on the Tapajoz."

29 Michael Polli, "Preliminary Report on Hevea Brasiliensis Areas in the State of Bahia," 13 October 1942, RG 166-FAR, Tech. Collab., box 4; R. D. Rands to Wallace E. Manis, Washington, DC, 12 January 1943, RG 166-FAR, box 92; Manifold to J. A. Russell, Jr., "Examination of the Hevea Area in the State of Bahia," 7 April 1943, RG 234-RFC, 271, box 6; Franklin E. Bradshaw to RDC-Rio de Janeiro, Ilhéus, 31 October 1943, Manifold to J. W. Bicknell, Ilhéus, 3 December 1943, and Bradshaw to H. J. Korkegi, Ilhéus, 26 October 1944, all in RG 234-RFC, 276, box 2.

30 Bradshaw to RDC-Rio, Ilhéus, 30 October 1943, RG 234-RFC, 276, box 2; Alphonse Buenzli, junior field technician, to B. V. Worth, senior field technician, Rio de Janeiro, Ilhéus, 2 November 1944, RG 234-RFC, 276, box 6; Bradshaw to Korkegi, "Dothidella Ulei or South American Leaf Disease," Rio de Janeiro, 13 December 1944, RG 166-RFC, Tech. Collab., box 4. Perhaps these planters were speculating in rubber with government loans; see the text below concerning V. Bouças and Camargo. No evidence was found that the USDA specialists from Belém practiced quarantine procedures to help protect southern Bahia against the introduction of further inoculum, therefore they may themselves have reintroduced it.

31 U.S. Embassy, "Coastwise Shipments of Rubber in July–September 1943," Rio de Janeiro, 26 January 1944, RG 166-FAR, box 92; Manifold to Russell, "Examination"; Bradshaw to Korkegi (see note 29). Hevea exports from Bahia were insignificant compared to exports of other rubbers, nearly all wild, which reached 391 tons in 1941: Ubaldino Q. Bonfim, "Borracha da Bahia," *Boletim do Serviço de Economia Rural* 2 (August–December, 1944): 121–5.

32 British Guiana, Department of Agriculture, *Administration Report[s] for the Year[s] 1943–1949* (Georgetown, 1943-[1950?]); Miles A. Walsh, special representative, "Monthly Operations Report – British Guiana," Caracas, 17 November 1945, RG 234-RFC, 272, Africa-British Honduras, box 28; Henry J. Fuller, field technician, "Reports on Rubber Plantations in British Guiana," Caracas, 12 July 1946, RG 234-RFC, 276, box 7. The latter appears to exaggerate output and undercount trees. Trinidad and Tobago, Director of Agriculture, *Administration Report[s] for the Year[s] 1945–1951* (Port-of-Spain, 1946–52); G. Lems, "Verleden, heden en toekomst van de rubbercultuur in Suriname," *Surinaamse Landbouw* 11 (1963): 19–26.

33 Nattier, memorandum CO no. 747; Brazil, *Coleção das leis*, Decreto-Lei 5200, 18 January 1943.

34 H. G. Sorensen and K. D. Butler, "Rubber Investigations, Research Line Project no. RI-1-1-4, Development of Clones or Varieties of Hevea and Other Rubber Plants Suitable to the Western Hemisphere," [Belém, 30 June 1942?], RG 54-BPI, box 731; Brandes to Camargo, Washington, DC, 25 January and 15 February 1943, both in RG 166-FAR, box 92.

35 Embassy Dispatch 11603 to secretary of state, Rio de Janeiro, 12 January 1943, RG 166-FAR, box 92. For Camargo's rosy recollections of his struggles with the USDA, see Camargo, *Medalla agrícola interamericana, 1967* (San José, Costa Rica, 1968), pp. 15–16.

36 Erwin P. Keeler, agricultural attaché, "Decree-Law Prohibiting the Exportation of Seeds or Seedlings of Hevea. . . Without Previous Authorization of the Ministry of Agriculture," Rio de Janeiro, 10 August 1943; Brandes to Fagundes, Washington, DC, 16 January 1943, and Brandes to Camargo, Washington, DC, 29 April 1943, all in RG 166-FAR, box 92; Rands to Manifold, Beltsville, MD, 28 December 1944, RG 234-RFC, 276, box 2; Brazil, *Coleção das leis*, Decreto-Lei 7946, 10 September 1944; Guy L. Buch, agricultural attaché, to secretary of state, 18 April 1944, RG 166-FAR, box 92. W. E. Klippert provides a sharp image of Camargo's wariness: When Camargo presented him with budwood to take back to Costa Rica, he affixed a misleading label to the package, even though he had permission from the Ministry of Agriculture to export.

37 Unsigned articles in the *Observador*: "A borracha, passado, presente e futuro," 8 (June 1943): 119–49; and "Plantações de borracha," 8 (July 1943): 100–3.

38 Camargo's reply: "Plantações da borracha," *Observador* 8 (July 1943): 92–100. Camargo had difficulty defending a curious recommendation he had made to plant Sapium trees until better Hevea clones were available. Sapium rubber is comparable to Hevea in quality, but takes longer to mature, yields much less latex, and is extremely difficult to tap.

39 Clipping file in box 13, PHW-P: See especially Ross Symontowne, "Rubber Deal with Brazil Proves Failure," *Washington Times Herald*, 16 November 1943; and

Charles C. Miller, "Behind the Scenes in Brazil," *Akron Beacon-Journal*, 30 November 1943. Official export figure from *Business Week*, no. 843 (27 October 1945): 118; Symontowne reported $4.5 million. Brazilian tire manufacturers sopped up all the rubber made available to them through the efforts of the RDC, turned it into tires, and exported them to Argentina. The U.S. State Department protested and extracted a commitment from Brazil to limit its consumption and export of rubber to 10,000 tons per year. Evidently the commitment had not been adhered to. Sumner Welles to Jefferson Caffery, 30 March 1942, and Caffery to Cordell Hull, 1 May 1942, both in U.S. Department of State, *Foreign Relations of the United States, 1942* (Washington, DC, 1962), pp. 697–700.

40 See three pamphlets by Camargo: *Considerações relativas ao problema de formação de seringais na Amazônia*, IAN Circular no. 1, 26 December 1943 (Belém, 1943); *Exploração extrativa de borracha*, Ministerio de Agricultura, Folheto no. 30 (Rio de Janeiro, 1943); *Plantação de seringueiras* (Rio de Janeiro, 1944).

41 Camargo, "Sugestão para planejamento econômico relativo à formação de seringais de cultura na região amazônica sob o regime de coletivismo," n.p., 4 July 1945, hectograph version reproduced by U.S. Embassy, RG 166-FAR, box 51. Later comments by Camargo in Brazil, Câmara de Deputados, Comissão Especial do Plano de Valorização da Amazônia, *Anais*, 2 vols. (Rio de Janeiro, 1948), 1:130–40.

42 R. D. Rands, "Hevea Rubber Culture," pp. 183–7. See also Randolph Kidder, U.S. consul, "Sale of Para Rubber Plantation," Belém, 4 December 1945, RG 166-FAR, acc. 3366, box 92.

43 Norman Bakkedahl, "Brazil's Research for Increased Rubber Production," *Scientific Monthly* 61 (September 1945): 199–209.

44 Hugh Butler, "Our Deep Dark Secrets in Latin America," *Reader's Digest* 43 (December 1943): 21–5; official estimate was sixty-nine cents a pound: U.S. War Production Board, *Report of the Special Director of Rubber Programs to the War Production Board* (Washington, DC, 1945), p. 5.

45 John H. Burns, vice consul, to secretary of state, "Transmission of Comparative Statistics," 7 February 1944, RG 54-BPI, box 729; D. H. Allen and F. A. Truslow, *Summarized History of Operations*, pp. 15–17; Henry J. Fuller, "War Time Rubber Exportation in Tropical America," *Economic Botany* 5 (October–December 1951): 311–37; "Report on the Operations of Rubber Development Corporation, February 23, 1943 to August 31, 1944," Washington, DC, 30 September 1944, mimeo., RG 234-RFC, 271, box 28. J. F. Rippy, "Some Rubber-Producing Fiascos in Tropical America," *Inter-American Economic Affairs* 10 (Summer 1956): 3–24. On Guayule, see National Academy of Sciences, *Guayule: An Alternative Source of Natural Rubber* (Washington, DC, 1977); William G. McGinnies and Jean L. Mills, *Guayule Rubber Production: The World War II Emergency Rubber Project* (Tucson, AR, 1980).

46 Price, Waterhouse, Peat and Company, Rio de Janeiro, "Report on the Examination of the Accounts as of June 30, 1945," RG 234-RFC, 283, box 3; "Aviation Budget," n.p., 3 July 1944, RG 234-RFC, 272, box 3; Frank Kelley, "U.S. and Brazil Spend 8 Million to Fight Disease on the Amazon," *New York Herald-Tribune*, 28 November 1943.

47 Alves Pinto, *Política da borracha*, pp. 101–2. "Did America Abandon 47,000 to

Death?'' and "What Price Rubber From Brazil?'' *Christian Century* 63 (19 June 1944): 772 and (31 July 1944): 932. Two Americans died, one of whom was Michael Polli. Paulo Sarasate, *A batalha da borracha (discursos proferidos na Assembléia Constituinte nas sessões de 28 de junho e 5 de julho de 1946)* (Rio de Janeiro, 1946).

48 Kenneth Wernimont, senior agricultural analyst, "Recent Accomplishments of the Instituto Agronômico do Norte,'' Rio de Janeiro, 31 May l944, RG 166-FAR, box 92; Bakkedahl, "Brazil's Research,'' pp. 199–209.

49 Bangham to Stallard, San José, Costa Rica, 26 May 1945, HFMA-D, Bud Grafting; F. Bruce Lamb, "Rubber Production in the Municipality of Santarem,'' n.p., 1 November 1943, RG 166-FAR, Tech. Collab., box 3.

50 Brazil, *Coleção das leis*, Decree-Law 8,440, 24 December 1945; "Statement of Increase in Advances to Companhia Ford Industrial do Brasil,'' Dearborn, 24 February 1941, and "Budget[s]'' 1940–1945, both in HFMA-D, 74-17, Yearly Budgets from 1933; compare Allan Nevins and Frank E. Hill, *Ford, Decline and Rebirth, 1933–1962* (New York, 1963), p. 323; Stallard to Richard P. Momsen, Belém, 17 December 1945, HFMA-D, 74-12, and [Johnston], "Belterra Estate,'' 8 November 1943, HFMA-D, 74-13.

51 Nevins and Hill, *Ford*, p. 323; Bangham, "Plantation Rubber in the New World,'' *Economic Botany* 1 (April–June 1947): 222; "Monthly Progress Report[s],'' Fordlandia and Belterra, 1945, HFMA-D, 74–5.

52 Luiz Osório da Silva, *A luta pela Amazônia* (São Paulo, 1963), p. 105; "Henry Ford's Rubber Plantations: After 15 Years of Struggle They Are Proving Themselves,'' *Ford Times* 1 (August 1944): 3; on Ford's embarrassment, see Barry Machado, "Farquahar and Ford in Brazil: Studies in Business Expansion and Foreign Policy'' (Ph.D. diss. in history, Northwestern University, 1975), p. 443.

7 Administrative discontinuities, 1946–1961

1 "The Rubber Cartel,'' *New Republic* 110 (27 March 1944): 430–4; "Reversal in Rubber,'' *Fortune* 33 (March 1946): 84–91; "Lesson For Socialists,'' *Time* 48 (18 November 1946): 94; "Rubber at 23½¢,'' *Business Week*, no. 878 (29 June 1946): 20; Dudley Maynard Phelps, *Rubber Developments in Latin America* (Ann Arbor, MI, 1957), pp. 3–24. The last is an excellent discussion of the postwar situation. See also United Nations, Secretariat, *Economic Development of Underdeveloped Countries; Impact of Selected Synthetics on Demand for Natural Products in International Trade* (New York, 1953), pp. 19–21.

2 Phelps, *Rubber Developments*, p. 28; Océlio de Medeiros, *A margem do planejamento econômico da Amazônia*, 2d ed. (Rio de Janeiro, 1948), p. 84.

3 Conferência Nacional da Borracha, 1, Rio de Janeiro, 1946, *Anais*, 2 vols. (Rio de Janeiro, n.d.). Essential analyses of this critical conference are Luiz A. de C. Carvalho, "História pouca conhecida da borracha natural brasileira,'' *Elastômeros* 5 (May–June 1979): 145–59; Cássio Fonseca, "Uma comédia de erros; a borracha natural no Brasil,'' *Elastômeros* 6 (May–June 1980): 20–4, (July–August 1980): 4–11, (September–October 1980): 9–13; and Nelson Prado Alves Pinto, *A política da borracha no Brasil* (São Paulo, 1984).

4 Manufacturers' complaints are in a bound file labeled "Conferência de Borracha''

at SUDHEVEA Library, Brasília, and in minutes of a joint meeting, "Reunião das bancadas dos estados da Região Amazônica e Presidente do Banco da Borracha, para estudar as medidas a serem postas em prática pelo governo, visando a defesa da Borracha, Ministério da Fazenda," [Rio de Janeiro], 27 May 1947, typed carbon, at Banco da Amazônia Library, Belém.

5 Conferência Nacional da Borracha, 1, *Anais*, 2:73.

6 Ibid., 2:202–3.

7 Phelps, *Rubber Developments*, pp. 111–12; Robert Delafield Rands and L. G. Polhamus, *Progress Report on the Cooperative Rubber Development Program in Latin America* (Washington, DC,1955), p. 28. J. C. Roberts to B. H. Larabee, "Report on Meeting of GSA Relative to Expanding Natural Rubber Production in the Western Hemisphere," n.p., 2 July 1952, Firestone Tire and Rubber Company Archives, Akron, OH [hereafter FTRC-A], Plantations Company, 1952, box 67.

8 Teodoro Brazão e Silva, "Nos domínios da Fordlândia," *Folha do Norte* (Belém), 21 April 1946, p. 1; Conferência Nacional da Borracha, 1, *Anais*, 2:72–3; George T. Coleman, U.S. vice-consul, "Visit to Ford Rubber Plantations," Belém, 28 November 1947, and U.S. Consulate, Belém, "Monthly Rubber Report, Brazil" [hereafter Belém-MRR], May 1948, U.S. National Archives, Washington, DC, Record Group 166, Foreign Agricultural Relations Reports [hereafter RG 166-FAR], box 537; Rands and Polhamus, *Progress Report*, pp. 7–14; Phelps, *Rubber Developments*, pp. 121, 122; Oswaldo Bastos de Menezes, "O problema da borracha brasileira," p. 21, and Mário Bocquet, "O problema da borracha no Brasil em 1951," p. 253, in Reunião de Estudos da Borracha para Aumento da Produção, *O problema da borracha brasileira* (Brasília, 1960) [hereafter REBAP]; Cláudio Rómulo Siqueira, "Borracha: relatório de viagem às zonas produtoras" n.p., 23 March 1964, mimeo., p. 6l.

9 Felisberto Cardoso de Camargo, "Report," n.p., 1 December 1944, Henry Ford Museum and Archives, Dearborn, MI [hereafter HFMA-D], 134-4; Edgar de Souza Cordeiro, "O plantio da *Hevea* no núcleo colonial de Guamá," in REBAP, p. 118; Charles H. T. Townsend, Jr., "Progresso do desenvolvimento no Brasil de clones superiores de *Hevea*," in Quarta Reunião de Fitotecnia, Santiago, Chile, November–December, 1958, partially transcribed by Paulo Ferreira de Souza, *Sementes de essências florestais* (Viçosa, MG, 1961), pp. 10–28; C. H. T. Townsend, Jr., "Progress in Developing Superior Rubber Clones in Brazil," *Economic Botany* 14 (July–September 1960): 189–96. George O'Neill Addison, at the time employed at the IAN, offers a criticism of Townsend's breeding strategy in: São Paulo, Secretaria de Agricultura, DPV-DATE, *Cultura da seringueira* (Campinas, 1958), p. 72. Eurico Pinheiro is often credited with introducing *H. pauciflora* in the breeding program, but he credits Townsend in Pinheiro and Virgílio F. Libonati, "O emprego da *Hevea pauciflora* M. A. como fonte genética de resistência ao mal das folhas," *Revista Polímeros* 1 (January–March 1961): 1–10. A summary of rubber research of the period is Brazil, Superintendência da Borracha, *Plano nacional de Borracha, Anexo XI, Pesquisas e experimentação com a seringueira* (Rio de Janeiro, 1971).

10 Vicente H. F. Moraes, "Seleção em seringais nativos," *Circular do IPEAN*, no. 7 (August 1963): 5.

11 R. A. Alston, "Memorandum on South American Leaf Disease of Rubber," RRIM

Ref. D.37//1(P.1269/48), Kuala Lumpur, 17 May 1948, mimeo., marked "Confidential not for publication," Malaysian Rubber Producers Research Association Library, Brickendonbury, Hertfordshire, England [hereafter MRPRA-B]. See also R. N. Hilton, "South American Leaf Blight, A Review of the Literature," *Journal of the RRIM* 14 (1955): 287–337.

12 "Minutes of Meeting of the Control of South American Leaf Disease (Ad Hoc) Committee, Held at RRIM," Kuala Lumpur, 4 December 1950, MRPRA-B; W. C. Heusden, "De Zuid-Amerikaanse Bladziekte (Dothidella ulei), een Brandende Kwestie," *De Bergcultures* 22 (1 May 1953): 171–7; Theodor G. E. Hoedt, "Opmerkingen over Hevea-Selectie in Z.O.-Azië en Latijns Amerika," *Archief voor de Rubbercultuur* 30 (March 1953): 1–37; H. E. Young, "South American Leaf Blight of Rubber, Notes of an Informal Meeting. . . by the SEA Research Institute Directors Liaison Committee," Bogor, 17 March 1954, mimeo., MRPRA-B. See also C. W. Brookson, "Import and Development of New Strains of Hevea Brasiliensis by the RRIM," *Journal of the RRIM* 14 (1965): 423, who notes more exchanges carried out in 1956 and 1958. Probably the IAN received RRIM series 500 and 600 clones in this exchange.

13 Brazil, Câmara de Deputados, Comissão Especial do Plano de Valorização da Amazônia, *Anais* (Rio de Janeiro, 1948), 1:159; Rands and Polhamus exaggerated Brazil's funding of rubber research, *Progress Report*, p. 28, 33; Felisberto C. Camargo, *Sugestões para o soerguimento econômico do vale amazônico* (Belém, 1948), pp. 45, 62–4; Brazil, Senado, *Plano de valorização econômica da Amazônia* (Belém, 1951), p. 38. See also Socrates Bonfim, *Valorização da Amazônia e sua Comissão de Planejamento* (Rio de Janeiro, 1958), pp. 2–4. The IAN nurseries were located at Utinga.

14 See Conferência Nacional da Borracha, 2, Manaus, 1948, *Anais* (Rio de Janeiro, n.d.), especially pp. 56–8, 69, 81, 84, 114, 165; and Conferência Nacional da Borracha, 3, Belém, 1949, *Anais* (Rio de Janeiro, n.d.), especially pp. 100, 102, 117–18, 121, 192–4, 198, 199. Comments by George T. Coleman, U.S. viceconsul, "Economic Rubber Congress Held at Manaus, Amazonas, Brazil," Belém, 9 April 1948, RG 199-FAR, box 537.

15 See article in *Folha do Norte* (Belém), 15 September 1949, enclosed by Coleman in dispatch of 20 September 1949, RG 166-FAR, box 537; Sílvio Meira, *Belterra, sua situação jurídica (tese aprovada pela III Conferência Econômica da Borracha, em 10 de setembro de 1949)* (Belém, 1949); Alves Pinto, *A política da borracha*, pp. 110–12. On Ferreira, see Brazil, SUDHEVEA, *Heveicultura no Brasil; relatório do GEPLASE* [hereafter GEPLASE] (Brasilia, 1970), p. 122. Interplanting of rubber in wild groves was frequently brought up by persons who had never tried it, or by seringalistas who saw it as a way of obtaining more funds from BASA. It was entirely impractical, since shaded trees grew extremely slowly or were eaten by animals, as Wickham himself had pointed out.

16 The law continuing monopoly was 1,184, 30 August 1950. On planning dilemmas, see Océlio de Medeiros, *A margem do planejamento*, pp. 80, 82; on bank operations, see Conferência Técnica sobre Valorização Econômica da Amazônia, Rio de Janeiro, 1951, *Valorização econômica da Amazônia; subsídios para seu planejamento* (Rio de Janeiro, 1954), pp. 30–1, 74–7, 78.

17 An example of the national security ploy: Cosme Ferreira's speeches reprinted in

Conferência Nacional da Borracha, 2, *Anais*, pp. 50, 52. Camargo's text in U.S. Embassy, Rio de Janeiro, "Translation of Text of Lecture Delivered at the Army Staff School, May 9, 1951," Foreign Service Dispatch no. 1821, 8 June 1951, RG 166-FAR, box 532. Army's reaction in João Bernardo Lobato Filho, *A borracha da Amazônia* (Rio de Janeiro, 1951), pp. 17, 45–8.

18 U.N., Economic Commission for Latin America, *Economic Survey of Latin America, 1954*, pp. 86–8; Belém-MRR, May 1951, RG 166-FAR, 1950–4, box 52.

19 U.N., Secretariat, *Economic Development*, pp. 23–4; Alves Pinto, *A política da borracha*, p. 113; U.S. Embassy, "Translation of Text."

20 U.S. Embassy, "Translation of Text"; Cássio Fonseca, *A economia da borracha*, 2d ed. (Rio de Janeiro, 1970), pp. 187, 227. On the successive internalization of Brazil's export crops, see Warren Dean, "The Brazilian economy, 1870–1930," in Leslie Bethell, ed., *Cambridge History of Latin America* (Cambridge, Eng., 1986), 5:711.

21 Conferência Técnica, *Valorização econômica*, pp. 4, 8, 82, 137–48; Brazil, Senado, *Plano*, pp. 29–38.

22 Conferência Técnica, *Valorização econômica*, p. 222; Richard Evans Schultes, "Wild Hevea: An Untapped Source of Germ Plasm," *Journal of the Rubber Research Institute of Sri Lanka* 54, pt. 1, no. 1 (1977): 257; GEPLASE, p. 100. On Camargo's management style, João Jacob Hoeltz, interview with author, Campinas, 1 June 1983.

23 Siqueira, "Borracha," p. 54; Instituto de Pesquisas e Experimentação Agropecuárias do Norte, *IPEAN – 25 anos de pesquisas na Amazônia* (Belém, 1964), pp. 19–25. K. G. MacIndoe, "Report on a Visit to Indústria Pneumáticos Firestone, S.A., with Notes on Incidental Visits," n.p., 25 July 1959, FTRC-A, Plantations Company, box 77. A more optimistic assessment was sent by B. O. Vipond, "Belém-Belterra Trip, February 1959," Ituberá, 4 March 1959, box 77.

24 Phelps, *Rubber Developments*, pp. 112, 113, 124–8. A cynical and not very well informed critique was provided by J. Fred Rippy, "Some Rubber-Planting Fiascos in Tropical America," *Inter-American Economic Affairs* 10 (Summer 1956): 3–24. He cites most of Brandes's testimony; see also U.S. Congress, House Committee on Appropriations, *Hearings, State Department Appropriations Bill, 6 March 1946*, pp. 536–7. Brazil bought out the U.S. government-owned minority share in BASA in 1959.

25 William MacKinnon and R. D. Rands, "Relatório geral sobre a proposta expansão da produção da borracha no Brasil," p. 286, and John Herbert Newman, "O programa da borracha no Território do Amapá," pp. 130–8, both in REBAP. Instituto Agronômico do Norte, *Notas sumárias sobre a cultura da seringueira na Amazônia* (Rio de Janeiro, 1952), pp. 10–11; Brazil, Superintendência do Plano Econômico da Amazônia, *SPVEA, 1954/1960: política de desenvolvimento da Amazônia*, 2 vols. (Rio de Janeiro, 1961), 2:325; Belém-MRR, June 1952, RG 166-FAR, 1950–4; Alarico José da Cunha, Jr., and Fernando A. Genshow, *Amapá, um estudo para colonisação* (Rio de Janeiro, 1958), pp. 87–95, 134.

26 José de Souza Pereira, clerk, U.S. Consulate, Belém, "Natural Rubber in the State of Bahia, Brazil," Belém, 28 April 1948, and Belém-MRR, May 1948, both in RG 166-FAR, box 537; Belém-MRR, July and August 1951, RG 166-FAR, 1950–4, box 5; GEPLASE, p. 19; "A Bahia na produção da borracha," and "Resultados

de dois anos de trabalho desde REBAP,'' in REBAP, pp. 196–201, 321–4; Renato Gonçalves Martins, "A borracha da Bahia," *Observador Econômico e Financeiro* 16 (December 1951): 60–7; Fundação Comissão de Planejamento Econômico da Bahia, *A seringueira na Bahia, alguns aspectos tecnico-econômicos* (Salvador, 1960), pp. 14–16, 33, 45–6; Rayfred L. Stevens and Paulo Rebouças Brandão, "Diversification of the Economy of the Cacao Coast of Bahia, Brazil," *Economic Geography* 37 (July 1961): 235.

27 Siqueira, "Borracha," p. 31; Belém-MRR, June 1952, RG 166-FAR, 1950–4, box 52; Phelps, *Rubber Developments*, pp. 143–5; Brazil, SPVEA, *SPVEA*, 2:324.

28 Brazil, SPVEA, *Primeiro plano qüinqüenal*, 2 vols. (Rio de Janeiro, 1955), 1:321; "O Projeto Borracha de SPVEA," pp. 81–3, Waldemar Cardoso, "O problema da heveicultura," pp. 124–9, and "Resultados de dois anos de trabalho desde a REBAP," pp. 316–17, all in REBAP; Brazil, SPVEA, *SPVEA*, 1:55–6; Sylvio Braga, *Borracha* (São Paulo, 1960), pp. 74–6. Escritório Técnico de Agricultura Brasil–Estados Unidos, *Borracha na Amazônia* (Belém, 1958), mimeo., with annexes.

29 Brazil, SPVEA, *SPVEA*, 2:321–38; Siqueira, "Borracha," p. 65; Braga, *Borracha*, p. 72; Cordeiro, "O plantio da *Hevea*," pp. 117–23. J. Biard and G. A. W. Wagenaar, *Report to the Government of Brazil in Crop Production in Selected Areas of the Amazon Valley* (Rome, 1960), pp. 37–9.

30 Rubens Rodrigues Lima, et al., "Plano para o incentivo ao plantio da seringueira na Amazônia," in REBAP, pp. 84–103; Siqueira, "Borracha," pp. 50–7; Brazil, SPVEA, *SPVEA*, p. 325; Orlando de Morais, *Amazônia espoliada* (Rio de Janeiro, 1960), pp. 55–7.

31 Belém-MRR, February 1951, RG 166-FAR, box 52; B. H. Larabee to B. O. Vipond, Akron, 1 February 1952, and Theodor G. E. Hoedt, Bert O. Vipond, and W. E. Klippert, "Natural Rubber in Brazil," [São Paulo?], 10 April 1952, mimeo., both in FTRC-A, Plantations Company, box 67.

32 Bert O. Vipond to H. Firestone, Jr., "Suggestions Reference Rubber Plantations in Brazil," [São Paulo?], 22 May 1952, box 67; G. E. Porteck to B. H. Larabee, São Paulo, 31 March 1953, box 67; E. Babcock to J. E. Turner, [Akron], 12 March 1953, box 69; Porteck to R. H. Mather, Santo André, 20 October 1953, box 69, "Recommendations to the Brazilian Government," n.p., 23 June 1953, box 69; Porteck, cable, Rio de Janeiro, 5 November 1953, box 69; all FTRC-A, Plantations Company. Fonseca, "Uma comédia de erros," p. 21. Relevant decrees are 30,694, 31 March 1952, and 35,371, 12 April 1954, in Brazil, *Coleção das leis*. The 1952 decree also required the smaller, Brazilian-owned tire and rubber companies to invest in planting, but that clause was never enforced.

33 W. E. Klippert, *Reflections of a Rubber Planter* (New York, 1972), pp. 167–8; Antônio Rocha Penteado, *O uso da terra na região Bragantina-Pará* (São Paulo, 1968), pp. 65–6. Hoedt, "Opmerkingen over Hevea-Selectie," pp. 8–10.

34 Keith Truettner to Walter J. LeVar, Beltsville, MD, 30 January 1953, and Truettner to B. O. Vipond, Salvador, 3 and 5 November 1953, both in FTRC-A, Plantations Company, box 69; Hoedt, Vipond, and Klippert, "Natural Rubber," Appendix A. See also Phelps, *Rubber Developments*, p. 138n. Firestone at the time was also planning estates in the Philippines and Guatemala: See "Return of the Native: Firestone Will Grow Rubber in Brazil," *Business Week* 36 (11 August

1956): 109. Brazil, Ministério de Agricultura, Indústria e Comêrcio, Commissão Junto á Missão Norte-Americana de Estudos do Valle do Amazonas, *Relatorio* (Rio de Janeiro, 1924), pp. 326, 337–8.

35 Vipond to Firestone, "Suggestions"; Walter J. LeVar, "As plantaçoes de seringueira da Firestone em Ituberá, Bahia," in REBAP, pp. 205–9; Alves Pinto, *A política da borracha*, pp. 116–17. The most consistent nationalist position was, of course, to oppose foreign tire companies: See Silvio Braga, *Borracha*, (São Paulo, 1960), pp. 24–5.

36 Stevens and Brandão, "Diversification," pp. 23–239.

37 Larabee to Porteck, Akron, 19 January 1956, and Larabee to Board of Directors, Akron, 11 June 1956, box 74; Vipond to K. G. MacIndoe, Salvador, 26 January 1959, box 77; Vipond, "Belém-Belterra Trip," box 77; Porteck to Richard P. Butrick, U.S. consul general, São Paulo, 13 March 1959, box 77; MacIndoe, "Report on a Visit to Indústria Pneumáticos Firestone"; Ross E. Wilson, "The Firestone Plantations of Brazil," n.p., 29 July 1959, box 77; A. C. Koenig to Larabee, n.p., 28 July 1960, box 78; MacIndoe to Larabee, Leesburg, FL, 11 August 1960, box 78; H. J. Dupré to Larabee, Ituberá, 2 September 1960 and 25 October 1960, box 78; all FTRC-A, Plantations Company. Robert J. Dunham, et al., "Comportamento das clones de seringueira e novos materiais recomendados para futuros plantios na fazenda Tres Pancadas," Ituberá, BA, 1982, xero.

38 H. Gustin, "A cultura da seringueira pela Goodyear na Amazônia," in REBAP, pp. 105–13; Biard and Wagenaar, *Report*, p. 40; Vipond, "Belém-Belterra Trip"; MacIndoe, "Report."

39 Th. G. E. Hoedt, "Material de plantio para propagação de seringais de cultura: o projeto de Pirelli," in REBAP, p. 188; Penteado, *O uso da terra*, pp. 59–61; Vipond, "Belém-Belterra Trip"; MacIndoe, "Report."

40 An assessment of these plantations is provided by Siqueira, "Borracha," pp. 43–4. On Firestone plans, see MacIndoe to Vipond, Ituberá, 18 July 1959, FTRC-A, Plantations Company, box 77. Alves Pinto suggested that the companies may have been acting with "ill will," *A política da borracha*, p. 117. MacIndoe reported that Dunlop's effort was in his and others' opinion, "token": See his "Report."

41 João Martins da Silva Coutinho, *Relatorio da Commisão Encarregada do Reconhecimento da Região do Oeste da Provincia de S. Paulo* (Rio de Janeiro, 1872), p. 15; Angelo Artur Martinez, "Cultura da seringueira, diagnóstico da situação, medidas correctivas," in São Paulo, Secretaria de Agricultura, Secção de Plantas Tropicais, *Programa de orientação técnica, 1969–1970* (Campinas, 1970), p. 14; "José Procópio de Araujo Ferraz conserva a mesma fé inquebrantável," *Folha de Manhã*, 14 July 1954; "Chegam do planalto paulista do litoral norte as primeiras mil seringueiras," *Correio Paulistano*, 1 April 1952; T. D. Mallery to E. W. Brandes, Belém, 25 May 1941, RG 54-BPI, box 729. João Ferreira da Cunha, "A seringueira na região de Campinas, sua adaptação e produtividade," *Bragantia* 22, pt. 2 (1963): 445; Octavio Ramos Nóbrega, "Comunicação," in Seminário Nacional da Seringueira, 1, Cuiabá, 1972, *Anais* [hereafter SNS-1] (n.p., 1973?), pp. 313–14.

42 MacKinnon and Rands, "Relatorio," pp. 296–9; "Deve ser considerado em primeiro lugar o litoral para a implantação dessa cultura," *Diário de São Paulo*, 11

October 1951. Louis Papy, "En marge de l'Empire du café," *Cahiers d'Outre-Mer* 5 (October–December 1952): 388–91.

43 Hoedt, Vipond, and Klippert, "Natural Rubber."

44 G. E. Porteck to S. Broers, São Paulo, 24 April and 29 August 1952, FTRC-A, Plantations Company, box 67; "Plantações experimentais de seringais em São Paulo," *Correio Paulistano*, 12 January 1956; A. Luytjes and G. N. Visser, "Rubberwinning in Brazilië," *De Bergcultures* 26 (1 February 1957): 57–68. de Menezes, "O problema da borracha brasileira," in REBAP, pp. 23–4.

45 Raul Gomes de Freitas Paranhos and Jayme Vázquez Cortez, "O Serviço de Expansão da Seringueira de São Paulo," in REBAP, pp. 212–31; João Jacob Hoelz and Angelo Artur Martinez, "A cultura da seringueira no Estado de São Paulo," in SNS-1, pp. 57–8; Angelo Artur Martinez, "Cultura da seringueira," pp. 15–16.

46 Hoelz, *Cultura da seringueira* (São Paulo, 1958), p. 7; Martinez, "Cultura da seringueira," p. 15.

47 Walter Ramos Jardim, secretary of agriculture, to Camargo, São Paulo, 4 July 1958, and Camargo to Jardim, n.d., Rio de Janeiro, both in FTRC-A, Plantations Company, 1959, box 77. Camargo, "Estudo das possibilidades da cultura da seringueira no estado de São Paulo," (Rio de Janeiro, 1958), mimeo., and another version, a file of notes, possibly based on an oral presentation, at which Firestone representatives were present, marked "Scheme of Subjects Discussed," undated, but apparently October 1958, both in FTRC-A, Plantations Company, box 77.

48 João Ferreira da Cunha, "Cultura experimental de seringueira no município de Caraguatatuba," and "Cultura experimental de seringueira em Iguape," *Bragântia* 22 (January 1963): 27–41, 43–51; "A Dothidella em São Paulo," *Estado de São Paulo*, 24 February 1960; J. F. da Cunha, "A seringueira no vale do Paraíba," *Bragântia* 25 (July 1966): 129–44; Angelo Paes de Camargo, et al., "Comportamento e ecologia do Mal das Folhas da Seringueira nas condições climáticas da planalto paulista," *Bragântia* 26 (1967): 1–18.

49 Camargo to Renato da Costa Lima, president of the Instituto Brasileiro de Café, n.p., 9 October 1958 [before Camargo's report was presented to the secretary of agriculture!], FTRC-A, Plantations Company, 1959, box 77; Camargo, "A formação de seringais no Estado de São Paulo," *Folha de São Paulo*, 9 October 1960; various articles in *Estado de São Paulo*, 1, 3, 8, 22 June, and 17, 22 December 1960, and 14 May 1961; Carlos Eduardo Siqueira Sampaio, "Novos horizontes para a borracha natural," [Campinas], 1980, xero. Escritório Técnico Brasil–Estados Unidos, *ETA em marcha* (Rio de Janeiro, 1958), p. 52. Charles H. Townsend, "Report on the Brazilian Rubber Situation," Belterra, 7 May 1958, typed ms., IAC Library.

50 Sylvio Braga, *Borracha*, p. 72; Brazil, SPVEA, *SPVEA*, 2:324; Alfonso Wisniewski, "Considerações sobre os princípios da economia nacional no setor borracha," *Circular do IPEAN*, no. 7 (August 1963): 58–9; Cosme Ferreira Filho, *Porque perdemos a batalha da borracha* (Manaus, 1965), pp. 356–9. Among other Amazonian defenders, see Orlando de Morais, *Amazônia espoliada*, pp. 37–9, 43–6; Luiz Osiris da Silva, *A luta pela Amazônia* (Rio de Janeiro, 1962), p. 120.

8 Complete perplexity, 1961–1972

1 The U.S. embassy in Rio de Janeiro had evidence of a Brazilian contact with a North American synthetics company in January 1951: See Isabel L. de Hartwig, economic assistant to Department of State, 24 August 1951, U.S. National Archives, Washington, DC, Record Group 166, Foreign Agricultural Relations Reports, Brazil, box 52. Brazil, Presidência, Serviço de Documentação, *Programa de Metas do Presidente Juscelino Kubitschek*, 3 vols. (Rio de Janeiro, 1958–9), 1:83–4, 2:83, 3:160–1. On planning for synthetic rubber, see discussions in Reunião de Estudos da Borracha para Aumento da Produção, *O problema da borracha brasileira* (Brasília, 1960) [hereafter REBAP]. On the execution of the synthetic projects, Cláudio Rómulo Siqueira, *Borracha: relatório de viagem realizada às zonas produtoras* (n.p., 23 March 1964), pp. 10, 15, 19, 21–4; and Economic Commission for Latin America, "Posição da borracha na América Latina," in International Rubber Study Group, Assembly, 19, São Paulo, 1967, *Documentos* (n.p., n.d.), pp. 93–7; Luiz Octávio Teixeira Mendes cites Fonseca in Brazil, SUDAM, *Reunião de instalação da Comissão Nacional da Seringueira* (Cruz das Almas, 1971), pp. 11–12. An important study of rubber policy in this period is Nelson Prado Alves Pinto, *Política da borracha no Brasil* (São Paulo, 1984), pp. 121–40. For general agricultural policy of the period, see G. E. Schuh, *Agricultural Development of Brazil* (New York, 1970), pp. 292–8.

Luiz A. de C. Carvalho, "Historia pouca conhecida da borracha natural brasileira," *Elastómeros* 5 (May–June 1979): 145–59; Brazil, SPVEA, *SPVEA, 1954– 1960: política de desenvolvimento da Amazônia*, 2 vols. (Rio de Janeiro, 1961), 2:334–8.

3 See Luis Osório da Silva, *A luta pela Amazônia* (Rio de Janeiro, 1962), p. 133; Sylvio Braga, *Borracha* (São Paulo, 1960), p. 7; and E. Chaves Neto, "Borracha," *Revista Brasiliense*, no. 32 (November–December 1960): 182–3, for nationalist arguments. IPEAN sought unsuccessfully to capture these feelings for planted rubber: See Alfonso Wisniewski, "Considerações sobre os princípios de economia nacional no setor borracha," *Circular do IPEAN*, no. 7 (August 1963): 56.

4 Banco da Amazônia, S.A., *Amazônia: instrumentos para o desenvolvimento* (Belém, 1969), p. 9; Brazil, *Diário do Congresso Nacional*, Seção I, Projeto de Resolução No. 114, de 1970 (1 May 1971), Supplemento, "Aprova as conclusões da Comissão Parlementar de Inquérito destinada a verificar as razões do desestímulo à produção da borracha" (Da CPI criada pela Resolução No. 49/67) [hereafter CPI-49/67], pp. 150–2, 177. BASA had been authorized to expand its operations in 1959, in fact. Brazil, SUDAM, *I Plano qüinqüenal de desenvolvimento (1967– 1971)* (Belém, 1967), p. 99. The COPERBO plant was designed to transform sugarcane-derived alcohol into polybutadiene. Technical difficulties obliged it to convert to petroleum feedstocks, however.

5 Brazil, Gabinete do Ministro Extraordinário para o Planejamento e Coordenação Econômica, Grupo de Estudos para a Reformulação da Política da Borracha, *Exposição de Motivos e Projeto de Lei* ([Brasília], 4 July 1966), pp. 5–6; Brazil, SUDHEVEA, *Legislação política-econômica da borracha* (Brasília, 1972); Cássio

Fonseca, "Uma comédia de erros; a borracha natural no Brasil," *Elastômeros* 6 (July–August, 1980): 8–10. See also his testimony before CPI-49/67, p. 214. On the contemporary market, see C. E. F. Manning, *The Market for Natural Rubber with Particular Reference to the Competitive Status of Natural Rubber* (London, 1970).

6 Alves Pinto, *Política*, p. 134; José Marcelino Monteiro da Costa and José das Neves Capela, *Acre e Rondônia: diagnôstico econômico* (Belém, 1967).

7 CPI-49/67, pp. 1–12, 70–1; the witness was Samuel Benchimol.

8 Camargo, "Agricultura na América do Sul," in E. J. Fittkau, et al., eds., *Biogeography and Ecology in South America* (The Hague, 1968), 1:312; Alves Pinto, *Política*, p. 138–40; see Brazil, *Coleção das leis*, Decree-Law 1106, 16 June 1970 (the Plan of National Integration). Brazil, SUDHEVEA, *Legislação político-econômica da borracha*; Fonseca, "Uma comédia" (September–October 1980), p. 9, notes that the price rise caused manufacturers to shift to substitutes like polyurethane. Law 5459, it should be noted, added a military representative to the CNB. On the inelasticity of wild rubber supply, see José M. Monteiro da Costa and José das Neves Capela, "Borracha vegetal, analise da oferta," *Revista Econômica da BASA* 1 (September–December 1970): 37–44. On COPERBO's difficulties, see testimony of Romeu Boto Dantas, director superintendent, CPI-49/67, pp. 124–30.

9 Brazil, SUDAM, *Plano*, pp. 99–100; CPI-49/67, pp. 10, 11, 118, 165–6, 207; Fernando Bezerra Teixeira, et al., *Plano geral de heveicultura para a Amazônia brasileira* ([Belém], 1965), pp. 9–11.

10 Brazil, SUDHEVEA, *Heveicultura no Brasil; relatório do GEPLASE* [hereafter GEPLASE] (n.p., 1970), pp. 3–9; Brazil, SUDHEVEA, *Plano nacional da borracha* [hereafter PNB] ([Rio de Janeiro], 1971). Brazil, SUDHEVEA, *Assistência técnica aos produtores de borracha vegetal na região amazônica (Projeto SUD-HEVEA No. 4 AT/AM)* (Rio de Janeiro, 1970), pp. 24–6, 239, 247.

11 Brazil, SUDAM, *Contribuição da SUDAM para o programa "Projeto Borracha" da BASA, para aplicação dos recursos do Proterra* ([Belém], 1971); Brazil, SU-DAM, *Subsídios ao plano regional de desenvolvimento (1972/1974)* (Belém, 1971), p. 79. Conferência Nacional das Classes Produtoras, 2, 1971, "Contribuição Regional-Amazonas: a problemâtica da borracha," (n.p., n.d.), mimeo., p. 2; CPI-49/67, p. 10.

12 GEPLASE, pp. 74–5, 97–100, 191, 200; Instituto de Pesquisas e Experimentação Agropecuárias do Norte, *IPEAN: 25 anos de pesquisas na Amazônia, histórico, organização, pesquisas* (Belém, 1969), pp. 69–70.

13 GEPLASE, pp. 6–8, 9–15, 102–6; Vicente H. F. Moraes, "Seleção em seringais nativos," *Circular do IPEAN*, no. 7 (August 1963): 5–6; Eurico Pinheiro, "Seringueira de plantação," in Brazil, Ministério de Agricultura, *Livro anual de agricultura, 1968* (Brasília, n.d.), pp. 178, 185. On loss of collections, Brazil, SUD-HEVEA, *Assistência*, pp. 61–2.

14 GEPLASE, pp. 40–5, 93–103, 108–9; L. O. T. Mendes, "Perspectivas sobre a utilização de clones poliploides em seringais industriais," Campinas, 1976, typed ms., Instituto Agronômico de Campinas Library, no. 69309.

15 H. Bos and K. G. M[a]cIndoe, "Breeding of Hevea for Resistance Against *Dothidella ulei* P. Henn.," *Journal of the RRIM* 19, pt. 2 (1965): 98–107; "Memo-

rando apresentado pelo govêrno da Libéria sobre a necessidade de medidas de proteção contra a introdução da *Dothidella ulei*, doença sul-americana das folhas," in International Rubber Study Group, Assembly, 19, São Paulo, 1967, *Documents* (n.p., n.d.), pp. 21–2, see also pp. 37–9, 71–2; K. H. Chee, "Combatting South American Leaf Blight of *Hevea* by Plant Breeding and Other Measures," *Planter*, no. 53 (1977): 288, 295; Ong Seng Huat, et al., "Breeding For Resistance Against *Hevea* Leaf Disease," paper presented at Workshop on International Collaboration in *Hevea* Breeding and the Collection and Establishment of Materials from the Neo-Tropics, Kuala Lumpur, 1977, xero. Note also Theodor G. E. Hoedt, "Dothidella Ulei and the Selection and Breeding of Hevea," in Natural Rubber Research Conference, Kuala Lumpur, 1960, *Proceedings* (Kuala Lumpur, 1961), pp. 446–52.

16 Pinheiro, "Seringueira," p. 185; John W. Miller, "Differential Clones of Hevea for Identifying Races of Dothidella ulei," *Plant Disease Reporter* 50 (March, 1966): 187–90; Miller, "Biology of *Dothidella ulei*" (Ph.D. diss. in agriculture, University of Florida, 1965); and Kenneth R. Langdon, "Culture and Pathogenicity of *Dothidella ulei*" (Ph.D. diss. in agriculture, University of Florida, 1966); P. R. Wycherley, "Breeding of Hevea," *Journal of the RRIM* 21 (1969): 50.

17 Bezerra Teixeira, *Plano geral*, p. 4; Pinheiro, "Seringueira," p. 180; see also testimony of IPEAN director A. Wisniewski, CPI-49/67, p. 145, and of J. W. Andrade, CPI-49/67, p. 164; GEPLASE, p. 132; CPI-49/67, final recommendations, p.8. Clone recommendations in PNB, Anexo XI, pp. 30–4. Foreign observers were unimpressed: See Patrice Compagnon, *Rapport de Mission au Brésil executée du 11 mars au 14 avril 1971* (Paris, 1971), p. 11. For a test of eight of these clones, see J. R. C. Gonçalves, "The Resistance of Fx and IAN Rubber Clones to Leaf Diseases in Brazil," *Tropical Agriculture* 45 (October 1968): 331–6.

18 C. N. Williams, *The Agronomy of the Major Tropical Crops* (Kuala Lumpur, 1975), pp. 142–3; Pinheiro, "Seringueira," p. 185; GEPLASE, pp. 98–9; Antônio Lemos Maia, *Normas básicas para a cultura da seringueira na Bahia* (Itabuna, BA, 1961), p. 25; CPI-49/67, p. 197; Eurico Pinheiro, interview with author, Belém, 11 July 1983, stated that the rubber obtained from Belterra trees could not be coagulated because the trees had suffered some sort of trauma upon being top grafted at the age of six or seven years. Belterra records show, however, that many trees had been top grafted at the customary one and one-half to two years of age.

19 Charles H. T. Townsend, Jr., "Progress in Developing Superior Hevea Clones in Brazil," *Economic Botany* 14 (July–September 1960): 189–90; Lemos Maia, *Normas*, pp. 14–15.

20 CPI-49/67, pp. 96–7, 148–9; J. H. Lloyd, "Problems of Controlling Leaf Diseases in Mature Hevea Rubber," in Congrès de la Protection des Cultures Tropicaux, Marseille, 1965, *Compte rendu des travaux* (Marseille, 1965), p. 491; David Ferreira Carvalho, et al., "Seringais de cultivo: uma análise crítica," *Elastômeros* 2 (November–December 1976): 6, reports Stanislau Prill, owner of a fazenda near Ituberá, introduced the first fungicide sprayer in 1969.

21 GEPLASE, p. 35; PNB, Anexo XI, pp. 65–6; Eurico Pinheiro, interview. On CEPEC, see Peter T. Knight, "Transforming Traditional Agriculture, The CEPLAC Experience," in H. J. Rosenbaum and W. G. Tyler, eds., *Contemporary*

Brazil: Issues in Economic and Political Development (New York, 1972), pp. 253–77.

22 Alves Pinto, *Política da borracha*, p. 131; CPI-49/67, p. 71. Itacoatiara's output reached 530 kilograms (latex?) in 1965, but in 1968 it dropped to 71 kilograms: Brazil, SUDHEVEA, *Projeto Sudhevea No. 2, AT/AM; Assistência técnica aos produtores e comerciantes de borracha nos altos rios do estado do Amazonas* ([Rio de Janeiro?], 1970), pp. 2–7. See also Brazil, SPVEA, *SPVEA*, 2:325, 333; Siqueira, *Borracha*, p. 3. Eurico Pinheiro, interview; João Walter de Andrade, "Planos de desenvolvimento: SUDAM," in Arthur Cezar Ferreira Reis, et al., *Problemática da Amazônia* (Rio de Janeiro, 1969), p. 142–3; Brazil, *Diário do Congresso Nacional*, Secção I, 26:18 (1 May 1971), Supplement, Projeto de Resolução No. 114, de 1970.

23 CPI-49/67, p. 71; GEPLASE, pp. 156–63; "Projeto de heveicultura da Amazônia (PROHEVEA), plano de trabalho para o período de janeiro a dezembro de 1971," n.p., n.d., Centro de Pesquisas Agronômicos do Trôpico Húmido, Belém [hereafter CPATU-B]. Brazil, EMBRAPA, *Anteprojeto de implantaçào do Centro Nacional de Pesquisa de Seringueira* (Brasília, 1974), p. 37.

24 Samuel Benchimol and G. Braga Dias, BASA, testimony, CPI-49/67, pp. 71, 85; Gabriel Hermes, "Borracha natural e sintética e heveicultura," in Brazil, *Diário do Congresso Nacional*, Seção II (4 May 1979), pp. 10–20; SPVEA, *SPVEA*, 2:336; Elias José Zagury, "Preço da mão de obra na heveicultura," paper presented at the Seminário Econômico da Borracha, [Belém, 1962?], mimeo. Siqueira, *Borracha*, pp. 4–6, suggests reforms.

25 Armando Nadler, "O problema da produção de borracha na Amazônia e suas relações socio-econômicas com todo o país," in Reunião de Estudos da Borracha para Aumento da Produção, *O problema da borracha brasileira* (Brasília, 1960), pp. 77–9; José Alfinito, *Produção e comercialização do seringal de cultivo da Base Física de Belterra* ([Santarém?], 1975); CPI-49/67, pp. 8, 81–2, 148, 196.

26 CPI-49/67, p. 199.

27 GEPLASE, pp. 61–2.

28 "Seringueira supera fase experimental," *Coopercotia* (May 1963): 41–3; GEPLASE, pp. 129–30; Angelo Artur Martinez, "Cultura da seringueira: diagnóstico da situação, medidas corretivas," in São Paulo, Secretaria de Agricultura, Secção de Plantas Tropicais, *Programa de Orientação Técnica, 1969–1970* (Campinas, 1970), pp. 17–22. Idem, "O mal-das-folhas da seringueira não constitui problema nas condições do Planalto Paulista," *O Agronômico* 20 (May–June 1968): 5; Angelo Artur Martinez, et al., "Produção e comercialização de seringueira nas C.A. e DIRAS" (Campinas, 1974), xero.

29 GEPLASE, p. 125; PNB, p. 120; Brazil, EMBRAPA, *Anteprojeto*, p. 31.

30 CPI-49/67, pp. 96–7, 185, 192–3; Brian Avery-Jones, interview with author, Granja Maraton, 9 July 1983; GEPLASE, pp. 55–6; J. R. C. Gonçalves, "Resistance of Fx and IAN Rubber Clones," p. 335.

31 CPI-49/67, p. 193; A. G. Lund, speech to Firestone World Management Conference, Akron, 7–9 November, 1966, Firestone Tire and Rubber Company Archives, Akron, OH [hereafter FTRC-A], Corporate Research and Planning Division, Folder 2; Lund to Robert E. Leoni, Akron, 10 March 1966, box 90; H. J. Dupré to E. H. Houser, "Turnover Report," Camamu, BA, 20 March 1965, box

88; C. E. Snyder to Lund, n.p., 14 June 1966, box 99; all in FTRC-A, Plantations Company. GEPLASE, pp. 62, 129; Robert J. Dunham, et al., "Relatório preliminar sobre o desenvolvimento da enxertia de copa da *Hevea brasiliensis* na fazenda Três Pancadas, BA," Brazil, SUDHEVEA, *Seminário sobre enxertia de copa da seringueira* (Brasília, 1982), pp. 92–134.

32 GEPLASE, p. 62.

33 CPI-49/67, p. 210; Siqueira, *Borracha*, pp. 34–6.

34 Dupré to Houser, 20 March 1965; Fundação Comissão de Planejamento Econômico da Bahia, *A seringueira na Bahia, alguns aspectos técnico-econômicos* (Salvador, 1960), pp. 1–2, 6, 17, 35, 49, 70; Siqueira, *Borracha*, pp. 68–76; Orlando G. Teixeira, *Cultura da seringueira no estado da Bahia* ([Salvador], 1961), pp. 5–8; Brazil, SUDHEVEA, *Projeto SUDHEVEA No. 3, AT/BA Assistência técnica aos produtores de borracha vegetal da Bahia* (n.p., 1969), p. 24; Associação dos plantadores de Seringueira da Bahia-SEPLAN, "Desenvolvimento dos problemas que envolvem a heveacultura na Bahia," in Encontro Nacional de Agropecuária, Brasília, 1975, *Anais* (Brasília, 1975), p. 73; Siqueira, *Borracha*, pp. 68–76; GEPLASE, pp. 30–1; Banco da Amazônia, S.A., *Desenvolvimento econômico da Amazônia* (Belém, 1966), p. 213. Carvalho, et al., "Seringais de cultivo," p. 3.

35 Arnaldo Gomes Medeiros and Djalma Batista Bahia, *Situação atual do cultivo da seringueira Hevea brasiliensis Muell. Arg. na Bahia em relação aos fungos Phytophthora palmivora (Butl.) Butl. e Microcyclus ulei (P. Henn.) Arx.* (Itabuna, BA, [1967?]), pp. 7–8, 13; GEPLASE, pp. 120, 126–7; SUDHEVEA, *Projeto SUDHEVEA No. 3*, pp. 26–8; PNB, Anexo XI, p. 64; Brazil, CNB, Grupo de Avaliação do PROBOR, *Estudo da Bahia: Relatório* (n.p., 1975), pp. 14–16.

36 CPI-49/67, pp. 155, 179.

37 Maria José Oliveira e Silva, *A sociedade amazônica e o problema social da desocupação e subocupação* (Belém, 1974), pp. 24, 36–9.

38 BASA, *Desenvolvimento econômico*, p. 202; CPI-49/67, p. 100; Conferência Técnica sobre Valorização Econômica da Amazônia, Rio de Janeiro, 1951, *Valorização econômica da Amazônia; subsídios para seu planejamento* (Rio de Janeiro, 1954), pp. 28–9; *A situação problemática do Acre em relação à produção da borracha – hoje* (Rio Branco, AC, 1971). The hunting of pelts was outlawed in 1967, further reducing gathering incomes.

39 CPI-49/67, pp. 79, 179; Siqueira, *Borracha*, p. 65.

40 World Bank, *Brazil: A Review of Agricultural Policies* (Washington, DC, 1984), p. 4.

9 Economically guaranteed, 1973–1986

1 Stésio Henri Guitton, *Política da borracha na Amazônia* (Brasília, 1975), p. 15; Brazil, SUDHEVEA, *Anuário estatístico: mercado nacional* 15 (1981): 7; Peter William Allen, et al., *A Study on Competition Between Natural and Synthetic Rubber*, IRRDB Monograph No. 1 (Kuala Lumpur, n.d.), pp. 1–54.

2 World Bank, *Brazil: A review of Agricultural Policies* (Washington, DC, 1984), pp. 12, 16, 17, 56.

3 Guitton, *Política*, pp. 18–19; comments unfavorable to SUDHEVEA in Brazil,

Congresso Nacional, *Diário do Congresso Nacional*, Secção II, 17 September 1977, p. 4707, and 23 September 1978, p. 4759.

4 Brazil, SUDHEVEA, *Programa de incentivos à produção de borracha vegetal* (Brasília, 1972).

5 Guitton, *Política*, p. 20; Brazil, Conselho Nacional de Borracha, Grupo de Avaliação do PROBOR, *Estado da Bahia: relatório* (n.p., 1975), pp. 32–3; Brazil, EMBRAPA, *Anteprojeto de implantação do Centro Nacional de Seringueira* (Brasília, 1974), p. 41; Francisco da Cunha Silva, "Borracha: riqueza que a tecnologia faz retornar," *Revista Brasileira de Extensão Rural* 2 (March–April, 1981): 14; Luiz A. de C. Carvalho, "História pouca conhecida da borracha natural brasileira," *Elastômeros* 5 (May–June 1979): 143–59; Brazil, Instituto de Planejamento Econômico e Social (IPEA), *Diagnóstico e sugestões para a auto-suficiência do setor da borracha no Brasil* (Brasília, 1976).

6 Guitton, *Política*, p. 12; Brazil, IPEA, *Diagnóstico*; Brazil, SUDHEVEA, *Relatório de atividades, 1982* (Brasília, 1983), p. 27; Brazil, SUDHEVEA, *PROBOR II – segundo programa de incentivo à produção de borracha nacional: fundamentos, objetivos, normas operativas* (n.p., 1978), pp. 6, 8, 47; Brazil, SUDHEVEA, *Encontro SUDHEVEA/BASA/EMATER, Manaus, 1978* (Rio de Janeiro, 1978); Pará, Associação de Crédito e Assistência Rural do Estado do Pará, *Projeto Heveicultura; plano anual de trabalho, 1975* (Belém, 1974).

7 Brazil, SUDHEVEA, *Relatório, 1982*, pp. 27, 29, 32; Associação dos Plantadores de Seringueira da Bahia, "Desenvolvimento dos problemas que involve a heveacultura na Bahia," in *Encontro Nacional de Agropecuária* (Brasília, 1975), pp. 73, 78; Eurico Pinheiro, FCAP, interview with author, Belém, 11 July 1983; Luadir Gasparotto, et al., "Relatorio de visita à propriedade do Sr. José Cesário de Menezes Barros [*sic*] no Distrito Agropecuário da SUFRAMA," Manaus, 14 December 1982, typed ms., CNPSD Library; Brian Avery-Jones, interview with author, São Francisco do Pará, PA, 9 July 1983.

8 [Brazil, SUDHEVEA], PROBOR 3, *Informações gerais* (Brasília, 1982); Brazil, SUDHEVEA, *Relatório de atividades, 1983* (Brasília, 1983), p. 5 (manuscript, xero., with corrections, in SUDHEVEA Library); José Cesário Menezes de Barros, "Para breve, a autosuficiência em borracha natural," *Revista Brasileira de Extensão Rural* 4 (January–February 1983): 12–13, 16, 17; Antônio Maria Gomes de Castro, "Excursão dos presidentes de sindicatos rurais da região norte aos seringais do sul da Bahia – resultados alcançados" ([Brasília, 1979?]), xero., SUDHEVEA Library.

9 Brazil, EMBRAPA, *Projeto de implantação do Centro Nacional de Pesquisa da Seringueira* (Brasília, [1975]), pp. 1–28; Brazil, SUDHEVEA, *Relatório de atividades, 1978* (Brasília, 1979), p. 46; Brazil, EMBRAPA, *Programa nacional de Pesquisa* (Brasília, 1981), pp. 15–16; Brazil, SUDHEVEA, *Relatório, 1982*, pp. 38–9. Nelson Prado Alves Pinto criticizes the organization of an entirely new center, rather than building on IPEAN or the National Institute of Amazon Research at Manaus, but a single-purpose center was probably a valid idea, and was evidently modeled on the RRIM. See Alves Pinto, *Política da borracha no Brasil* (São Paulo, 1984), p. 158. The CNPSD soon added research in African oil palm (or Dendê, *Elaeis guineensis*) to its responsibilities.

10 J. Keith Templeton, *Natural Rubber; Organizations and Research in Producing*

Countries (Arlington, VA, 1978), pp. 84–94 (which surveys all important rubber institutions worldwide); R. L. Wastie, "Diseases of Rubber in Brazil: Report on Consultancy Visit in October/November 1978," n.p., 10 December 1978, xero., CNPSD Library; Theodore Goering, et al., *Natural Rubber*, World Bank Sector Policy Paper (Washington, DC, 1982), annex 6; World Bank, *Brazil*, pp. 66–7. In November 1969, the World Bank sent to Brazil an agronomist who apparently recommended funding for rubber research. Brazil, SUDHEVEA, *Assistência técnica aos produtores de borracha vegetal na região amazônica, Projeto SUD-HEVEA No. 4-AT/AM* (Rio de Janeiro, 1970), p. 256.

11 J. E. van der Plank, *Plant Diseases: Epidemics and Control* (New York, 1963), pp. 223–59; Raoul A. Robinson, "Vertical Resistance," *Review of Plant Pathology* 50 (May 1971): 233–9; idem, "New Concepts in Breeding for Disease Resistance," *Annual Review of Phytopathology* 18 (1980): 189–210; J. E. Parlevliet and J. C. Zadoks, "Resistance, Horizontal and Vertical," *Euphytica* 26 (February 1977): 5–21.

12 Fábio Zenaide Maia, "A experiência de CULTROSA," in Brazil, SUDHEVEA, Seminário Sobre Enxertia de Copa da Seringueira, Brasília, 1982, *Anais* (Brasília, 1982), p. 79; A. de S. Lynage and K. H. Chee, "A ocorrência de uma estirpe virulenta de *Microcyclus ulei* em *Hevea* em Trinidad," in Brazil, SUDHEVEA, Seminário Nacional da Seringueira, 3, Manaus, *Anais* (Brasília, 1980) [hereafter SNS-3], pp. 52–61; K. H. Chee, interview with author, Itabuna, BA, 21 June 1983.

13 Ismail Hashim, et al., "Reaction of *Hevea* Leaves to Infection with *Microcyclus ulei*," *Journal of the RRIM* 26, no. 2 (1978): 67–75; Alfonso Wisniewski, "*Hevea benthamiana* e *Hevea pauciflora* como fontes potenciais de produção de borracha," *Boletim da Faculdade de Ciências Agrárias do Pará*, no. 9 (December 1977): 18. The reaction was biochemical, based on a phenol, either kaempferol or quercetin. Rosa Maria Gaioso Cardoso, "Doenças da seringueira no Estado de São Paulo," in Brazil, Ministrério da Agricultura, Seminário Nacional da Seringueira, 1, Cuiabá, 1972, *Anais* (n.p., n.d.), p. 129; Hashim, "Possible Mechanisms of Hevea Resistance to South American Leaf Blight," in Association of Natural Rubber Producing Countries [ANPRC], Third Meeting of the ANPRC Technical Committee on SALB, Kuala Lumpur, 1979, *Report* ([Kuala Lumpur, 1979]), Appendix 13.

14 N. W. Simmonds, "Some Ideas on Botanical Research on Rubber," *Tropical Agriculture* 59 (January 1982): 2–8; Affonso Celso Candeira Valois, "Expressão de caracteres em seringueira e obtenção de clones produtivos e resistentes ao mal-das-folhas," *Pesquisa Agropecuária Brasileira* [hereafter *PAB*], 18 (September 1983): 1015–20; Fernando Carneiro de Albuquerque, *Possibilidade de emprego da resistência vertical e horizontal no melhoramento da seringueira*, XI Curso de Especialização em Heveicultura, Doenças da Seringueira, III (Belem, 1983), pp. 1–6.

15 Colin Barlow cites Wycherley: *The Natural Rubber Industry* (Kuala Lumpur, 1978), p. 119; J. R. de Paiva, et al., "Avaliação do desempenho de clones de seringueira através de índices de seleção," *PAB* 17 (June 1982): 865–72; Moacyr Eurípedes Medri and Eduardo Lleras, "Quantificação e uso de caracteres anatômicos e fisiológicos de folhas na determinação de eficiência hídrica em clones de *Hevea*

spp.," *Acta Amazônica* 13 (April 1983): 261–88; Wastie, "Diseases," pp. 25, 29–30; Robert J. Dunham, et al., *Comportamento dos clones de seringueira e novos materiais recomendados para futuros plantios na Fazenda Três Pancadas* (Camamu, BA, 1982).

16 Valois, "Expressão de caracteres," p. 1017; P. de S. Gonçalves, "Interspecific Crosses in the Genus Hevea," *PAB* 17 (May 1982): 775–81; Wisniewski, "*Hevea benthamiana,*" pp. 15–26; idem, "Borrachas naturais brasileiras," *CPATU-Miscelânea,* no. 7 (1981).

17 Teixeira Mendes, "Perspectivas sobre a utilização de clones poliploides em serin-gais industriais," in Brazil, Conselho Nacional da Borracha, Seminário Nacional da Seringueira, 2, Rio Branco, 1976, *Anais* (Rio de Janeiro, 1978) [hereafter SNS-2], pp. 440–1; Medri and Lleras, "Comparação anatômica entre folhas de um clone diploide (IAN 873) e dois clones poliploides (IAC 207, 222)," *Acta Ama-zônica* 11 (January 1981): 35–47; Valois, "Expressão de caracteres," p. 1016; Carlos Eduardo Siqueira Sampaio, CATI, interview with author, Campinas, 1 June 1983; Templeton, *Natural Rubber,* p. 91.

18 Brazil, IPEAL, *Expedição à Amazônia: relatório* [Cruz das Almas, BA, 1974]; Paulo de Souza Gonçalves, et al., *II coleta de material nativo de alta produção em seringais do estado do Acre e território federal de Rondônia, relatório* (Belem, 1973); Gonçalves, "Collection of Hevea Materials from Rondônia Territory in Brazil," *PAB* 17 (April 1982): 575–82; idem, *Seleção e coleta de seringueiras nativas na região de Ouro Preto – território federal de Rondônia (relatório de viagem)* (Manaus, 1979); and Gonçalves, interview with author, Manaus, 18 July 1983.

19 Ismael de Jesus Matos Viégas, et al., *III coleta de material nativo de alta produção em seringais do estado do Acre e território federal de Rondônia, relatório* (Belem, 1974).

20 F. Hallé and J. C. Combe, "Mission en Amazonie brésilienne pour la récolte de matèrial génétique nouveau destiné à l'amelioration de l'Hevea," Paris, 1974, xero., CNPSD Library; International Rubber Research and Development Board [IRRDB], IRRDB Project for the Identification, Collection and Establishment of Hevea Materials from South America, *Report of the Preliminary Mission to South America* [Brickendonbury, Hert., 1978], p. 25

21 Barlow, *Natural Rubber Industry,* pp. 24–5; Abdul Aziz Kadir, et al., "Estrategia para o controle de doenças de *Hevea* na Malásia," in SNS-3, pp. 178–87; Ong Seng Huat and A. M. Tan, "Performance of Ford, Fx and IAN Series Clones in RRIM Trial," paper presented to IRRDB Symposium, Bogor, 1976, xero., MRPRA Library, Brickendonbury, Herts. Malayan researchers were reporting an increase in severity and distribution. It is significant that they thought it worthwhile to engage in aerial spraying experiments to control leaf disease: T. M. Lim, et al., "Thermal Fogging as a New Technique in Controlling Rubber Disease," *Planters Bulletin,* no. 155 (1978): 75–7.

22 S. Subramaniam, "Breeding for resistance against SALB – Recent Develop-ment," in ANPRC, *Report,* Appendix 15; "South American Leaf Blight of Rub-ber," *Planters Bulletin,* no. 127 (July 1973): n.p.; K. H. Chee, "The Suitability of Environmental Conditions in Asia for the Spread of South American Leaf Blight of Hevea Rubber," *The Planter* 56 (1980): 445–54.

23 M. S. Swaminathan, "Recent Trends in Plant Breeding," in International Rubber Conference, Kuala Lumpur, 1975, *Proceedings* (Kuala Lumpur, 1976), 1:147–9; K. H. Chee, "Combatting South American Leaf Blight of Hevea by Plant Breeding and other Measures," *The Planter* 53 (1977): 292; Subramaniam, "Hevea Introduction from South America to Conserve Germplasm – Tentative Project Proposal," in Workshop on International Collaboration in Hevea Breeding and the Collection and Establishment of Materials from the Neo-Tropics, Kuala Lumpur, 1977, *Report* (Kuala Lumpur, 1978); IRRDB Project, *Report*, pp. 41, 42; Brazil, SUDHEVEA, *Relatório de atividades, 1981* (Brasília, [1982?]), p. 17; IRRDB, *Report for 1979–1981* [Brickendonbury, Herts., 1982], pp. 4, 6, 8, 16.

24 RRIM, *1982 Annual Report* (Kuala Lumpur, 1983), p. 25, and *1983 Annual Report* (Kuala Lumpur, 1984), p. 6; P. de S. Gonçalves, *Expedição internacional à Amazônia no território federal de Rondônia para coleta de material botânico de seringueira (Hevea brasiliensis)* (Manaus, 1981); idem, "Report on Present Status of *Hevea* Germplasm in Brazil Collected in IRRDB Expedition," Manaus, 1982, xero., CNPSD Library. It was decided to undertake no further expeditions until the significance of the 1981 expedition had been absorbed, although the concerns about wild germplasm extermination continued strong.

25 P. de S. Gonçalves, interview with author, Manaus, 19 July 1983; K. H. Chee, interview with author, Itabuna, BA, 22 June 1983.

26 João Rodrigues de Paiva, et al., "Variação genética entre procedências de seringueira," *PAB* 20 (January 1985): 97–108; de Paiva, et al., "Avaliação preliminar do comportamento de novos clones de seringueira em Manaus," *PAB* 18 (February 1983): 147–58; Gonçalves, "Report," p. 4. Southeast Asian specialists at Bahia initiated their SALB studies by testing their suspicion that SALB had not appeared in their region simply because it experienced higher temperature ranges there.

27 Eduardo Lleras, interview with author, Manaus, 15 September 1981; Brazil, SUDHEVEA, Seminário sobre Enxertia de Copa da Seringueira, *Anais* (Brasília, 1982).

28 Avery-Jones, interview, 9 July 1983.

29 J. L. Bezerra, "Controle químico de *Microcyclus ulei* no Brasil através do PROMASE," in SNS-3, pp. 130–61; R. Romano, et al., "South American Leaf Blight and its Control," paper presented at ANPRC Meeting, 1983, n.p., n.d., typed ms., CNPSD Library; Johan Joseph Begeer, "Realidade sobre a borracha natural; uma contribuição dos produtores de borracha natural do Sul da Bahia sobre os problemas atuais e com sugestões para melhorar a situação," n.p., [1975], xero., CEPLAC Library; R. L. Wastie, "Diseases," pp. 15–16.

30 Hermínio Maia Rocha, et al., "Controle do Mal-das-Folhas da seringueira na Bahia," *Revista Theobroma* 5 (July–September 1975): 3–11; Laércio Pinho Lima, "Análise da produção e da produtividade de seringais no litoral sul da Bahia, submetidos ao controle de 'mal das folhas' (*Microcyclus ulei*) por via aérea," in SNS-2, pp. 133–51; K. H. Chee and R. L. Wastie, "Situação atual e panorama futuro das doenças de *Hevea* no Novo Mundo," in SNS-3, p. 292; Brazil, SUDHEVEA, *Relatório de atividades, 1978*, pp. 48–9; Brazil, SUDHEVEA, *Anuário estatístico; mercado nacional, 1980* (Rio de Janeiro, n.d.), p. 8; Bezerra, "Controle químico," p. 158; Assis Ramos de Souza, et al., "Avaliação do Programa Especial de Pulverização Aérea de Seringueira (PROMASE) na Bahia em 1979," in SNS-3, pp. 62–81. B. Sripathi Rao, "Novos enfoques sobre o controle das prin-

cipais doenças foliares em seringueira na Bahia," in SNS-3, pp. 234–8; Brazil, SUDHEVEA, Programa especial de controle do mal das folhas da seringueira – PROMASE *Relatório, 1980* (Brasília, 1981); Ronaldo Romano and Sripathi Rao, "Desfolhamento químico em seringueira na Bahia," *PAB* 18 (May 1983): 507–14.

31 E. H. Houser to C. E. Snyder, Camamu, 10 January 1970, Firestone Tire and Rubber Company Archives, Akron, OH [hereafter FTRC-A], 1970, Fl-1, 111; J. M. H. Conduru Neto, et al., *Controle do mal-das-folhas da seringueira pela termonebularização do fungicida Triadimefon* (Belém, 1983); K. H. Chee, "Management of South American Leaf Blight," *The Planter* 56 (August 1980): 321; Brazil, SUDHEVEA, *Relatório de atividades, 1982*, p. 38, and 1985 (Brasília, 1986), manuscript, p. 76.

32 Brazil, SUDHEVEA, *Plano Nacional da Borracha* (Rio de Janeiro, 1970), Anexo 10A, B, C; V. H. Figueiredo Moraes and Therezinha Xavier Bastos, "Viabilidade e limitações climáticas para as culturas permanentes e anuais com possibilidades de expansão na Amazônia brasileira," *Boletim Técnico do IPEAN*, no. 54 (January 1972): 138; Moraes and Valois, "Prioridades nacionais de pesquisa em heveicultura," in SNS-2, p. 119; Moraes, "Rubber," in Paulo de T. Alvim and T. T. Koslowski, eds., *Ecophysiology of Tropical Crops* (New York, 1977), p. 319; Eurico Pinheiro, et al., "Comportamento de alguns clones de seringueira em Açailândia, na região pre-amazônica maranhenses – dados preliminares," in SNS-3, pp. 103–29; J. M. H. Conduru Neto, "Observações preliminares sobre ocorrência de doenças em viveiros de seringueira em Açailândia," in SNS-3, p. 253.

33 Derrick Mahinda Fernando, "Project: Strengthening Agricultural Research in Brazil," Memorandum to IICA, Manaus, [1980], xero., CNPSD Library; R. Romano, et al., "South American Leaf Blight"; Moacyr Eurípedes Medri and Eduardo Lleras, "Aspectos da anatomia ecológica de folhas de *Hevea brasiliensis* Müell. Arg.," *Acta Amazônica* 10 (September 1980): 463–93.

34 Colin Barlow, *Natural Rubber Industry*, p. 158; Y. D. A. Senanayake, "The Influence of Rainfall on Yield of Rubber," *Journal of Plantation Crops* 6 (June 1978): 21–3; F. Hallé and J. C. Combe, "Mission en Amazonie"; Ruth Linda Benchimol, "Ocorrência de *Microcyclus ulei* em Açailândia-MA," *FCAP: Nota Prévia*, no. 3 (1983). In fact, R. L. Wastie reported seeing SALB there in 1978, "Diseases," p. 9.

35 Brazil, CNPSD, *Síntese de problemas, ações desenvolvidas e resultados alcançados com a pesquisa de seringueira* (Manaus, 1980), pp. 1–19; J. K. Templeton, *Natural Rubber; Organizations and Research in Producing Countries* (Arlington, VA, 1978), p. 92. Studies were also being undertaken to come to grips with the problem of relatively slow growth, commonly observed in the Amazon, but not yet recognized as a problem. At a well-managed plantation in Acre that had not yet been attacked by Microcyclus, plant researchers from the Agricultural school at Piracicaba, São Paulo, measured the growth of Fx 3864 clones and found that the weight of plant matter after four years was 5 to 7 percent of averages reported in Malaysia. Henrique Paulo Haag, et al., *Nutrição mineral da seringueira* (Campinas, SP, 1982), p. 23.

36 A. C. Derr, managing director, to A. G. Lund, São Paulo, 17 August 1973, D-215/75, and Derr to H. E. Hunt, São Paulo, 9 November 1973, FTRC-A, Planta-

tions Companies, 1973, box 119. "Special Report No. 3, The Rubber Market and Industry in Brazil," *Rubber Trends*, no. 88 (1980): 45.

37 Lund to R. A. Riley, n.p., 7 March 1973, and Lund to F. A. LePage, n.p., 3 May 1973, FTRC-A, Plantations Companies, 1973, box 119; Firestone News Service, 15 March 1973 and 14 January 1978.

38 Robert J. Dunham, et al., "Relatório preliminar sobre o desenvolvimento da enxertia de copa da *Hevea brasiliensis* na Fazenda Três Pancadas," in Brazil, SUDHEVEA, Seminário sobre Enxertia de Copa da Seringueira, Brasília, 1982, *Anais* (Brasília, 1982), pp. 92–134; "Firestone Fazenda Tres Pancadas, Fact Booklet, 1982"; Templeton, *Natural Rubber*, p. 75; Firestone Tire and Rubber Company, *Annual Report*, 1975, 1978, 1979, 1980, 1981, 1983, for information on plantations. All the Firestone plantations have been sold, save the Liberian. Firestone began experimenting with Guayule rubber in the U.S. Southwest in 1978. Wastie, "Diseases," p. 19.

39 *Rubber Trends Quarterly*, no. 100 (December 1983): 50–1; Milton F. da Rocha Filho, "BCN e Goodyear unem-se para plantar seringueiras," *Jornal do Brasil* (30 June 1983). John Webster, Firestone Tire and Rubber Company, interview with author, Akron, OH, 28 January 1985. There were five smaller, Brazilianowned tire companies in Brazil, none of which planted rubber.

40 Goodyear Tire and Rubber Company, *SEC Report* (1984), p. 11; Avery-Jones, interview, 9 July 1983. In some quarters the idea persisted that the foreign tire companies were deliberately refusing to grow more rubber: See speech by E. Carreira, in Brazil, *Diário*, pp. 4704, 4706.

41 Brazil, EMBRAPA, *Anteprojeto*, p. 30; Piruna Agro-Industrial, "Comportamento de clones de seringueiras na Plantação Pirelli-Una," Una, BA, 1982, xero., CEPLAC Library; Armando Comparato, Pirelli, interview with author, São Paulo, 24 October 1986.

42 Bahia, Bahia-Alcool Empreendimentos Energéticos e Agroindustriais, S.A., *Borracha natural na Bahia: situação atual e perspectivas* (Salvador, 1982), pp. 55, 60, 68; Johan Joseph Begeer, "Realidade sobre a borracha natural; uma contribuição dos produtores de borracha natural do Sul da Bahia sobre os problemas atuais e com sugestões para melhorar a situação," n.p., [1975], xero., CEPLAC Library (a modified version appears in SNS-2, pp. 585–98); José Alexandre de Souza Menezes, et al., *Cadastro dos seringueiros do estado da Bahia: atualização e análise* (Itabuna, BA, 1975), p. 19.

43 Aureo L. de A. Brandão, et al., *Determinação dos custos de exploração de seringais no litoral sul da Bahia*, CEPEC Boletim Técnico, no. 69 (Itabuna, BA, 1980), pp. 1–27; "O desafio da borracha natural," *Elastômeros* 4 (November–December 1978): 14–20; Associação dos Plantadores de Seringueira da Bahia – SEPLAN, "Desenvolvimento dos problemas que envolvem a heveacultura na Bahia," in Encontro Nacional de Agropecuária, Brasília, 1975, *Anais* (Brasília, 1975), pp. 72–80.

44 Brazil, CEPLAC, *CEPLAC: 12 anos ajudando Rondônia a crescer* (Brasília, [1983?]); World Bank, *Brazil: Integrated Development of the Northwestern Frontier* (Washington, DC, 1981), pp. 61, 64, 72, 80, 167; Orlando Valverde, ed., *Organização do espaço na faixa da Transamazônica* (Rio de Janeiro, 1979), 1:83, 108, 127–9, 137, 147, 154, 159, 163, 170, 174, 176, 210; José Rufino Borges

and M. F. Araripe Leite, "Importância do 'Proborzinho' para a heveicultura acreana," in Brazil, EMBRAPA, Seminário Agropecuário do Acre, 1, Rio Branco, 1983, *Anais* (Rio Branco, AC, 1983), pp. 175–9. José Carlos Nascimento, "Uma possível estratégia para vencer o problema de indicação de clones para o território brasileiro," paper presented at Seminário Brasileiro para Recomendações de Clones de Seringueira, 1, Brasília, 1982, xero.; Antônio Maria Gomes de Castro, SUD-HEVEA, interview with author, Brasília, 27 June 1983; Brazil, EMBRAPA, Seminário, *Anais* (1983), p. 438.

45 Odilon Soares Favoreto, *A heveicultura no Espírito Santo* (Vitória, 1978), xero., Empresa Capixaba de Pesquisa Agropecuária (EMCAPA) Library, p. 2; Francisco Xavier Hemerly and João Maurício Rodrigues, *Considerações com vista à expansão da heveicultura no estado do Espírito Santo* (Vitória, 1977), pp. 8, 16–17; Hemerly, *Expansão da heveicultura no estado do Espírito Santo* (Vitória, 1978), pp. 7–8; Renan F. Brito, SUDHEVEA, interview with author, Vitória, 16 June 1983.

46 G. M. Sá Filho, et al., *Considerações sobre a introdução da cultura da seringueira nos municípios de Colatina, Boa Esperança, Pinheiro, Nova Venécia, Montanha e São Gabriel da Palha* (Cariacica, ES, 1981); Paulo Cézar Marques and O. S. Favoreto, "Problemas nutricionais em seringal adulto no Espírito Santo," *Comunicado EMCAPA* 2 (2 June 1980): 4; Francisco Xavier Hemerly, EMCAPA, interview with author, Vitória, 16 June 1983; P. W. Allen, IRRDB, interview with author, Brickendonbury, Herts., 6 June 1984.

47 Pará, Secretaria de Estado de Agricultura, *Projeto Seringueira, 1973–1978* ([Belém, 1973]), pp. 1–6, 7; "Governo cria a cidade da borracha para plantar 500,000 seringueiras," *Jornal do Comêrcio* (Manaus) (12 November 1978).

48 Alfredo Kingo Oyama Homma, et al., "Estrutura produtiva de seringais no município de Santarem, PA" *CPATU Circular Técnico*, no. 3 (1980). This data conflicts with personal observations by Stephen G. Bunker, who disparages the problem of Microcyclus: See his *Underdeveloping the Amazon* (Urbana, IL, 1985), pp. 65–6.

49 Ethrel stimulation was developed in Southeast Asia (Ethrel = 2–chloroethylphosphonic acid). See Vicente H. F. Moraes, "Estimulação da produção de látex em seringais nativos," *Comunicado Técnico-EMBRAPA*, no. 2 (May 1982); Brazil, SUDHEVEA, *Guia para a introdução do cernambi virgem prensado em seringais nativos* (Rio de Janeiro, 1976); Olinto Gomes da Rocha Neto, CNPSD, interview with author, Manaus, 17 September 1981; Brazil, SUDAM, *II Plano de Desenvolvimento da Amazônia (1975–1979)* (Belém, 1976), pp. 64, 147–8. One CNPSD researcher reports continuing coercion against seringueiros, however, including murder of those who try to abandon the wild groves: Paulo de S. Gonçalves, interview, 18 July 1983. On wild rubber quality: Armando Comparato, interview, 24 October 1986.

50 Lúcio Flâvio Pinto, "Ford, o império perdido no meio do vale," *O Estado de São Paulo* (25 March 1979); Francisco Chagas, interview with author, Belterra, 13 July 1983.

51 Angelo Paes de Camargo, et al., "South American Leaf Blight Epidemics and Rubber Phenology in São Paulo," in International Rubber Conference, Kuala Lumpur, 1975, *Proceedings* (Kuala Lumpur, 1976), 3:251–66; Rosa Maria G.

Cardoso, "Estágios ontogénicos do fungo Microcyclus ulei V. Arx em seringueira nas condições do vale do Ribeira em São Paulo," in Congresso Paulista de Fitopatologia, 4, Campinas, 1981, *Resumos dos trabalhos* (n.p., n.d.); A. A. Martinez, et al., "Produção e comercialização do latex de seringueira," Campinas, 1974, xero., Instituto de Biologia Library; Mário Cardoso, "Nota prévia sobre a produtividade de seringueiras em São Paulo," in SNS-2, pp. 383–90; "Seringueira pode ser plantada em terras ociosas do Estado," *O Estado de São Paulo* (4 January 1976); "São Paulo já tem polo com 2 milhões de seringueiras," *O Estado de São Paulo* (12 July 1981).

52 Guitton, *Política*, pp. 34, 43; Mário Cardoso, "Subsídios ao desenvolvimento da heveicultura no estado de São Paulo," Campinas, 1979, mimeo., IAC Library; Carlos Eduardo Siqueira Sampaio, *Novos horizontes para a borracha natural* (Campinas, 1980), pp. 2, 7; Brazil, SUDHEVEA, *Anuário estatístico; mercado nacional* 14 (1980): 13; Mário Cardoso, *Instruções para a cultura da seringueira*, 2d ed. (Campinas, 1980), p. 35; Mário Cardoso, interview with author, Campinas, 31 May 1983.

53 José Cesário Menezes de Barros, "Para breve, a autosuficiência em borracha natural," *Revista Brasileira de Extensão Rural* 4 (January–February 1983): 13–15, 18; Antônio Maria Gomes de Castro, *Estudo da viabilidade técnica e econômica da heveicultura em áreas não tradicionais de exploração no Brasil* (Rio de Janeiro, 1979), p. 2; Vilson de Oliveira, *Cultura de seringueira nos cerrados de Mato Grosso* (Cuiabá, 1982), p. 1.

54 Brazil, SUDHEVEA, *Relatório, 1982*, p. 32.

55 Brazil, SUDHEVEA, *Relatório, 1983*, manuscript, xero., pp. 5, 8; Theodore Goering, et al., *Natural Rubber*; U. N., Food and Agricultural Organization, *Commodity Review and Outlook, 1982–1983* (Rome, 1983), p. 85; J. C. Menezes de Barros, speech, in SNS-3, pp. 2–21; Eurico Pinheiro, interview, 11 July 1983. On dismissals, see *Veja* (5 November 1986): 127.

56 Aureo Luiz de Azevedo, et al., "Estimativa das despesas diretas de capital para estabelecimento de seringais no litoral sul da Bahia," *CEPEC-Boletim Técnico*, no. 47 (1976); Francisco (last name unknown), interview with author, Granja Marathon, São Francisco do Pará, PA, 9 July 1983.

Conclusion

1 The principal limiting factor in cacao planting in the Amazon is witches'-broom, *Crinipellis perniciosa*.

2 Paulo de Tarso Alvim, "Desafio agrícola da região amazônica," *Geografia e Planejamento*, no. 7 (1973): 2.

3 Among more or less deliberate attempts to confuse the issue, see Cássio Fonseca, *A economia da borracha*, 2d ed. (Rio de Janeiro, 1970), pp. 43–4. For an example of F. Camargo's attempts to forget his role in rubber, see Instituto Interamericano de Cooperación Agrícola, *Medalla agrícola* (San José, 1968).

4 Banco de Amazônia, *Desenvolvimento econômico da Amazônia (redação preliminar)* (Belém, 1966), p. 167; Brazil, Convênio Ministério Agricultura/SUDAM, Unidade Regional de Supervisão Norte (URS/N), *Estudos sobre os produtos po-*

tênciais da Amazônia (Primeira Fase) (Belém, 1978); *Ciência Hoje* 1 (July–August 1982): 5.

5 For the convenience of the casual reader, who may be inclined to affix the label *determinism* to a historical explanation based upon ecological principles, the following definition of the term is hereby presented, along with the author's formal plea of not guilty: "Scientific principle according to which each fact has one cause and, under the same conditions, the same causes always produce the same effects, from which it results that facts are ruled by necessary and universal laws," *Grand Larousse Encyclopédique; Trois volumes en couleurs* (Paris, 1965), 1:n.p.

6 Luiz A. de C. Carvalho, "História pouco conhecida da borracha brasileira," *Elastômeros* 6 (May-June 1980): 20; Townsend worried about sabotage, see "Report on the Brazilian Rubber Situation," Belterra, 7 May 1958, typed ms., IAC Library.

7 The author hopes that this last grim remark will not be taken as advocacy for a policy of forest devastation.

Glossary

African oil palm (see *Elaeis guineensis*)

Aviador
> A commercial forwarder and broker in the rubber trade, intermediary between the exporter and seringalista. He usually owned steamboats and launches as well.

Balata (see *Manilkara*)

Bordeaux mixture
> A fungicide consisting of blue vitriol (copper sulphate) mixed with lime and water.

Castilla elastica: Castilloa, Caucho
> A species of latex-bearing tree, native to tropical Central and South America, formerly tapped in the wild for its rubber.

Caucho (see *Castilla elastica*)

Ceara rubber (see *Manihot glaziovii*)

Clone
> A group of cultivated plants of which the individuals are transplants of a single original plant. There is, unfortunately, no unified list of all the clones in experimental or commercial use in Brazil. Clones are identified with a letter code indicating the orginating organization or location and a series of numerals, e.g., Fx 25 = Fordlandia cross, number 25.

Dendê (see *Elaeis guineensis*)

Dothidella ulei (see *Microcyclus ulei*)

Elaeis guineensis: Dendê, African oil palm
> An African palm species, whose fruits have numerous applications.

Elastomer
> All rubbers, natural and synthetic, considered collectively.

223

Glossary

Erynnis ello: mandarová caterpillar
> A pest in manioc plantations, it also attacks Hevea.

Ficus elastica: rubber plant, rubber tree
> A latex-bearing tree native to Southeast Asia, formerly tapped in the wild for its rubber. Now widely planted in city streets in the American tropics as an ornamental, and indoors in colder climates.

Hancornia speciosa: Mangabeira
> A latex-bearing tree native to eastern Brazil. Formerly tapped in the wild for its rubber.

Hevea brasiliensis: Seringueira, Seringueira verdadeira, Seringa, Para rubber tree, Hevea rubber tree
> The tree that is the source of cultivated commercial rubber. It is native to the forested region south of the Amazon. Other species of this genus also have been tapped in the wild, or employed for hybridization with *H. brasiliensis*.

Hevea rubber tree (see *Hevea brasiliensis*)

Mal-das-Folhas (see *Microcyclus ulei*)

Mandarová caterpillar (see *Erynnis ello*)

Mangabeira (see *Hancornia speciosa*)

Maniçoba (see *Manihot glaziovii*)

Manihot glaziovii: Maniçoba, Ceara rubber
> A latex-bearing tree native to the dry northeastern region of Brazil. Formerly tapped in the wild for its rubber.

Manilkara: Massaranduba, Balata
> A genus of latex-bearing tree native to the eastern Amazon and the Guianas that yields Balata, a substance similar to rubber.

Massaranduba (see *Manilkara*)

Microcyclus ulei (also *Dothidella ulei*)
> A fungus that parasitizes leaves of the genus *Hevea* and causes South American Leaf Blight, or Mal-das-Folhas.

Murupita (see *Sapium*)

Para rubber tree (see *Hevea brasiliensis*)

Patrão (see seringalista)

Sapium: Murupita
> A genus of latex-bearing tree native to the eastern Amazon, formerly tapped in the wild for its rubber.

Seringalista (also patrão, obsolete)
> Owner or manager of a grove, or groves, of wild rubber trees, with

the attendant functions of employer of wild rubber tappers and store-keeper.

Seringueira (see *Hevea brasileira*)

Seringueiro
 A tapper of wild rubber.

South American Leaf Blight (see *Microcyclus ulei*)

Index

Abati, 7
Abreu, Luiz d', 177
Acre, 40, 42, 48
Adamson, William, 28
aerial dusting, see South American Leaf
  Blight, chemical control
African Oil Palm, 152, 164
Agassiz, Louis, 11
agricultural growth, 143, 164–5
Agronomic Institute of Campinas, 123, 134,
  139, 159–60
Agronomic Institute of the East, 118, see
  also Institute for Agricultural Research
  and Experimentation of the East
Agronomic Institute of the North, see also
  Institute for Agricultural Research and
  Experimentation of the North
  funding, 114
  organized, 88
  research, 112, 113–14, 118
  rubber development, 116, 119, 120
  in World War II, 89, 91, 92, 99, 102, 104
alcohol, 129, 131
Alencar, J. Virgolino de, 48
Allen, Douglas H., 101
Almeida, Manuel Pereira de, 140
Alston, R. A., 113
Amazon Credit Bank, 115, 118, 128, 129,
  see also Bank of Amazônia
Amazon region
  agriculture, 6, 50, 164–5
  bourgeoisie, 49
  despair, 164
  development fund, 102, 109–10, 114,
    116, 130
  extractive economy, 11, 36, 47, 131
  foreign adventurers in, 51
  forest destruction, 167
  government, 11, 42, 47, 73
  labor, 39, 42–3, 141

regionalism, 100, 127, 160
tax incentives, 130
Amazon Rubber Cultivation Project
  (PROHEVEA), 132–3, 136–7
Amazon Steam Navigation Company, 43
Amazonas, steamship, 17–18, 21
Amorim, Alexandre Brito de, 18
Araujo, Imar Cezar, 158
Argau, Jean Mueller von, 10
Association of Employers of the Wild
  Rubber Industry, 110
Association of Seringalistas of Mato Grosso,
  110
Aublet, Fusée, 10
Avery-Jones, Brian, 152, 156
aviadores, 40, 94, 99

Bakkedahl, Norman, 103
Balata, 38, 50, 53
Baldwin, James, 99, 100
Bancroft, C. K., 55, 57, 58–9
Bangham, W. N., 78–9, 80–1, 85, 113
Bank of Amazônia (BASA), 130, 131, 136,
  137, 141, 144, 145
Bank of Brazil, 118
Barros, José Cesário Menezes de, 146
base grafting, see bud grafting
Bastos, A. C. Tavares, 45
Bates, Henry, 11
Beery, Lawrence A., Jr., 91–2
Behrman, Wilhelm, 48
Belém, Botanical Garden, 22–3, 42, 55
Belgrave, W. N. C., 61
Belterra, 76–7, 80, 81, 112, 114, 117, 138,
  147, 159, 210, see also rubber
  plantations; Rural Establishment of the
  Tapajós
Benchimol, Samuel, 132, 137, 142
Bentes, Dionísio, 73
Bentham, George, 10

227

Index

Index

232

Index

Technical Conference on the Economic Valorization of the Amazon, 116
Thanatephoris cucumeris, 151, 154
"theft" of rubber seeds, 20–3, 151, 166
thermal fogging, 153, 155
Thiselton-Dyer, W., 26, 28
Thurn, Everard im, 53
Thwaites, H. K., 26
tire manufacturers, 50, 108, 120–3, 127, 128, 131, 139–40, 143, 155, 166–7, 200, 205
top grafting, 79, 97, 105, 112, 121, 122, 135, 140, 141, 152–3 210
TORMB rubber tax, 131, 132, 145, 162
Townsend, Charles H. T., 79
Townsend, Charles H. T., Jr., 79, 91, 97, 112, 117, 119
Trans-Amazon highway, 132
transfer of plant domesticates, 1, 22–3, 34, 60, 166, 188
Treadwell, John C., 69
Trimen, Henry, 29
Trinidad, 53
Truettner, Keith, 121
Turrialba, research station, 88, 91, 92, 118, 135

Ule, Ernst, 34, 56, 162
United Fruit Company, 84
United States
    Department of Agriculture, 59–60, 69, 70, 87–9, 90–2, 99, 103, 111, 112, 118, 166
    Department of Commerce, 69, 70
    Embassy, Rio de Janeiro, 94, 95, 100, 103
    enters World War II, 92
    Point Four, 117
    purchases of wild rubber, 93–4
    rubber research efforts, 5–6, 87–8, 117
    State Department, 79–80
    survey of 1923, 62, 69, 71
    survey of 1940, 87–8
United States Rubber Company, 48, 67, 69, 73
Universal Exposition
    of 1855, 41
    of 1867, 11
University of Florida, 88, 135

Valle, Eurico de Freitas, 73
Valois, A. C. Candeira, 154
van der Plank, J. E., 147
Vargas, Getúlio, 73, 83, 89, 100, 102, 110, 116, 121–2
Villares, Jorge Dumont, 71–3

Vincens, François, 56
Vipond, Bert, 120
vulcanization of rubber, 4, 9

Wallace, Alfred Russel, 11
Wallace, Henry A., 87, 103
Washington Accords, 93–4, 108–9, 110
Wastie, R. L., 155–6
Weir, James R., 70, 75–6, 77, 78, 79–80, 85, 113, 153
    photograph, 74
Wibel, A. M., 75
Wickham, Henry Alexander (*see also* Wickham's selection), 13, 14–22, 24–5, 30, 61, 162, 179–80
    myth of, 7, 90, 166, 176, 177
    photograph, 37
    report, 29, 45
Wickham, Violet Cave, 14, 15, 17
Wickham's selection, 24–8, 31, 33, 34, 43, 46, 66, 150–1, 180
wild rubber gathering, 36–8, 39, 44, 93, 115, 119, 127
    eradication, 149–50, 182–3
    recuperation, 145, 159
    techniques, 10, 36–8, 159
wild rubber tappers, *see* seringueiros
wild rubber trade, 4, 9, 11, 39, 40
    capital inputs, 40, 47–8, 50, 133
    coalition with Northeast, 131
    collapse, 35, 46, 130, 131
    costs, 44
    hostility to planted rubber, 111, 114, 123, 126, 141, 165
    hostility to synthetic rubber, 130–1
    labor, 40, 41, 93, 96, 104, 130, 182
    lobby, 43, 44, 47, 86, 110–11, 114–15, 131–2, 145
    output, 144, 159
    in postwar, 108–10, 114, 119
    strategic importance, 132
    in World War II, 93, 94, 95, 96, 99, 101, 103, 104, 106, 108
Willdenow, Carl Ludwig, 10
Williams, J. P., 32
Willis, John, 29
Wisniewski, Alfredo, 127, 136, 148
World Bank, 147
Wycherley, P. R., 148

Yan, Tan Chay, 30

Zaire, Guilherme, 131
Zehntner, Leo, 48
Zilles, J. A., 97

234